From Experience to Expression

A College Rhetoric

From Experience

A College Rhetoric

Wm. C. Brown Company Publishers

to Expression

by Joseph Comprone

University of Cincinnati

Dubuque, Iowa

for Pamela and Raphael

Contents

APPENDIX I

APPENDIX II

Preface

From Experience to Expression is based upon the principle that a writer works from self-discovery—both a discovery of his purpose and his subject and a discovery of what he or she wants to say about that subject—to public expression. Both elements are important; both need to be naturally integrated in a successful writing program. And such an integrated program should help students learn more about themselves and their experience as they also learn the rhetorical skills they will need to communicate effectively. A writer without requisite rhetorical skills is like a politician with the best of intentions and moral qualities who cannot persuade people to listen to or believe him. The writer who knows rhetoric but has nothing to say and very little understanding of himself is like the politician of questionable ethics who persuades people to believe him to their own detriment.

Learning to write can be exciting as well as instructive. Excitement comes with the writer's thrill of discovery and his intense desire to communicate those discoveries to others. But that excitement and pleasure can sometimes lead only to frustration if the writer fails to communicate the process of discovering and the product of those discoveries to others.

This book develops a structured, rhetorical approach to writing; it retains, however, the pleasure of discovery by having students apply rhetorical principles to readings, paintings, cartoons, and other contemporary cultural artifacts. These artifacts are not included merely to "interest" students—although they should surely accomplish that—but also to provide sensory experience that can lead naturally, by an application of rhetorical skills, to effective expression. From Experience to Expression constructs a context in which both self-discovery and rhetoric work together, with ideas developing from immediate observations, organizational patterns developing naturally from a writer's personal reactions to what he reads or sees, and even grammatical competence growing naturally out of a desire to express experience that has been carefully observed and analyzed. In every instance, contemporary artifacts and reading are surrounded by rhetorical analyses, discussion questions, and thematic commentary to help students develop their responses in writing.

The five major sections of the book classify different, progressively developed approaches to writing from experience. In these sections contemporary cultural artifacts are used to motivate the discussion and to provide for the application of rhetorical principles.

Within the five sections are twelve chapters. Each chapter discusses a particular rhetorical principle or skill and applies that principle or skill to some model cultural artifact. The dual organization should help teachers and students locate and use whatever they require—whether an essay or story to use as a basis for class discussion, or a rhetorical principle to help organize and present an idea or feeling in writing.

Arguments about how to teach writing are numerous. *From Experience to Expression* tries to take the best of the traditional *and* the contemporary, the best of student experience and the best of what the experts find useful, and to combine them naturally in one book. The result, I hope, is a *useful* book; one that will develop better thinkers, more perceptive students and teachers, and writers who have both something to say and a variety of techniques and styles to use as they say it.

Acknowledgments

Acknowledgments are always an impossible task. I shall pay special respects to Walker Gibson: he helped me through a dissertation at the University of Massachusetts that in an indirect way made this book possible. He has continued to help me over the years with kind advice and good words. His thinking permeates the final section of *From Experience to Expression*.

Many people provided specific help in the preparation of this manuscript. The University of Minnesota provided a small summer research grant that allowed me to continue writing during the summer of 1971. I submit my grateful thanks to all those on the composition staff at the University of Minnesota, Morris, who contributed ideas, criticisms, and encouragement to me as I wrote this book. I especially acknowledge the creative example of Jim Gremmels, who teaches composition with energy, talent, and conviction every year at the University of Minnesota at Morris. Finally, I give more than thanks to the secretarial staff at the University of Cincinnati, especially Mari Niehaus and Alvena Stanfield, who typed a long and often difficult-to-read manuscript with good grace and considerable patience. And my gratitude goes as well to the English Department of the University of Cincinnati for its help in preparing the original manuscript.

Several teachers provided useful suggestions as I revised and edited *From Experience to Expression:* Al Rosa of the University of Vermont, Don Good of Ohio State University, and Brian Short of Northern Arizona University. Most of the strengths of *From Experience to Expression* were either encouraged or suggested by them. I also am indebted to Valerie Goldzung, a very close friend and a valued colleague, who read and remarked upon a large part of the original manuscript.

Finally, my thanks to Dick Crews, an editor who is patient, prodding, and a fine conversationalist. He was also born and raised, like the author, in Philadelphia. And he seems to believe in this book almost as much as I do. His good faith and patience kept me working.

April 1974   Joseph Comprone

From Experience to Expression

A College Rhetoric

The roving eye:

I

An overview of the writing process

> While I talk and the flies buzz, a seagull catches a fish at the mouth of the Amazon, a tree falls in the Adirondack wilderness, a man sneezes in Germany, a horse dies in Tartary, and twins are born in France. What does that mean? Does the contemporaneity of these events with one another, and with a million others as disjointed, form a rational bond between them, and unite them into anything that means for us a world? Yet just such a collateral contemporaneity, and nothing else, is the real order of the world.
>
> —William James

1

You and
your experience

A rich variety of events and sensations surround us at any moment of our lives. Our personal experiences are determined by which of these events and sensations we decide to give our attention. We often attend only to practical concerns such as making a living, being a student, buying the groceries, or reading the newspaper. This attention to practical matters is necessary in order for us to carry them out in the best way. When you, for example, set out to do your laundry, you need to be efficient. You need to remember what type of machine to use, when to put in the soap, how to use and time the dryer, how to sort and fold the clothes. But when we attend only to such practical concerns, we may become bored; and then we are missing many of the pleasures that a rich variety of experiences would give to us.

Starting to write

Writing depends upon careful attention to experience beyond the chores and exercises of everyday living. Each of you at one time or another has had the uncomfortable experience of sitting down to write something—a personal letter, a class assignment, an article for your school or local newspaper—and not knowing how to begin. You stare at the page, doodle a bit, think about your girl or last week's basketball game; you do just about everything but write. There is a way to turn at least some of these private daydreams and rambles into material for writing. But to begin to do that, you need to pay closer attention to those experiences.

Thinking Exercise

Try this experiment. Consider these three questions:

1. What particular images came into your mind as you read this page? Be specific. Did a person's face appear for a moment? What exactly did it look like?

2. Why did these images come to your mind's eye? Were they connected to what you were reading or were they totally extraneous?

3. How do these images relate either to what you were reading or to some aspect of your personal experience? Again, be specific. Does the image relate to some current problem, for instance an argument you just had with your boy friend or girl friend?

Now write a paragraph describing what it felt like inside as you read these pages. Use the answers to the questions above as your base material.

Recording an experience

If you train your mind to probe the evidence of your senses this way, you will almost always find *something* to say. But, of course, there is much more to effective writing than merely recording an experience. The *way* you record that experience is also important. Imagine writing a paragraph about some simple experience of the previous day. You've decided a trip to the laundromat would make good copy.

> Yesterday I went to the laundromat. The day was terribly bleak, a good day to do a wash. It took me fifteen minutes to get the clothes together and another ten minutes to get to the laundromat. When I got there, every machine was taken, so I had to wait another ten minutes. Finally, I jammed my clothes into two vacant machines, added the soap, and went out for a Coke. I came back a half-hour later and found the clothes on the top of the washer. I picked them up, put them in a dryer, and waited twenty minutes more. Finally, with clean clothes neatly stacked, I returned to my room. Three hours to do a very boring job.

There's a good deal of interesting activity described in this paragraph. But, overall, the paragraph is too general. The writer seems to be filling out a form rather than writing in detail what happened. A thousand people, we might say, could have had this experience. Especially in descriptive writing, a reader usually wants details; he wants to know the little things that made the experience described by the writer really his own.

Thinking Exercise

Imagine yourself the author of this paragraph. Ask yourself these questions:

1. What does a *bleak day* look and feel like?
2. What was happening while you got the clothes together and went to the laundromat? What did you see, feel, touch, or hear?
3. What did the washing machine look or sound like?
4. How did the clothes feel when you returned? Were they warm, wet, and sweet-smelling?

These questions, and questions like them, help to create your material. They give you something to write about that is bound to be different from what other writers might produce. They really tell your readers something about your experience.

Using descriptive details

Now read the following paragraph according to the approach we used in the first paragraph.

> Grocery shopping can be quite an experience. Once you enter the store, a barrage of colors, shapes, and interesting language assaults your senses. Paul Newman asks you to "Join the Pepsi Generation"; a soap seller asks you to *feel* the difference; a frozen pizza representative asks you to *taste* some hot pizza. Smells of cheese, fresh vegetables, and meats blend with those of detergents and ammonia. When you're finished you feel as though you've been through a commercial sauna. Every sensory organ tingles with awakened anticipation.

Use these questions to help you evaluate the two paragraphs.

Thinking Exercise

1. Is one paragraph better written mechanically (grammar, sentence structure, vocabulary) or are they about the same on this level?
2. Does the second writer use more detail? Does he appeal to more senses? Which ones?
3. How might the second paragraph be developed in more detail? What questions would you ask the second writer about his experience?

Careful observation of your experience *before* you write makes it easier to write in detail, to choose which details you will use and which you will ignore, to remember what your experience was really like. The writer who takes preliminary notes is like the artist who makes preliminary sketches. Even when we have no pencil and paper, however, we can train our minds to observe the forms and details of everyday experiences.

But paying close attention to experience is not in itself enough. A writer must also recognize the importance of whatever he experiences. He must be able to relate the little things that happen to him to a larger context or meaning. The poet William Carlos Williams, who was also a doctor often out on house calls late at night, wrote a little poem called "This Is Just To Say."

> I have eaten
> the plums
> that were in
> the icebox
>
> and which
> you were probably
> saving
> for breakfast
>
> Forgive me
> they were delicious
> so sweet
> and so cold

Ask yourself why this brief note is a poem. What gives it the power and expressiveness that make people continue to read it? How does the poet manage to get so much expressed in so little space? We can suggest two answers to those questions.

First, notice how the poet has remembered and described the concrete detail—the *delicious, sweet, cold* plums. These few words are very powerful and sensuous. Don't they help you to taste and smell the plums yourself? The sounds of the words—try pronouncing *delicious, sweet,* and *cold* right now—are themselves sensuous and tasty. The poet has selected these descriptive words carefully; he's put them in emphatic, final positions in the poem to emphasize the appeal to our senses; and he has kept the language of the rest of the poem spare and factual to set off those scrumptious plums.

Secondly, the poet must be the kind of person who notices and remembers what he sees and experiences. He must train his powers of observation so that he *feels* when and how an experience can be made to mean something to others.

Experience, then, is something to which you must be sensitive.

1. You must recognize and appreciate its complexity.

2. You must combat the chaos of immediate experience by finding details which can re-create that experience in a form your readers can understand.

3. You must somehow connect feeling and idea, the senses and the intellect, in whatever writing you do. Your writing must combine the way you felt and the way you thought about the experience.

Subjective and objective description

Sometimes we take the concrete elements of our experience and try to communicate to others our inner, or *subjective*, impressions. At other times we want to describe what we see, feel, hear, touch, or smell in an *objective* way, with accurate representations of as much concrete, physical detail as we can manage. When we are describing subjectively, we are describing three different qualities at once: at least some of the physical detail of the experience, the emotional attitudes we feel because of the experience, and the physical sensations we feel inside ourselves because of the experience. When we describe objectively, we usually try to remain neutral, to leave our emotional and personal reactions out, and to concentrate on recreating exactly the physical nature of our experiences.

Thinking Exercise

Look closely at Stuart Davis' *New York Waterfront* and Ben Shahn's *Handball*. To apply the principles of subjective and objective description to these paintings, ask yourself these questions:

1. Which painting is more subjective?

2. What subjective statement of emotion is each painter trying to express?

3. Can you find objective bits of detail in the subjective painting?

4. What is the main difference between the manner in which the objects are arranged in the subjective painting and in the objective one?

Figure 1-1

New York Waterfront
by Stuart Davis

Courtesy The Museum of Modern Art, New York.

5. Does the objective painting express emotion as well? How would you describe that emotion? Where do you find it suggested in the painting?

Think about this interpretation of *New York Waterfront:*

What did Stuart Davis want to say about city life in *New York Waterfront?* A city, to Davis, is a conglomerate of mechanical forms, angles, and curves. But the entire composite picture maintains its own life-force, just as a city is always moving and changing, at least to the human eye. The bends and curves, the flowing lines create in the viewer a feel for the movement and life carried out on this waterfront. The blockish building shapes, with rectangular window-like dark spots, the numerous angular poles and pipe-like tubes, the horizontally lettered sign figure make the background seem to function like an erector set.

The artist feels something for his subject—in this case a mechanical emotion; he is surrounded by gears and lines of force that make him feel a part of a machine. The artist takes the physical detail of the environment and combines it with or into his own mental picture of that scene.

Topics for Writing and Discussion

1. Shahn's *Handball* also shows a city scene. What do you think he is

Figure 1-2

Handball
by Ben Shahn

Courtesy The Museum of Modern Art, New York, Donated by Mrs. John D. Rockefeller, Jr. Fund.

trying to say about city life? Compare your answer to this question to the class' previous analysis of *New York Waterfront*.

2. Write a one-page essay on how you think the artist feels about the men in *Handball*. First, ask yourself what the painting means to you. Then find a thesis statement, preferably a brief sentence, that defines that meaning. Then look over the painting for specific details that you can use to support that thesis.

3. Write a concrete analysis of the forms in this painting. Spend some time describing the forms as accurately as possible; then provide some analysis of how these forms affect you. Appeal to your reader's senses; get him or her to feel, see, and hear along with you.

4. Write an introductory paragraph in which you describe the central objects in Shahn's painting and then a concluding paragraph in which you offer your evidence for what you say the artist emphasizes. Analyze visual relationships, what the artist has included, what you imagine might have been found in the actual scene which the artist has left out. Then, go out and observe a scene around you, selecting and arranging what you see so that particular details are emphasized in a way that creates the effect you want.

In all these exercises, you should, above all, aim to be specific. Let the details in the paintings help you organize your writing. For example, what specific details did you first notice as you looked at the painting? Did the artist intend for you to respond to those details first? How do you know? What evidence of this do you find in the painting itself?

Keeping a Journal

This is a good time for you to begin keeping a journal. To understand how a journal should function and why it is useful in a writing class, turn to "Appendix II: The Everyday Eye," page 417. You can begin by taking your journal with you into the city, town, or countryside that surrounds your campus. First spend about twenty minutes recording your subjective impressions of the scene you choose to observe. Then ask yourself where these impressions come from. Some will relate directly to physical parts of your environment. Others will come more from inside you—from past scenes that you are reminded of or emotions you feel because of other immediate concerns. Now spend another twenty minutes observing as objectively as you can. Record your observations in short, concrete sentences. When you finish, you might try composing a few very short poems in which you relate one of your impressions to a few, selected concrete details. If you're willing, let your teacher see a few of your poems. Perhaps a few of them can be reproduced for class discussion.

Writing from experience: A comparison of painting and writing

Both a painting and a piece of descriptive writing are copies of experience. One uses words, the other uses painted images, space, and visual arrangement to describe experiences that were originally received through the senses. The person who looks at a painting, however, can take in the entire canvas almost at once. The reader, on the other hand, receives information word-by-word, in parts. He doesn't get the entire "picture" before him at one time as the person looking at a painting does.

Does that mean that a writer works with an automatic disadvantage? Not necessarily. When you write you can put words and their references together in ways that make the reader feel he has the whole picture in front of him at once. What the painter shows visually the descriptive writer shows by using concrete language that appeals directly to the senses of his reader. He or she can write *coherently*: by being sure that his material is connected in space and time, by being sure that as his readers receive the specific details, they also have some sense of the entire picture or experience. And, even when the writer carefully organizes and relates his material, the reader might still rearrange the image or picture by the time it reaches his mind. The same is true of nondescriptive or expository writing whose purpose is to illustrate or explain an argument or point of view. One idea leads naturally to another, just as the bowl in a still-life painting has to be related visually to the fruit in it. To observe the principles of coherence and concretion, look closely at the painting by Roy Lichtenstein and *Still Life* by Henri Fantin-Latour.

Color figure 1-4
STILL LIFE
Henri Fantin-Latour
follows page 14.

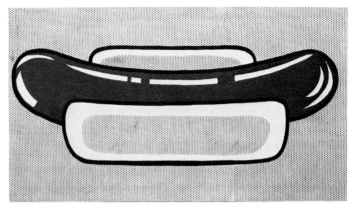

Figure 1-3

Hot Dog
by Roy Lichtenstein

Courtesy of the Leo Castelli Gallery. New York. Owned by René de Montagu, Paris.

Both paintings are carefully planned and unified, though the objects painted in each are themselves very different. Fantin-Latour paints objects we expect to see in a still life; Lichtenstein magnifies and presents in realistic detail a common object which isn't usually the subject of art.

Thinking Exercise

Ask yourself these questions:

1. What do you think Lichtenstein is trying to say to you about the world around you merely through his emphasis on the common? Do you laugh or are you puzzled when you see it? Is *Hot Dog* a joke? How do you know?

2. Could a writer get the same response by writing an essay on some very common, usually taken-for-granted, object? Could you write an essay on a hot dog that would create the same effect on your readers as this painting does on you? Try it.

3. Fantin-Latour carefully places and arranges the parts of his painting. Find a common object and write one paragraph in which you objectively describe the object, showing the relationships between its parts, how it might look, feel, or smell. Be sure to describe its physical arrangement. Then change your intention and use the object to describe something else, or to satirize or ridicule an idea, an emotion, or an action. For example, you might use the statement, "The game was so monotonous it reminded me of a still-life trying to be *Bonnie and Clyde*."

4. In sports, a showy or flashy athlete is often called a "hot dog." As you look at Lichtenstein's painting, try to explain what people mean when they use "hot dog" this way.

Writing Exercise

1. Find another painting or photograph. Describe it as objectively as possible before showing it to the class. Then show it to the class and let them discuss the differences between your description and the painting or photograph.

2. Write a brief essay or paragraph in which you describe as closely as possible any one of the objects in the painting.

3. Look through some magazines and find a flashy ad, one that strikes your attention almost immediately. First, write two or three paragraphs that describe how the appeal to your senses is organized in the ad. Then find one object or image in the ad and magnify it. Describe its imaginary, gigantic proportions in as much detail as you can.

4. A metaphor is a comparison between two objects used to highlight a similarity that explains an idea. Find two common, concrete objects—some objects like Lichtenstein's hot dog—and describe their similarities and differences. Then think of an idea, an attitude, or an opinion that you can develop from your comparison of the two objects. How does a box of cleanser compare with your best friend? What would a Virginia Slims cigarette tell you about one of your relatives? Do hot dogs and baseball bats have much in common?

Effective visual description in poetry can create for the reader a vivid picture. Read the following poem by Wallace Stevens and notice how the poet uses words to achieve a visual effect.

A Study of Two Pears

WALLACE STEVENS

I

Opusculum paedagogum.[1]
The pears are not viols,
Nudes or bottles.
They resemble nothing else.

II

They are yellow forms
Composed of curves
Bulging toward the base.
They are touched red.

Copyright © 1942 by Wallace Stevens. Reprinted from *The Collected Poems of Wallace Stevens* by permission of Alfred A. Knopf, Inc.

[1]A small instructive work.

STILL LIFE by Henri Fantin-Latour. Courtesy The National Gallery of Art, Washington, D.C. Chester Dale Collection.

FAMILY OF SALTIMBANQUES
by Picasso
Courtesy The National Gallery of
Art, Washington, D.C. Chester Dale
Collection.

LE VERTIGE D'EROS by Matta. Courtesy The Museum of Modern Art, New York.

III

They are not flat surfaces
Having curved outlines.
They are round
Tapering toward the top.

IV

In the way they are modelled
There are bits of blue.
A hard dry leaf hangs
From the stem.

V

The yellow glistens.
It glistens with various yellows,
Citrons, oranges and greens
Flowering over the skin.

VI

The shadows of the pears
are blobs on the green cloth.
The pears are not seen
As the observer wills.

Stevens calls his poem "a small instructive work"; the subject for instruction, we might say, is language itself. The pears are probably lying upon a table before the poet. First, the speaker/poet tells us what the pears are not—"not viols, Nudes or bottles./They resemble nothing else." He can't use metaphor, at least not explicitly, for he can think of nothing that captures the pears by simple comparison. Yet, of course, there are similarities among viols, nudes, bottles, and pears. In some ways the three items *are* like pears; they often are subjects for still-life paintings: they have shapes that are similar. Stevens, in the poem, points out a truth about all metaphor: the two things described are alike in some ways, different in others. And we learn something about the objects described because of their similarities *and* their differences.

The rest of the poem gives us, in piecemeal form, a visual description of the pears: they are "yellow forms . . . bulging . . . touched red . . . round . . . tapering . . . bits of blue . . . a hard dry leaf hangs from the stem . . . citrons . . . and greens flowering over the skin . . . shadows . . . blobs on the green cloth." Here we find appeals to the viewer's senses of color, shape, texture, touch, and form. But in written words we don't receive these forms and qualities as simultaneously as we do in Stuart Davis' *New York Water-*

front. Instead, we receive each descriptive item separately, one carefully distinguished from the other, in categorized form.

Why the final two lines of the poem? "The pears are not seen/As the observer wills." Here Stevens admits an essential shortcoming in written language. In written words, we observe almost mechanically. We tick off descriptive items or qualities one by one, as if they were actually separate and easily distinguishable in themselves. Stevens knows that as we receive experience the objects themselves constantly interact and change. Perhaps more importantly, he knows that when he changes the way he looks at the pears, or anything for that matter, the pears as he sees them seem to change. They are not "seen as the observer wills." In fact, they are nearly too powerful for language; the poet would rather look at the pears themselves than describe them.

But Stevens *did* write his poem. Why? Probably because the act of composing and communicating told him and his readers something about those pears they didn't know before. Ask yourself what the poet put into his poem that you might not have noticed had you looked at the pears yourself. Would you have appreciated the pears as much? Why or why not?

Activity Exercise

Give yourself this test. Find an everyday object—a piece of fruit, a vase in your living room, a painting, a poster or photo in your room. Look at it for only a few moments. Then jot down the concrete, sensory detail—colors, shapes, textures—that you would try to get into a painting based on the subject. How much do you remember? How close do you feel the words come to a painting of the subject?

The personal touch

Before we finish our discussion of the paintings, *Still-Life* and *Hot Dog*, and Stevens' poem, consider how these artists make the experience they express their own, without destroying the accuracy of their works. Besides looking closely at the original experience to find an order that is natural, they also strive to express their attitudes toward that experience. All three works are primarily objective: the artists try to represent accurately what they have received through their senses. Still, we can detect personal attitudes toward the subjects if we look closely. Stevens, although he is looking only at what most people would consider unimportant—two pears—manages to convey his deep feelings about the pears, their simple beauty, their sometimes complex appeal to almost all our senses, especially the visual. His admiration for the pears builds up until climaxed in the final lines: "The pears are not seen/ As the observer wills." Here we find a clearly articulated attitude toward all nature. Without respect for what he experiences, a person misses a great deal; he sees what he wants to see and sometimes he sees what isn't there. To observe well, we need to be careful not to allow our emotions and the limitations of our senses and our language to distort experience.

Fantin-Latour also describes objectively. He copies the structural order of the objects in his still life and the relationships among them. Yet we can also detect his attitude. The careful way he expresses texture, which appeals to our sense of touch, the deep shades of color, and the careful attention to details combine to make us feel the respect the painter has for these objects. His attitude in some ways might be like Stevens'.

Finally, Lichtenstein doesn't copy the dimensions of a hot dog, but he pays very close attention to its details. He's looked closely at and probably eaten a good many hot dogs. He uses common, everyday objects like hot dogs to express an attitude about the world.

Principles to follow in writing from experience

Once again take a quick look at the paintings and the poem. Then see if these principles, which you can also apply to your writing, are supported by what you see.

1. Before you begin to write, observe what you will write about carefully, recording what you think are important details and dimensions.

2. *Don't* try to include all that detail. Find a purpose—some general attitude or impression—and go back over your recorded detail and select items to fit that purpose.

3. As you write, follow the organizational plan which you set up for yourself. Also look closely at the experience itself. Are there hints for organizing in the experience itself?

4. For the most part, describe what you see and experience as objectively as possible. But always leave some time to express your opinion or attitude, as Stevens, Fantin-Latour, and Lichtenstein have done in their works. Too much personal opinion can cause you to ignore your subject and to omit the evidence you need to get from the experience itself. But, on the other hand, completely objective or factual writing can be dull and mechanical.

Using metaphors

We use metaphors over and over whenever we speak or write. When you use one object, action, or idea to represent another, you are using a *metaphor*. Some examples are: "My love is like a red, red rose," "Every time that happens I feel like a wet rag," "That guy's a real winner." In common speech or everyday writing we usually use metaphors to express something we either don't wish to or can't describe directly. So we use a common object or happening and let it stand in place of the literal explanation. Suppose you meet a friend in the hall between classes. You want to tell him as quickly and as emphatically as possible about your ride on a friend's cycle: "Man, it was like a roller-coaster ride and a Keystone Cops' chase all wrapped in one. I felt like I'd gone fifteen with Muhammad Ali when we had finished." If it's difficult finding words to say what you've felt or finding just the right words to express your meaning, then look around you for some concrete object or action to suggest what you mean. Of course, there are also dangers in using metaphors.

Thinking Exercise

Consider these questions whenever you use metaphors that are obvious and will attract your reader's attention:

1. Will your readers be bothered by your metaphors? Is the situation suited to metaphorical description? Don't, for example, use a metaphor when your readers want exact, factual information. You'd be annoyed if your college registrar used metaphors to tell you how to register.

2. Will your readers feel that you're a show-off, a "hot dog," if you use certain metaphors or too many metaphors?

3. What do *you* want to accomplish? Do you want to give information, to entertain, or to provide both? Select and use metaphors accordingly.

4. Sometimes our metaphors tell our readers as much about ourselves as they do about our subjects. Are your metaphors clichéd or dead? If you've heard them yourself a thousand times before, they probably are. Would you use these metaphors: "I *plumbed the depths* of the problem by *grabbing the bull by the horns* and *crossing the bridges* as I came to them"? What do these metaphors tell you about this writer?

About thirty years ago, I. A. Richards coined the terms *tenor* and *vehicle* to explain how metaphors work. The *tenor* of a metaphor is the subject or underlying meaning of the metaphor. The *vehicle* is the object, action, or idea the writer uses to express that tenor. Take Robert Burns' "my love is like a red rose." The purpose of the metaphor is to explain what his love is like. The rose, the vehicle, tells us by comparison what she is like.

Metaphors can be classified in three groups: *fresh, dead,* and *dying* (terms which of course are metaphors themselves).

Fresh: a metaphor that you or your readers haven't heard a thousand times before. You can freshen up a dying or dead metaphor by using it in an unfamiliar or new context.

Dead: a metaphor that you or your readers have heard so many times that you groan when you hear it. Examples are: He runs *like a rabbit;* He's *as slow as a turtle;* She's *as ugly as sin.*

Dying: a metaphor you've heard a couple of hundred times but that might be worth salvaging. *Don't* salvage it unless you're sure that it expresses what you want to say accurately and that your readers have not pronounced it dead.

Activity Exercise

Read the following ten sentences and do these three things. First, underline the metaphor. Then, mark the tenor and the vehicle by putting a *t* or a *v* over the proper word. Finally, note whether the metaphor is fresh, dead, or dying.

1. If you try that again, I'll squash you like a bug. (spoken by Matt Dillon in an early *Gunsmoke* show)

2. As Jimmy Clarke's car came round the curve, it seemed like a squat little animal scrambling to safety.

3. The Mustang handles like a dream.

4. When you get knocked out, you feel just like the television when it has just been turned off.

5. The cliffrose is a sturdy shrub with gnarled trunk and twisting branches, growing sometimes to twice a man's height.

6. He was not tall. And he appeared to walk on his toes—his nut-colored legs were bowed and skinny and made him hobble like a jerky little spider.

7. His hands were rough, black, and flinty like the side of a barren mountain.

8. He's a real drag.

9. If you want to stay out of trouble, don't rock the boat.

10. It was like a locomotive about ten miles away. It was the Hell's Angels in "running formation" coming over the mountain on Harley-Davidson 74s.

You might want to discuss with the class what these sentences tell you about the writer. What kind of writers would make these specific comparisons?

Look at Claes Oldenburg's sculpture, *Baked Potato*, before you do the next exercise.

Activity Exercise

1. Compare the photograph of Oldenburg's *Baked Potato* with a person you know well. Relate specific details of the potato to specific aspects of the person. Decide before you begin what impression you would like to create about the person.

2. Find an object (for example, a penny, a lemon, any everyday object) and compare it to a person in class. Begin by observing the person very closely, perhaps even taking notes. Then find and observe the object closely and draw a comparison between the two. Again, you should decide before you begin what impression you would like to get across.

Figure 1-5

Baked Potato
by Claes Oldenburg

Courtesy of the Pasadena Art Museum. Owned by Claes Oldenburg.

3. Develop an essay, on any subject that interests you, in which you use *Baked Potato* as a vehicle to describe or introduce the main subject. For example, you might use a description of the potato as a lead-in to a character sketch of a person you once knew. The first half of your essay might roughly describe the vehicle; the second half might describe the tenor (your main subject in the essay). Remember, you need to develop a careful transition between the vehicle and tenor.

2

Expressing your experience

Chapter 1 should have helped you understand what the word *experience* means when we apply it to writing. It should have helped you begin finding something to say and introduced a few skills to assist you in transferring that experience to writing. Now we can move to more specific ways of organizing your experience in writing. The aim of most writers is two-fold. First, we want to say something personal, something that draws from *our* own way of looking at the world. Second, we want to express it clearly and effectively to someone else. Sometimes we can achieve both those aims by finding means of organization and expression that naturally fit our subjects.

Take, for example, a writer who loves nature and wants to express that love by describing what he observes in nature to a general audience. To make what he says effective, he'll need to organize and form his description. Still, he doesn't want to *force* his material—what he sees around him in the trees, grass, the shapes and color of nature—into an unnatural pattern. When we're faced with such writing situations, when we want to express just how it felt to experience something without having the writing become disordered, unclear or ineffective, we can look very closely at the subject itself and usually find some natural organizing principle. Put yourself in the following classroom situation.

Two students costumed themselves in symbolic dress. One wore black, somber clothing, developed a contemplative expression, and constantly scratched the side of his head with his right hand. His eyes were glassy, almost dreamy; he seemed always engaged in faraway thoughts, seldom bothered by whatever touched his senses.

The second student wore colorful clothing, constantly leaped up and down, and strutted from side to side. He occasionally burst into song, his eyes darting from person to person in the audience, and shrieked whenever experiencing some immediate stimulus. He wore bright red, bell-bottom slacks and skinny black boots that creaked sharply as he walked. His broad leather belt was fronted by a large brass buckle that glistened in the sunlight everytime he passed a window; his shirt had flared sleeves and ruffles. The class just enjoyed watching him because he enjoyed being alive. Here was our "feeling" man.

Now certainly these are exaggerated stereotypes. That's easy to see. But read the following skit in the hope of discovering some way of getting these two so different people together. For the sake of drama, we will call our thinking man "Howard" and our feeling man "Hal."

Howard moves slowly on stage from the left, makes two slow and trudging circles around the stage and finally approaches a single flower, something like a rose, which rests in a glass cup precisely in the middle of the stage. He kneels down, gauges the rose with his eyes, delicately sniffs it, then seems to calibrate its position in the room. Finally he touches it very lightly, then gets up, strolls contemplatively about the room, deep in thought, sometimes sighing.

Hal enters from the right with a shriek; he stops short after brushing Howard and knocking his glasses awry. He gasps, lurches a bit, then sighs as his eyes strike the rose. Meanwhile Howard continues to walk and ruminate, scratching his head and mumbling. Hal leaps toward the rose and spills water from the glass, with a light splash, as he swings the cup up to eye level with his right hand, all the while gesticulating with his left hand and arching his black eyebrows. Finally, Hal puts the rose in his vest pocket; he throws the glass away and follows Howard about the room, finally collaring him near center stage. A conversation consisting of Howard's continual ruminations and Hal's groans and shrieks begins to become more violent as both refuse to listen to one another. Howard pushes Hal's face away. Hal replies by ripping off Howard's thin black tie and pulling two buttons off his shirt. Howard, still ruminating, absent-mindedly kicks Hal's shin. Hal tweaks Howard's nose violently. Howard knees Hal in the groin and punches Hal in the stomach, then quickly resumes a contemplative pose, with his eyes glassy and staring into the audience, his left hand rubbing his chin. Hal crumbles to the floor but reaches his head up to spit in the face of Howard, who wipes away the spit and in one motion slaps the face of Hal. Howard calmly pulls a gun and fires into the stomach of Hal, but as Hal dies he pulls out a black and silver five-and-dime rubber dagger and stabs Howard in the foot. Howard groans to a slow, ritualized death, still contemplating, rubbing his brow with one hand, his foot with the other. As the scene closes, Hal's hand reaches slowly for the crushed rose in his lapel, grasps it and flings it weakly into the air.

Now read this transcribed classroom dialogue and see where you agree, disagree, or where you can think of other interpretations or points.

A class dialogue on Howard and Hal

Terry: The way I see it Howard's the culprit. He keeps all his fancy thoughts to himself while Hal wants to share his feelings about the rose.

Mike: On the surface, it seems that way. But I wonder. Just what did hepped-up Hal expect Howard to do about that rose anyhow? Kiss it, or him, or what?

Terry: Well, at least he could have acknowledged that he liked it. After all, if it is a symbol of beauty and all . . .

Lonnie: That's where I have trouble. The symbolism is pretty obvious, I get that. The flashy feeling man and the boorish thinking man trying to get together over a rose. But they can't hack it. OK. But why the ritualized violence? That really wouldn't happen, not over some goofy rose anyhow. Even if it is supposed to be a symbol of *Beauty*.

Barb: Maybe the violence is purposely exaggerated. I helped write this skit and I think we exaggerated purposely. Because people can't communicate, even about something as simple as the beauty of a rose. Maybe the purpose of the whole skit was to get you talking about why the violence comes about. So let's try to answer Lonnie's question.

Dale: OK. I helped write the skit too, so I'll try to get us started on answering that question. What's wrong with Howard? Well, he at least notices the rose; he stops his thinking and brooding long enough to sense the rose. But he won't stop long enough to share those sensations with another, at least not with Hal.

Terry: Right. I mean he's so caught up with his own thoughts about the rose that he's useless, boring, dull—just not worth it . . .

Mike: Wait a minute, though. I don't think Hal's so hot either. Sure he looks with it and cool, fun to be with and all that. But just what does *he* do to communicate

	his perceptions of the rose? Grunts a lot, jumps around, big deal . . .
Barb:	Now I think you're getting at what we are trying to say . . .
Dale:	Yeah. They're both pretty inept. One gets so caught up in his mind, his thinking, that he's tongue-tied; the other is so caught up in his feelings, his sensations, that he's tongue-tied.

Here are several writing principles which the class formulated from the "Howard and Hal" skit.

1. Think *and* feel; more importantly, cause your readers to think and feel.

2. Combine thought and feeling by being careful to include concrete support with your more abstract generalizations.

3. Carefully select your concrete data. Fit them to your thesis, which is usually a general principle or opinion under which you organize your materials carefully.

4. Develop a personality when you write. That will help you make your opinions and your detail interesting.

Finding a thesis

Before we leave the Howard-Hal skit, try this exercise. It should help you bring your impressions, your ideas, and the specifications of your subject together into a natural order.

Activity Exercise

Read over the skit once again. Then jot down a general sentence that you think describes what the skit tells you about writing. Now look over the skit and select five or six of its parts and show how they support or relate to your general statement. You're ready to narrow down even more now. Ask yourself a question which is related to the skit and to writing. Make the question as brief and as succinct as possible. Finally, write a thesis statement which you believe answers your questions; make it a simple, declarative statement around which you can plan and outline a short essay. A thesis statement describes the writer's purpose. And, it can help you to control and organize an essay. Be sure that your thesis can be covered in a short essay. Also, select your supporting evidence carefully and plan paragraphs in your essay around the pieces of evidence you select. You should come up with a plan that looks something like this:

Rough, general statement: This skit deals with the split between the feeling and the thinking man and how that split applies to writing.

General evidence: Howard's gestures; his thoughts, his daydreaming; his thin black tie; the fight; each participant's actions in the fight; the rose and what happens to it.

Thesis question: How is the split between the feeling man and the thinking man shown in this skit?

Final thesis: Howard, the thinking man, and Hal, the feeling man, do not communicate with each other or understand each other's point of view.

Final list of evidence: the rose as symbol of misunderstanding and differing attitudes; the beginning of the fight as growing out of lack of communication; Howard's and Hal's actions as they portray the desire to dominate rather than to communicate.

Activity Exercise

Of course, the real test is how well you put together and relate your thesis and your evidence. Now look at Claes Oldenburg's *Giant Saw.* Apply the above process to the photograph in any way you wish. Build some thesis statement from your initial impression of the sculpture, finding evidence and asking questions according to the "finding a thesis" process which is outlined above.

Figure 2-1

Giant Saw
by Claes Oldenburg

Courtesy of the Vancouver Art Gallery, Vancouver.

Selecting your evidence

You wouldn't expect to read a novel without a setting. Settings are usually concrete; they consist of the material objects of our everyday lives. A really good writer brings those objects alive. He describes them carefully, closely, almost lovingly. Notice the intricate, careful way that William Carlos Williams describes a number that he saw briefly on a passing firetruck. And, more importantly, notice how he surrounds that number with sensory appeals which create a *setting* for his poem. The background or setting of our writing serves as the flesh on the bone. Our ideas, theses, and subjects need that flesh; skeletons usually don't interest readers.

The Great Figure

WILLIAM CARLOS WILLIAMS

Among the rain
and lights
I saw the figure 5
in gold
on a red
firetruck
moving
tense
unheeded
to gong clangs
siren howls
and wheels rumbling
through the dark city.

Williams captures the sensory appeals of the moment in a series of modifying phrases. He begins by describing the "I" of the poem as he sees the figure 5; the rest of the poem adds concrete detail—some that appeals to the eye, some to the ear, some to our sense of touch—to the figure 5. Williams re-creates the experience and leaves the general interpretation to you, the reader. In some things you write, you may wish to define the general thought or feeling and relate it directly to those concrete objects that caused the thought or feeling.

Strive to do more than include concrete detail, however. No writer, after all, can include every detail; experience is so crammed with details that a writer must select, and select carefully. Generally, you can go about selecting detail in two ways. One, select a group of concrete details which seem initially important. Then develop from the group of details an abstraction—sometimes a reasoned thesis, sometimes a more general statement of feeling. Or, two, compose a statement of general feeling or a concept and then search for specific details or examples to support your abstraction.

Perhaps even more effective is the method that Williams uses in "The Great Figure." He describes the details of the experience as carefully as he can using concrete nouns, verbs, and adjectives. A concrete word corresponds directly to some physical object, person, or action or to some physical property (color, size, shape) of an object, person, or action. Most descriptive writing relies on concrete language as a base or foundation. The writer develops his ideas—the generalities and abstractions of his writing—directly from these concrete references to his subject. Williams doesn't interpret the experience he describes for his readers; he merely puts together a few selected images and lets the reader draw his own conclusions. Williams is at least in part one of a long tradition of twentieth century poets who try to strip their poems down to bare essentials, to words that appeal to experience as directly as possible. Although such a method wouldn't work in every writing situation, you can usually benefit when you allow your reader to *induce* the interpretation himself—as long as you supply him with enough concrete detail.

Activity Exercise

As an exercise in appreciating William Carlos Williams' "The Great Figure," list the objects represented in the poem and the physical properties of those objects. Point out the adjectives and other modifiers and discuss with the class whether the modifiers are concrete. Then decide why you think the poet chose these objects over the many others that he might have included from the actual scene. Does he want his readers to take a specific feeling or meaning from the poem? What is that feeling or meaning? How is it developed?

Writing Exercise

1. The exercises that you've tried so far have asked you to describe stationary physical objects. Now try to describe an action or an entire real-life scene. You'll want to describe motion and change as well as stationary objects and properties in this exercise. Take your journal with you and observe some scene or action on a city street, in a department store, or in some busy place on campus. Look around. Then jot down the broad

outlines or limits of the scene or action and the important details: how many people are involved, what objects in the surroundings are most notable, and what the spatial arrangements are. Then plot out how the action or scene takes place: who goes where, what visual changes or rearrangements in the scene occur. Then write two descriptive essays. In the first one, describe the scene objectively but in a manner, as Williams does in "The Great Figure," that will encourage a certain emotional or intellectual response from your readers. In the second essay, begin with your abstract response to the experience and go on to include supporting evidence. In the first essay, you will be organizing your materials objectively and allowing your readers to interpret *inductively*—by drawing their general interpretations of the experience from its details, from what actually happened. In the second essay, you'll be organizing *deductively* by beginning with a general interpretation and supplying concrete evidence as support.

2. Now try to apply either inductive or deductive organization to another kind of writing. So far you've been writing mostly description; you've been working with concrete physical experience transferred directly to words. Now you can apply what you've learned from those exercises to argumentative or expository writing. Choose one of these general argumentative statements:

a. William Carlos Williams' poetry is far too simple.
b. Life becomes meaningless when living conditions are too crowded.
c. The Democratic Party is the poor man's party.
d. Students at large universities are often up-tight and unfriendly.
e. Freshmen in college usually look confused, homesick, or bored.

Next, find experiences around you that you can use to argue for or against the statement. As you write your essay, work from a general statement of your position back through your supporting evidence, including personal observations, factual material, and illustrations from readings and your past experience.

3. As you listen to others talk in any crowded place (a restaurant, a study room in a library, wherever), be alert for an opinion or an idea with which you disagree. Listen also to hear *how* the person talking says his opinion or idea. Then write two brief papers. In one, make up a dialogue between yourself and the person you heard talking in which you either agree or disagree with the speaker. In the second, make the opinion you overheard into a thesis for a short paper; think up as much evidence as you can to support the thesis and write a brief expository essay.

Drawing inferences, building compositions

Pulling together your observations and experiences *before* you write—what many call "pre-writing"—is important. Organizing what you write is a complex process that begins when you've just started to think about your subject. Many of you may be used to organizing only *after* you write. But revising and editing are merely last steps in the whole process of putting experience together on paper.

There are two general processes you can use to begin forming your thoughts. *Induction* is a natural process of organization and reasoning that moves from particular instances to more general conclusions, impressions, or opinions. *Deduction* is a more artificial way of thinking and ordering. When you use deduction you usually move from general premises to specific rules.

All of us use induction almost every day. We observe particular instances or examples of some experience and gradually move toward an interpretation that makes some connection among those particulars. Someone, for example, is bothered as he walks to work every day by a neighbor's noisy, snapping cocker spaniel. As weeks pass, he notices other equally noisy, bothersome cocker spaniels. Soon he begins to develop an *inference,* that cocker spaniels are as a rule noisy and bothersome. An inference is a conclusion that you've drawn from a particular set of experiences, either from particular examples as in induction or from some set formula or logical equation as in deduction.

Activity Exercise

Look back or ahead to two or three of the paintings, cartoons, and ads in this book. Very quickly try to think of other pieces of visual experience—another ad or cartoon, an experience similar to one of the scenes you see in a painting—and develop, in a sentence or two, some general inference from these similar objects.

Not all experience can be evaluated, ordered, or analyzed by natural, inductive methods. Sometimes, for example, we don't have enough particulars to draw accurate inferences. Sometimes the problem is generalization. In the latter case, we can turn to deduction.

Deduction begins with assumptions. You *assume* that certain things are true.

All slaves are men.

All dogs have four legs.

Air conditioners produce cold air.

Assumptions have to be *self-evident;* in other words, you and your readers must accept them as true without doubt or question. Then, once you are sure there is agreement on your assumptions, you can link together a chain of assumptions to produce an inevitable, logical conclusion.

All slaves are men. → John Deforest is a slave. → John Deforest is a man.

All dogs have four legs. → Scotty is a dog. → Scotty has four legs.

Air conditioners produce cold air. → That machine is an air conditioner. → That machine produces cold air.

Obviously, a primary danger in all deductive reasoning is the misuse of basic assumptions. If there is legitimate cause for disagreement over basic assumptions, or if there are important exceptions to your assumptions, you must try to offer your readers evidence and illustrations in support of your assumptions. Unless you do, you're expecting your reader to agree with a deductive chain which may be valid in itself but not based on a valid foundation of assumptions.

Let's imagine a few possible exceptions to the above rather simple assumptions.

All slaves are men. (Some slaves are not men because they've lost the ability to think for themselves.)

All dogs have four legs. (Some dogs are deformed by accident, birth, or disease and have more or less than four legs.)

Air conditioners produce cold air. (Broken air conditioners may produce hot air or no air at all.)

The first example shows that people sometimes use different definitions of key terms in their assumptions. *Men* can refer to a class of mammals, human beings, in a general, biological way. But, as the exception demonstrates, *men* can also be used to refer to members of the class *man* who are different sexually and socially from women, also members of that large, general class *men*. Be sure you find words that represent your experience without confusion. Check your deductive assumptions for confusing wording. Make sure you *define* carefully any words that might be taken two or more ways by your readers.

The second and third exceptions to the above assumptions point out that *some* dogs don't have four legs and that *some* air conditioners don't produce cold air. These are *factual* exceptions. Whenever we generalize we run the risk of ignoring some particular instances that do not fit our general inferences. Be sure that you recognize important exceptions when you form your basic assumptions. If the factual exceptions are directly related to what you are trying to establish by deduction, then rewrite the assumption. If, for example, deformed dogs are not important to your argument, you can stay with your basic assumption. But, if Scotty *is* a deformed dog, your deductive chain may be faulty because you've begun with a premise that assumes he is healthy. He may, in other words, have been born with *two* legs, an important exception to your assumption about the number of legs.

Here are short, simple lists of the characteristics of inductive and deductive reasoning. Don't try to memorize them. Just absorb the characteristics in a general way so that you will be able to use them in organizing your experience before you write.

Induction

1. Works from the particular instance to the general conclusion, interpretation, or thesis.

2. Fits the *usual*, everyday way of reasoning—what we sometimes call *common sense*.

3. Every piece of inductive reasoning includes some *inductive leap*. We begin with particulars and form general conclusions from them. Somewhere we have to jump or leap from one to the other. Make sure that leap isn't too far or your reasoning will be fatal.

4. *All* inductive reasoning produces only *probable* conclusions. You can't be *sure* that a particular conclusion will be proven by every example; you can only examine your examples carefully and try to select those that are representative and reach *probable* conclusions.

Deduction

1. Works from general assumptions in a series of related statements to a general conclusion.

2. If the assumptions can be proven, the conclusion is *certain beyond doubt* in deduction.

3. Deduction can only be applied to smaller aspects of larger problems. Because we can usually be certain of only a few basic assumptions in any particular writing situation, we must be sure to begin our deductive chains of reasoning with clear, agreed-upon assumptions.

Argument: Details and oppositions

Sometimes we make the mistake of assuming that reasoning processes such as induction and deduction apply only to argument or to writing situations in which we plan to explain and persuade rather than to describe objectively. But that's not true. Even when we are writing to describe we have to develop some kind of organizational plan. Sometimes we organize descriptions spatially or tell a story chronologically, relating events in the order they occurred. But we must remember that argumentative writing and informative writing also use some description. Suppose you want to argue that a good magazine article usually assumes a very general audience. The best way to prove that is to *describe* very carefully a few typical magazine readers and a few typical magazine articles. In this way you're *showing* your readers why they should agree with you. You're sharing your opinions *and* your experience with them. You'll need to describe and illustrate quickly—that means you'll have to select and organize your descriptions carefully—*and* you'll have to connect the illustrations to your general argument clearly. To accomplish economy and to establish the relationships between what you describe and your argument, you will sometimes resort to inductive or deductive methods of organization.

Often the best way to write a strong argument is to first take the opposite of the argument you would support yourself. Taking the opposite position can help you understand and subsequently to oppose the arguments of the other side. Otherwise, you might omit answers to important questions or underestimate the appeal of an opposing view.

Activity Exercise

Here are several theses which seem popular with many people now. Imagine yourself defending the opposite of these theses. What arguments might you use? What evidence could you cite?

1. Smoking is dangerous to your health and should be banned.
2. Women should not be used as sex symbols in advertising.
3. War is unhealthy for living things.
4. Cities, because they are overcrowded and run-down, are the cause of most modern social problems.
5. More people should "go back to the land," to farming, gardening, to living with and in nature.
6. Boxing is an inhuman sport; it should be abolished by state laws.
7. Racism is evil and the cause of much human suffering and injustice.

Thinking what you see

Color figure 2-2
LE VERTIGE D'EROS
Matta
follows page 14.

Here you can apply a few reasoning processes to a common experience—viewing a contemporary painting. Begin with this simple exercise. Look over Matta's painting carefully. As this painting demonstrates, the artist doesn't imitate or copy objects as they appear to us in everyday life. At first you'll feel that the painting has no focus or organization of its own, that the artist had no clear purpose. But as you look, let your mind wander freely. We think about and absorb what we see and experience all the time. But we are often not *conscious* of our mind's working and, as a result, lose much of the meaning of experience. Jot down a few of your thoughts. More than likely your mind will do some organizing. You'll make some kind of sense out of the painting. But you'll need to capture that sense and begin to transfer it to paper.

Now try this exercise in word association. Record any nouns (words that represent objects, people, places) that come to mind as you look over the painting. You may come up with a list something like this:

dizzy	matter
flow	brown
motion	green
glass	violet
abyss	springs
future	tubes
death	cloths
life	sticks
birth	
egg	

Look over your list and sort the words into groups of abstract and concrete nouns. An *abstract* word represents a large class of objects or ideas. *Freedom,* for example, and *honesty* are abstract because they include a great variety of meanings and applications. "Honesty" doesn't refer to any specific, concrete action or object but to a generally understood virtue that can be applied to a great number of people and actions. *Concrete* nouns refer to specific physical objects—a stone, a particular color, usually something we can experience directly through our senses. Here is the above list separated into abstract and concrete groupings.

Abstract	*Concrete*
death	glass
life	springs
birth	tubes
future	sticks
dizziness	brown
flow	green
matter	violet
	abyss
	egg

Now try to work out either an inductive plan, from particular example to more general conclusion or impression, or a deductive plan, from general thesis back through supporting evidence, for a short essay on the painting. In either case, stay very close to the painting. Describe it carefully; refer to objects or details in it.

Here are two sample paragraphs, both built around words in the above lists.

Any painting that doesn't show the world the way it appears to us every day is what I'd call an "abstract" work. In other words, the artist takes a natural, common scene and, rather than just copy it, mixes up the elements in the scene to try and capture its essence, what it *really* is underneath. Matta's painting is definitely abstract. When you look at it, you just barely recognize a few familiar shapes—coils, springs, lines of force—that probably existed in some other design in a real-life situation. I think the painter is trying to describe a fantastic future world, one we can just barely imagine.

I see weird designs. I feel pressures that I've never felt before——ones that make me dizzy and slightly tipsy. I feel light, almost airy. I'm lost in a swirling, emptier-than-air atmosphere. This has to be a picture of outer space, something someone in the twenty-first century might feel. In fact, maybe this would qualify as a rather traditional, everyday landscape painting in the twenty-first century.

Both these paragraphs were written spontaneously. Both show that even our initial responses to experience demonstrate some sense of order. We need to discover whatever natural order our experience exhibits and then develop it, adding flesh to that basic organizational skeleton of experience.

The first paragraph is a bit more formal than the second. The writer gives us an equation that he thinks explains what kind of painting *Le Vertige D'Eros* is. The equation begins with a basic assumption, one that the writer proposes without much discussion as a conventional definition: "Any painting that doesn't show the world the way it appears to us every day is what I'd call an 'abstract' work." Then he goes on to offer evidence that shows how the painting fits that assumption. The paragraph moves from basic premise and assumption, through supporting evidence, to a logical conclusion: that the painting *is* abstract and that it tries to show a future, abstract world. The conclusion or answer to the equation is simplified in the last sentence rather than directly stated. We might plot the paragraph like this:

Assumption: Any painting that doesn't represent the world as we experience it every day is abstract.

Middle term of equation: When we analyze the painting, we find that it does not represent an everyday version of the world.
Conclusion: The painting is abstract.

The second paragraph follows a natural organizing process. The "I," or observer-writer, records his physical sensations as he responds to the painting. Then he moves quickly to a general conclusion. If the exercise were longer, we'd expect more evidence, more careful attention to how evidence and specifics are related to generalities. But in both examples, however short, we find generally successful inductive and deductive plans.

There are three general stages in learning to organize inductively and deductively. First, you've got to look for and clarify patterns of organization in your actual experience, *before* you actually write. That helps you to clarify and direct your outlines and plans.

Second, and this is what we've been treating in these exercises, you've got to begin to apply the natural order to the writing situation. How can you rework the material and plan to fit a particular audience? How do you want to sound as you write—objective and detached, involved and argumentative, sophisticated and formal? To answer these questions, you'll need to figure out your attitude toward the subject and the reasons behind it.

Finally, you'll need to read and revise your rough draft, to make sure you're following an organizational plan consistently and clearly. We begin with very basic patterns, the inductive and the deductive, and gradually develop more complex organizing strategies, perhaps combinations of inductive and deductive strategies, all geared to specific situations.

Organizing Exercise

1. Look over any painting, cartoon, or advertisement in this book. Write freely about it for some fifteen or twenty minutes. Don't worry yet about unity, coherence, or order. Just let the ideas, opinions, observations, and creative responses come. If you have trouble getting started, ask yourself pointed questions about objects in the painting, about what is going on in the cartoon or ad, about what you think might be the creator's intentions. Then go back and select one of your more general statements, make it the main sentence of your paragraph, and find particulars to support your generality. Be selective. Revise your paragraph using a simple inductive plan.

2. Go for a stroll in the neighborhood around your campus. Find a scene (for example, an animated conversation going on across the street, a scene in a quiet barber shop or in a busy department store) and take

particular, concrete notes on what you see. When you've finished, quickly jot down your general interpretation of what's going on. Are the participants arguing, will the lady looking over the underwear finally buy some? Then go back and rewrite following some deductive or inductive plan.

3. Turn on your television set with the sound turned down. Then, watch the speakers and imagine what they are saying. As you watch, take notes on what you think the speakers or actors are saying, what their subjects and opinions are. Sometimes you'll even have to guess at what they're doing. Singers, interviewers, and news commentators make excellent subjects. What are the sentiments of the song being sung, the subject of a discussion on a talk show, the import of the news being described? What specific or general impressions make you think so?

4. Begin with some general premise. For example: "Almost every person who rides a bike and is over forty is eccentric." Then go out and try to find instances that either verify or contradict the premise—"A perfectly conservative man wearing a thin, gray tie and a dark brown suit came by today on his bike." Or find experiences that lead you to some logical conclusions about bike-riders: "Bike-riding is physically tiring and good, everyday physical activity. Most people who have bikes around this campus use them every day instead of automobiles. Most bike-riders on this campus are physically fit." Then, plan and write a brief essay either working inductively from examples to conclusions or working deductively through a logical formula.

5. Form in your mind some generality about language as it is used every day, perhaps something like "most waitresses in city diners, cafés, and snack bars use a great deal of slang." Next, go out, eat at a downtown diner and purposely engage a few waiters or waitresses in conversation. Ask them leading questions, ones that you think will elicit colorful responses. Then, look up *slang*, in your dictionary. Did you actually hear it? Or did you hear other language traits? Look up *dialect, idiolect,* and a few other terms that might be used to describe the different styles of language we hear every day.

Logical fallacies

Before we apply our understanding of induction and deduction to some professional writing, we should give some attention to the more common fallacies in both kinds of reasoning.

Common inductive fallacies

1. Reasoning from too few examples: You've all met people who jump too quickly to general opinions about people, objects, or ideas. "I met a very talented and sophisticated Indian girl in New Mexico. Certainly Indians are

extremely talented people." They may be and probably are, but this particular argument or line of thinking doesn't prove it. Or how about the person who thinks he's helping all blacks by referring to the "nice black guy he once met in Paterson, New Jersey"? Be sure you have enough evidence to make a case for your opinions. When you describe a single object or scene, don't be too quick to draw general conclusions from it.

2. Reasoning from atypical examples: Be sure your examples are selected to make a fair representation or sample of the experience from which you are generalizing. We've all heard of the opinion survey that failed to make a truly random sampling. They happened to talk only to Democrats when evaluating the popularity of a Republican president. Ask yourself if your examples *do* represent all the possible examples fairly. Are you stacking the cards against or for your subject?

3. Ignoring counter-reasoning: The last general inductive fallacy occurs when a writer ignores an example that counters his line of reasoning: For example, several graduates of a particular school have gone on to become successful doctors. But many others have failed after trying for several years. A writer who tries to argue that the school should be recommended to potential medical students must somehow explain the failures as well as refer to the successes.

4. Reasoning from faulty analogies: Sometimes we use analogies to clarify our interpretations or descriptions. An *analogy* explains a puzzling or unfamiliar experience by comparing or relating it to a familiar experience. In this way, the reader learns the unfamiliar by comparing it with the familiar—"Those pears taste like green apples (green apples are usually sour; the pears must be sour as well)." Reasoning by analogy usually depends upon the idea that if two instances agree on a number of points they are likely to agree on the point in question. If the two instances are alike in what both writer and reader would agree are *important* respects, the analogy will usually be effective.

Thinking Exercise

Pick out an analogy in the following poem and ask yourself these questions about it:

1. Why did the writer use an analogy rather than a literal description?

2. Is it a clear analogy—are you familiar enough with both sides of the analogy to judge its accuracy?

3. Does the analogy really help to clarify what's being described? What *is* being described?

4. Could you think up a better analogy to describe the object of this poem?

5. What does the analogy tell you about the writer? What kind of person is he? How do you know?

6. Translate this poem into a literal description of the action. Be concrete and specific and try to capture the drama in the situation.

The Base Stealer

ROBERT FRANCIS

Poised between going on and back, pulled
Both ways taut like a tightrope-walker,
Fingertips pointing the opposites,
Now bouncing tiptoe like a dropped ball
Or a kid skipping rope, come on, come on,
Running a scattering of steps sidewise.
How he teeters, skitters, tingles, teases
Taunts them, hovers like an ecstatic bird,
He's only flirting, crowd him, crowd him,
Delicate, delicate, delicate, delicate—now!

Writing Exercise

As a brief exercise in developing and using analogy to help you describe, choose an action similar to the one in this poem. Limit the scope of the action to something you can describe in a page—a tennis player returning a difficult serve, a boy eating an ice cream cone, a mother pushing her small child on a swing. After you've written a few paragraphs describing the action factually or objectively, make a list of objects or scenes to which you might compare your subject. Next, list the concrete details of that object or scene. Then, just as Robert Francis compares a tightrope-walker and a base-stealer, write an analogy into your description and use it to clarify the objective description in your previous paragraph.

Obviously, when you're reasoning inductively from examples to conclusions, you've got to test your analogies carefully. An ill-chosen analogy might destroy your argument. And above all, select analogies carefully and mix them with objective description and clear logic. In this way, your reader doesn't feel that you are using analogies to show off or sound literary, but rather to help him see and experience what you are saying.

Common deductive fallacies

1. False or unproven assumptions: You can't expect a reader to agree with an interpretation that is not founded on an assumption with which he also agrees. Someone who expects another to respond negatively to a person because he has proven that person to be a Communist may be ignoring the fact that not all people believe that Communists are naturally bad. The writer must prove the assumption—that Communists are bad——before he goes on to his argument. Consider also what debaters often call the "red herring." Someone begins by assuming that a particular word, idea, object, person, or group is bad. Then he merely mentions that word to get an emotional and negative response from his readers. For example, a speaker might use the term "sex education" to get an emotional outcry from an audience he knows is anti-sex education. If he hasn't really proven that the term deserves censure, he's using a "red herring."

2. If-then fallacies: It does not follow because one premise is true, a second, perhaps unrelated, premise is also true. For example, the player batting third in the Mets line-up is usually a good hitter. If Jones bats third, then he must be a good hitter. But, Cleon Jones may be having a bad year. The reasoning fails to acknowledge an important exception, an important "if," so the thinking proves false. Another example: "If you don't water the flowers they'll die. The flowers are dead. You didn't water them." This is faulty deductive reasoning because lack of watering is not the *only* cause of dead flowers. If you set up a deductive line of thought, be sure that you consider *all* possible causes of an effect, not just the one that first occurs to you.

3. Either-or thinking: This is probably the most common deductive fallacy. Don't allow yourself to limit your thinking to only two solutions for any particular problem: "Either he killed him or he didn't." Perhaps he helped to kill him or had him killed by someone else or accidentally killed him or only tried to kill him. Either-or thinking is an especially dangerous fallacy when you try to describe or analyze an immediate experience; it can cause you to ignore too much, to limit your analysis to only those alternatives the fallacy allows. We sometimes see *only* what we are looking for. And we sometimes read only to find what we want to find.

4. Emotional appeals: Always consider the emotions of your reader. But don't appeal to your reader's emotions in order to distract him from your real subject. Hitler blamed the Jews, not the German economy or poor German leadership, for all Germany's problems. He, in other words, appealed to his people's emotions to make them avoid rather than confront the real issues. The German Jews under Hitler became what historians call "scapegoats." They became the objects of all their countrymen's resent-

ment, despair, and prejudice because Hitler was at least partially successful in appealing to emotions, often at the expense of reason.

Finding patterns in what you read

Most good writing uses both inductive and deductive patterns of organization. The two essays that follow are crammed with numerous examples of the process: the writers use particular instances to illustrate, prove, and clarify a general interpretation. James Agee describes how it feels to sleep late at night on the front porch of a poor tenant farmer's home in the South. He records sights, sounds, smells, and feelings very carefully, and through his recordings he shares a personal experience completely. Soon the recorded detail adds up and forms for the reader and Agee a general feeling: that the quiet of the night, the sky, the stars, the sounds and small movements of insects and birds accumulate and smother the observer—both Agee and his readers—in a dream-like revery, a very close relationship with the world around them. Tom Wolfe believes that Americans are using machines and technology—motorcycles, closed-circuit television, mass-produced clothing and beauty aids—to create private and personal life-styles. Everybody escapes into his own little pleasure-world, turns on, and leaves the rest of society behind. He describes motorcycle racers, topless Go-Go dancers, and the editor of *Playboy* magazine as people all searching for a world of private pleasures amidst a sea of people and confusion.

Readers can find deductive patterns of thought behind these essays as well. Agee's respect for the poor families he describes throughout *Let Us Now Praise Famous Men* and his empathy with and understanding of how they live and what they feel and do, grow naturally from both what he sees and from a basic belief in the equality of all men, in the essential worth and dignity of the poor and unnoticed. In a sense, he finds in his observations of poor farmers what he more than likely believed from the very beginning—that a thorough study and description of such people would be interesting and basically heroic and would prove him right. He follows a general deductive pattern: it is good to live simply, to struggle for one's existence, to feel close to your environment; the poor live close to the earth and simply, the poor will make interesting and noble subjects of study because they live simply in a very complex age. This pattern is hidden in the essay; the reader must discover it for himself. But it is there, controlling the language.

Tom Wolfe works back and forth through his essay from illustration to thesis, from thesis to illustration. He has traveled throughout this country and England finding evidence, asking questions, observing carefully, writing. Americans and British alike, with few exceptions, are living escapist lives in what he calls "statuspheres"—little, isolated compartments of pleasure—which are found in San Francisco night club scenes, on the Sunset Strip, at the beaches, in the London mod-clothing cliques. Wolfe groups every example under his thesis, explains how and why it works, and ends with a brief account of how the "important" people—leaders, politicians and intellectuals alike—remain ignorant of what's really going on around them.

from *Let Us Now Praise Famous Men*

JAMES AGEE

On the Porch

The house and all that was in it had now descended deep beneath the gradual spiral it had sunk through; it lay formal under the order of entire silence. In the square pine room at the back the bodies of the man of thirty and of his wife and of their children lay on shallow mattresses on their iron beds and on the rigid floor, and they were sleeping, and the dog lay asleep in the hallway. Most human beings, most animals and birds who live in the sheltering ring of human influence, and a great portion of all the branched tribes of living in earth and air and water upon a half of the world, were stunned with sleep. That region of the earth on which we were at this time transient was some hours fallen beneath the fascination of the stone, steady shadow of the planet, and lay now listing toward the last depth; and now by a blockade of the sun were clearly disclosed those discharges of light which teach us what little we can learn of the stars and of the true nature of our surroundings. There was no longer any sound of the settling or ticking of any part of the structure of the house; the bone pine hung on its nails like an abandoned Christ. There was no longer any sound of the sinking and settling, like gently foundering fatal boats, of the bodies and brains of this human family through the late stages of fatigue unharnessed or the early phases of sleep; nor was there any longer the sense of any of these sounds, nor was there, even, the sound or the sense of breathing. Bone and bone, blood and blood, life and life disjointed and abandoned they lay graven in so final depth, that dreams attend them seemed not plausible. Fish halted on the middle and serene of blind sea water sleeping lidless lensed; their breathing, their sleeping subsistence, the effortless nursing of ignorant plants; entirely silenced, sleepers, delicate planets, insects, cherished in amber, mured in night, autumn of action, sorrow's short winter, waterhole where gather the weak wild beasts; night; night: sleep; sleep.

In their prodigious realm, their field, bashfully at first, less timorous, later, rashly, all calmly boldly now, like the tingling and standing up of plants, leaves, planted crops out of the earth into the yearly approach of the sun, the noises and natures of the dark had with the ceremonial gestures of music and of erosion lifted forth the thousand several forms of their entrancement, and had so resonantly taken over the world that this domestic, this human silence obtained, prevailed, only locally, shallowly, and with the childlike and frugal dignity of a coal-oil lamp stood out on a wide night meadow and of a star sustained, unraveling in one rivery sigh its irremediable vitality, on the alien size of space.

Where beneath the ghosts of millennial rain the clay land lay down in the creek and the trees ran thick there disposed upon the sky the cloud and black shadow of nature, hostile encampment whose fires were drenched, drawn close, held sleeping, near, helots; and it was feasible that within a few hours now, at the signaling of the primary changes of the air, the wave which summer and darkness had already so heavily overcrested that it leaned above us, snaring its snake-tongued branches, birnam wood, casually would lounge in and suddenly and forever subdue us: at most, some obscure act of guerrilla warfare, some prowler, detached from his regiment, picked off in a back country orchard, some straggling camp whore taken, had; for the sky:

The sky was withdrawn from us with all her strength. Against some scarcely conceivable imprisoning wall this woman held herself away from us and watched us: wide, high, light with her stars as milk above our heavy dark; and like the bristling and glass breakage on the mouth of stone spring water: broached on grand heaven their mental fires.

And now as by the slipping of a button, the snapping and failures on air of a spider's cable, there broke loose from the room, shaken, a long sigh closed in silence. On some ledge overleaning that gulf which is more profound than the remembrance of imagination they had lain in sleep and at length the sand, that by degrees had crumpled and rifted, had broken from beneath them and they sank. There was now no further extreme and they were sunken not singularly but companionate among the whole enchanted swarm of the living, into a region prior to the youngest quaverings of creation.

Discussion Questions and Writing Exercises

1. Many readers would find Agee's description corny if it weren't for his extensive use of concrete detail to support his subjective feelings. Find three sentences that you believe show Agee's opinions, his attitudes toward the scene he describes. Then find at least one concrete detail or appeal to your senses that supports his attitude. Can you find general statements of feeling that you believe Agee failed to support adequately?

2. Write down a general fact about something that matters to you—an

object, an idea, a feeling, a deep emotion. Then begin to record other facts that come along, trying to use more and more specific language. If you began by thinking of a car or poster you own, record details and feelings that come to your mind naturally. Keep moving back and forth, as Agee does, between your personal opinions or feelings and the object or experience itself. Make what you have experienced come to the aid of what you think.

3. Try this with a few friends, perhaps someone in class. Ask them to name and describe factually a past incident that was important to them in a few words. *You* listen carefully. Can you tell just by their tone of voice, their gestures, and the words they use *why* the incident was important? Try this several times and discuss how attitude was communicated even when the speaker wanted to be objective and factual.

4. James Agee was primarily a journalist; he traveled the country recording what he saw and felt, working up interesting subjects, and writing feature articles for newspapers and magazines. He had to be interesting as well as accurate. Where do you think the passage we just read would fit in your local newspaper? Would it fit at all? How would you grade Agee on accuracy and interest if you were his editor? Compare Agee's piece with the story by Tom Wolfe, who is also a traveling, free-lance writer-journalist commenting on different aspects of modern culture.

from *The Pump House Gang*

TOM WOLFE

I wrote all but two[1] of these stories in one ten-month stretch after the publication of my first book, *The Kandy-Kolored Tangerine-Flake Streamline Baby*. It was a strange time for me. Many rogue volts of euphoria. I went from one side of this country to the other and then from one side of England to the other. The people I met—the things they did—I was entranced. I met Carol Doda. She blew up her breasts with emulsified silicone, the main ingredient in Silly Putty, and became the greatest resource of the San Francisco tourist industry. I met a group of surfers, the Pump House Gang. They attended the Watts riot as if it were the Rose Bowl game in Pasadena. They came to watch "the drunk niggers" and were reprimanded by the same for their rowdiness. In London I met a competitive 17-year-old named Nicki who got one-up on her schoolgirl chums by taking a Kurdish clubfoot lover. I met a £9-a-week office boy named Larry Lynch. He spent his lunch hour every day with hundreds of other child laborers in the crazed pitchblack innards of a noonday nightclub called Tiles. All of them

[1]"The Automated Hotel" and "Tom Wolfe's New Book of Etiquette."

in ecstasies from the frug, the rock 'n' roll, and God knows what else, for an hour—then back to work. In Chicago I met Hugh Hefner. He revolved on his bed, offering scenic notes as his head floated by—

Now, about Hefner. I was heading for California from New York and I happened to stop off in Chicago. I was walking down North Michigan Avenue when I ran into a man from the Playboy organization, Lee Gottlieb. Something he said made me assume that Hefner was out of town.

"Out of town?" said Gottlieb. "Hef never leaves his house."

"Never?

Never, said Gottlieb. At least not for months at a time, and even then only long enough to get in a limousine and go to the airport and fly to New York for a TV show or to some place or other for the opening of a new Playboy Club. This fascinated me, the idea that Hefner, the Main Playboy himself, was now a recluse. The next afternoon I went to the Playboy offices on East Ohio Street to see about getting in to see him. In the office they kept track of Hefner's physical posture in his Mansion, which was over on North State Parkway, as if by play-by-play Telex. He was flat out in bed asleep, they told me, and wouldn't be awake until around midnight. That night I was killing time in a dive in downtown Chicago when a courier materialized and told me Hefner was now on his feet and could see me.

Hefner's Playboy Mansion had a TV eye at the front portals and huge black guards or major-domos inside. *Nubian slaves,* I kept saying to myself. One of the blacks led me up a grand staircase covered in red wall-to-wall, to a massive carved-wood doorway bearing the inscription, *Si Non Oscillas, Noli Tintinnare,* "If you don't swing, don't ring." Inside were Hefner's private chambers. Hefner came charging out of a pair of glass doors within. He was wound up and ready to go. "Look at this!" he said. "Isn't this fantastic!" It was an issue of *Ramparts* magazine that had just come. It had a glossy foldout, like the one in *Playboy.* Only this one had a picture of Hefner. In the picture he was wearing a suit and smoking a pipe. "Isn't this fantastic!" Hefner kept saying. Right now he was wearing silk pajamas, a bathrobe, and a pair of slippers with what looked like embroidered wolf heads on them. This was not, however, because he had just gotten up. It was his standard wear for the day, this day, every day, the uniform of the contemporary recluse.

There were several people in attendance at the midnight hour. The *dame d'honneur* of the palace, who was named Michele; Gottlieb; a couple of other *Playboy* personnel; the blacks: they were all dressed, however. Hefner showed me through his chambers. The place was kept completely draped and shuttered. The only light, day or night, was electric. It would be impossible to keep track of the days in there. And presently Hefner jumped onto . . . the center of his world, the bed in his bedroom. Aimed at the bed was a TV camera he was very proud of. Later on *Playboy* ran a cartoon showing a nude man and woman in a huge bed with a TV set facing them, and the man is saying, "And now, darling, how about an instant replay." Hefner hit a dial and the bed started revolving . . .

All I could think of at that moment was Jay Gatsby in the Fitzgerald novel. Both were scramblers who came up from out of nowhere to make their fortunes and build their palaces and ended up in regal isolation. But there was a major difference between Hefner and Gatsby. Hefner no longer dreamed, if he ever did, of making the big social leap to East Egg. It was at least plausible for Gatsby to hope to make it into Society. But Hefner? He has made a fortune, created an empire, and the Playboy Beacon shines out over the city and the Great Lakes. But socially Hefner is still a man who runs a tit magazine and a string of clubs that recall the parlor floor; not the upper floors but the parlor floor—of a red-flock whorehouse. There is no Society in Chicago for Hugh Hefner.

So he has gone them one better. He has started his own league. He has created his own world, in his own palace. He has created his own status-phere. The outside world comes to him, including the talented and the celebrated. Jules Feiffer stays awhile in his scarlet guest suite. Norman Mailer skinnydips in his Playboy swimming pool. He has his courtiers, his girls, and his Nubian slaves. Not even God's own diurnal light rhythm intrudes upon the order that Hefner has founded inside.

What a marvelous idea! After all, the community has never been one great happy family for all men. In fact, I would say the opposite has been true. Community status systems have been games with few winners, and many who feel like losers. What an intriguing thought—for a man to take his new riches and free time and his machines and *split* from *communitas* and start his own league. He will still have status competition—but he invents the rules.

Why has no one ever done it before? Well, of course, people have. Robin Hood did it. Spades, homosexuals, artists, and street gangs have done it. All sorts of outlaws, and outcasts, by necessity or choice. The intriguing thing today, I was to find, is that so many Americans and Englishmen of middle and lower incomes are now doing the same thing. Not out of "rebellion" or "alienation"—they just want to be happy winners for a change.

What is a California electronics worker making $18,000 a year supposed to do with his new riches? Set about getting his son into Culver Military and himself and the wife into the Doral Beach Country Club? Socially, he is a glorified mechanic. Why not, à la Hefner, put it all into turning his home into a palace of technological glories—and extend that abroad in the land with a Buick Estate Wagon and a Pontiac GTO—and upon the seas with an Evinrude cruiser and even into the air with a Cessna 172? Why not surround the palace with my favorite piece of landscaping of the happy worker suburbs of the American West, the Home Moat. It is about three feet wide and a foot and a half deep. Instructions for placing rocks, flowers, and shrubs are available. The Home Moat is a psychological safeguard against the intrusion of the outside world. The Home Moat guards against the fear that *It* is going to creep up in the night and press its nose against your picture window.

Southern California, I found, is a veritable paradise of statuspheres.

For example, the move to age segregation. There are old people's housing developments, private developments, in which no one under 50 may buy a home. There are apartment developments for single persons 20 to 30 only. The Sunset Strip in Los Angeles has become the exclusive hangout of the 16 to 25 set. In 1966 they came close to street warfare to keep it that way, against the police who moved in to "clean up."

And . . . the Pump House Gang. Here was a group of boys and girls who had banded together in a way that superficially resembled a street gang's. They had very little of the street gang's motivation, however. They came from middle-class and upper-middle-class homes in perhaps the most high-class beach community in California, La Jolla. They had very little sense of resentment toward their parents or "society" and weren't rebels. Their only "alienation" was the usual hassle of the adolescent, the feeling that he is being prodded into adulthood on somebody else's terms. So they did the latest thing. They split off—*to the beach! into the garages!*—and started their own league, based on the esoterica of surfing. They didn't resent the older people around them; they came to pity the old bastards because they couldn't partake of this esoteric statusphere.

The day I met the Pump House Gang, a group of them had just been thrown out of "Tom Coman's garage," as it was known. The next summer they moved up from the garage life to a group of apartments near the beach, a complex they named "La Colonia Tijuana." But this time some were shifting from the surfing life to the advance guard of something else—the psychedelic *head* world of California. That is another story. But even the *hippies,* as the heads came to be known, did not develop *sui generis.* Their so-called "dropping out" was nothing more than a still further elaboration of the kind of worlds that the surfers and the car kids I met—"The Hair Boys"—had been creating the decade before.

The Pump House Gang lived as though age segregation were a permanent state, as if it were inconceivable that any of them would ever grow old, i.e., 25. I foresaw the day when the California coastline would be littered with the bodies of aged and abandoned *Surferkinder,* like so many beached whales.

In fact, however, many of these kids seem to be able to bring the mental atmosphere of the surfer life forward with them into adulthood—even into the adult world where you have to make a living. I remember going to the motorcycle races at Gardena, California, which is just south of Watts with a surfer who is now about 30 and has developed a large water-sport equipment business. This was a month after the Watts riots. We were sitting in the stands at Gardena. The motorcycles were roaring around the half-mile track below and flashing under the lights. Just beyond the track from where we sat were Watts and Compton.

"Tom," he said to me, "you should have been here last month."

"Why?"

"The riots," he said. "You should have been here. We were all sitting here right where we are now and the bikes were going around down below here. And over here"—over to the left you could look over the edge of the stands and see the highway—"the National Guard units were pulling up and jumping off the trucks and getting into formation and everything with the bayonets and all. It was terrific. And then, there"—and his gaze and his voice got a far-off quality, going beyond the track and toward Watts—"and there, there in the distance, was Los Angeles . . . . *burning!*"

A few minutes later ten motorcycles came into the first turn, right in front of where we were sitting. Five went down in a pile-up. Bodies shot through the air every which way. I saw one, a rider in black and white racing leathers, get hit in midair by one motorcycle and run over by the one behind it. This was a kid named Cleemie Jackson. He was dead. Everybody could see that. His neck was broken like a stick. Two other riders were seriously injured. The p.a. announcer didn't mention those who were lying there, however. He only mentioned those who got up. "There's No. 353, Rog Rogarogarog, he's up and his bike looks O.K. . . ." As soon as the bodies were removed, the race resumed. Luckily they hadn't had to take both the ambulances. They have two ambulances at the track, and if both have to leave, the races have to stop until one returns. They were able to get the three worst bodies into one ambulance. The ambulance, a big white Cadillac, left very quietly. It didn't even flash a light. About three minutes later you could hear the siren start up, way down the highway. Off in the distance, as they say. It was a freaking ghastly sound, under the circumstances. Within seconds, however, the race was on again, with five bikes instead of ten, and all was forgotten. As usual, there were only a couple of paragraphs in the papers about the death.

I don't think that is a very morbid incident, taken in context. The half-mile racers are the wildest and most suicidal crowd in the motorcycle life, but all the motorcycle crowds get a lot of their juice out of the luxury of risking their necks. The motorcycle life has been perfect as a statusphere. It is dangerous and therefore daring. It is as esoteric as surfing. It can liberate you physically from the *communitas*.

When you mention the motorcycle life, people tend to think —again—of outlaws. Namely, the Hell's Angels. The Angels and other motorcycle outlaws, however, make up only a small part of the people who have started their own league with their bikes. I'll never forget the Harley-Davidson agency in Columbus, Ohio. A guy came in the back there dragging a big Harley. It was all bent and mashed, the spokes, the headers, the cylinder heads, the sprocket, the drive chain. Everybody said, You had a wreck! The guy said, Naw, it was my wife. Everybody said, Was she hurt bad! The guy said, Naw, she took a block of cement about this big and she—well, it seems she had smashed the hell out of it. He had first bought the Harley just for a little recreation away from the wife and kids. Then he had discovered hundreds of motorcyclists around Columbus—all drifting away from the wife and kids. Pretty soon he was meeting the boys every day after work at a place called Gully's and they would drink beer and ride up to Lake Erie before coming home, a mere 200-mile trip. By and by they had a whole new life for themselves—blissful liberation—based on the motorcycle. Until his wife decided to sort that little situation out . . .

Columbus is the world capital of the motorcycle life. This statement, I find, comes as a surprise and an annoyance—the damnable Hell's Angels again—to a lot of people in Columbus, despite the fact that the American Motorcycle Association has its headquarters there. On the surface, Columbus could not be more conservative and traditional. A few big property-owning families seem to control everything. Well, they don't control the motorcycle life, which has proliferated in and around the town over the past ten years in full rich variety, from half-mile racing daredevils to Honda touring clubs. They also have a local version of the Hell's Angels, the Road Rogues. The vast majority of Columbus motorcyclists, however, are perfectly law-abiding citizens who happen to have found an infinitely richer existence than being a standard wagemule for whoever does run Columbus.

The two great motorcyclists of Columbus are Dick Klamforth, a former half-mile racing champion and now owner of the Honda agency there, the biggest in the country, and Tom Reiser. Reiser is truly one of the greats. He built "Tom's Bomb." He achieved an ultimate. He flew through the air of the American Midwest, astride a 300-horsepower Chevrolet V-8 engine . . . riding bareback . . .

Now, this is not exactly what the great Utopian thinkers of the nineteenth century, the Saint-Simons, the Fouriers, and the Owens, had in mind when they envisioned a world of the future in which the ordinary working man would have the time and the money to extend his God-given potential to the fullest. The old Utopians believed in industrialism. In fact, it was Saint-Simon who coined the word. Yet the worker paradise industrialism would make possible was to take a somewhat more pastoral form. They saw it as a kind of Rousseauvian happy-primitive village with modern conveniences. In short, a community, with everyone, great and small, knit together forever after, grateful as spaniels. More recently, in the 1920s and 1930s, the vision was amended. It now put the happy workers into neat lead-white blocks of Bauhaus apartments and added Culture. Every night, in this vision, the family would gather around the hearth and listen to Dad read from John Starchey or Mayakovsky while WQXR droned in the background. The high point of the week would be Saturday afternoon, when Dad would put on his electric-blue suit—slightly gauche, you understand, but neat and clean and pressed, "touching," as it were—and the whole family would hold hands and walk up to the Culture Center to watch the Shock Workers of the Dance do a ballet called "Factory." Well, today, in the 1960s, the Culture Centers have sprouted up, sure enough. We have them in most of the metropolises of America. But where have all the happy workers gone? These temples to breeding and taste are usually constructed at great cost, in the name of "the people." But the people, the happy people, have left them to the cultivated, educated classes, the "diploma elite," who created them.

And even the cultivated classes—the term "upper classes" no longer works—are in a state of rather amusing confusion on the subject. When great fame—the certification of status—is available without great property, it is very bad news for the old idea of a class structure. In New York, for example, it is done for, but no one has bothered to announce its death. As a result, New York "Society" is now made up of a number of statuspheres- —all busily raiding the old class order for trappings to make their fame look genuine. Business and other corporate statuspheres have been so busy cannibalizing the old aristocratic modes, I have had to write an entire new gull's handbook on the subject ("Tom Wolfe's New Book of Etiquette"). The great hotel corporations now advertise Luxury (equals "class") to the same crowd who used to go to the durable second-raters, the commercial or businessman's hotel. It is a pretty amusing invention, this second-class *class,* unless you happen to stay at The Automated Hotel without knowing the name of the game. Meanwhile, individual climbers are busy moving into separate little preserves that once made up the happy monolith of "the upper class"—such as charities and *Yes!* Culture—and I offer the golden example of Bob and Spite Scull for those who want to make it *Now,* without having to wait three generations, as old-fashioned sorts, such as the Kennedy family, had to do. Of course, with so many statuspheres now in operation, and so many short cuts available, there is a chronic chaos in Society. People are now reaching the top without quite knowing what on earth they have reached the top of. They don't know whether they have reached *The* Top or whether they have just had a wonderful fast ride up the service elevator. But as Bob Scull himself says: "Enjoy!"

What struck me throughout America and England was that so many people have found such novel ways of doing just that, *enjoying,* extending their egos way out on the best terms available, namely, their own. It is curious how many serious thinkers—and politicians—resist this rather obvious fact. Sheer ego extension—especially if attempted by all those rancid proles and suburban petty burghers—is a perplexing prospect. Even scary, one might say. Intellectuals and politicians currently exhibit a vast gummy nostaligia for the old restraints, the old limits, of the ancient ego-crusher: *Calamity.* Historically, calamity has been the one serious concern of serious people. War, Pestilence—Apocalypse! I was impressed by the profound relief with which intellectuals and politicians discovered poverty in America in 1963, courtesy of Michael Harrington's book *The Other America.* And, as I say, it was *discovered.* Eureka! We have found it again! We thought we had lost it. That was the spirit of the enterprise. When the race riots erupted—and when the war in Vietnam grew into a good-sized hell—intellectuals welcomed all that with a ghastly embrace, too. War! Poverty! Insurrection! Alienation! O Four Horsemen, you have not deserted us entirely. The game can go on.

One night, in the middle of the period when I was writing these stories, I put on *my* electric-blue suit—it is truly electric blue—and took part in a symposium at Princeton with Günter Grass, Allen Ginsberg, and Gregory Markopoulos, who is an "underground" filmmaker, before 1,200 students. The subject was "The Style of the Sixties." Paul Krassner was the moderator, and Krassner has a sense of humor, but the Horsemen charged on. Very soon the entire discussion was centered on police repression, Gestapo tactics, the knock on the door, the Triumph of the Knout. I couldn't believe what was happening, but there it was.

"What are you talking about?" I said. "We're in the middle of a . . . Happiness Explosion!" But I didn't know where to begin. I might as well have said let's talk about the Fisher King. Happiness, said Saint-Just a century ago, is a new concept in Europe. Apparently it was new here, unheard-of almost. Ah, *philosophes!*—if we want to be *serious*, let us discuss the real apocalyptic future and things truly scary: ego extension, the politics of pleasure, the self-realization racket, the pharmacology of Overjoy . . .

But why discuss it now. I, for one, will be content merely to watch the faces of our leaders, political and intellectual, the day they wake up and look over their shoulders and catch the first glimpse of their erstwhile followers—streaking—*happy workers!*—in precisely the opposite direction, through God's own American ozone—*apocalyptic riders!*—astride their own custom versions—*enjoy!*—of the 300-horsepower Chevrolet V-8 engines of this world . . . riding bareback . . .

Discussion Questions and Writing Exercises

1. Tom Wolfe knows what he wants to say about the people he describes before he even begins to write. Every group or individual he has described fits his thesis—modern man has the ability and the desire to wipe out class distinctions by creating little, isolated personal worlds built upon private or small-group values. Yet Wolfe never betrays his thesis or his evidence openly. He jumps around, develops his thesis here ("What an intriguing thought—for a man to take his new riches and free time and his machines and *split* from *communitas* and starts his own league"), gives illustrations and examples here ("Here was a group of boys and girls who had banded together in a way that superficially resembled a street gang's."), constantly fuses what he thinks and what he sees. Could you defend Wolfe against the charge that he's disorganized, that he writes like a modern madman? Do *you* like the way he organizes his material? Can you make sense of it? Can you draw up an outline of Wolfe's essay? Can you find a design or form in it?

2. The last few pages of this passage are deductively organized. Wolfe explains the development of his thesis and cites examples of intellectuals and politicians who can't themselves comprehend it. Would these pages work *without* the examples cited in the earlier pages?

3. Read closely and analyze *one* of Wolfe's concrete descriptions—his description of Hugh Hefner's pad in Chicago or his brief references to the Pump House Gang in California. How would you grade his selection and use of detail, his style (the way he uses words to get across his attitude)?

Does he ever seem to notice only what he wants to notice to fit his thesis? Go out and find some examples similar to the ones Wolfe uses. You might observe a group of local high school "hair boys," as Wolfe calls them, or a group of housewives at a museum. Describe them. Then try to relate what you describe to the society-at-large, as Wolfe does. You might begin this exercise in your journal and finish with a two- or three-page essay. Or take your journal to a local drive-in restaurant and record some of what you see. Draw some inferences from what you see and then develop an essay, with a thesis, from your observations.

Finding material in current events

The writer who says he has nothing to say is really saying that he hasn't paid much attention to what goes on around him. He's missed a lot, ignored a lot. The exercises, analyses, and discussions in the previous sections of this chapter should have helped you find material to write about.

Now turn your attention to the following display of brief newspaper articles (page 55). Read them carefully; try to absorb what they mean to you, especially when you consider that newspapers contain such articles every day. Analyze the experiences much as you would a passing, everyday happening, but with intensified attention to the background suggested by the words. Imagine yourself actually at the scene of the action. What would you see, hear, smell, or think? We can summarize what being conscious means to a writer by analyzing our responses to these newspaper clippings. Newspapers are especially useful sources for subject matter. The front page presents a variety of happenings as if they were occurring simultaneously before you. Any one item might lead to arguments and discussions with other readers. Present your opinions to others; try to find out *why* you think as you do and use the information to convince someone else.

The newspaper is an everyday experience you can enjoy. The variety of voices—the irate letter to the editor, the gossipy social columnist, the sarcastic or ironic political columnist, or the objective reporter—are parts of experience readers have become accustomed to every morning or evening.

Remember, the important difference between an experience in real life and what you read in a brief newspaper article is usually the amount of detail. The article condenses information, reveals just a few significant facts; the reader fills in the rest. Articles like the following present a series of condensed, factual experiences. You be the social critic. Draw some inferences about social problems from what you read. But, remember, the idea is not to arrive at a *right* answer. Rather, it is to see how well you can explain the opinions you carry around with you every day, even those on subjects that are not particularly familiar to you. Pull the facts together into an interpretation.

Here are several one-sentence responses, casual and familiar, to the experiences expressed in these articles.

These articles are sick.

They show the violent side of American culture.

Everything on this page shows that violence is natural to men.

Some violence is funny, some of it is terrifying, but all of it is dangerous.

A lot of what we read in the newspaper is garbage and junk.

Without violence society would die of boredom. Some of it is necessary.

Before you draw opinions of your own from these and articles like these, think about their implications. Talk to your friends. Discuss the articles and responses in class or with a wife, husband, or roommate over coffee. These "off the top of your head" opinions would need to be explained and supported in writing. Can you improve any of them so that they would function as supportable theses for a longer essay? Consider this response: "Everything on this page shows that violence is natural to man." Why "everything"? Yes, and why "natural"? A revised thesis might read: "Violence is an undeniably large part of society as we know it." No, that's too vague; it's not worth proving or supporting. A second revised thesis might be: "The abundance of violence, as shown in our newspapers every day, results from life in a fast-moving, tension-filled society, one that forces individuals to resort, out of frustration, to violent acts." It's a good thesis, but not all the articles would support it.

This brief account gives you some idea of the variety of responses possible. Different people respond differently to the same experience. The good writer knows this; he observes everyday experiences carefully and tries to imagine how other people might respond to an experience he is presently having.

Bring to class other everyday artifacts—newspapers, magazines, letters, anything—and analyze different reactions. These differences should convince you that you'll need to remember details to make your opinions convincing.

Kidnapped Coed Found Closed in Trunk of Car

OCALA, Fla. Dec. 31 (UPI) —A college coed kidnaped from a birthday party by a gunman early Sunday was found disheveled but unharmed today in the trunk of a car 90 miles from where she was abducted.

Marion County Sheriff Don Moreland said Kathy Morris, 20, of South Daytona, "told us she had been in the car since Sunday."

The girl was abducted by a masked gunman who terrorized four coeds during a birthday party early Sunday at a home in South Daytona.

The hostess's parents slept through the 90 minutes of terror in an upstairs bedroom.

The sheriff said there was no sign of the gunman, who had fled the home in a car belonging to one of the girls.

"He may have fled on foot," he said.

The girl was found by passersby who heard scuffling noises coming from the trunk of the car.

The incident began at a party to celebrate the 20th birthday of Pattie Malarney. She, Miss Morris, Anna Farrell and Valerie Potter, all 20 years old and friends since grammar school, were in the kitchen of the Malarney home playing cards.

About 12:30 a.m. a young man wearing a hat, mask and gloves burst into the room, having entered the house through an unlocked door in stocking feet, the girls told officers.

"Shut up—don't look at me and don't turn around," he snapped He ordered them to lie on the floor while he went through their pocketbooks, removing a small amount of money.

Man charged in slaying of bartender

Mark R. Amason, 20, of Price Hill, arrested yesterday after allegedly threatening to kill a man in a Price Hill lounge, has been charged with aggravated murder in the Monday night shooting death of Matt Monahan, 76, bartender and caretaker at the Trio Lakes Tavern, 5156 Foley Road, Delhi Hills.

Monahan, who lived above the tavern, was found shot in the head behind the bar about 11:30 a.m. yesterday. He was last seen alive at 1 a.m. yesterday.

AMASON was apprehended at 1:40 a.m. yesterday by off-duty Cincinnati Patrolman Floyd Phelps in Mr. Z's Lounge, 3509 Warsaw Avenue, Price Hill. Phelps walked in the lounge and was told by a waitress that a man was pointing a gun at Leonard Borgelt Jr., 28, of 8425 Cottonwood Drive, Finneytown, in the rear of the building.

Phelps disarmed Amason who had a loaded pistol. Borgelt, who had been working at the lounge during a New Year's Eve party, told police Amason pointed a gun at him and said he was going to kill him.

CINCINNATI police charged Amason with aggravated menacing in connection with pointing the gun at Borgelt. While Amason was in custody, Delhi Township police charged him with the Monahan killing.

Amason gave Delhi police an address of 569 Rosemont Avenue and gave Cincinnati police an address of 1770 Ashbrook Drive, both in Price Hill.

Fostoria Man Arrested After Chase In Auto

From The Blade Correspondent

FOSTORIA, O. — A Fostoria man was arrested Sunday morning after a car reported stolen here was involved in a police chase and a three-car accident on U.S. 23 in southern Marion County, police said.

The car, owned by Andy Veres, was taken about 9:15 a.m. from near the Veres home. Highway patrolmen from the Marion and Delaware posts pursued the vehicle south on U.S. 23 to Waldo, where the accident occurred at about 10:15 a.m. No one was injured.

The driver of the stolen car, Elman Craddolth, was to be returned to Fostoria today to face an auto theft charge, police said.

Argentine guerrillas ask $10 million for hostage

BUENOS AIRES (AP) — The People's Revolutionary Army, a guerrilla group, has asked $10 million in goods for the release of Victor Samuelson, a kidnaped American Esso executive, sources said yesterday.

The company reportedly is negotiating the demands.

The sum was believed the highest ransom demand made in Argentina by kidnapers, political or criminal, who hold four foreigners and two major Argentine victims.

Samuelson, 36, manager of the Esso oil refinery in Campana, was seized by about 12 armed men Dec. 6.

U. S. Girl Linked To Terrorists

LONDON (AP) — Scotland Yard said Wednesday it is holding an 18-year-old American girl and two other persons arrested at London airport as suspected members of an international arms ring.

The British Press Association said the three were believed to be part of an Arab guerrilla group ordered to Britain to attack prominent Zionists.

The official statement from Scotland Yard said two of the group were arrested Saturday. They were an American girl who arrived on a flight from Los Angeles, and a Moroccan man she allegedly contacted on an airport bus.

British authorities did not identify the girl, but three London newspapers identified her as Allison Thompson of Santa Barbara, Calif.

The Santa Barbara News-Press quoted the manager of a restaurant where Miss Allison had worked as saying he fired her after a man, who he described as an Arab about 30 years old, interfered with her work.

Customs officials found five automatic pistols and 150 rounds of ammunition hidden in the girl's baggage, the statement said. A third suspect, a Pakistani man, was arrested two days later, also arriving from Los Angeles, the statement added.

The Press Association, the national news agency, said the American girl was thought to be a courier for an Arab group briefed to step up attacks on Jews in Britain.

London Jews say they feared guerrillas had drawn up a death list of leading British Zionists.

Meanwhile Kuwait has rejected an Italian request for extradition of the five Arab terrorists who fire-bombed a plane and shot up the Rome airport December 17, Foreign Ministry sources said in Rome.

Kuwait called the massacre of 31 persons a political crime, the sources said. The decision drew an immediate and strongly worded reply from the Italian government, they added.

LONDONDERRY, NORTHERN IRELAND (Reuter) — Guerrillas of the outlawed Irish Republican Army have passed a "death sentence" on Britain's Northern Ireland administrator, Francis Pym declaring: "We will not rest until it has been carried out."

2 Killed; Homicides Total 744

Detroit's homicide toll continued to climb on the weekend as police were told that a jealous man shot his ex-wife's new husband and a west side man was slain by a guest.

Police said James Lawson, 23, of 1560 Lee Place, was gunned down about 10:40 p.m. Saturday when two men who had been visiting him and his wife, Karen, 23, began leaving their apartment.

One of the men allegedly put a knife to Mrs. Lawson's throat while the other man entered the hallway with Lawson, where two shots were fired.

Police are searching for two 22-year-old black men, one known only as Morgan.

ABOUT AN HOUR after Lawson's killing, Rahim Avduli, 36, became the city's 744th homicide of 1973.

When Avduli and his wife, Violet, 19, entered their house at 11:30 p.m., Mrs. Avduli told police, Dali Kola, 27, of Brooklyn, N.Y. was standing in their living room, armed with two pistols.

Kola, Mrs. Avduli's former husband, shot twice, fatally wounding Avduli in the head, then escaped out a front window, police were told.

Police confiscated one .357 magnum pistol.

Detroit's homicide record was 693 in 1972, but the slaying toll could hit 750 by the end of 1973.

The city's homicide has climbed steadily since 1964, when 232 persons were slain.

Tear gas quells revelry by youths in Florida

FORT LAUDERDALE, Fla. (AP) — Fourteen persons, including four policemen, were slightly injured and 27 young people were arrested early yesterday after police used tear gas to disperse a crowd of New Year's revelers.

Police said about 3,000 young people gathered on highway A1A and began rocking cars and throwing bottles and rocks.

About 20 miles farther south on Miami Beach police also used tear gas to break up a crowd of unruly youths. Seven persons were arrested and four policemen injured slightly in that incident.

Bomb explodes in Belfast shopping center

BELFAST (UPI): A 200-pound bomb exploded in Belfast's biggest shopping center yesterday and the Irish Republican Army pledged to increase the campaign of violence that has plagued Northern Ireland for more than four years. No one was injured in the bomb blast but damage was heavy.

In the following brief essay the writer develops a personal response to these articles, supports the response with specific references to the articles themselves, and concludes with a moving description of a personal experience.

> No one can say exactly why violence is so widespread in our society. But I believe there are two dominant reasons for violence in American culture.
>
> We can all do each other in without really caring because we have machines to do our killing. The cowboy at least had to stare at his victim before he drew his six-gun and fired. Even the cavalry, though having all kinds of technological advantages, usually had to engage in some hand-to-hand fighting with Indians. But now we do violence with electronic gadgets, "Mission Impossible" technology of all kinds, or with bombs from airplanes.
>
> Just as we are able to kill so impersonally, we also have more opportunity to avoid each other, especially enemies, day by day. Cities are crammed with people, many of whom are frustrated and potentially violent, who never really have to face people they dislike, disagree with, or hate.
>
> Yesterday I analyzed my own reactions to a television program. I, too, enjoy "mechanical overkill"—the desire to control and even injure others with clever electronic devices, tapes that self-destruct, bombs that destroy, anything that is clever and puts me, as a viewer, in *control*. The show was an international spy intrigue. The "heroes" had science on their side; they destroyed or defeated their enemies— and who the enemies were didn't matter much—with wired doorknobs, an exploding car, a bugged electric shaver. They were clever, even brilliant. They were cold and calculating. They never got dirty. And they never once saw who they were killing.

This essay develops its points carefully. The writer has read the articles, thought them over, developed an interpretation, and thought up personal experiences of his own, perhaps related only very generally to the newspaper articles, that support his interpretation. As a piece of formed experience, it's effective. We know what the writer wants to say and we can follow his support easily. Writing, however, needs more than a clear plan. We want to know the personality of the writer as well. We want to know that he recognizes other possibilities and will listen to other interpretations. In a very basic way, this writer accomplishes those objectives as well. His first sentence admits the complexity of the topic. Using a straightforward, factual, "tough" style, especially highlighted in the simple repetitions in the last four short sentences, he gets to the point quickly and clearly.

Writing Exercise

This assignment should help you organize the components of some everyday experience and make writing about that experience easier. Spend thirty minutes undertaking an everyday activity, such as reading the sports pages, preparing breakfast, eating a sandwich and drinking a glass of milk, watching a favorite television program. But, pay more attention than you normally would to *how* you do it, your actions and thoughts. Open *all* your senses to the experience. Ask yourself these questions and briefly jot down the answers.

1. How does the experience *feel* to you? (Use your hands more. Touch as much as you can.)

3. Do you *see* things you normally miss? What are they? (Try to see what you're doing from as many perspectives as possible.)

3. Can you *hear* small sounds that you normally miss? (You might even exaggerate a few of these sounds.)

4. Are there any *smells* related to the experience? (If you're feeding the cat, what does his catfood smell like?)

5. Are there *tastes* involved in this activity? (Remember, we sometimes taste even when we are not eating or drinking.)

Now analyze your recorded notes. You might expand a few of them on separate note paper by adding adjectives or phrases that fill in even more detail. Select those details in your notes which you think will best re-create the experience for a reader. Finally, put these selected details into separate sentences. Ask your classmates to help you select and develop your sentences into complete descriptive paragraphs, adding more detail all the time.

Sharing your experience

Inductive and deductive patterns of organization give you an overall plan. But you've got to put flesh on the skeleton of that plan. And the flesh has to be your experience, described carefully, planned carefully, and geared to achieve your purpose. You draw on your experience in many forms. Sometimes you state a thesis and carefully select and explain examples that prove that thesis. Or, sometimes you go back over your thinking process, step by step. This section deals with a third way to draw on your experience: by going back over and *sharing* the whole event. In this way the reader re-lives the experience with you. On a basic level, that's what all fiction does. It *shows* rather than *tells*. It shares rather than summarizes. In all your writing you'll want to share what you've experienced, whether to support an argument or merely to tell a story.

Principles to remember

Here are three principles to remember when you're writing to share an experience:

1. Make clear to the reader *where you stand* in relation to the experience you describe. Clarify your perspective, both your physical perspective as you originally went through the experience and your present mental perspective. Are you going to be looking back? Remembering? Then, use the past tense *consistently*. Are you going to describe an event as if the experience were happening on the page right before the reader? Then you'll want to use the present tense and very direct, factual, fast description. Will you be looking down on the action or will you be right in the midst of it? Then you'll want to describe accordingly, relating only those actions you would naturally see from your chosen perspective. A man in an airplane sees everything, but not the man on the ground.

2. *Arrange detail and action* so that they lead up to a climax. Don't summarize everything in the first sentence and then retell the experience step by step. Work out a plan and stick to it.

3. Above all, *select plenty of specific detail* to support your plan. Don't include everything that you can remember, but do include what counts for you and describe it carefully. Notice how one of the following sentences shows and the other tells: "They started way over at the far end of the course and there was some trouble at the barrier. Something with goggle blinders on was making a great fuss and rearing around and busted the barrier once, but I could see my old man in our black jacket, with a white cross and a black cap, sitting up on Gilford, and patting him with his hand." The first sentence summarizes. The second supports it with concrete, telling facts, facts that count because they *show* the reader why and what.

Selecting what you share

Here is a forceful piece of action-description. Notice how the writer keeps the physical perspective clear—he's watching the race from the side of the track. Notice how he mixes the storyteller's own feelings ("Gosh, I was so excited") with very concrete, factual descriptions of what he sees ("I fixed the glasses on where they would come out back of the trees . . .").

Finally, notice how all the detail and action builds up, bit by bit, sentence by sentence. The telling facts stack up and lead us dramatically to the climax.

from *My Old Man*

ERNEST HEMINGWAY

    Second time Gilford and my old man started, was a rainy Sunday at Auteuil, in the Prix du Marat, a 4,500 meter steeplechase. As soon as he'd gone out I beat it up in the stand with the new glasses my old man had bought for me to watch them. They started way over at the far end of the course and there was some trouble at the barrier. Something with goggle blinders on was making a great fuss and rearing around and busted the barrier once, but I could see my old man in our black jacket, with a white cross and a black cap, sitting up on Gilford, and patting him with his hand. Then they were off in a jump and out of sight behind the trees and the gong going for dear life and the pari-mutuel wickets rattling down. Gosh, I was so excited, I was afraid to look at them, but I fixed the glasses on the place where they would come out back of the trees and then out they came with the old black jacket going third and they all sailing over the jump like birds. Then they went out of sight again and then they came pounding out and down the hill and all going nice and sweet and easy and taking the fence smooth in a bunch, and moving away from us all solid. Looked as though you could walk across on their backs they were all so bunched and going so smooth. Then they bellied over the big double Bullfinch and something came down. I couldn't see who it was, but in a minute the horse was up and galloping free and the field, all bunched still, sweeping around the long left turn into the straightaway. They jumped the stone wall and came jammed down the stretch toward the big water-jump right in front of the stands. I saw them coming and hollered at my old man as he went by, and he was leading by about a length and riding way out, and light as a monkey, and they were racing for the water-jump. They took off over the big hedge of the water-jump in a pack and then there was a crash, and two horses pulled sideways out off it, and kept on going, and three others were piled up. I couldn't see my old man anywhere. One horse kneed himself up and the jock had hold of the bridle and mounted and went slamming on after the place money. The other horse was up and away by himself, jerking his head and galloping with the bridle rein hanging and the jock staggered over to one side of the track against the fence. Then Gilford rolled over to one side off my old man and got up and started to run on three legs with his off hoof dangling and there was my old man laying there on the grass flat out with his face up and blood all over the side of his head. I ran down the stand and bumped into a jam of people and got to the rail and a cop grabbed me and held me and two big stretcher-bearers were going out after my old man and around on the other side of the course I saw three horses, strung way out, coming out of the trees and taking the jump.

My old man was dead when they brought him in and while a doctor was listening to his heart with a thing plugged in his ears, I heard a shot up the track that meant they'd killed Gilford. I lay down beside my old man, when they carried the stretcher into the hospital room, and hung onto the stretcher and cried and cried, and he looked so white and gone and so awfully dead, and I couldn't help feeling that if my old man was dead maybe they didn't need to have shot Gilford. His hoof might have got well. I don't know. I loved my old man so much.

Then a couple of guys came in and one of them patted me on the back and then went over and looked at my old man and then pulled a sheet off the cot and spread it over him; and the other was telephoning in French for them to send the ambulance to take him out to Maisons. And I couldn't stop crying, crying and choking, sort of, and George Gardner came in and sat down beside me on the floor and put his arms around me and says, "Come on, Joe, old boy. Get up and we'll go out and wait for the ambulance."

George and I went out to the gate and I was trying to stop bawling and George wiped off my face with his handkerchief and we were standing back a little ways while the crowd was going out of the gate and a couple of guys stopped near us while we were waiting for the crowd to get through the gate and one of them was counting a bunch of mutuel tickets and he said, "Well, Butler got his, all right."

The other guy said, "I don't give a good god dam if he did, the crook. He had it coming to him on the stuff he's pulled."

"I'll say he had," said the other guy, and tore the bunch of tickets in two.

And George Gardner looked at me to see if I'd heard and I had all right and he said, "Don't you listen to what those bums said, Joe. Your old man was one swell guy."

But I don't know. Seems like when they get started they don't leave a guy nothing.

Writing Exercise

1. You've read part of the story. Now think about its purpose. What does the experience tell you about racing? What do you think Hemingway wanted to say about racing? Go back over the excerpt and pick out sentences that support your interpretation. Write down at least five sentences. Then write an introductory paragraph which explains your interpretation, follow it with a couple of paragraphs that refer to and explain your example sentences, and then write a concluding sentence that rounds out your thesis and supporting evidence.

2. Select a very brief action, such as a man hanging up his coat or a boy petting his dog. Then imitate Hemingway's style as you describe it. Find facts and details that you believe reveal meaning. Find a physical perspective; select detail and build to a climax. Make your sentences flow naturally, like Hemingway's, with just a bit of your own feelings as you describe. Connect your sentences by keeping what you describe before your reader. Appeal to his senses.

The following essay by Robert Campbell also shares personal experience. But Campbell's purpose is different from Hemingway's. Campbell wants to explain, to write *exposition;* the essay form is best suited to his purpose. Writers of fiction put the sharing of experience above all else, whereas writers of exposition share only those bits and pieces of an experience that will help explain the meaning or significance of that experience. The expository writer is more selective and arranges his illustrations of experience so that they support his purpose. As you read Robert Campbell's "With Thee . . . I Plight My Troth," notice how he weaves his interpretations ("Such are the incidents that keep the true Bugatti owner going") with bits of past experience, explained carefully and in detail.

Thinking Exercise

Ask yourself these questions as you read:

1. What is Campbell really saying about people who own rare, classic cars like Bugattis?
2. Why does Campbell select only a few of his past experiences with his Bugatti and describe them very closely?
3. Can you imagine this story written seriously, without humor, as everyday tragedy?

With Thee . . . I Plight My Troth

ROBERT CAMPBELL

The two young cyclists came to a skidding halt and turned to stare as I eased the throbbing, supercharged Bugatti into the elevator of a New York garage.

"What's *dat?*" asked the girl incredulously.

"With Thee . . . I Plight My Troth" by Robert Campbell. Reprinted by permission from *Sports Illustrated,* November 9, 1970. © 1970 Time Inc.

"San ahmah'd cah," replied her boy companion.

"Ha'jah know san ahmah'd cah?" persisted the girl, somewhat dubiously.

"I know an ahmah'd cah when I sees one," snapped the boy, shutting off any further questions.

Such are the incidents that keep the true Bugatti owner going. It doesn't much matter whether the observations are accurate. The important thing is that they should occur with a high rate of frequency, for they provide a direct transfusion to what otherwise would be a seriously damaged ego. Without these little interludes few mortals could withstand the doubts, frustrations and anguish that assail a Bugatti owner as he sets out on the open road, the loneliest driver there because he knows full well that in so doing he is putting himself several hundred, or perhaps a thousand, miles away from the nearest human being who has the faintest idea of what makes this particular machine tick.

By now it is almost common knowledge that the Bugatti is the greatest automobile ever made. There is an aura and mystique about these cars that applies to no other known vehicle. Throughout the 1920s and 1930s they swept the racing circuits of Europe, amassing an overall victory total that has yet to be surpassed. Top speed in some of the last models reached 180 mph, quite a clip even for today. To own a Bugatti was to possess what Sir Malcolm Campbell described as "a car in a class by itself." *"Pur sang"* was the term the aficionados used—thoroughbred. There is a story, possibly apocryphal but completely credible, about a Frenchwoman who poisoned her husband to collect his insurance—so she could buy her lover a Bugatti.

World War II put an end to the Bugatti era when the factory at Molsheim in eastern France was overrun by the German army. Ettore Bugatti, the Italian automotive genius who moved to France as a young man and designed the cars that bore his name, died shortly afterward. Hugh Conway, a Briton and world authority on the cars, estimates that around 6,000 were produced during the 30-odd years of the era and that roughly 1,200 have survived. A few models even appeared in the postwar years. But the spark was gone. Yet, though more than a quarter century has passed, the Bugatti mystique remains as alive as ever. Two magazines in circulation today are devoted purely to Bugatti matters, a fact unique in automotive history. It is as though the era never ended. And in a way it hasn't, for some people anyway, as I discovered on seeing my first Bugatti.

The encounter took place in the summer of 1952. The car, a sleek gray convertible, had been brought to New York from Europe by an engineer friend who was also a sometime racing driver. I had practically lost all interest in automobiles at that point, though I retained vivid childhood memories of the classic American cars of the '30s—my first hair-raising ride in a boat-tailed Auburn Speedster, then hours of curbside watching with the gang in our small town, hoping for a glimpse of one of the great Packards or Cadillacs or Lincolns and later the Cords. But something happened to cars after World War II.

One day in New York I met my friend's Bug (a frequently used diminutive, not a mechanical term). My first reaction was: "What a queer-looking automobile!'' And indeed it was, completely unlike any other machine I had ever seen or even imagined. I circled the car warily, looked under it and sat in it as my friend chatted about finned racing brakes, the unique front axle, precise steering, instruments and so on. I still didn't get the idea though. Then he took me for a ride.

We headed uptown through Central Park. The engine made quite a racket. The springs were unyielding. We stopped for a red light just short of the S turns at the north end of the park. Two hopped-up motorcyclists on gooked-up motorcycles pulled alongside, gave us the eye and emitted a challenging ''vroom, vroom.'' The light changed and the Bugatti took off, accelerating with breathtaking speed. It took the sharp curves effortlessly, with but a slight movement of the steering wheel, as though the whole car were hung on rails. The motorcyclists fell behind and dropped from view. We returned to my friend's apartment and I took a second look at the car. This time I got the point.

The car looked exactly like what it had just done. Its design gave the impression of something light and poised, impatient and self-confident, capable, ready to spring alive at the slightest touch and take you whistling down the road at top speed, negotiating the tightest curve with ease, on and on to the end of the world if need be—and you'd better hop in right now or it might just up and depart without you. This pure expression of function and purpose had resulted in a uniquely beautiful automobile. There wasn't a single false note to the design. Every feature served and was subservient to the basics: acceleration, speed, road holding and endurance. Moreover, the design represented what would be called in mathematicians' terms the elegant solution to a problem, as opposed to solving it by brute force. Ettore Bugatti achieved his racing objectives with elegance and finesse, and that is just the way his cars look.

This, I think, is what lies at the core of the Bugatti mystique. There is a look about a Bugatti that says, ''I am the Eternal Machine.'' Closer scrutiny will reveal the barest trace of a smile that says, ''I am the Infernal Machine, too.'' But a novice like myself would not notice that. I was simply hooked. I had to have one of those cars. I had been bitten by the Bug bug but had no way of realizing the virulence of this disease. It has no known cure. It runs a long course, periodically racking the host in feverish convulsions until, hopefully, some immunity sets in. Even then the patient is never quite the same again.

The Bugatti hangup is a transcendental experience in the true sense, with the pilgrim progressing through levels of understanding as though through a series of veils, moving ever onward toward the True Reality, the Ultimate, the One—in this case a true perception of the Eternal Machine. Only a few make it through the full course of this disease. In this respect the Bug hangup is different from more popular indulgences such as glue sniffing and LSD popping, which produce hallucinations. But however gaudy and exciting these hallucinations may be, they have no objective reality. This is merely a form of self-induced schizophrenia. Bugatti owners, on the other hand, are not the least bit schizzed. A Bug is, after all, a real thing—just as real as Ahab's whale.

At the time I got hooked I realized I lacked several important qualifications for owning a Bugatti. It seemed to me that to maintain such a machine it was necessary to be either rich or a good mechanic, and preferably both. Since the latter course was the only one reasonably open to me, I set out to acquire some knowledge about automobile engines. I read a book. Then, for $150, I bought a disheveled 1927 Rolls-Royce touring car and hauled it out to a small garage in New Jersey. I took it apart—and over a year of weekend work went by before I got the Rolls back together. Surprisingly enough it actually ran. I drove the car around the block and back to the garage. Then I returned proudly to the city. The next day it turned cold and the Rolls' block cracked.

The week after that I sold it to a fellow from Wilkes-Barre for $75. It was a beautiful sunny day and as the Rolls disappeared I sat down on the curb and almost cried. Had I known at the time the true meaning of all the weekends I had invested I might very well have shot myself. For one could spend a whole lifetime working on Rolls-Royces and hardly learn anything relating to Bugattis, as I found out later on.

Now thinking myself prepared, I set out in search of a Bugatti. And five years after being bitten by the Bug bug I had a shot at one—a sleek, white, supercharged, four-door bomb, a late 1939 tourer and one of the last Bugattis made. I phoned a crotchety old Alsatian mechanic I had become acquainted with; I was at least smart enough to know I would need a consultant.

"Charlie, I'd like you to take a look at a Bugatti I want to buy."
"Dun't buy it."
"But I want to buy it."
"Dun't buy it."
"But I *want* it!"
"Are you rich?"
"No."
"Dun't buy it."
"But I'm in love with the car, Charlie."
"So marry it. But dun't buy it."

I brought the car to Charlie's shop. He contemplated it dubiously. He stuck a finger up the tail pipe and looked at the black smudge that resulted. Dubiously. He lifted the hood, picked up a yard-long stick of wood, pressed one end to the engine and the other to his ear, and listened, dubiously. The stethoscope effect, I thought to myself cheerily, admiring Charlie. "What do you think of her, Charlie?" He arched his eyebrows, hunched his shoulders and curled down the corners of his mouth, all dubiously. "It runs," he said. Then he walked away.

For a modest investment of $2,000 I became what is known in some quarters as a *Bugattiste*. I experienced instantly what might be described, in transcendental terms, as the "novitiate's bends." I finally had my hands on the Ultimate Automobile. And I felt I now stood in the presence of some Final Revelation.

The Bugatti did everything in its power to encourage this deception—by continuing to run, for example. In buying it I had also become a member of what must be the world's most exclusive key club. The ignition keys of most of the later-model cars are identical. A distinct touch! *Un vrai beau geste!* What owner of a Bugatti would conceivably make off with another's machine?

Our first outings together were a success, both socially and sonically. Driving along to the supercharged whine of the engine was pure joy. It was also marvelous for the ego. Pedestrians stared. Crowds gathered. Notes with messages and phone numbers were stuck under the windshield wipers: "Call me immediately! Desperate!" "Take $6,000 cash?" A Britisher with a highly pinstriped suit, a spanking-new Rolls-Royce and a complete Arthur Treacher accent pulled alongside one evening:

"Oh, I say! Booghhatti, isn't it?"

"Yes it is."

"Late model, what?"

"Fifty-seven C—late '39."

"Thought so. Mahhhvelus to see one. Simply mahhhhvelus. Luck, old chap!"

There are, one should admit, sexual overtones to such an ego-expanding machine. "Good God!" exclaimed a friend's wife at her first sight of the car. "That's the biggest phallic symbol I've ever seen!" A stop at a favorite French restaurant one evening produced similar results. Guy the bartender, the *patron* and his wife and half the clientele poured out to the sidewalk to admire this particular piece of French pastry. Guy drew me aside and whispered with an air of Gallic savoir faire, "She eez gude for getteeng zee girls, *non*?"

I began to venture out on longer trips, explaining to my wife all the instruments, levers and buttons on the dash, the trick of revving up the engine, double-clutching and shifting down just at the right sound (which, if missed, produces a nerve-shattering grind from the gearbox) and other features of the car. I even let her drive it (she's a good driver). She accepted the hangup with a kind of serene confidence that I wasn't totally balmy or worse and even came to enjoy the car to some extent, I think. That's important. For, short of bringing some young thing home to live with you, I can't imagine anything that could break up a marriage quicker than a Bugatti. It is totally impossible to explain the hours over at the shop doing little things like polishing the brake drums or repacking the water pump or searching through store after store for some obscure kind of grease that hasn't been made in 30 years. In all that time who knows what you've been up to?

A notice appeared once in the sports section of the Sunday *Times* advertising two Bugattis for sale. It concluded with: "Wife says must go." I couldn't help feeling that if that was the way it was with them the fellow would have been better off keeping the cars instead.

On the open road I developed a facile habit of turning small defects into large virtues that, at the least, must have been mildly infuriating. One Christmas we started out for Maryland in a light snowstorm to spend a few days with my mother. We were hardly under way when the windshield-wiper motor quit. "Ha!" I said to my wife. "Now you'll see that Mr. Bugatti thought of everything." I reached for a walnut knob on the walnut dash. This knob connected directly with the wipers and by turning it left right, left right the wipers did the same. For 250 miles I worked the wipers by hand. A pessimist might have said the car needed that knob because the wiper motor was none too reliable. But I didn't look at it that way. I couldn't afford to, emotionally.

We arrived at my mother's house and were greeted with the news that my old friend Bill was having a cocktail party and we were definitely expected. We went, and my old friend Bill held out a drink for me. I accepted it in the wiper hand, curling my stiff fingers around the glass. Immediately and automatically the hand rotated gently to the left and dumped the drink down my old friend Bill's shirt.

In the course of such trips I became superstitious about the car, convinced that it was inhabited by some druidlike spirit. Once I took it out while a bit tipsy. The motor gradually died and the Bug refused to budge. I attributed this to a kind of self-preservation instinct on the part of the car. The next day it ran perfectly. On one of those hypnotic hauls up the New Jersey Turnpike the sound of the motor seemed to rise and fall rhythmically. It alarmed me. I couldn't understand it. I popped my ears. The rhythm persisted. I finally concluded that the car had undertaken to keep the driver awake.

Approaching New York at dawn I glanced in the rearview mirror. An enormous cloud of white smoke was billowing out behind the Bugatti. "My God!" I thought. "The Red Baron has shot us down!" I pulled off the road and lifted the hood. Nothing. I started up again. Nothing. No smoke, no nothing. We finished the trip, wide awake but quite without incident.

This mixture of awe and superstition, fantasy, fright and rationalization presents a reasonably accurate sketch of the classic fool's paradise. Somewhere in the back of my mind was developing a terrible, unformulated thought, "I really don't know a blinking thing about this automobile." My ego bubble was about to burst. One "pop" and all that élan would vanish. It was time for me to be graduated from the Lower Level to the Second Stage. I was quite unaware of this, thinking somewhat foolishly that I had already arrived.

Graduation exercises took place on a trip to Richmond with a film producer friend named Larry Madison. I picked up Larry at his house, handed him a stick of gum and asked if he would mind chewing some. "We have an oil leak," I explained as we headed south. (Charlie had told me that gum was a good leak sealer in a pinch.) We made Richmond with only a few stops for gum and water for the radiator and headed back the next afternoon. In the middle of nowhere, the bad news came in the form of a loud rapping sound in the engine. "Sounds like a connecting rod," said Larry. We limped into a little one-horse town and up to a garage. A mechanic came out.

"My friend is sick," I said.

"Mebbe I can hep ya."

"No, sir, I don't think you can."

The mechanic seemed insulted. He lifted the hood, took one look at the supercharged Bugatti engine and slammed the hood down again.

"No, suh, I don't think I can eitheh."

"Well, tell us how to get the bus to Fredericksburg and mail me the car."

The next morning, back in New York, I called Charlie:

"Our mutual friend is sick."

"*Qu'est-ce qu'il y a?*"

"*Il y a un* burned-out bearing, I think."

Charlie just whistled.

Several days later the Bugatti arrived at Charlie's shop on a truck. It was pushed against the side wall along with a Lagonda, a Delahaye, a Hispano-Suiza, a Packard tourer and several Rolls-Royces that awaited the Master's attention. I asked him what he thought a job like mine would run. "Don't count on getting out of here for less than $750" was as far as he would go. I volunteered to help out on weekends, doing uncritical chores like taking off nuts and bolts and cleaning up parts and so on, with some vague idea that I would thereby learn something and possibly also cut costs. Charlie agreed.

My racing friend took a dim view of this plan, pointing out that there were a lot of things about Bugatti engines that you really have to know in order to rebuild one properly, that tolerances, nut tightnesses and things like that are critical in a racing engine, even a detuned touring version of the engine. He urged me to send the engine back to the factory in France. I refused, feeling that if I did I would end up knowing no more about the car than I did to start with, whereas if I helped out around Charlie's shop I would discover what made the thing tick. Secretly, of course, I was actually blowing up a new ego balloon to replace the one that had just popped. This balloon, appropriate to the Second Stage, would be labeled with the following doubtful proposition:

List all possible false starts. What then remains is the right way. The proposition is suspect because with a Bugatti there are an infinite number of possible false starts.

Work began in Charlie's shop, which on a Bugatti is not easy, because the engine must be removed completely from the car before anything significant can be accomplished. To get it out, the hood, side panels, front fenders and radiator have to come off. Only then comes the really unique challenge of the celebrated Bugatti power plant. It is put together with dozens and dozens of little nuts and bolts, like an airplane engine, instead of a lesser number of larger ones. "Must have had someone working full time just making nuts and bolts," muttered Charlie. The nuts and bolts also come in a fantastic variety of sizes, requiring not only a full complement of European metric wrenches but some British and American wrenches and a few pure Bugatti wrenches. Some nuts are almost impossible to get at without hiring a part-time midget or bending a perfectly good wrench into some corkscrew shape. Watching Charlie struggle with one particularly inaccessible nut behind the water pump, I remarked with some pride: "I guess Mr. Bugatti built his cars to stay together, not come apart." Charlie exploded: "Damn guinea ought to have been a Swiss watchmaker!"

After several weeks of this the famous Bugatti crankshaft came out. Unlike most crankshafts, which are cast, this remarkable object was machined out of a solid billet of steel—journals, counterweights and all. "It's beautiful," I said. "A work of art," commented Charlie grudgingly. "Didn't nobody make *that* in a day. Well, no use just standing here looking at it." Somehow that's what happened, though, for almost two years.

In an effort to keep things going I fiddled around with trivial matters like scraping 25 years of gook off the chassis with a putty knife, getting small parts rebuilt and taking the eight-day stop clock to the watchmaker. From time to time Charlie would look at the parts scattered about his old dingy shop and remark: "Yes sir. We gotta be sober when we put *that* back together."

Finally Charlie got around to me. I found him with my pistons lined up on a workbench. "Watcha doin'?" I asked with as much casualness as I could muster. "Knurling up your pistons. Makes 'em a little larger." This, Charlie had reasoned, would compensate for the fact that pistons and cylinder walls had undoubtedly become somewhat worn through use. I pointed out to Charlie that I had backtracked on the history of the car and discovered it already had oversized pistons in it. A previous owner had demanded that it run quieter. "When you leave here you're gonna have a nice tight engine, son" was Charlie's only response.

The engine gradually resumed its original shape. And then came the problem of getting it back into the car. Charlie devoted a whole day to squeezing the engine back in—pulling, pushing, turning, wiggling and kicking at it in the process. Every now and then his pressure valve let go: "A lot of other people made automobiles that stood up, didn't they? Him and his crazy ideas." Later, in a muffled singsong from beneath the car: "*La Misère. La Misère de Bugatti*" (imparting to the name the full flavor of its proper pronunciation—Boo-gha-tee). Finally he succeeded, crawled out from under the car and kicked it viciously. "Any man ever made a crazy automobile, this is it! Mr. Bugatti, I hate you!"

Charlie started the car. It ran, in a somewhat ragged fashion. Charlie fiddled around, and the engine sounded smoother. His assistant suggested that maybe now the fenders and hood could go back on. "No sir," snapped Charlie, "not until the engine is running perfectly."

The car was run in the shop periodically for several days, and then the old man took it out and drove it around the block. Hood and fenders went back on. After that the Bugatti refused to run at all. Charlie stared at the car in disbelief. "Heartbreaking automobile," he said. He fiddled some more. "It's some damn little thing about this big," he said, holding up two fingers about two inches apart.

I called a Bugatti expert in Connecticut to ask if he would take a look. He couldn't but said he would send someone. The next day a little man arrived with a little Bugatti emblem in the lapel of his coat, which somehow infuriated me. The little man removed a sparkplug and took a compression check. There was a slight whistling sound but no compression. The same was true in other cylinders. "The valves are all bent," the little man said. Then he went home.

Charlie couldn't believe it. Summer came and went and he still couldn't believe it. Apparently there are things about a Bugatti that elude a good Rolls-Royce man. But in the fall he went at it again, took the engine out, dismantled it, straightened the valves and reassembled the car once more. In the latter operation he followed a suggestion made by the Connecticut consultant to make assembly easier. He glued the piston rings to the cylinders to make inserting them easier. Then he poured solvent through the sparkplug holes to dissolve the cement and release the rings, draining the resulting gunk out of the bottom of the engine. Then came the day for the Great Road Test.

I had a business date at a research lab in New Jersey, and Charlie agreed that a run out there would be a good first trip. Early the next morning I arrived at the shop. The car was poised and ready to go, all warmed up and with a blanket over the classic, horseshoe-shaped radiator. Charlie was ready to go, too. No coveralls for a classy test like this. Instead a tweed suit and golf cap. We made the 35-mile trip without incident, and I waved goodby to Charlie as he headed back to the city. By mid-afternoon, unable to bear the suspense any longer, I called the shop.

"How are things?"

"Not so good."

"What happened?"

"You know that long, slow grade up to the George Washington Bridge?"

"Yes."

"Burned out a bearing."

This time it was my turn to whistle. I returned to the city, got to the shop as soon as I could and looked at the fine-mesh wire screen that forms the car's oil filter. It was completely covered with a kind of gooey slop. The recommended solvent had dissolved the glue, all right. But Charlie had not gotten it all out of the engine. The residue had clogged off all oil circulation, which is as good a way as any to burn out a bearing. Charlie took the hood and fenders off again.

I made the next road test myself, down the West Side Highway, around the Battery and up the FDR Drive, where I knew I could keep moving and the car would not overheat. But at the Battery it began to overheat. And by the time I reached the 96th Street exit it was boiling. I pulled off and stopped. The car spat out several quarts of boiling water. I sat there waiting for it to cool down. "Charlie made me a nice, tight engine all right," I thought, "and it'll take about 10,000 miles to break it in."

I speculated briefly on what people would think of an ad in the *Times* that read: "*Owner* says must go!" I rejected the idea as being unfair to the Bugatti—humiliating, even. After all, it was not *its* fault that it had become involved in some affair of the halt leading the blind into one cul-de-sac after another. It was not *its* fault if it became overheated. To hell with élan and all that. To hell with *my* ego. What about *its* ego? The car deserved better than this.

At this point, unaware as ever, I was beginning to move from the Second Level to the Third Level, where the split occurs between Bugatti fanciers and Bugatti lovers. I very well might have decided that the car was just too much trouble, persuaded Charlie to get it running somehow and unloaded it on the next unsuspecting fancier. I imagine quite a few Bugattis change hands at this stage. But I couldn't do it. I cared about the car and wanted to see it functioning properly. And, despite the hangups, I had learned enough to become convinced of something that is the definition of the Third Level: No matter what anyone says, there is a Right Way.

"Bugattis run hot," Charlie had said. I was quite certain by this point that only sick Bugattis ran hot. After all, the engine was designed to run wide open for 24 hours straight in a race like Le Mans, for example. So why should it boil over tooling around Manhattan at 35 or 40 mph? Charlie had obviously made the pistons too tight. And there were probably several dozen other things wrong with the engine that I didn't know about. But I was quite sure by now that there was a Right to it and that in some ultimate way a Bugatti engine did make sense. Further, I was hooked on the thought of one day knowing what *that* engine would be like.

I tried to start the car but the engine had seized and would not turn over at all. A tow truck hauled us back to Charlie's shop. Charlie broke the engine loose by applying a crowbar to the flywheel and presented his bill—$1,500. My jaw sagged. Charlie was a sport about it, though. He knew I wanted to keep the car in his shop. There was still a million little things to attend to. And he let me pay him in the course of the next month or so.

Good times returned. I ran the car carefully and managed to keep it below boiling. Gradually it loosened up and cooled down, and the joys of the open road returned. We had the car on Nantucket one whole summer, and it enjoyed the cool climate. The Bugatti went to the store and performed other minor errands, just like any family car. But time finally ran out on another trip back from Maryland. The oil pressure dropped, and again came the telltale hammering. This time the engine went back to the factory. Quite a few letters were exchanged. A query as to what had gone wrong evoked the stark reply: *"Le passage d'huile des manetons du vilebrequin était complètement bouché."* Which is to say that the oil channels of the crankshaft were plugged up. More of that glue-and solvent gunk, no doubt.

In due time the engine returned from the factory completely rebuilt to original Bugatti specifications. It sounded great—very strong. It ran at a cool 65° centigrade, just like my old manual said it should. I broke it in carefully and began to take it up slowly to the higher rpms. It, in turn, began to run hot. The radiator was flushed out. Still it ran hot. Once on the open road it boiled over quite unaccountably. After that a slight rapping sound could be heard when the engine was cold. The sound disappeared once it was warmed up, which meant that when I took the car to a mechanic to ask about it, it wouldn't make its noise.

Disaster came on a long trip to upstate New York with a friend named Dunbar. We were climbing a long grade near the little town of Herkimer when suddenly smoke began to pour up from beneath the floorboards, accompanied by a death rattle from the engine. Dunbar remarked: "Bubbie, I do believe we're afire." I pulled off the road. The engine stopped with a clunk that had all the finality of a prison gate being slammed shut. I lifted the hood. The No. 1 spark was covered with a whitish paste that I could only imagine was vaporized aluminum from a piston. We were only a few miles short of our destination and soon managed to get a push to the motel. I put in a call to Bob Schultze, the best mechanic I know, who has a shop in New Jersey near where I now live. "We've come a cropper," I said.

Bob closed his shop at noon the next day and came to fetch us.

Quite unbelievably it turned out that The Works, as the Bugatti factory is sometimes called, had blundered. Someone had installed the No. 1 piston and connecting rod backward, which put a lot of pressure on the weak side of the piston. This, in turn, had made for excessive friction and explained the overheating. Under the strain the piston had finally exploded into fragments. This discovery restored my confidence in the rightness of the engine. Once more a defect in execution, not in design.

A month later I set out on a business trip to the West Coast. I wrapped up one of the good pistons and rods in a paper bag and put it in my suitcase. "If anything happens to the airplane," I told my wife, "and the FAA finds the piston while they're poking around in the rubble, it'll take them three months and cost the Government $10,000 to figure out where it came from." I had a side destination on the Coast, the shop of O. A. Phillips near Padadena. Bunny, as he's called, is the honorary chairman of the American Bugatti Club. He had the original Bugatti agency in Hollywood in the late 1930s, raced the cars then and has worked on practically nothing but Bugattis since. If anyone in the world knows the Right of it, I figured, it's got to be Bunny.

We talked for three hours about little details and touches I'd never heard of or even imagined, and when I returned home I shipped Bunny my engine.

Later, Bob and I contemplated the body. It, too, clearly needed attention to prevent it from deteriorating. We put it on a truck and carted it off to the obvious mecca for bodies, Earl Lewis' Restoration Shop near Princeton. Ultimately the chassis, too, will be towed to still a third mecca for rewiring and a few other things, a place known as Vintage Auto Restorations, Inc. run by an East Coast Bug expert named Donald Lefferts.

That's about as far as you can scatter an automobile. But I know now that it's the Right Way. Old Charlie was right about one thing at least, asking, "Are you rich?" But I cannot let that nagging question interfere now. For somewhere along the line I took another piece of his advice and married the car, for better or worse (and in sickness and in health). I now stand on the threshold of the Fourth Level where, like Ahab's whale, the Eternal Machine beckons. I know now that there is indeed such a thing as a real Bugatti, a car that will run to the end of the world if need be, with that feeling of joy and response I have had but the faintest glimpse of so far. And I have my hands on one—almost. All that remains is for it to come together. Somewhere in my future there is the Ultimate Automobile. Name: Bugatti. I hope we make it.

Writing Exercise

1. Find a possession, anything from your car to your favorite drinking glass, that seems to own you more than you own it. Write a tongue-in-cheek essay, somewhat like Campbell's, in which you develop an explanation of why you own the object and *how,* with frequent descriptive examples, it owns you.

2. Write a one-page action-description that shows how a possession owns you. Be specific. *Don't* jump in and interpret the way Campbell does. Let the action suggest what you feel about the possession.

3. Try to draw some larger conclusions from this essay. Does it say something about human nature? About our relationships with machines? About what materialism can do to a man? Write a straightforward clear thesis statement in answer to one of these questions. Then find parts of Campbell's essay that support your thesis. Organize your material and write an interpretive essay.

4. Campbell uses dialogue to add both humor and dramatic force to his writing. On page 67, Campbell describes a phone conversation he had with Charlie, his mechanic, about one in the long series of Bugatti breakdowns. Charlie is French; he speaks a colorful and sarcastic mixture of English and French and clearly expresses his disgust with fancy classic automobile-owners and the Bugatti throughout the essay. Look over the entire essay and define Charlie's function in the essay. What does he tell us about the narrator, the Bugatti, and the general situation?

5. Often, the professional writer explains what an object or idea *is* by describing what it looks like, sounds like, or how it works out in everyday life. Campbell's essay describes the kind of person who would buy and maintain a classic car by showing you what happens to him when he buys it. On page 63, Campbell uses a long series of metaphors and analogies to add to his definition of "the Bugatti mystique." Write a brief essay in which you demonstrate how Campbell's figurative language—his metaphors and analogies—work to define that mystique. Here are just a few of Campbell's analogies and metaphors:

"Eternal Machine/Infernal Machine"

"Novice like myself"

"I was simply *hooked*"

"bitten by the Bug bug"

"It [the mistique] runs a *long course*"

"racking the host in feverish convulsions"

"The Bugatti hangup is a transcendental experience . . . with the pilgrim progressing through levels of understanding . . ."

"as though a series of veils"

"moving ever onward toward the True Reality"

"through the full-course of this disease"

"more popular indulgences such as glue-sniffing and LSD popping"

"This is merely a form of self-induced schizophrenia"

"just as real as Ahab's whale"

Don't try to define the function of each metaphor, but rather select a few that are related because they tell similar information about "the mystique." Use a dictionary to find the meaning of words that might be unfamiliar, such as "schizophrenia." Ask your teacher to explain unfamiliar analogies, such as "Ahab's whale." Then ask yourself a general question about the metaphors you have chosen to analyze and make your answer the thesis of your paper. A working outline might look something like this:

Q. How are Ahab's whale, LSD, glue-sniffing, schizophrenia, and True Reality related in these paragraphs?

A. (thesis) All these points of analogy are used to define the mystique of owning a Bugatti, and they help us to understand the *irrationality* of owning this type of car. The Bugatti, like Ahab's whale, is never owned and always elusive.

Thesis—Introduction

Analysis of Metaphor Number One

Analysis of Metaphor Number Two

Analysis of Metaphor Number Three

Conclusion—Thesis Restatement

Remember to connect your paragraphs and to explain specifically how the referent in the metaphor (the whale or the Bug bug) adds to what we know about the Bugatti mystique.

Great Bronze Dead Man

Look at the photograph of a sculpture—Leonard Baskin's *Great Bronze Dead Man*—on page 74. All of us think once in a while about death, mostly our own or those of close friends or family. Because death is close to all of us, it can be difficult to discuss. If we exaggerate our response to death, we sound a bit sentimental or corny for, after all, everyone has to die sometime. But we can sound too cold, too clinical as well, like a mortician filling out one of a long series of body reports.

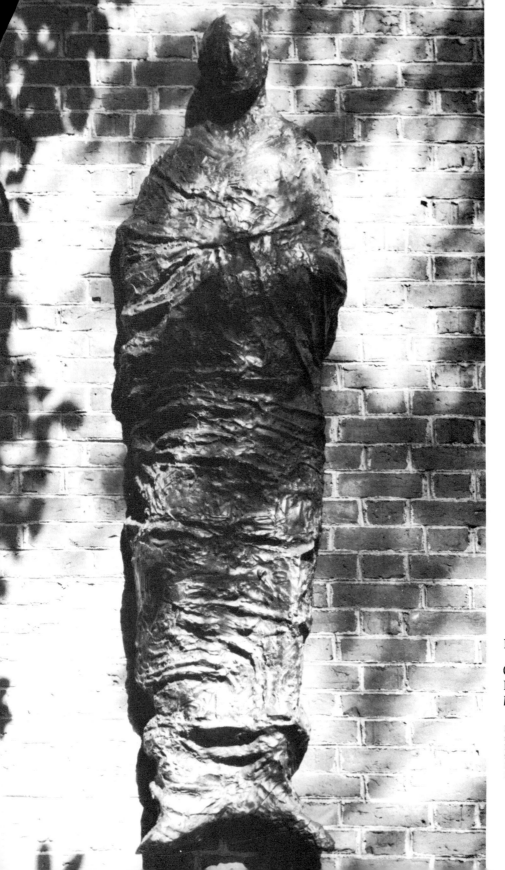

Figure 2-3

Great Bronze
Dead Man
by Leonard Baskin

Photograph reprinted by per
mission of The University o
Massachusetts Press, Amherst
from *Figures of Dead Men* b
Leonard Baskin; photograph b
Hyman Edelstein.

Somehow we try to work a balance between both extremes. A good way to find and keep that balance is to use specific experience to connect what you feel inside about death to some concrete experience outside yourself. Then, if you describe and tell the experience clearly, the reader will know what you feel indirectly, from the way you describe and from the experience itself. When you can find specific, personal experiences to support your ideas, emotions, and opinions, you're on your way to effective writing.

Thinking Exercise

1. *Great Bronze Dead Man* is one artist's attempt to express what he feels about death in concrete terms. What do you think Baskin's attitude is toward death? Can you express his general attitude in a sentence and then expand it to a paragraph by pointing to visual details in the painting that support that attitude?

2. How do you know this man is dead from what you see in the photograph? Could the man be alive and merely playing dead?

3. How would you feel about the bronze dead man if you had to walk by him on the way to class every morning? Could you describe your sensations in concrete language?

Writing Exercise

1. Death is a very general, broad subject. You need to narrow it if you hope to write effectively about it. Spend a few minutes just thinking privately about death. Then write down anything that comes to your mind, first in mere notes, then in complete sentences. Select one of the sentences and develop it into a thesis for a short essay. Work on it until it is clear and you know what you want to say in your essay. Then look around you for one or two very specific examples to support your thesis, to carry the weight of example in your essay. Look in the newspaper you read every day, think about material you've had in other classes—biology, physics, anything that relates. Consider novels or essays you've read, or a poem or story. Go over recent experiences that might qualify—the death of a family pet, a relative, the changing of seasons, winter, anything that you can describe very specifically and use to support your thesis. Take notes and organize your experiences *before* you include them in your essay.

2. Review our earlier discussion of deduction (pages 30–34). Then work out a deductive plan for a short essay on death. Your plan might go something like this: death is universal throughout nature; somehow every

individual has to come to some understanding of and compromise with the fact of death; here are several examples of how some individuals face death and a conclusion that I have drawn from them. Now plan your essay. Stick to the formula you've outlined and be sure to use specific supporting examples. Include a final paragraph that summarizes your plan and emphasizes your conclusion.

3. Make a list of general topics, such as death. Find specific examples of supporting experiences. Then apply either exercise described above to one of the topics.

Facts, opinions, and convention

Once we discover what we want to say, we begin to shape it to our audience. Even our very personal experiences must be reworked if we want them to convince an audience.

To begin, you must be able to distinguish between statements of fact, opinion, and convention. You've got to be able to tell when a sentence is factual and doesn't need further support, when a sentence is opinion and requires illustration, evidence, and examples, and when a sentence is a convention—a statement that everyone in your audience would accept without proof or evidence.

Imagine your audience. In a sense, we assume or create an audience for everything we write. Even in writing which is supposed to be factual description, you'll have to ask yourself some questions about your readers.

1. In the experience I have decided to describe, what would be familiar or unfamiliar to my readers?

2. How can I appeal directly to the senses? How can I get my readers involved? To answer that question, you've got to know *some* things about your readers. For example, you'll need to know what their general interests are, whether they expect a certain kind of approach. Are they, for example, already interested in your topic? Do they expect you to be subjective or objective?

3. What would be the opinions, at least in general, of my readers toward the experience? How can I make the experience come alive for them?

4. How much interpreting do I have to do for my readers? Can I afford to let the experience speak for itself, or should I be sure to explain what every bit of the experience meant to me?

We must also be on our guard against pitfalls involving our attitude toward an audience. Some writers interpret too much. They become preachy and beat their readers over the head. They don't know when they can let an experience, a concrete detail, or a specific fact or example speak for itself. In other words, they talk down to their readers.

Other writers write as if their readers had gone through the experience themselves. They take too much for granted. They include only the broad outlines of experience and ignore specific details. This tendency exists because writers have the experience clearly in their own mind's eye and forget that their readers don't.

Still others record their experience in very mechanical, dry forms. They sometimes include detail haphazardly, almost too completely, without a sense of direction or purpose. Often, they include *too much* detail; they forget that a reader doesn't want to be immersed in factual information without any sense of where he's going. Remember to appeal directly to the senses of your readers, but don't overdo it. Give your readers signals to tell them where you're going next and why. Details, examples, facts, and exemplifying materials must be carefully selected, arranged, and related; otherwise, the reader feels abused and confused.

Finally, a writer treats his readers best when he can imagine what they need to have developed and explained and what he can assume they will develop and explain for themselves. A sportswriter covering a baseball game wouldn't need to define the term *home run* to readers who follow the sport daily. He may, however, need to include much discussion and explanation if he is going to argue that a favorite player ought to be traded. And the writer who casually refers to a female jockey in describing a horse race will probably annoy his readers by ignoring their curiosity. Jockeys haven't traditionally been women.

Here are some suggestions for evaluating the way you treat your readers. Ask yourself if what you have written is a fact, an opinion, or a statement of convention.

Fact: something you believe you and your readers would know with certainty. Be careful, for you may be sure of the certainty of a fact that a reader may question. Question yourself as you would expect to be questioned by an intelligent reader. Some facts are provable by simple observation—"the sun comes up every day." Others might demand reference to sources—"the weather bureau says there were ninety-three rainy days last year." Example: *Abraham Lincoln was assassinated in 1865 by John Wilkes Booth.*

Opinion: a belief held with confidence, but not substantiated by positive knowledge or proof. Of course, some opinions will be more questionable than others. A careful writer evaluates his opinions to gauge the amount of support he will need to give them. Example:

Abraham Lincoln was not free of racism himself, despite his renown as the "Great Emancipator."

Convention: a statement that a writer can assume most readers will accept as truth without much argument. Custom, items of general usage, and established practice would be material for statements of convention. Remember, in some situations you may want to question statements of convention that you believe are superficial or wrong. Expect the same questioning response from your readers. Example: *Abraham Lincoln was a great American statesman.*

Once you decide what your statement is, you'll need to consider how you'll offer support, if it needs it. Perhaps an even more important decision will be the kind of support you decide to give your statements. Obvious facts—"there is a stop sign on the corner"—need very little substantiation. Most readers will take your word for it, at least in most situations. (There are exceptions, of course. When a witness is describing an automobile accident in court, a lawyer may well demand proof—photographs or substantiation from a traffic officer—that indeed there is a stop sign on a particular corner.) Other kinds of facts, however, must be supported, sometimes by reference to sources, sometimes by an explanation or description of the writer's fact-finding process. Consider, for example, the following statement: "According to Alcoholics Anonymous, alcoholism is America's most serious disease." Such statements pose difficulties for any writer. Certainly the reference to Alcoholics Anonymous is factual since A.A., according to the writer, did make the statement. But most readers would want to see the reasoning behind the statement, since the statement itself is an opinion.

Opinions are usually the focus of writing in which the purpose is to explain or to argue. The first step is to develop the ability to recognize opinions as opinions, to know that readers will want your opinions supported and explained. Once you have separated opinion from fact and convention, move on to decide which opinions are most important in your essay. Find the most general of your preliminary opinions and refine it into a thesis sentence. Then, supporting opinions, which might demand paragraphs of support in themselves, can be arranged under the thesis. Finally, decide how you wish to develop each opinion. You may choose to *exemplify* with further discussion or analysis, to provide specific facts and examples in support of an opinion, to tell a story or describe an experience that supports the opinion. Whatever form of development you choose, you should use detail and appeal to both the senses and the intellect of your reader.

The following steps will help you in developing statements of opinion:

1974 THUNDERBIRD BURGUNDY SPECIAL EDITION

Most of the luxuries in Thunderbird come *standard:* things like air conditioning. The vinyl roof. Steel-belted radial ply tires. And it doesn't require premium gas. Now, for a little more, you can have this very limited Special Edition. The Burgundy Luxury Group is sumptuous, from its discreet gold stripes and distinctive wire wheel covers, to its deep Victoria Velour seating surfaces (or choose red leather and vinyl). Here's the car to remember. Better still, to own. Thunderbird 1974. *In the world of personal luxury cars, it's the unique value.*

This is your year. Make a little Thunder of your own.

THUNDERBIRD

The Sensuous Car by "D"

If you knew cars before your alphabet. If the Paris Auto Show is more important than the Rose Bowl. If you take two parking slots because you're paranoid about dings. If you enjoy getting where you're going rather than arriving there.

If this is the way you are, our machine is lovingly designed for you. It's not just a car, because a car performs ordinary functions, like a refrigerator or washing machine. Rather, 240-Z is a gran turismo automobile, designed and built by gentlemen to whom an automobile is a work of enduring art.

Another word about 240-Z. It is not a plaything of the idle rich. It is not painstakingly handcrafted over a period of months, which as you know can result in ill-fitting parts and high costs. What it is, however, is a mass-produced automobile of exceptionally high quality. The best of two apparently contradictory worlds: affordable price and mystique... a Datsun Original. **Drive a Datsun, then decide.**

1. Distinguish statements of opinion from those of fact and convention.

2. Decide upon your most important opinion, usually in general form, and list more specific supporting opinions under it.

3. Decide upon methods or strategies of development for each opinion—by examples, by concrete descriptions, or by step-by-step illustrations. (These specific strategies, and others, will be covered in the final chapter of the book.)

Many writers get into the most trouble with statements of convention. Often they mistakenly believe they should develop and support the obvious, the agreed upon and conventional statement. This tendency bores the reader. Someone writing an essay on Mark Twain does not need to support the claim that Twain was a great writer. Most people would agree. He would be better off going on to more specific and pointed statements.

A second and more serious danger is to use statements of convention too often. As a result, your entire essay becomes conventional; it says nothing that a reader wouldn't know himself. A writer should keep conventional statements to a minimum, unless his purpose in the essay is to criticize the conventional and offer opposing opinions.

Organizing Exercise

We've discussed ways to organize and develop experience in written form, mostly in the essay form. Let's return now to a specific piece of experience and try to apply the principles we have learned to our writing. Most critics of Max Ernst's painting, *The Horse, He's Sick* (page 80), believe that he is trying to say something in the painting about modern society. Begin by listing a group of statements that you feel capture what the painting says. You might produce a list something like this:

"The horse is sick because it represents modern, mechanical man." (opinion)

"This is an animate object—a horse—painted as if it were an inanimate object—a machine." (fact)

"This mechanical contraption represents man's place in the modern world." (opinion)

"The dove, usually a symbol of love and sensitivity, contrasts with the mechanical horse to show the split in modern culture between the mechanical and the living." (opinion)

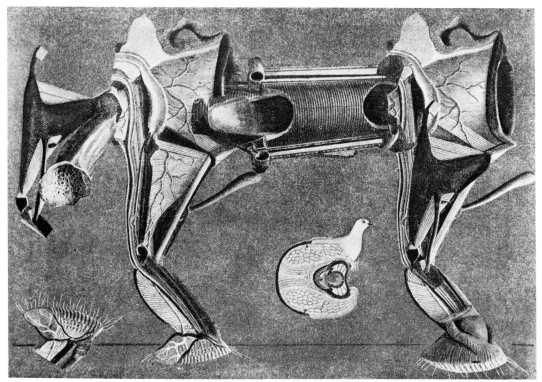

Courtesy The Museum of Modern Art, New York.

Figure 2-4   The Horse, He's Sick *by Max Ernst*

Here we have three statements of opinion and one of descriptive fact. The clearest, and in several ways the most general, is the fourth, a statement of opinion which argues a split in modern culture between the machine and living organisms. Let's propose a strategy for developing two paragraphs under this statement.

Paragraph One: Develop the split as it is represented in the painting itself.

1. The shapes and forms of the horse, here portrayed in detail, create a sterile, lifeless impression.

2. The dark background seems to blend with the mechanical horse more than it does with the dove, which seems stuck on to the painting like an afterthought.

3. The gaping holes and the hard cylinder in the center give the horse a devouring look.

Paragraph Two: Relate the specifics of the painting to what you feel would be examples of this split in culture.

1. The way our environment has come to be dominated by machinery—from roads and street mechanisms to our kitchens and houses.

2. The way human feelings seem separated from social functions—the dove is pasted on to the painting to show that our feelings are often no longer connected to people and living things but to machines.

Such an exercise produces a conceptual outline for an expository essay on this painting. You might produce several similar outlines as you work in workshops with other members of the class to refine your initial reactions to the painting. Find an everyday object that you feel demonstrates something about our society, for example, a garbage can with a "Dump Nixon" sticker on it or an old, oil-burning car with a green and white ecology flag pasted on the bumper. Take specific notes and write a preliminary description of the object. Then work out a thesis on how this object offers a comment on our society. Put your thesis material and your concrete description together in one essay.

Writing where you find it

Experience surrounds us. Part of the writer's job is to pay attention to it, observe it sensitively, and follow it where it takes him. Then he's got something to write about. To help you put in practice a few of these everyday habits, turn your attention to the selections that begin on page 82. You'll find all types of language. Every selection presents experience concretely and directly. The represented experience speaks for itself; the writer doesn't jump in to interpret or preach; he describes carefully, letting his description suggest his attitude.

What do we mean by *attitude*? Attitude describes a writer's feelings, his opinions about his subject. Sometimes attitude is perfectly clear:

I don't care for scotch. It tastes smoky, burned, and flat. I'd rather drink beer.

Sometimes attitude is *too* clear:

Anything I can't stand I ignore. The guy sitting next to me on the bus was a creep, dirty, unintelligent, and crude. But he kept asking me questions that I couldn't ignore. I sneered when I answered.

In the example above, the writer's attitude toward certain kinds of people is clear, perhaps a bit repulsive, but clear. We can reveal more about ourselves when we describe other people, objects, and scenes than we often realize. Get used to looking for words, images, and general ways of speaking that reveal *you* and *your* attitudes as you describe. When you do, you'll be better able to control and direct your readers. You won't be revealing attitudes you don't even recognize yourself.

Each of the following selections develops an attitude, not directly or openly, but suggestively in a between-the-lines way. That's probably the most effective way to develop attitude. Your reader is persuaded by the concrete experience itself, not by your telling him what to think.

But to persuade without telling or preaching means that you've got to select and plan your description. You've got to consider what your reader needs in order to get a full picture. More importantly, you've got to consider your words and your style in relation to your attitude, what you want to say between-the-lines about your subject. This consideration involves going over your experiences carefully, thinking about what they mean to you, and planning what to use and how to use it—all *before* you write.

Consider the following selections carefully. Think about the purpose of each and how the described experience—visual or verbal—achieves or fails to achieve that purpose.

In back of the real

ALLEN GINSBERG

railroad yard in San Jose.
    I wandered desolate
in front of a tank factory
    and sat on a bench
near the switchman's shack.

A flower lay on the hay on
    the asphalt highway
—the dread hay flower
    I thought—It had a
brittle black stem and
    corolla of yellowish dirty
spikes like Jesus' inchlong
    crown, and a soiled
dry center cotton tuft

           like a used shaving brush
       that's been lying under
           the garage for a year.

       Yellow, yellow flower, and
           flower of industry,
       tough spikey ugly flower,
           flower nonetheless,
       with the form of the great yellow
           Rose in your brain!
       This is the flower of the World.

The flower is the central object in Ginsberg's poem. It carries the weight of the meaning and through it we know what the poem says. Look closely at the way Ginsberg describes the flower, at the words he uses, especially adjectives, at the way he contrasts the flower's concrete, yellow beauty with the grime of the railroad yard.

Activity Exercise

Now write a general sentence that describes Ginsberg's attitude toward the flower and another that describes his attitude toward the railroad yard. Then go back and find support in the poem for your general statements of attitude. Look at the words Ginsberg uses and the tension in the poem between the flower and the dirt that surrounds it.

You might also consider comparing Ginsberg's poem to Max Ernst's painting *The Horse, He's Sick*. Ernst, if we take his horse as symbolic of modern man and society, makes a joke out of the same material that Ginsberg treats seriously. Are their purposes similar or different? How can you tell? Does the fact that Ginsberg uses a flower to represent his ideas and Ernst a horse say anything to you about their respective purposes?

Activity Exercise

1. What does Christianson say about modern life-styles in the cartoon on the following page? Write a few sentences describing the dress of the two main figures. Exchange papers with another person in class and evaluate each other's accuracy.

2. Block out the print and write your own caption for the cartoon, one that develops a different theme.

Christianson

"I was into awareness. Now I'm into money."   **Figure 2-5**

Reproduced by permission of *Playboy* magazine; Copyright © 1972 by *Playboy*.

3. Try developing a thesis statement for an argumentative essay on the theme represented in the original caption. Before you start, define *awareness* and *money* as they are used in the caption.

4. Try writing an extended dialogue between the two main figures in the Christianson cartoon. Use actual phrases you've overheard in public places. Recall your own conversations and those of friends.

next to of course god america i

e. e. cummings

"next to of course god america i
love you land of the pilgrims' and so forth oh
say can you see by the dawn's early my
country 'tis of centuries come and go

and are no more what of it we should worry
in every language even deafanddumb
thy sons acclaim your glorious name by gorry
by jingo by gee by gosh by gum
why talk of beauty what could be more beautiful than these heroic happy dead
who rushed like lions to the roaring slaughter
they did not stop to think they died instead
then shall the voice of liberty be mute?"

He spoke. And drank rapidly a glass of water

In many of his poems, E.E. Cummings mixes bits and pieces of conversations he has overheard, perhaps at a restaurant, a ballgame, on a subway,
or in an airport lounge. He's developed an attentive ear, always waiting to
hear something that will help him write.

Thinking Exercise

Ask yourself these questions: Do you recognize any of the phrases in
the poem? Do they give you any indication of where the words originally
were spoken? Does the glass of water give you a hint as well? Does the
language sound like everyday talk or formal, ceremonious speech?

Tom Martin Creek

RICHARD BRAUTIGAN

I walked down one morning from Steelhead, following the Klamath
River that was high and murky and had the intelligence of a dinosaur. Tom
Martin Creek was a small creek with cold, clear water and poured out of
a canyon and through a culvert under the highway and then into the
Klamath.

I dropped a fly in a small pool just below where the creek flowed out of
the culvert and took a nine-inch trout. It was a good-looking fish and fought
all over the top of the pool.

Even though the creek was very small and poured out of a steep
brushy canyon filled with poison oak, I decided to follow the creek up a
ways because I liked the feel and motion of the creek.

I liked the name, too.

Tom Martin Creek.

It's good to name creeks after people and then later to follow them for a while seeing what they have to offer, what they know and have made of themselves.

But that creek turned out to be a real son-of-a-bitch. I had to fight it all the God-damn way: brush, poison oak and hardly any good places to fish, and sometimes the canyon was so narrow the creek poured out like water from a faucet. Sometimes it was so bad that it just left me standing there, not knowing which way to jump.

You had to be a plumber to fish that creek.

After that first trout I was alone in there. But I didn't know it until later.

Activity Exercise

Richard Brautigan gives us a concrete description of a walk along a small creek. Yet he tells us a good deal about himself along the way. What kind of guy is Richard Brautigan? Try to imagine what he looks like, what he wears, and a few of his attitudes just from this brief sketch. Separate his statements of opinion—"You had to be a plumber to fish that creek"—from his concrete description—"Tom Martin Creek was a small creek with cold, clear water. . . ." Then try to determine his attitude toward nature *through* the attitudes he expresses toward Tom Martin Creek. Is he a nature-lover? If so, why the sense of struggle and pain?

Figure 2-6

"Also in all times and in all places to condemn war, pollution, and non-biodegradable containers, to support the Third World, and to fight for a better life for the migrant farm worker."

Drawing by William Hamilton; © 1972 The New Yorker Magazine, Inc.

In this cartoon, we find a traditionally ceremonious occasion—a wedding—transformed by a change in language. The scene looks familiar. But we don't hear the words we expect to hear. Instead, we hear a pledge to support several contemporary and popular movements. This couple joins together, not to support one another as much as to support their ideas. Do you think William Hamilton is against ceremonies or against the people who misuse them? Is the ceremony misused here? How do you know? Should nonconformist ideas be institutionalized? Does that destroy their impact, make them seem establishment?

Activity Exercise

1. Think of any situation, ritual, or occasion in which changing the words would both alter the meaning of the ritual itself and create a humorous comment on some contemporary idea, fad, movement, or issue.

2. Write a sentence that describes what Hamilton thinks about some element of the cartoon—the issues or items mentioned in the ceremony, the couple, the onlookers. Then develop support for that interpretation. Use examples from the cartoon or your own experience.

Waking From Sleep

ROBERT BLY

Inside the veins there are navies setting forth,
Tiny explosions at the water lines,
And seagulls weaving in the wind of the salty blood.

It is the morning. The country has slept the whole winter.
Window seats were covered with fur skins, the yard was full
Of stiff dogs, and hands that clumsily held heavy books.

Now we wake, and rise from bed, and eat breakfast!—
Shouts rise from the harbor of the blood,
Mist, and masts rising, the knock of wooden tackle in the sunlight.

Now we sing, and do tiny dances on the kitchen floor.
Our whole body is like a harbor at dawn;
We know that our master has left us for the day

Activity Exercise

Robert Bly tries to describe with metaphors and analogies, the sensations he feels inside himself as he awakens in the morning. (If you still feel unsure of metaphors, look back over the material on pages 17–21.) Choose a few of Bly's metaphors—"the navies setting forth inside the veins, the seagulls weaving in the wind of the salty blood"—and explain how they work. Do they give you an accurate and lively idea of how Bly feels when he wakes? Do they really help him to *share* that experience? Try analyzing your own sensations as you go through some common experience. Can you find metaphors that will help you explain those sensations? A sensation is an inner response, something you feel along the nerve lines of your body, the sinking feeling in the pit of your stomach just before your appearance on stage, or as the opening kickoff heads toward you, or perhaps as you prepare to deliver the final words in a debate. Sometimes the only way to describe a sensation is to find an objective experience that will describe it by comparison—Bly's blood moving in his veins in the morning feels like "navies setting forth/ Tiny explosions at the water lines." Have you ever seen a torpedo hit a battleship and cause an explosion at the water line, perhaps in an old movie on television? If so, does that memory help you to understand how Bly feels as he awakens?

In most advertisements, the writer's attitude is not hidden. We all know he wants to sell us something; we all know he likes the product and feels it is superior to others. If we're at all experienced, we don't expect to get the whole truth. In fact, we expect an appeal to our senses and emotions, not an appeal to reason. Some of us ridicule and ignore advertisements, and certainly many ads demonstrate simple-minded, exaggerated appeals. But we often ridicule without realizing how clever and effective these appeals are, how they "sell" without our realizing it. Analyze the sensory appeal in the Thunderbird advertisement. How do the colors and other visual appeals—the picture of the interior and the woman, for example—reinforce the words? Notice how every statement of fact—"Most of the luxuries in Thunderbird come standard"—is usually followed by some form of sensory appeal (which we are meant to assume is a factual statement as well)—"deep Victoria Velour seating surfaces, Burgundy Luxury Group, discreet gold stripes, distinctive wire wheel covers." Attitudes are supported by physical details which are, in turn, described in emotionally charged words. *Deep, velour, sumptuous* create the sound and meaning of comfort; the repetition of s's and rich vowel clusters (*ee, ou, uou*) thrust us bodily into Thunderbird seats.

Activity Exercise

Write a short paper describing the kind of man who drives a Thunder-bird. How does he dress? What are his values? Where does he work and live? Or, more importantly, where will he want to live once he has looked at enough ads of this type? Select your details carefully and be specific.

Highway 61 Revisited
BOB DYLAN

I'm standing there watching the parade/
feeling combination of sleepy john estes.
jayne mansfield. humphrey bogart/morti-
mer snurd, murph the surf and so forth/
erotic hitchhiker wearing japanese
blanket. gets my attention by asking didn't
he see me at this hootenanny down in
puerto vallarta, mexico/i say no you must
be mistaken. i happen to be one of the
Supremes/then he rips off his blanket
an suddenly becomes a middle-aged druggist.
up for district attorney. he starts screaming at me you're the one. you're the one
that's been causing all them riots over in
vietnam. immediately turns to a bunch of
people an says if elected, he'll have me
electrocuted publicly on the next fourth
of july. i look around at all these people
he's talking to are carrying blowtorches/
needless t say, i split fast go back t the
nice quiet country. am standing there writing
WHAAAT? on my favorite wall when who
    should
pass by in a jet plane but my recording
engineer "i'm here t pick up you and your
latest works of art. do you need any help
with anything?"
my songs're written with the kettledrum
in mind/ a touch of any anxious color. un-
mentionable. obvious. an people perhaps

like a soft brazilian singer . . . i have
given up at making any attempt at perfection/
the fact that the white house is filled with
leaders that've never been t the apollo
theater amazes me. why allen ginsberg was
not chosen t read poetry at the inauguration
boggles my mind/if someone thinks norman
mailer is more important than hank williams,
that's fine. i have no arguments and i
never drink milk. i would rather model harmonica holders than discuss aztec anthropology/
english literature. or history of the united
nations i accept chaos i am not sure whether
it accepts me. i know there's some people terrified
of the bomb. but there are other people terrified
t be seen carrying a modern screen magazine.
experience teaches that silence terrifies people
the most . . . i am convinced that all souls have
some superior t deal with/like the school
system, an invisible circle of which no one
can think without consulting someone/in the
face of this, responsibility/security. success
mean absolutely nothing . . . i would not want
t be bach. mozart. tolstoy. joe hill. gertrude
stein or james dean/they are all dead. the
Great books've been written. the Great sayings
have all been said/I am about to sketch You
a picture of what goes on around here sometimes. tho I don't understand too well
myself what's really happening. i do know
that we're all gonna die someday an that no
death has ever stopped the world. my poems
are written in a rhythm of unpoetic distortion/
divided by pierced ears. false eyelashes/sub-
tracted by people constantly torturing each
other. with a melodic purring line of descriptive
hollowness—seen at times thru dark sunglasses
an other forms of psychic explosion. a song is
anything that can walk by itself/i am called
a songwriter. a poem is a naked person . . . some
people say that i am a poet
            (end of pause)
an so i answer my recording engineer
"yes. well i could use some help in getting
this wall in the plane"

We now move from the language of an ad to the language of a popular performer as he expresses a few of his personal feelings and sensations and tries to tell us where those feelings and sensations come from. Again we find metaphors. The sentences read like lines of poetry. Dylan describes a confusing swirl of events: people he meets, people he reads about, sees in movies (Bogart and Mansfield, hitchhikers, his recording engineer), incidents that he's gone through, bits of conversation, public events (the reference to Allen Ginsberg, the beatnik poet, reading at a presidential inauguration, for example, is a recalling of Robert Frost's address at the Inauguration of John Kenendy in 1961). And he links them to his personal attitudes, to why he "accepts chaos" and "would rather model harmonica holders than discuss aztec anthropology" (a slap at intellectuals and the academic world?).

Activity Exercise

The second half of Dylan's monologue states his attitudes more directly than the first. Select one of those attitudes—for example, that he "would not want to be bach. mozart. tolstoy. joe hill. gertrude stein or james dean/they are all dead"—and write a page explaining it. Don't argue, just explain. Try to point out in concrete terms what Dylan means and why he says it the way he does. Then try putting together some of your own personal attitudes and the reasons and experiences behind them in a free-form monologue like Dylan's.

Activity Exercise

1. The Datsun ad doesn't mince words. Everybody, of course, wants a car that's "a gran turismo automobile designed and built by gentlemen to whom an automobile is a work of enduring art." Right? If you think not, write an essay in which you criticize the ad by disagreeing with its underlying assumption—that we all want gran turismo cars. By the way, keep in mind the possibilities of irony. Maybe the people who make Datsuns have figured out the market. Some people buy cars for power or sex, and others for economy, transportation, and survival. Could this ad appeal to both types of these perspective buyers?

2. Imagine yourself the owner of this car. Put yourself in the driver's seat of the Datsun 240-Z and write an essay in which you describe a single, extended experience with the car. (You might use parts of Campbell's essay on page 61 as a model.) Be specific and have some general purpose in mind—either to entertain or to express some attitude toward sporty cars. If you can, work in some dialogue with a passenger, a service station attendant, or another driver.

Color figure 2-8
DATSUN AD
follows page 78.

The exploring eye

II

Finding and
limiting your subject

"The insight that we can never get away from ourselves is an insight which the human race through its long history has been deliberately, one is tempted to say willfully, refusing to admit. But the ostensibly timeless absolutes are formulated and apprehended by us, and the vision which the mystic says is revealed by the direct intervention of God is still a vision apprehended by him. When we talk about getting away from ourselves it is we who are talking."

—*P. W. Bridgman*

LIBERTY LEADING THE PEOPLE by Delacroix. Courtesy The Louvre.

WINTER (RETURN OF THE HUNTERS) by Pieter Brueghel. Courtesy Art Reference Bureau.

3

Discovering something to say

Have you ever returned from an exciting movie, or a basketball game that your favorite team won in the final seconds, and tried very unsuccessfully to tell another person what happened? You didn't know where to begin. In fact, you didn't really remember very clearly what actually happened, except that what did happen had been exciting.

First, you resorted to adjectives: "that was a *fantastic* game" or "I just saw a *super* flick." But adjectives don't really do the job. They may tell your reader how *you* feel, but they don't tell him much about the movie or game.

Then, you tried summarizing what happened: "Johnson won the game with a foul shot with only seven seconds left. The fans were in an uproar the whole time." That's better, but still nothing like what *you* experienced at the game itself. The person you are talking to has only the bare facts, and he can read the sports page for those. You haven't done very much to share the experience with him. The minute-by-minute feelings of being at that game or movie are gone, perhaps never to be recalled in the particular and personal way that you experienced them. Why is it often difficult to explain an experience to a person who hasn't gone through that experience himself?

There are many answers to that question. But one we often ignore is probably the most obvious answer. Such explanations are difficult because we don't remember much of the experience ourselves. I remember a college roommate of mine who came charging into my room eager to explain his reaction to a film. But as he explained, he found he hadn't really noticed much. Had the hero been wearing black in the final scene? Maybe. Was the car he drove green or blue? A Ford or a Pontiac? How did the hero walk, jerkily or smoothly? What my roommate finally discovered was that he had been so immersed in the experience himself that he really hadn't noticed much. He resorted, then, to summarizing and *telling* me about the experience rather than basing his response on actual, concrete observation. After we had talked, I may have had a general idea of what happened, but I hadn't *shared in* the experience.

This chapter should help you become more sensitive, more observant, and more conscious of what's happening to you *as it happens.* That means we will give attention to the way we receive experience through our senses. Then, you'll have more to say simply because you'll remember more. You'll be more perceptive, better able to see *why* things happen as well as *how* they happen. To find material we've got to be attentive and observant, like the artist who carries his sketch pad with him all the time or the novelist who is never without his notebook. As your eyes explore, follow them with your mind. As your senses reach out, keep your imagination as close behind them as possible.

The discovering process

In order to train your senses and to train your mind to follow and analyze your senses, you need first of all to subject your experience to some very mechanical exercises. Here is what we'll aim to develop with these exercises and related discussion:

1. the ability to record details *as* we receive experience
2. the ability to understand *why* our experiences occur as they do, again *as* we receive them
3. the ability to share in writing the actual, concrete details of experience along with our personal opinions and attitudes.

As you become more accustomed to careful perception and observation, you'll be less mechanical. You'll be able to retain more of what you experience; you'll have more to say, more concrete support to use in your writing.

We can break the process of receiving experience into four distinct units. In everyday life, these units overlap. But distinguishing them should help you to organize what you receive through your senses.

Stimuli: the concrete details of our immediate environment, *before* our minds change or reorganize them.

Sensation: feelings as we experience them inside ourselves through our senses and nervous system. Sensations are, of course, usually caused by some physical or mental stimuli, either from our immediate environment or from our memories.

Perception: larger blocks of experience in which we find some physical or mental relationships—combinations of related stimuli and sensation.

Conception: perceptual units which are combined into completed thoughts, ideas, or images and which are often composed of numerous stimuli and sensations.

Before we analyze these subdivisions, we need to know something about how the whole receiving process operates. We seldom are conscious of the entire process. In fact, most of us respond unconsciously to most stimuli; we are often only vaguely aware of sensations. Even full perceptions sometimes never are fully conscious; we are "half-aware" of them, in a subconscious way. Only under rare conditions are we fully open to experience, do we recognize the smallest stimuli, savor the briefest sensation, recognize why we perceive experience as we do. Poets often call these "moments of insight," sometimes "moments of vision." They are times of heightened perception, times when we are fully alive to the "world out there."

Ambrose Bierce, a late nineteenth-century American writer, wrote a short story in which a young, southern civilian is hung by the Union Army during the Civil War. The complete story is included in Section IV. Here is a brief excerpt. It demonstrates very well the "moment of insight," a brief period in which the hero, the man being hanged, has turned all his senses on, is gloriously open and sensitive to every detail of experience, every stimuli and sensation, every completed perception.

> He was now in full possession of his physical senses. They were, indeed, preternaturally keen and alert. Something in the awful disturbance of his organic system had so exalted and refined them that they made record of things never before perceived. He felt the ripples upon his face and heard their separate sounds as they struck. He looked at the forest on the bank of the stream, saw the individual trees, the leaves and the veining of each leaf—saw the very insects upon them: the locusts, the brilliant-bodied flies, the gray spiders stretching their webs from twig to twig. He noted the prismatic colors in all the dewdrops upon a million blades of grass. The humming of the gnats that danced above the eddies of the stream, the beating of the drangonflies' wings, the strokes of the water spiders' legs, like oars which had lifted their boat—all these made audible music. A fish slid along beneath his eyes and he heard the rush of its body parting the water.

Just before hanging, Bierce's main character becomes suddenly and fully alive. He recognizes, consciously evaluates, and enjoys even the smallest stimuli in his environment. His physical senses, as the narrator tells us, had been rudely awakened by the shock of the rope: "they made record of things never before perceived." Bierce records three kinds of sensory appeal —touch, sight, sound—in extended detail.

First, we read how the hero *feels* the ripples of the water and *hears* the sound they make as they struck his face. He sees the forest for the first time, although he had lived near it all his life, sees the individual trees, the leaves, the tiniest bugs on the leaves. He notices spider-webs, brilliant colors, a million blades of grass. And he notices each individually, respects its beauty, loves it for what it is in itself. Here we see stimuli—the actual bits of experience, the blades of grass, leaves, etc.—not only recorded but related directly to the heightened sensations of the perceiver. The hero senses the world fully; each group of stimuli causes deep emotion, a full response from his nervous system. We know how intensely he feels his immediate environment because we share with him many of the stimuli in his environment.

A writer, like the hero of this story, must learn to feel the rope about his neck. He must develop the ability to observe the stimuli of experience, even when his life is not being threatened. Then, he must be able to record those stimuli accurately in words and sentences.

Recording in Your Journal

Your journal is a good place to record your everyday impressions as accurately as possible. Be careful to observe the objects and details in your everyday experience which *stimulate* sensations and perceptions. Get in the habit of recording experiential stimuli quickly and without much effort. Have your journal in a convenient place so that it will be easy for you to record stimuli on the spot. Record after a basketball game, a date, a pizza break, a movie, after walking across campus, anything anytime. Your journal is one way to become conscious of experience *as* it happens. Then, when you write longer papers, you will have concrete experience near at hand in your journal.

There is another aspect of receiving experience that you should consider as you write in your journal. Experience usually comes to our senses in simultaneous form. Of course, even our senses, especially our eyes, record experience sequentially, with some order already imposed. But in actual experience, the order exists simultaneously with the occurrence. The hero in Bierce's story receives stimuli in a chaos of sense impressions—shots ring out, he hears water rippling, sees insects and leaves, feels the water on his body—all simultaneously. Yet, in reading the story, we are able to follow the experience because Bierce has recreated it for us. In writing the words automatically slow down and sort out what we sense. We feel as the main character feels because we follow his experience from raw stimuli to felt sensation to ordered perception. Notice the way stimuli, sensation, and perception are combined in this sentence.

> The humming of the gnats [stimuli], that danced above the eddies of the stream [stimuli], the beating [stimuli] of the dragonflies' wings [stimuli], the strokes [stimuli] of the water spiders' legs [stimuli], like oars which had lifted their boat [perception]—all these made audible music [conception].

The bits of unrelated objects and images are raw stimuli. The comparison between the spiders' legs and the oars of a boat represents a fusing of two unlike stimuli to point up a similarity. That's a perception. The summarizing ("all these made audible music") is a concept built from the preceding stimuli and perceptions. The writer sorts and reorders the chaos of experience; he helps the reader to experience in detail and discover order for himself. The writer must take in experience with his senses open; he must recreate experience to appeal to the reader's senses, without making the experience seem artificial. Review the Bierce excerpt and follow the way the writer builds from raw stimuli to completed conception in other sentences.

Ambrose Bierce doesn't rely on general adjectives or quick summaries. He has a point to make and he takes the time necessary to *show* where the point came from, to share the experience that led up to that message. The man being hanged lives intensely because Ambrose Bierce writes intensely of real, concrete, sensory experiences.

Activity Exercise

Spend a few minutes looking over Delacroix' *Liberty Leading the People.* Just let your eyes scan the painting freely. Then give yourself five minutes and write down as rapidly as you can, in rough form, as many conceptual statements as possible, all based on the painting. Then go back over the painting and try to find stimuli that you think might have been the foundation of some of your conceptions. Here are a few example conceptions. These sentences were produced rapidly during a class period.

Color figure 3-1
LIBERTY LEADING THE PEOPLE
Delacroix
follows page 94.

> Liberty is noble and beautiful and many people die for it.
> War, even in the name of liberty, is cruel and inhuman.
> The woman is a striking symbol of liberty.
> The painter is a romantic who loves individuals but hates mankind.

These are telling, not showing, sentences. They tell what the writer thinks without showing us where the thought or conception comes from. Can you fill in and support these conceptions with sentences that point to stimuli? Can you find images in the painting that might lead to feelings or sensations which might, in turn, lead to some general conception? Can you find particular stimuli, particular details and images, that are related to form perceptions? How do particular perceptual chains work together to create the completed conception?

Here are a few example supporting sentences. Try to relate them to particular conceptual statements.

Haze and smoke cover the scene; a city looms dimly in the background.
Every sword, every gun glistens and points up toward the woman.

These example sentences capture isolated stimuli; they have not been combined or related, except in sentence two in which the swords and guns have been related to the woman. The purpose of these sentences is to capture the objective stimuli of the painting and to describe the stimuli in as much detail as possible. The above sentences, and perhaps the ones you wrote, are not as detailed or as descriptive as they might be. To help you produce more detail, so that the stimuli you describe can be seen and experienced by an audience which has not even seen the painting, try this activity. Isolate the basic units of your sentences in this manner:

subject: every *sword*, every *gun*
verb: *points*

Now look for simple adjectives, descriptive words, which will add visual detail to your subject. Try to find adjectives that add as much concrete, visual detail as possible.

Every *bright* sword and *flashing* gun pointed toward the *noble* woman.

Let's turn now to the verb and try to discover simple modifiers that will add detail to our basic sentence. You can simply add "ly" to an adjective and make an adverb. Again, try to find concrete verbal modifiers, ones that will contribute visual detail to your description.

Every bright sword and flashing gun pointed *sharply* toward the noble woman.

That's not an astounding sentence, but in it we find stimuli described specifically in a clear pattern. It is a strong support sentence for a potential conceptual sentence, one that shares the stimuli in the painting. You can probably produce much better support sentences with some practice and planning.

Keep this suggestion in mind: be careful not to overload your writing with single-word modifiers, especially adjectives. Too many adjectives and adverbs give a sentence a crammed, confusing structure. The reader loses himself in the mass of modifiers and can't get a complete, unified perspective. Choose many concrete adjectives that describe physical properties (color, size, shape, texture) and avoid overusing general and vague adjectives like "wonderful," "great," "tremendous" or "fantastic." They just don't give the reader enough to go on. They tell, rather than show and share.

Activity Exercise

Try writing specific responses, about a paragraph in length and in rough draft form, to the class interpretations of the painting given on page 103. If you agree, show why by referring to the specifics in the painting. Do the same if you don't agree. Also, try to qualify your paragraphs so that, in turn, you will *qualify* the interpretations. You can qualify in three ways—by *adding* to what the reader knows about the painting's detail, by *comparing* details of the painting to other objects or ideas, and by narrowing a generality with qualifying words such as *almost, sometimes,* and *probably.* When we qualify, we *add* something to the interpretation without actually agreeing or disagreeing.

Then, try discussing the painting in class. A group of students can discuss whether they like the painting or not. Then other members of the class can question the group on their taste, either arguing or agreeing with them by referring to specific details in the painting itself. What makes you like or dislike the painting? Is it some visual detail? Some confusing aspect in perspective? The point of view of the artist reflected in the painting?

Sentences describing sensations

Sensations are the feelings or physical responses that we experience inside because of stimuli. The writer may decide to describe stimuli objectively and to leave sensations to the reader. If the writer selects, arranges, and controls stimuli carefully, he can usually predict what sensations his readers will experience as they respond to those stimuli. But in many writing situations, as in the Ambrose Bierce excerpt we analyzed previously, the writer may want to describe his sensations and experiences, to recreate them for the reader. Words which aptly describe feelings are not easy to find.

Perhaps the most useful suggestion for the writer who wishes to describe sensations accurately is to relate sensations directly to stimuli, to actual, concrete bits of experience. In this way, the reader will have a focal point upon which to base what he knows about the writer's sensations. A writer who describes sensations must also be sure to analyze them thoroughly; he must search carefully for descriptive words that bring out the right responses in his readers. That means careful scrutiny of word denotation and connotation.

When we look up a word in a dictionary, we find its denotative meanings. But words usually have suggestive, or connotative, meanings as well. Take, for example, the word *rat*. Denotatively, the word refers to "various long-tailed rodents, resembling, but larger than, mice; especially one of the genus *rattus*." Certainly, we don't always use the word that way. Sometimes we apply it metaphorically to other people. When we do that, we use the connotation of the word, for rats down through the ages have gained fairly notorious reputations as carriers of diseases, as frequenters of garbage dumps, as common pests. When a reader sees the word *rat*, he not only thinks of "long-tailed rodents larger than mice," but also of all those negative connotations—disease, dirt, infested garbage dumps. Very few of the words we use in everyday situations have only one connotative meaning. To describe our sensations accurately we need to control the meanings of important words.

Many words have a single, explicit definition, but these same words may *imply* different things. Take the words *brilliance* and *radiance*, for example. Both have very similar denotative, explicit definitions, especially if we limit the meaning to "quality of light." Both denote a brightness or intensity of light spread over an area of space. But their connotations are quite different. *Radiance* connotes beams radiating from a source; *brilliance* connotes an intensity of light, but does not include any reference to source or movement of light. A careful writer might select *radiance* to describe how he feels when he is extremely happy and is able to radiate the happiness out into his environment. He would not choose *brilliance* because he would lose the connotation of sending his happy feelings out to others.

Generally, a consideration of context can help us control the meaning of a word. For example, you will respond to a discussion of rats, genus *rattus*, in a biology text much differently than you would to a reference to rats in a description of a slum building. In the biology text, you want to learn more about the rat as a rodent, how and what it eats, where it usually lives, whether it is dangerous and will attack. When you read the textbook you consciously exclude the negative, everyday connotations. But if a novelist mentions rats while he describes the living quarters of one of his characters, you probably exclude the textbook meaning and unconsciously emphasize the everyday associations: dirt, disease, shabby tenements in a city neighborhood.

Here are two sentences which describe sensations that some class observers have felt while looking at *Liberty Leading the People.*

> I feel the excitement of people who are fighting for a cause.
> My head reels as I look over the tangled figures.

These are simple descriptions of sensations. What can we add to these sentences? What will help the reader to share the sensations described in the sentences? First, we can add detail and modify the sensation itself. The following sentence is a rewritten version of sentence two above.

> My head reels, my senses burn, as I look over the tangled figures in the painting.

But more importantly, we should try to connect our descriptions of sensations to the sentences that describe stimuli. A writer can fuse stimuli and sensation in two ways: by connecting stimuli and sensation in one sentence; or by relating stimuli and sensation in several sentences, with careful attention to connecting or transitional structures. Here are two examples.

> The haze and smoke in the background, the extended arms and hands of the people, make me feel dizzy.
> When I look at this painting I feel a part of the action. The human figures are all in the midst of doing something, and I feel I should complete their actions for them. The ends of my fingers feel the rifle; my arm stretches to hold the flag up; my back feels the cold ground beneath me.

In these examples, we find simple visual stimuli related directly to the writer's sensations. In this way the reader at least knows the source of the writer's feelings. Sometimes, however, you'll want to avoid *telling* your reader how you feel and prefer to let your description speak for itself. Look over the following student paragraphs. Both describe the same incident, but one tells directly how the writer felt about the subject, whereas the second allows the language to suggest how the writer felt. Can you find places where the writer emphasizes certain word connotations to reinforce what he feels?

> Yesterday I saw something that made me sick. An older man pushed a child, a young girl, almost to the ground while he rushed to get to a

bus. She cried and I felt like finding that guy and setting him straight. It's things like that that make large cities unbearable.

He walked rapidly ahead of me as I approached the corner, his arms flapping out with each step. I followed, my eyes carelessly scanning the intersection ahead. Suddenly, his fast walk became a run; he headed for the bus as it slowly pulled away from the curb. A small child, about as high as his waist, stepped in front of him. He nervously slowed, his body lurched and hesitated for a moment, and he brushed by. His momentum forced her down to the sidewalk.

She picked herself up slowly. The bus faded with a rumble down the road. And I stepped more slowly across the intersection.

Writing Exercise

Write a paragraph in which you tell how you feel about some object around you. Then revise the paragraph so that you describe the object and get across your feeling about the object simultaneously. Try to find words that will suggest how you feel as well as what you see.

Sentences describing perceptions

Perceptions are often difficult to separate from stimuli and sensations, at least in writing. The easiest way to separate stimuli and sensation from perception in actual experience is to remember that perceptions are more complete; they represent a further stage in the development of completed conceptions. A sensitive observer notices the smallest stimuli; a careful writer describes those observed stimuli accurately, in detail. A person who experiences deeply and sensitively analyzes his sensations closely and becomes familiar with his feelings or sensations; a writer who wishes to describe sensations records feelings accurately and connects them to concrete stimuli. An intelligent and sensitive perceiver analyzes the ways in which he forms raw materials (stimuli) and feelings (sensations) into completed perceptions; the writer who is conscious of the perceptual processes will be careful to recreate in whatever he writes the whole perceptual process, the completed perception of formed units in experience.

The following two sentences capture completed perceptual units (combinations of stimuli perceived as a completed whole by the observer). Each sentence is followed by a diagram that charts the relationships among the visual stimuli, the perceptions, and the overall conception.

The mass of human figures lying in confusion at the bottom of the painting represent those who have died for liberty.

Stimuli:	the mass of human figures
Perception:	that the figures are in confusion
Perception:	that they are clustered at the bottom of the painting, below the symbolic figure of liberty
Conception:	that the masses have died for liberty; that freedom demands such personal sacrifice

All types of people, men and women, must band together to fight tyranny; liberty is a woman with breast bared and is supported partially by a half-nude man who lies wounded on the ground.

Stimuli:	the woman with bared breast and the partially nude man
Perception:	that the woman who represents liberty is supported by a partially clothed man
Conception:	that all types of people must unite to fight for liberty

These sentences are relatively simple examples of how our sentences, even in everyday talk, are built from fairly complex strings or series of experience and thought. Become accustomed to following what you say and write back to its origins in experience. This method will help you discover numerous ways to support what you think and feel. The stimuli you experience, the sensations you feel, and the thoughts and opinions you hold are all related. Your writing ought to *show* those relationships to your readers.

Activity Exercise

See if you can find perceptual units in the Delacroix painting. These perceptions will take the form of visual areas that you perceive as related subunits within the entire painting.

Back to the raw materials

Now that we have traced the process of receiving experience from stimuli through conception, let's consider again the stimuli themselves. They are the raw materials in the writer's "gold mine." But they are often difficult to capture in words, sometimes even difficult to *see* and *experience* clearly before we write.

William James, in a lecture he gave to a group of religious people about a century ago, described the chaos of a mere moment in anyone's existence: "While I talk," James said, "and the flies buzz, a seagull catches a fish at the mouth of the Amazon, a tree falls in the Adirondack wilderness, a man sneezes in Germany, a horse dies in Tartary, and twins are born in France. What does that mean? Does the contemporaneity of these events with one another, and with a million others as disjointed, form a rational bond between them. . . ?" We make sense out of the world primarily through words. We take the basic stimuli of our experience and transform them into ordered language. Before we get too far from experience itself, we need to pinpoint and analyze the basic stimuli, to see what it is we really see. That usually means stripping away our attitudes and prejudices and analyzing the experience as if through a microscope.

Let's try to clarify with an example. Suppose that you are sitting in your student center busily reading a letter from your boyfriend or girl friend, simultaneously engaging in conversation with friends, and eating dinner. Here, you've isolated several simultaneous experiences, with a look back over the experience, to recapture essential stimuli, to choose just those elements of the situation which you thought were important. Certainly, you can't say everything all at once; your reader would then be immersed in a chaos of indistinct detail. He would be confused, disoriented and, as a result, the experience would mean little to him. Therefore, you select several concrete stimuli—an important word or phrase from the letter, a passing remark in the conversation, a bit of food, a particularly distinctive taste—from the combined stimuli of the experience.

You select according to your purpose in composing. If the letter you were reading held particularly bad news, say a "Dear John" from your steady, you might take in the entire scene differently from the way you would if the letter brought good news, say that you had gotten an important job offer. For example, as reader of a "Dear John," you might notice a particularly monotonous voice droning on at a nearby table. After good news, however, you might give more attention to a particularly good-looking person or an attractive meal. Remember that your emotions do influence how and what you perceive, which stimuli you give attention to, which stimuli you ignore or barely notice. Before you write about an experience, question your observations; ask yourself whether you have ignored important stimuli or exaggerated others. Evaluate the total experience and select important stimuli, those that will help you to communicate your attitudes and feelings.

Activity Exercise

One way to test your powers of observation is to create classroom scenes and ask individual members of your class to record their impressions of those scenes. Here are two that have worked for other classes. You should be able to develop others in group discussions.

1. Have three or four class members devise a skit. Have one or two other class members leave the room before the class prepares the skit. The class members who have left can then be recalled during the presentation, having no previous knowledge of what is to happen in the skit. At times, the skit may call for some immediate reaction from the recently returned classmates. The class can then analyze the skit in follow-up discussion and writing. Here is an example skit.

Bill and Tom leave class. The rest of the class stages a mock fist-fight and argument, as if on a streetcorner, in front of the room. Bill and Tom are called back in the midst of the action. How do they respond, both verbally and nonverbally? Why do they respond as they do?

2. Look at Robert Rauschenberg's *Storyline I.* Try to absorb as much of the detail in the painting as you can—objects, shapes, people you might recognize, shades, anything. Then close your book and jot down as much as you can remember. Several people might read their lists until the class feels the description is complete. Then, open to the painting and compare your list with the original. Why did you miss certain details and perhaps over-emphasize others? Was it because of your past experience or your attitudes toward objects in the painting?

Details and stories

Narrative is writing that tells a story. A good narrative never preaches, just as a good storyteller never stops his story to tell the listener what he means or to lecture about the significance of his story. His main aim is to *share* the experience of the story. He finds those physical details that will evoke the listener's senses in response. He tells his story so that the listener eagerly waits for the next word. Once in a while, the storyteller repeats a phrase, emphasizes a detail, or focuses on an action. In other words, he lets the experience of his story tell itself. He is dramatic, not philosophic.

When you are writing a narrative, you've got to select and organize your detail before you begin. Otherwise, your story will wander and so will your reader. You select according to how you want your reader to feel in response to your detail. If you want him to feel gloomy, select and describe "gloomy" details. Don't ever tell your reader to be gloomy. That's cheating. That's like the halfback who scores a touchdown because all eleven oppos-

Figure 3-2

Storyline I
by Robert Rauschenberg

Courtesy of the Leo Castelli Gallery.

ing players tripped and fell. You pick details that will get the right senses operating—sounds, sights, smells, tastes.

Then, you organize the detail you select to make a good story—one that leads logically to a climax but never gives itself away before then. Sometimes we can support an opinion or thesis in an expository or argumentative essay by telling a little story to give an example of why and how your opinion developed.

Writing Exercise

Here is the beginning of a little story.

Mike came into the Prof's office with his eyes flashing, a nervous twitching around his mouth. Professor Digby had his back turned to him as he read student papers. He slowly shifted his weight, made a few final marks on the paper which he was grading, and swung his chair toward Mike. His face seemed pale; his eyes a bit blurry and red. Mike took a sheaf of papers from his bag, shook them in his hand from side to side, and said "Ah . . . I wanted . . . to ask you about the marks I got on these quizzes . . ." "Oh, yeah," Digby said, lowering his glasses and leaning forward toward Mike. The clock on his desk ticked solemnly.

1. Write a second and third paragraph briefly completing the narrative which begins above. Then, look back over the opening paragraph and ask yourself which stimuli suggest the content of the concluding paragraphs. What does Mike *notice* that gives you an indication of his state of mind, his feelings about and relationship to Professor Digby?

2. Suppose Professor Digby's office contained the following items: a very colorful psychedelic poster, a large photo of a very pretty young woman, a large wall plaque which read, "If you're not part of the solution, you're part of the problem." Suppose Professor Digby was wearing a wide, bright tie and mod shirt and smiled as he moved around in his chair to speak to Mike. Why do you imagine Mike might have ignored these stimuli? Write a paragraph or two in which you explain why Mike, who was worried about his grades, noticed Digby's blurry eyes, his exhaustion, while he seemed to ignore other stimuli—the poster, Digby's clothes, and so on.

Journal Exercise

The journal can give you everyday practice in examining how you perceive the world around you. Use your journal, at least occasionally, as a writer's sketchbook. When you expect to go through a particularly noteworthy experience—an important party, a rehearsal with your music instructor, a trip to the dentist, a difficult exam, or a job interview—jot down ahead of time what you expect from the experience. Then go back and compare what actually did happen to your recorded expectations.

Occasionally, you'll want to practice finding words for your inner feelings, trying to relate what you feel at a specific moment to some physical or emotional stimuli. At these times, try writing an occasional poem in which you use basic, concrete words to describe that feeling or sensation.

Once or twice a week, try to record changes in the way that you perceive a familiar object, perhaps a tree you pass every day as you enter a classroom building. Sometimes you'll have a flash perception or notice a quick connection between two objects as you write down what you see. Writing can make us more observant and less like everyday sleepwalkers. Observant people always have more to write about. Here are several examples of brief, one- or two-sentence journal entries that capture quick, elusive perceptions.

> Today my small child grabbed his red fire truck from a friend. Kids naturally feel a territorial imperative; they want to protect their property, which is an extension of their territory.

> Paul bothers me in class every day. He wants to answer everything. I think he's insecure.

> My wife gave me a glass of beer during a violent argument today. I guess that's what love is all about.

> I saw a girl reading *Love Story* and eating a salami sandwich at lunch. Every time she took a bite she got more mustard on her lip. I wish Ali McGraw would get mustard on her lip. Just once. Maybe even ketchup.

> I never shave, even with my electric razor, without washing my face first. It feels better that way. But when I'm finished, I wash my face again. The face-soap people love me.

These brief observations might be turned to good use later. They can be expanded and made into personal essays, especially if you find several related instances and combine them. But, more importantly, the habit of composing a few of your everyday perceptions will help you to observe more, to discover the raw materials of essays in your everyday life. (For further information on keeping a journal, see Appendix II, page 417.)

Activity Exercise

1. Find a small object (an apple, a raisin, a comb, a matchstick, a baseball) and describe it as closely as you can. Begin with general, perceptual statements and add specific detail as you proceed. Find nouns and verbs that will capture what you see and feel; then try to add modifiers (adjectives, adverbs, or modifying phrases and clauses) that will capture detail accurately and clearly.

2. Find a spot where you can observe your immediate environment relatively uninterrupted. Open all your senses for about fifteen minutes. Listen for sounds, look at objects closely and register details, touch things around you, taste and smell if you can. Record stimuli in brief sentences, adding detail upon detail as you go along. When you're finished, write a conceptual sentence that is based on your recorded stimuli.

3. Spend fifteen or twenty minutes observing a particular object carefully. Occasionally, your mind will wander; try to capture the stimulus which triggered your mind-wandering. Can you relate the content of your mind-wandering in any direct way to the object you were observing? Write a paragraph in which you explain how your conscious streams of thought are related to your subconscious streams of thought.

4. Find some common objects that are usually repugnant to you—a picture of an ant or spider, a snake, any object that you normally avoid. Describe it as closely as possible. Do your feelings about the object change as you write?

5. Go to a crowded place where you can observe someone without being noticed. Find the person around you whom you find most unattractive. Write one paragraph explaining why and another paragraph pointing to physical details and features that create your dislike. Now, turn the tables. Imagine you find the person attractive. Describe why, even if you have to imagine a bit; then describe the person's attractive physical characteristics. How do you feel about the person now that you have considered both points of view?

6. Have a friend or classmate choose a common object. You should be blindfolded. Then your friend can hand you the object, and he or she can record your description of that object as closely as possible. Use a tape recorder, if one is available, to record the description.

7. Take a photograph of a simple object or scene, perhaps from a newspaper or a magazine, and write a detailed description of it. Sometimes a simple drawing or geometric shape will work as well. Once you have finished your description, pass it on to another class member. He or she can either try to draw the shape or to describe the object or scene verbally.

Writing Exercise

To use personal experience to write exposition, you've got to select according to a clearly-defined purpose. Go back to any one of the seven activity exercises above and rewrite it in expository form. Since exposition intends to inform readers, to show them how or why something is done, or to explain or illustrate an idea or opinion, you'll want to develop a purpose before you begin. Then proceed to revise your original observation to suit that purpose. For example, if you have already written up your observation of an unattractive person in a crowded place, you might decide to make it into an essay on a certain *type* of person. Your expository purpose would be to characterize the type generally and to use your specific subject to illustrate that type. Or you might wish to rework your written description of a photograph into an expository essay on how two different observers can look at the same photograph and see different things. In other words, you'd be writing an essay on perception and using the two descriptions as support for your thesis. Be sure to relate your thesis and evidence carefully and define your key terms.

Getting your experience into sentences

Looking around you to find material is the first step toward effective writing. Now you can begin to work on getting that material into words. We can begin by making effective sentences.

You don't need to know very many rules to write effective sentences. And most of us know a good deal of grammar already, although we might have a difficult time diagraming and parsing sentences. We all use language every day—to register for courses, to ask the cashier the price of an item in a supermarket line, to share a good story or joke, and, of course, to share ideas and knowledge in our classes. But to transform our experience into written language is a bit more difficult. To do it well we need at least to become more conscious of how we control the parts of our sentences: how we choose words that fit the raw materials of our experience, how we control the parts of sentences (subjects, predicates, clauses, and phrases) to be sure our readers receive our experience in a form that corresponds to the way *we* receive it before we write.

If you don't remember what a few of these grammatical terms mean, ask your instructor or check a basic handbook. Generally, just remember that a *clause* always has a complete subject and verb. An *independent clause* can stand alone as a sentence; it doesn't contain a word like "because" or "which" to make it dependent on something else in the sentence. A *dependent clause* can't stand by itself *because,* as in this clause, it does have a word, usually a conjunction, that joins it to another sentence part.

Because it was raining (dependent clause), I wore my raincoat (independent clause). A *phrase* doesn't have a complete subject or predicate; it can never stand alone as a sentence. There are many forms of phrases —prepositional, participial, absolute—but we'll deal more specifically with the variety of phrases in later sections. At this point, be sure you can identify as phrases groups of words such as:

He went *to the store* to buy a piece *of candy, his money jangling in his pocket.* (two prepositional phrases and one absolute phrase)

Most likely, you'll recognize phrases without much trouble. Effective writing depends upon your developing control over such sentence elements, so that you can put details from your experience exactly where you want them in your sentences. Your readers will then receive your experience in the form you want.

Choosing words

Don't rely on the first word that comes to mind. Suppose you want to describe a man as he rides a horse across a field. What subject/noun do you want? Is "man" too general? Would "rider" be more accurate? Or perhaps you'd prefer "horseman"? How might you modify the subject/noun? Would "elegant" fit the outfit he wears? Or would you prefer a description such as "wearing tight breeches and carrying a riding stick"? Do you want a simple verb like "ride" or a more specific and action-filled verb like "gallop"? Do you want to modify the verb, perhaps using an adverb—"jerkily galloping"? You answer these questions by deciding just what effect you want your description to have on the reader. Do you want to make your reader feel as if he is riding that horse? Then choose specific nouns, verbs, and modifiers so that he'll feel the same feelings and physical sensations that the rider feels. If you don't want to emphasize the drama of the ride, use less specific, more conventional words that will keep your reader at a distance from the rider.

As you begin to transcribe experience into words, go through your sentences and ask questions like the ones above about your subjects, verbs, and modifiers. If careful, effective description is your main purpose, try to use concrete words that appeal directly to your reader's senses. Use words your reader can see, touch, taste, feel, or smell.

Controlling your basic sentence patterns

To become an effective writer, you'll need to combine the right word with the right sentence structure. Good sentences usually contain concrete words when sensory appeal is stressed and abstract words when a summary is necessary. Putting the right words in the right places is also important. You don't want to put a minor idea in a main clause, or a major physical detail in a dependent or subordinate clause. You want to be sure that your reader sees what you see *the way you see it*. If you describe an auto accident and spend more time telling how you got to the scene of the accident than actually describing the accident, you annoy your readers.

On the following pages, you'll find a painting and brief definitions of five basic sentence patterns. Every English sentence contains some variation of these five patterns. The possible variations are numerous, and that's where the creativity and skill of the writer are most important. Three basic sentence elements are found in the five patterns: a *subject/noun* (a simple or compound subject); *a predicate* (a single or compound verb and optional related modifiers); and an *object/noun* or *complement* (an object/noun is in some way related to the subject by the predicate; a complement is a noun or adjective that can replace the subject/noun). All sentences require subject/nouns and predicates to be grammatically sound, but not all sentences require object/nouns or complements.

As you read through the basic patterns that follow, try forming your own model sentences. Use *Storyline I* by Robert Rauschenberg as the experience in your model sentences. Look over the painting carefully and notice familiar objects in it, trying to describe them as concretely as possible in your model sentences.

Pattern I:	Subject—Intransitive Verb
Sample:	S The *boy,* who is leaning his head slightly for- In V ward, *stares* into the space before him.
Explanation:	"The boy stares" is complete in itself. A sentence containing an intransitive verb needs no object/noun or complement to complete its meaning, no adjective or noun-equivalent to identify the subject further. The other parts of the sample sentence are *modifiers* that are related either to the subject or the predicate. As you read through these examples, remember that an intransitive verb completes an action, and requires no noun or clause to complete the meaning; a transitive verb *does* require an object/noun to complete the action of the subject and verb.
Pattern 2:	Subject—Linking Verb—Subject Complement
Sample:	S LV SC SC The man's *tie is black* and *straight.*
Explanation:	A linking verb (ususally a form of *be* or a word like *taste, sound, smell, seem, appear*) demands a complement; it must connect the subject to something else in the sentence. The complement following a linking verb answers what the subject does or is. (Note that forms of *be* are not always linking verbs. *Is* sometimes means *exists,* as in the sentence *At the front is the group known as the Green Berets.*) Remember, almost any part of speech can be used as a linking verb complement—verb forms, nouns, adjectives,

and so forth. Example: *The man's face is darkly shadowed.*

Pattern 3:	Subject—Transitive Verb—Direct Object
Sample:	S TrV DO The slim, dark *cheeks indicate that this is a* determined, quiet *man.*
Explanation:	Unlike pattern two in which subject and complement have the same referent, in this pattern the direct object is *different from* the subject noun. As shown in the sample sentence, a *noun clause* can be used as a direct object, including a subject and verb of its own (. . . that *this is* a determined, quiet man).
Pattern 4:	Subject—Transitive Verb—Indirect Object—Direct Object
Sample:	S Tr V IO DO This *portrait gives me* the *feeling* that this person is sensitive and intelligent.
Explanation:	Sometimes it takes two nouns or noun clusters to complete the meaning of a verb. An indirect object has a secondary referent—the person receiving the action of the verb *give* in the sample sentence. A direct object has a primary referent—the *action* given by the portrait in the above sentence. An easy way to distinguish indirect objects from direct objects is to place "to" before the first noun in normal word order. If the sentence still makes sense, that word is an indirect object. Remember, even when a sentence contains an indirect object, a direct object can include more than one word, say, a noun cluster or a clause.
Pattern 5:	Subject—Transitive Verb—Direct Object—Object Complement
Sample:	S TrV This *man*, at least from my point of view, *makes* DO OC a *person uneasy.*
Explanation:	In pattern five, the noun or noun cluster that is used as an object complement identifies or classifies the noun referred to by the direct object. The direct object *person* is somehow qualified by the following complement *uneasy;* both words have a single referent—the "uneasy per-

son" produced by the man's portrait. Again, remember that more than one word can function
as either the direct object or the object complement.

Activity Exercise

Just for practice write a descriptive paragraph based on *Storyline I* in
which you use the five basic sentence patterns. Begin with a general
description of the painting. Then, in the remaining four sentences, describe
supporting qualities or details in the painting. Keep the sentences short
and don't vary the patterns. Now, go back over the paragraph and rewrite
the sentences to emphasize your attitude toward the painting. Change the
basic patterns in your sentences if you feel the changes will help you say
what you want about the painting. The initial exercise of imitating the five
sentence patterns should make your finished product more varied, even if
you change structure radically from rough draft to final copy.

Now revise your paragraph adding a few, specific details to your basic
sentences. Perhaps you'll add a concrete adjective or adverb, a prepositional phrase that locates or clarifies a more general detail in your basic
sentence, or an entire clause that adds to what the reader knows about some
aspect of the painting.

Thinking Exercise

With these preliminary exercises as background, ask yourself these
questions about *Storyline I:*

1. If you've seen the film *Bonnie and Clyde,* what do you recall as you
look at the collage? Be specific.

2. Why do you think Rauschenberg chose to include these specific
objects? Are they related in any way that you can immediately explain?

3. The objects fall into three general categories—hero, heroine, and
automobile. Why?

Writing Exercise

1. A collage is an art work that combines in one picture a group of
distinct visual images, usually on one general theme. It's a group of related

pictures put together inside one frame. In *Storyline I*, Rauschenberg uses a Bonnie-and-Clyde theme; he puts together a group of photos from the film to make a statement on American society. Write an essay in which you tell what this collage says about our culture. Try to relate your interpretation to specific scenes and shots in the collage.

2. Pick one object or person in the collage and describe it objectively in two or three paragraphs. Show the reader as much as you can. Appeal to his senses. Choose the right descriptive words and emphasize those aspects of the object which you think are most important. Then, write two or three additional paragraphs in which you describe how this object fits into the general purpose of the collage. Think about the theme of the collage *before* you write.

Getting feelings into words

Suppose you were covering an important baseball game for a local newspaper. The game is won by a dramatic ninth-inning home run.

Your purposes would be, first, to inform your reader, to tell him what actually happened. For that you need to get the facts straight. A left-hander was pitching, the batter *wasn't* a noted power hitter, he hit from the right side, the count was 2 and 2, there were two out, the crowd was tense, both managers were pacing in the dugout. These are all physical, concrete facts that will help you set the stage for that home run. You won't need *all* the facts; instead, you will want to select and emphasize only those facts that will create drama and let your reader know what he needs to follow the action. You might include the fact that two pitchers were warming up in the opposing bullpen because that adds to the tension. You might ignore the fact that the batter had a low batting average, especially if you have mentioned that he had struck out the three previous times he had batted. That last detail will help the reader to sympathize with the batter and get under his skin as he hits the homer.

Second, you'd want to share the concrete detail of the action itself. Perhaps a nervous gesture by the pitcher immediately before he delivers the fatal pitch. Or a piercing catcall from the crowd—"Hit it you bum!" Or the way the sun glanced off the bat as it came off the hitter's shoulders. Again, you won't need *all* the stimuli. You'll want just those that create drama and bring the reader into the batter's shoes. You'll probably select details that will carry the reader all the way through the action, from the gesture by the pitcher to the tip of the batter's hat as he enters the dugout.

What's important is that you **suggest** to your readers how you feel. Don't tell them outright, at least not all the way through. If you do, you have summary and too much outright sentiment; and both can be boring and corny. Instead, write directly *from* the experience.

Compare these examples of action description. The first *tells*; the second *shows*. The first summarizes and tells the reader what to think. The second shares sensory detail and suggests.

I knew as soon as I set foot in the car that something terrible was going to happen. As we came to the fatal turn, the car swerved to the right and I thought "Oh God, this is it." Then the next thing I remember is coming to in the hospital bed.

The car door thudded closed with a dull, grating sound. I squeezed in next to my buddies, our thighs compressed like soft cushions against one another. As we drove and talked loudly, I remember noticing a small stain, light brown with a star-pattern, on top of the seat in front of me. Our feet were tangled about on the floor. As I watched the spot fade in and out of my vision, the car began to pull to the right. Someone screamed. But I was calm all the way, even through the skidding sound of rubber on cement and through the crazy feeling we experienced as the car leaned over and then dropped, like a lid, on its top.

The second description appeals to the reader's senses—to touch, hearing, and sight. It also *surprises*. The details are carefully recorded and selected; the writer was calm even during the accident. He is like the eye in the midst of a hurricane. We know by the action he describes that he must be excited, but his rationality through the excitement is a surprising, refreshing opposition. It gives us something to think about as we read on.

Feelings and sensations are often very difficult to get into words effectively. Remember these suggestions as you write.

1. Try to *show* the reader how you feel by selecting important details and arranging them dramatically. Don't use too much or too little descirption.

2. Limit your telling statements. If you finish a descriptive paragraph and still feel that you should tell your reader how you feel, you've probably failed to describe suggestively. Go back and see if you can control your stimuli, describing the action in a way that will suggest your emotions.

Summary principles

You can improve your writing by learning to explore systematically the world around you. Such explorations provide you with material, with plans for organizing what you write, and with examples to help you support what you think. Read over the following list and try to apply the principles as you consider the paintings on the next few pages.

1. For writing purposes, we can say we receive and organize experience in four related stages: stimuli, sensation, perception, conception.

2. We write more effectively when we share at least parts of all four stages with our readers.

3. As we observe we also discover what we think. We can improve our writing by selecting and arranging our experience to fit what we think. No writer says or includes everything.

4. We can shape sentences to fit both what we think and what we experience. Experimenting with different sentence patterns can help us find the right words for the right places.

5. Good writing usually includes more showing than telling, more actual experience than abstract thought. Your conceptions can be outlined quickly; showing where they come from in detail takes more time and space.

Activity Exercise

1. Robert Motherwell is usually considered an "abstract expressionist." An abstract artist breaks his subject down into parts and reorganizes those parts in a way that he feels expresses the true meaning or "feeling" of that subject. He leaves out some things, emphasizes or exaggerates others,

Figure 3-3   Black on White *by Robert Motherwell*

Courtesy The Museum of Fine Arts, Houston, Texas.

and ends up with a work that he believes expresses how he felt when he originally perceived the subject. In *Black on White,* Motherwell takes two simple colors and creates a design on canvas. Write down your immediate feelings as you look at the painting. Can you find words that tell how you feel when you look at it? Make a list of words that at least come close to explaining how you feel.

2. Now go through the painting and try to find visual details that support your feelings. What about the various designs? What do the blotches, dots, and smears add to the painting? Are there shapes that bring other shapes to your mind? Write an objective description in rough form, selecting only those details you think are important and describing them specifically.

3. Now put your objective observations together with your descriptions of how you feel when you look at the painting. Do they make sense together? Work up a plan for an expository essay. First, go over your descriptions of feeling and develop a thesis for your essay. Then go back over your objective description and select details that you think will help your reader understand *why* you feel that way. Use your details to illustrate your thesis.

4. Imagine that you are giving an address to a local women's club on this painting. All you want to do is show how the painting works, what it tries to say, and how it says it. Write down a casual presentation, either in outline form or as a brief speech, and try it out on your classmates. How effective do they think the address will be? Why?

5. Show this painting briefly to at least one person. Ask for a quick response. Watch the person as he or she responds. Is he hesitant? Immediately repulsed or attracted? Then, explain to the class why you think your subject responded as he or she did. What did he like about the painting? What did he dislike? What in the respondent influenced his perception of the painting? Was there some personal reason for the response? Might the context in which you showed your subject the painting have influenced the reaction?

Activity Exercise

Color figure 3-4
WINTER (RETURN OF THE HUNTERS)
Pieter Brueghel
follows page 94.

1. Take a close look at Brueghel's *Winter (Return of the Hunters)* and imagine yourself walking home after the hunt. You are one of the men who walk in front of the dogs, looking over the crowded valley before you. Write a description of your feelings using the third person pronoun *he.*

2. What senses are most active? Do you *feel* the cold? What do you hear—the birds above you? The skaters in the distance? What seems most inviting? Is there anything in the painting you can smell?

3. Organize your observations of this painting into an explanation of the general life-style of the main figures. First, describe their personalities

as you would imagine them to be. What do they most enjoy? What do they do for a living? Would *you* enjoy living in this place? Why or why not? Organize your essay around some central plan that is related to your description of the life-styles of the figures. Can you, for example, classify the lives of these characters under some general headings—perhaps *work, play, eating, sleeping, romance?* What would their habits and customs be in each case? How can you tell from the painting? Work out a general thesis—for example: "these people live rugged, struggling lives"—*before* you begin.

4

Controlling your discoveries

Chapter 3 should have helped you find stimuli and sensations that can become the backbone of what you write. By analyzing what you experience, you come to know, understand, and use your experience more efficiently. In this way, you can be more specific and do more actual sharing in your writing.

This chapter should help you take those specific details and feelings and transfer them to completed pieces of writing. In essence, the chapter should give you models and theories for reshaping the basic elements of experience into complete essays. You'll find a series of language items: a few short poems, two brief descriptive pieces, some visual materials, a longer, dramatic poem, and a complete essay. As you absorb these materials, try first to consider physical stimuli and sensations. What does the writer make you feel and sense? What does *he* feel or sense as he writes? How does he get that feeling across? Second, analyze how the writer puts together his immediate experience and feeling; in other words, ask yourself what his formed *perceptions* are as he writes. Finally, move to conceptions and consider the general purpose, theme, or thesis of what you read or see. How does the writer put together his perceptions to form an entire composition, a complete message?

Remember, basic stimuli and sensations are the skeleton of what you write. Perceptions and conceptions are the flesh on the bones. One should never be seen without the other, for then you have only half a composition.

Using everyday experience

The two personal essays which follow might be taken as examples of polished and revised journal writing. The writers—Henry David Thoreau and Mark Twain—are experienced observers and recorders who find an effective general form for their experience. They appeal to your senses, carefully and purposely. They do, however, have in mind a larger purpose than the sharing of those observations. If they are successful, you should come to share their general attitudes toward their subjects even without being told directly what those attitudes are.

Thoreau is often considered "a literary naturalist": someone who records and observes the life around him objectively, step by step, almost as a scientist. But, of course, he goes far beyond mere recording and observing. As you read ask yourself what Thoreau's attitude is toward nature and man, toward everything he senses and feels. Try to cite specific examples to support your answers. Thoreau takes a "winter walk" and shares the experience. And, as he shares, you come to think like him.

from *A Winter Walk*
HENRY DAVID THOREAU

The wind has gently murmured through the blinds, or puffed with feathery softness against the windows, and occasionally sighed like a summer zephyr lifting the leaves along, the live-long night. The meadow mouse has slept in his snug gallery in the sod, the owl has sat in a hollow tree in the depth of the swamp, the rabbit, the squirrel, and the fox have all been housed. The watch dog has lain quiet on the hearth, and the cattle have stood silent in their stalls. The earth itself has slept, as it were its first, not its last sleep, save when some streetsign or wood house door has faintly creaked upon its hinge, cheering forlorn nature at her midnight work,—the only sound awake twixt Venus and Mars,—advertising us of a remote inward warmth, a divine cheer and fellowship, where gods are met together, but where it is very bleak for men to stand. But while the earth has slumbered, all the air has been alive with feathery flakes descending, as if some northern Ceres reigned, showering her silvery grain over all the fields.

We sleep, and at length awake to the still reality of a winter morning. The snow lies warm as cotton or down upon the window sill; the broadened sash and frosted panes admit a dim and private light,

Reprinted from *Excursions* by Henry David Thoreau, Introduction by Leo Marx (New York, 1962), pp. 109-131.

which enhances the snug cheer within. The stillness of the morning is impressive. The floor creaks under our feet as we move toward the window to look abroad through some clear space over the fields. We see the roofs stand under their snow burden. From the eaves and fences hang stalactites of snow, and in the yard stand stalagmites covering some concealed core. The trees and shrubs rear white arms to the sky on every side; and where were walls and fences, we see fantastic forms stretching in frolic gambols across the dusky landscape, as if nature had strewn her fresh designs over the fields by night as models for man's art.

Silently we unlatch the door, letting the drift fall in, and step abroad to face the cutting air. Already the stars have lost some of their sparkle, and a dull, leaden mist skirts the horizon. A lurid brazen light in the east proclaims the approach of day, while the western landscape is dim and spectral still, and clothed in a sombre Tartarian light, like the shadowy realms. They are Infernal sounds only that you hear,—the crowing of cocks, the barking of dogs, the chopping of wood, the lowing of kine, all seem to come from Pluto's barnyard and beyond the Styx;—not for any melancholy they suggest, but their twilight bustle is too solemn and mysterious for earth. The recent tracks of the fox or otter, in the yard, remind us that each hour of the night is crowded with events, and the primeval nature is still working and making tracks in the snow. Opening the gate, we tread briskly along the lone country road, crunching the dry and crisped snow under our feet, or aroused by the sharp clear creak of the wood sled, just starting for the distant market, from the early farmer's door, where it has lain the summer long, dreaming amid the chips and stubble; while far through the drifts and powdered windows we see the farmer's early candle, like a paled star, emitting a lonely beam, as if some severe virtue were at its matins there. And one by one the smokes begin to ascend from the chimneys amidst the trees and snows.

And now we descend again to the brink of this woodland lake, which lies in a hollow of the hills, as if it were their expressed juice, and that of the leaves, which are annually steeped in it. Without outlet or inlet to the eye, it has still its history, in the lapse of its waves, in the rounded pebbles on its shore, and in the pines which grow down to its brink. It has not been idle, though sedentary, but, like Abu Musa, teaches that "sitting still at home is the heavenly way; the going out is the way of the world." Yet in its evaporation it travels as far as any. In summer it is the earth's liquid eye; a mirror in the breast of nature. The sins of the wood are washed out in it. See how the woods form an amphitheatre about it, and it is an arena for all the genialness of nature. All trees direct the traveler to its brink, all paths seek it out, birds fly to it, quadrupeds flee to it, and the very ground inclines toward it. It is nature's saloon, where she has sat down to her toilet. Consider her silent economy and tidiness; how the sun comes with his evaporation to sweep the dust from its surface each morning, and a fresh surface is constantly welling up;

and annually, after whatever impurities have accumulated herein, its liquid transparency appears again in the spring. In summer a hushed music seems to sweep across its surface. But now a plain sheet of snow conceals it from our eyes, except where the wind has swept the ice bare, and the sere leaves are gliding from side to side, tacking and veering on their tiny voyages. Here is one just keeled up against a pebble on shore, a dry beech leaf, rocking still, as if it would start again. A skilful engineer, methinks, might project its course since it fell from the parent stem. Here are all the elements for such a calculation. Its present position, the direction of the wind, the level of the pond, and how much more is given. In its scarred edges and veins is its log rolled up.

We fancy ourselves in the interior of a larger house. The surface of the pond is our deal table or sanded floor, and the woods rise abruptly from its edge, like the walls of a cottage. The lines set to catch pickerel through the ice look like a larger culinary preparation, and the men stand about on the white ground like pieces of forest furniture. The actions of these men, at the distance of half a mile over the ice and snow, impress us as when we read the exploits of Alexander in history. They seem not unworthy of the scenery, and as momentous as the conquest of kingdoms.

Again we have wandered through the arches of the wood, until from its skirts we hear the distant booming of ice from yonder bay of the river, as if it were moved by some other and subtler tide than oceans know. To me it has a strange sound of home, thrilling as the voice of one's distant and noble kindred. A mild summer sun shines over forest and lake, and though there is but one green leaf for many rods, yet nature enjoys a serene health. Every sound is fraught with the same mysterious assurance of health, as well now the creaking of the boughs in January, as the soft sough of the wind in July.

The sun at length rises through the distant woods, as if with the faint clashing swinging sound of cymbals, melting the air with his beams, and with such rapid steps the morning travels, that already his rays are gilding the distant western mountains. Meanwhile we step hastily along through the powdery snow, warmed by an inward heat, enjoying an Indian summer still, in the increased glow of thought and feeling. Probably if our lives were more conformed to nature, we should not need to defend ourselves against her heats and colds, but find her our constant nurse and friend, as do plants and quadrupeds. If our bodies were fed with pure and simple elements, and not with a stimulating and heating diet, they would afford no more pasture for cold than a leafless twig, but thrive like the trees, which find even winter genial to their expansion.

The wonderful purity of nature at this season is a most pleasing fact. Every decayed stump and moss-grown stone and rail, and the dead leaves of autumn, are concealed by a clean napkin of snow. In the bare fields and tinkling woods, see what virtue survives. In the coldest and bleakest places, the warmest charities still maintain a foothold. A cold and searching wind drives away all contagion, and nothing can withstand it but what has a virtue in it; and accordingly, whatever we meet with in cold and bleak places, as the tops of mountains, we respect for a sort of sturdy innocence, a Puritan toughness. All things beside seem to be called in for shelter, and what stays out must be part of the original frame of the universe, and of such valor as God himself. It is invigorating to breathe the cleansed air. Its greater fineness and purity are visible to the eye, and we would fain stay out long and late, that the gales may sigh through us, too, as through the leafless trees, and fit us for the winter:—as if we hoped so to borrow some pure and steadfast virtue, which will stead us in all seasons.

There is a slumbering subterranean fire in nature which never goes out, and which no cold can chill. It finally melts the great snow, and in January or July is only buried under a thicker or thinner covering. In the coldest day it flows somewhere, and the snow melts around every tree. This field of winter rye, which sprouted late in the fall, and now speedily dissolves the snow, is where the fire is very thinly covered. We feel warmed by it. In the winter, warmth stands for all virtue, and we resort in thought to a trickling rill, with its bare stones shining in the sun, and to warm springs in the woods, with as much eagerness as rabbits and robins. The steam which rises from swamps and pools, is as dear and domestic as that of our own kettle. What fire could ever equal the sunshine of a winter's day, when the meadow mice come out by the wallsides, and the chicadee lisps in the defiles of the wood? The warmth comes directly from the sun, and is not radiated from the earth, as in summer; and when we feel his beams on our backs as we are treading some snowy dell, we are grateful as for a special kindness, and bless the sun which has followed us into that byplace.

This subterranean fire has its altar in each man's breast, for in the coldest day, and on the bleakest hill, the traveler cherishes a warmer fire within the folds of his cloak than is kindled on any hearth. A healthy man, indeed, is the complement of the seasons, and in winter, summer is in his heart. There is the south. Thither have all birds and insects migrated, and around the warm springs in his breast are gathered the robin and the lark.

Occasionally we wade through fields of snow, under whose depths the river is lost for many rods, to appear again to the right or left, where we least expected; still holding on its way underneath, with a faint, stertorous, rumbling sound, as if, like the bear and marmot, it too had hibernated, and we had followed its faint summer trail to where it earthed itself in snow and ice. At first we should have thought that rivers would be empty and dry in midwinter, or else frozen solid till the spring thawed them; but their volume is not diminished even, for only a superficial cold bridges their surface. The thousand springs which feed the lakes and streams are flowing still. The issues of a few surface springs only are closed, and they go to swell the deep reservoirs. Nature's wells are below the frost. The summer brooks are not filled with snow water, nor does the mower quench his thirst with that alone. The streams are swollen when the snow melts in the spring, because nature's work has been delayed, the water being turned into ice and snow, whose particles are less smooth and round, and do not find their level so soon.

Far over the ice, between the hemlock woods and snow-clad hills, stands the pickerel fisher, his lines set in some retired cove, like a Finlander, with his arms thrust into the pouches of his dreadnought; with dull, snowy, fishy thoughts, himself a finless fish, separated a few inches from his race; dumb, erect, and made to be enveloped in clouds and snows, like the pines on shore. In these wild scenes, men stand about in the scenery, or move deliberately and heavily, having sacrificed the sprightliness and vivacity of towns to the dumb sobriety of nature. He does not make the scenery less wild, more than the jays and muskrats, but stands there as a part of it, as the natives are represented in the voyages of early navigators, at Nootka Sound, and on the Northwest coast, with their furs about them, before they were tempted to loquacity by a scrap of iron. He belongs to the natural family of man, and is planted deeper in nature and has more root than the inhabitants of towns. Go to him, ask what luck, and you will learn that he too is a worshiper of the unseen. Hear with what sincere deference and waving gesture in his tone, he speaks of the lake pickerel, which he has never seen, his primitive and ideal race of pickerel. He is connected with the shore still, as by a fish line, and yet remembers the season when he took fish through the ice on the pond, while the peas were up in his garden at home.

Activity Exercise

1. Consider Thoreau's choice of words. Do the words he uses to describe stimuli help to convey his *feelings* about what he describes? Consider sentences like these: "But while the earth has slumbered, all the air has been alive with feathery flakes descending, as if some northern Ceres reigned, showering her silvery grain over all the fields."

2. Thoreau uses metaphors to tell us how he feels. He takes an objectively-observed experience and compares it to something else. The comparison tells us how Thoreau feels about what he is describing. Do Thoreau's metaphors help you to figure out how he feels about winter? Find a few winter metaphors and show how they express Thoreau's

attitude. Consider "the sere leaves are gliding from side to side, tacking and veering on their tiny voyages" and the sentence in which Thoreau says that the pond "is nature's saloon, where she has sat down to her toilet."

3. Do you find Thoreau's descriptions corny or sentimental? If so, why? If not, why not? Does he include enough details to make his assertions of feeling convincing? Consider "This subterranean fire has its altar in each man's breast, for in the coldest day, and on the bleakest hill, the traveler cherishes a warmer fire within the folds of his cloak than is kindled on any hearth." What is Thoreau saying about winter in this sentence? Have you ever felt this way? How would you describe the same thought and feeling?

4. When you describe, you'll want to select certain physical details and emphasize them. You might even repeat them to get the reader to see things your way. Can you pick out any important repetitions in this essay? Do you notice any physical object that is mentioned several times? Does Thoreau use a particular metaphor several times? If you find a few repeated patterns, what do you think they mean? What does Thoreau say through them? Consider the pickerel-fishers who are described twice in depth.

5. Try mapping out or charting the stimuli in just one of Thoreau's paragraphs. List the details and then relate them to some sensation you feel as you read the paragraph. Then, go back over your list and try to decide whether Thoreau is trying to control what you feel and think by the way he arranges and uses stimuli.

6. Write an essay in which you explain the purpose of Thoreau's journal. Your thesis might explain what value a journal like Thoreau's would have to others. Be sure to cite specific sections of the journal to explain your main points.

7. You might want to look over Brueghel's *Winter* once again. His subject is somewhat similar to Thoreau's. And he certainly observes with equal care. Perhaps Thoreau's journal and Brueghel's painting have a similar purpose and function, however different their locales and historical periods. Write a comparison of the two.

In the following excerpt from *Life on the Mississippi*, Mark Twain shares the experience of guiding a clumsy steamboat down the Mississippi through a dense fog. First, he wants you to experience the ride through your senses. Then, he wants you to develop a general attitude toward steamboats, the Mississippi, and being a riverboat captain. He develops a talky, witty, down-home voice to go along with what he describes. He uses fancy and common words together—"All through your watch you are tortured with the *exquisite* misery of uncertainty." We usually don't see "exquisite" used to modify "misery." We share a little joke with Twain's narrator, and that makes us feel a bit closer to him. Sometimes, he addresses you as a friend, not as an "average" reader: "I thought I had finished this chapter, but I wish to add a curious thing while it is in my mind." The narrator's way of talking, along with his very specific sharing of stimuli and sensation, helps us to see things his way. We share his voice—his particular way of talking—and his experience: we learn about his attitude toward riverboats, as well as his experience with them.

from *Life on the Mississippi*

MARK TWAIN

An embankment ten or fifteen feet high guards both banks of the Mississippi all the way down that lower end of the river, and this embankment is set back from the edge of the shore from ten to perhaps a hundred feet, according to circumstances; say thirty or forty feet, as a general thing. Fill that whole region with an impenetrable gloom of smoke from a hundred miles of burning bagasse piles, when the river is over the banks, and turn a steamboat loose along there at midnight and see how she will feel. And see how you will feel, too! You find yourself away out in the midst of a vague, dim sea that is shoreless, that fades out and loses itself in the murky distances; for you cannot discern the thin rib of embankment, and you are always imagining you see a straggling tree when you don't. The plantations themselves are transformed by the smoke, and look like a part of the sea. All through your watch you are tortured with the exquisite misery of uncertainty. You hope you are keeping in the river, but you do not know. All that you are sure about is that you are likely to be within six feet of the bank *and* destruction, when you think you are a good half-mile from shore. And you are sure, also, that if you chance suddenly to fetch up against the embankment and topple your chimneys overboard, you will have the small comfort of knowing that it is about what you were expecting to do. One of the great Vicksburg packets darted out into a sugar plantation one night, at such a time, and had to stay there a week. But there was no novelty about it; it had often been done before.

I thought I had finished this chapter, but I wish to add a curious thing, while it is in my mind. It is only relevant in that it is connected with piloting. There used to be an excellent pilot on the river, a Mr. X, who was a somnambulist. It was said that if his mind was troubled about a bad piece of river, he was pretty sure to get up and walk in his sleep and do strange things. He was once fellow-pilot for a trip or two with

Reprinted from *Life on the Mississippi* by Mark Twain (New York: P. F. Collier and Son Company, 1874), pp. 93-97.

George Ealer, on a great New Orleans passenger-packet. During a considerable part of the first trip George was uneasy, but got over it by and by, as X seemed content to stay in his bed when asleep. Late one night the boat was approaching Helena, Ark.; the water was low, and the crossing above the town in a very blind and tangled condition. X had seen the crossing since Ealer had, and as the night was particularly drizzly, sullen, and dark, Ealer was considering whether he had not better have X called to assist in running the place, when the door opened and X walked in. Now, on very dark nights, light is a deadly enemy to piloting; you are aware that if you stand in a lighted room, on such a night, you cannot see things in the street to any purpose; but if you put out the lights and stand in the gloom you can make out objects in the street pretty well. So, on very dark nights, pilots do not smoke; they allow no fire in the pilot-house stove, if there is a crack which can allow the least ray to escape; they order the furnaces to be curtained with huge tarpaulins and the skylights to be closely blinded. Then no light whatever issues from the boat. The undefinable shape that now entered the pilot-house had Mr. X's voice. This said:

"Let me take her, George; I've seen this place since you have, and it is so crooked that I reckon I can run it myself easier than I could tell you how to do it."

"It is kind of you, and I swear I am willing. I haven't got another drop of perspiration left in me. I have been spinning around and around the wheel like a squirrel. It is so dark I can't tell which way she is swinging till she is coming around like a whirligig."

So Ealer took a seat on the bench, panting and breathless. The black phantom assumed the wheel without saying anything, steadied the waltzing steamer with a turn or two, and then stood at ease, coaxing her a little to this side and then to that, as gently and as sweetly as if the time had been noonday. When Ealer observed this marvel of steering, he wished he had not confessed! He stared, and wondered, and finally said:

"Well, I thought I knew how to steer a steamboat, but that was another mistake of mine."

X said nothing, but went serenely on with his work. He rang for the leads; he rang to slow down the steam; he worked the boat carefully and neatly into invisible marks, then stood at the center of the wheel and peered blandly out into the blackness, fore and aft, to verify his position; as the leads shoaled more and more, he stopped the engines entirely, and the dead silence and suspense of "drifting" followed; when the shoalest water was struck, he cracked on the steam, carried her handsomely over, and then began to work her warily into the next system of shoal-marks; the same patient, heedful use of leads and engines followed, the boat slipped through without touching bottom, and entered upon the third and last intricacy of the crossing; imperceptibly she moved through the gloom, crept by inches into her marks, drifted tediously till the shoalest water was cried, and then, under a tremendous head of steam, went swinging over the reef and away into deep water and safety!

Ealer let his long-pent breath pour in a great relieving sigh, and said:

"That's the sweetest piece of piloting that was ever done on the Mississippi River! I wouldn't believe it could be done, if I hadn't seen it."

There was no reply, and he added:

"Just hold her five minutes longer, partner, and let me run down and get a cup of coffee."

A minute later Ealer was biting into a pie, down in the "texas," and comforting himself with coffee. Just then the night watchman happened in, and was about to happen out again, when he noticed Ealer and exclaimed:

"Who is at the wheel, sir?"

"X."

"Dart for the pilot-house, quicker than lightning!"

The next moment both men were flying up the pilot-house companionway, three steps at a jump! Nobody there! The great steamer was whistling down the middle of the river at her own sweet will! The watchman shot out of the place again; Ealer seized the wheel, set an engine back with power, and held his breath while the boat reluctantly swung away from a "towhead," which she was about to knock into the middle of the Gulf of Mexico!

By and by the watchman came back and said:

"Didn't that lunatic tell you he was asleep, when he first came up here?"

"No."

"Well, he was. I found him walking along on top of the railings, just as unconcerned as another man would walk a pavement; and I put him to bed; now just this minute there he was again, away astern, going through that sort of tight-rope deviltry the same as before."

"Well, I think I'll stay by next time he has one of those fits. But I hope he'll have them often. You just ought to have seen him take this boat through Helena crossing. *I* never saw anything so gaudy before. And if he can do such gold-leaf, kid-glove, diamond-breastpin piloting when he is sound asleep, what *couldn't* he do if he was dead!"

Thinking Exercise

1. This excerpt transforms an observed experience into a story: the experience is retold as if it were happening. Do you think specific stimuli are important in this excerpt? Would the excerpt be as effective if Twain had focused on the sensations of the helmsmen and ignored much of the detail? Consider especially the paragraph in which the narrator describes how "X" guides the ship through the reefs and shoals outside of Helena, Arkansas.

2. What specific sensations are you supposed to feel as you read various parts of this excerpt? How does Twain assure that you will feel these sensations? The description of "X" is again a good example; read the paragraph and ask yourself just what sensations Twain hoped you would experience. How successful is he?

3. What kind of person is Mark Twain as he speaks in this piece? Describe his personality and the personality of George Ealer, who takes Twain's place in the anecdote. What does he enjoy? Does he like or dislike riverboating? Can you imagine characters similar to Twain or Ealer in any present-day situations—say, bus drivers or cabbies or farmers you might know?

Journal Exercise

1. Take a walk, notebook in hand, and record your sensory impressions as carefully as you can, in short form. Then, write two separate entries, one in which you describe what you saw in objective terms, the other describing the walk as if it were happening as you write, the way Thoreau does. Consider the impression you want to create and try to control, arrange, and select stimuli to fit the experience.

2. Isolate yourself in a quiet place and record your inner sensations for about ten minutes. Don't worry about mechanics or form. Then revise what you have recorded into two paragraphs in which you try to develop a particular voice—humorous and witty like Twain's, loose and talky as you would sound in an everyday situation, or somewhat formal as you would sound in more serious situations. In the revision, keep some of the detail you first recorded.

3. Describe and narrate a past experience—something you remember fairly accurately, an experience that seemed important to you at the time. You probably won't remember many details, but be as specific as you can with what you do remember. Try to create a voice that helps to tell the reader how you feel *now* about the experience. Imagine yourself retelling the experience to prove a point, much as Twain recites the anecdote in the previous reading.

4. Record just one funny or peculiar incident each day for several successive days. Be specific. Then, as you go back over what you've written, look for patterns and repetitions. Do you find only certain kinds of incidents funny? Why? What can you say about yourself and about your sense of humor by rereading these entries? Do you find striking oppositions in what you record? Surprises? People who act differently than you expected?

5. Experiment with an expository essay on a past experience. First, go back and piece the experience together in your memory. Who and what was involved? Where did it happen? Why? Remember as many

specific details as you can by compiling an inventory or checklist. As a writer, you'll be most interested in *recreating;* your reader wants essence, not facts. You'll need to use some details, reject others, merely mention some, emphasize and repeat others. After you've gone through the memory process, look over your list of facts and experiences and search for some dominant idea or impression. Can you phrase a thesis from your accumulated detail? Perhaps you've gotten together materials for an essay on hospital emergency rooms. Perhaps your thesis will be that they are too sterile, too grotesquely clean and bright for the mangled people who enter. The contrast, however logical, seems grotesque. Once you've chosen a thesis or dominant idea, inform your reader by going back and selecting detail, arranging it carefully under your thesis paragraph.

Working perceptions into your writing

Imagine yourself crossing a busy intersection. You are confronted with a barrage of detail; you feel a variety of fragmented sensations. The street may be crowded with automobiles, their engines throbbing, drivers hunched over the wheels ready to move through the intersection. Other people brush by you, pulling against your sleeves, crushing your toes. Perhaps you feel the heat of the sun, notice a speck of dust on your glasses, or see a woman with a funny hat. You had an early breakfast and now feel hungry. Your senses receive numerous stimuli; you experience a variety of sensations, some related to immediate stimuli and others to past experiences.

As you cross the intersection, you begin to select from these sensations and stimuli. You may notice, especially if you are hungry, a restaurant sign a half-block away. If you are late for a meeting, the clock on the bank building across the intersection may attract your attention. In other words, what you notice, let us say what you *perceive,* is at least partially controlled by several factors: your immediate concerns, your past experiences, and certain feelings, like hunger, which are related to bodily processes. In everyday life, you miss a lot. You may ignore the new traffic light, just installed the previous day, as you cross an intersection.

Let's turn our attention to perception as a process which is distinct from the processes of receiving stimuli and sensations. A *perception* is a group of related stimuli and sensations combined into an ordered and related pattern. The hunger you experience as you cross the intersection fuses with the restaurant sign to attract your attention. You may, as you drive, pass a service station and glance at your gas gauge. These scattered units of received experience represent an intermediate stage within the ordering of experience. Usually, perceptions do not depend as much on language as on completed thoughts. In any case, perceptions become foundation blocks for our completed thoughts; they represent an individual's first, sometimes subconscious, attempts to order the chaos of experience. In writing, we also compose bits of experience (stimuli and sensation) into larger, more ordered perceptual blocks. Finally, we either imply or directly express complete thoughts. When you write, you often want to carry your reader back through the entire process. You want to show him where your perceptions come from and how they were put together. A friend, you say, is flighty and nervous. What particular details made you think that? How does he talk? How does he walk? Are there nervous gestures that he can't control? Have you seen him drop one project after another, although he seems enthusiastic at the onset? The same type of questions apply when you try to support a perception you've had while reading a poem or novel or while listening to a political speech. Perceptions are quick little insights. Put together successfully and explained in detail, they build strong general conceptions.

Here are some suggestions that might help you analyze your everyday perceptions and discover how they are produced.

1. Try to notice details you might ordinarily ignore. Plan a few controlled experiments. Go into a crowded department store and consciously *listen* as well as look. Do you hear any peculiar or repeated sounds that you hadn't noticed before? If you live in an apartment, a house, or a dormitory that overlooks a fairly busy street, look out and observe for ten minutes straight. What is there that you see for the first time? Go into a supermarket or corner store and be sensitive to what you can *smell*. Why don't you use *all* your senses all the time? Even though most of us are visually oriented, we can increase our abilities to smell, hear, touch, and taste.

2. As you go through daily experiences, try to keep your senses moving from the general to the specific. If you see a large elm, go on to look closely at its leaves, smell its fragrance, touch its bark. If you drive by a large billboard every day, read what's on it. If you ride a bicycle or motorcycle, consciously evaluate what you feel as you drive—the bumps, the wind, the road beneath you.

3. Every once in a while change your usual perspectives. If you're close enough, try walking to class when you usually drive. If you usually walk up a particular hill, try walking down it. Try looking *up* at your bedroom or dormitory window rather than *down* out of it. Record in your journal any significant discoveries these changes in perspective produce.

4. To test whether your reactions to certain objects or people are caused by some prejudice in you or by that object or person, try to write an objective description of something or someone you dislike. Record some journal observations on that annoying girl who sits next to you in history. Have another student read your entry and tell you whether the entry is objective.

5. How does your immediate state of mind affect what you perceive? If you have an important exam, do you ignore most of what is around you? Or do you exaggerate your reaction to a stimulus—say, a long traffic light—when your money is short or you are having some problems with a friend?

The photo and the painting on the opposite page should help you sharpen your perceptions. They should also help you use your perceptions, and the experience behind them, as you write.

Activity Exercise

1. What differences do you perceive in the painting and the photo you've just looked at?

2. Are the differences meaningful? If so, what do they mean to you?

3. Write two paragraphs telling your readers how the pictures say different things about America. Base your judgment on the differences you perceive between the photograph and the painting.

4. Compose funny or ironic captions for both pictures. What do the captions say, indirectly, about our culture?

5. Write an essay in which you compare the two pictures. Develop a thesis to organize your comparison before you begin; take notes on detail in the painting and in the photo. Be sure to select and arrange the details to support your thesis.

6. What does *American Gothic* say to you about the people in the painting? About the society in which they live? Which specific details control your response? Can you describe how these people feel about their homesteads? What desires might they have for the future? How do you know? Apply these questions to the photograph as well.

The sentence modifier

Most of us find single-word modifiers—especially adverbs and adjectives—fairly easy to use. The more concrete the modifier, the more powerful the effect on a reader's senses.

Figure 4-1

American Gothic
by Grant Wood

Figure 4-2

New American Gothic
photograph by author

But there are many other ways to modify the main parts of your sentences—your subjects, verbs, and objects or complements. In fact, any larger group of words that in some way qualifies or adds to what we know about some main element of the sentence is a *sentence modifier*. How well you discover and control longer sentence modifiers will often decide how much variation and specific detail you can get into your sentences and essays. Look at the following sentence. The main clause is italicized.

> *The Texan turned to the nearest gatepost and climbed to the top of it,* his alternate thighs thick and bulging in the tight trousers, the butt of the pistol catching and losing the sun in pearly gleams.[1]
> —William Faulkner

Faulkner describes an action. He finds the subject he wants (a "Texan," not just a man or a cowboy) and the verbs ("turned" and "climbed"). He then builds on those basic elements by qualifying them, adding specific physical details, mostly long, multiword sentence modifiers.

The sentence begins with a main action described in the right subject and verbs and moves on to fill in the gaps, bringing the reader in closer to the main action. Watch Faulkner as he moves you in closer to the action, shows you the Texan's bulging thighs, his tight trousers, his pistol as it catches the sun. Every visual stimulus relates back to the main action and qualifies by adding more specific information to that main action. We might diagram the relation between the complete perception—the Texan turning and climbing to the top of the gatepost—and the modifying details like this:

Most general: Texan turns and climbs to the top of the gatepost. . .
Second level of generality: his thighs are thick and bulging in his trousers. . .
Second level of generality: his pistol gleams in the sun. . .

Obviously, both the added details need more than a single word. But the writer wants them in the same sentence because together they give a more unified, clearer picture of the Texan than they would in

---

[1] I acknowledge Francis Christensen's use of this model sentence in *Notes Toward A New Rhetoric.*

separate sentences. Also, the reader, when he reads the longer sentence, gets the feel of the action. It seems to go on right in front of him, as if he were noticing the main action and then the minor actions himself. Notice the different effect when the sentence is broken up.

> The Texan turned to the nearest gatepost. He climbed to the top of it. His thighs were thick and bulging. His pistol caught and lost the sun in pearly gleams.

In the shorter sentences, we don't see the action in sequence, smoothly connected as it would meet the eye.

Here are two suggestions that are based on this discussion. Apply them to your own descriptions—both of static objects or scenes and of continuous action.

1. When you write, include at least a few sentences in which you begin with a main action and move to a minor action. Work from a *general* perception back through to *specific* stimuli in one sentence.

2. Get a few multiword modifiers into some of your sentences. Don't depend on adjectives and adverbs alone. Use a few prepositional phrases, a few dependent clauses, or other types of phrases—as Faulkner used in the sentence above. As you observe before you write, try to break objects or actions into major and minor sequences and details. What do you want your reader to see or experience first? Then where do you want his attention to go?

Activity Exercise

1. Write several brief action-descriptions. First, observe someone performing an action—a young child climbing a flight of stairs, an older person crossing a busy street, a pitcher in his windup, an outfielder making a difficult catch, a violinist tuning up before a concert. Record what you think are major and minor actions, including details and sequences. Then make sentences, building main clauses out of major actions and supporting modifiers out of minor actions. Try your sentences out on your classmates.

2. Using the following sample list of basic clauses, all based on Picasso's *Family of Saltimbanques,* add sentence modifiers that expand and clarify the general impression. Look at the painting closely and decide how you will direct the reader's senses. Make a preliminary chart of your visual details and make a plan for your description. The first clause has been completed to give you an idea of how to add modifiers to those that follow.

Color figure 4-3
FAMILY OF SALTIMBANQUES
Picasso
follows page 14.

The circus family reminds me of a group of gypsies (main clause), their differently shaped bodies poised in various performing positions.

The tall, thin man holds his arm behind his back. . .

The sky is cloudy and light blue. . .

The little girl's head is bent forward. . .

3. Make one of the above sentences the main sentence in a paragraph. Then go on to add more and more detail in each sentence until you have a complete paragraph. Imagine yourself your own reader. Is the detail you are using coming together to form a unified picture?

4. Write an essay on circuses. Use Picasso's painting to get started. You might read a bit from books about circuses and famous circus families before you begin. You can write your essay in one of two ways. You can develop an explicit thesis about the way circus families live and survive, introducing the thesis in your opening paragraph. Then you can select various descriptive and defining details, from the painting or your reading, and arrange them to support your thesis. Or you might write a description of one circus family, perhaps the Saltimbanques, and use it to develop a hidden thesis about circus families. You can form detail in a way that will suggest to your readers a general impression of circus families.

Developing larger meanings

Perceptions are intermediate steps. Conceptions are larger, more concrete steps, composed of stimuli and perceptions. Conceptions are what we think of as "ideas" or "meanings." Animals recognize and respond to stimuli. In fact many animals have better developed senses than we have. The rabbit hears sensitively, the bloodhound smells sensitively. Some animals are capable of simple perception; the horse who is fed by a particular barn door may return to that door before feeding every night and morning. He perceives a sensory association —the barn door is connected in his mind with food. When he craves food, he makes the connection and returns to that door. Primates —monkeys, baboons, and gorillas—have even more perceptual powers. They often make somewhat complex "decisions" and develop sophisticated behavioral habits and patterns. Rodents, under the pressure of a laboratory environment, solve surprisingly complex perceptual problems, finding their way through complex mazes and obstacles. Generally, however, only humans are capable of high-level conceptual performance.

Effective writing, like effective thinking, often depends most upon the writer's ability to connect his general thoughts and main ideas with his concrete experience. A writer is often concerned with the relationship between an idea and an object, between a main idea in a sentence and its various parts. Occasionally, he wants to bring a large group of ideas and experiences under some paragraph order. And, of course, he often wants to give an entire thought process a general heading, or thesis, in an essay. But, at whatever level he is working, his goal is to connect his experiences with his thoughts. Effective writing carries the reader back over a complete experience—from initial stimuli to final conception—and lets him *share* a good deal more than the final product of thought and feeling.

Exposition and narration

Usually, the paragraph is the unit through which a writer shares conceptions, just as the sentence is the unit through which a writer shares perceptions. In essence, a paragraph shows relationships among perceptions. Read this paragraph from *Successful Wine-Making At Home* by H. E. Bravery.

> When you bottle, bottle only perfectly clear wine and don't use any old bottle which happens to be available. It is worth while taking the trouble to use wine bottles all the time; dark ones for red wines, clear glass for lighter wines—and they should be the sort that have an indenture or "punt" at the bottom. A punt is the part of the bottle which has been pushed up inside. Use decent labels, even if they are plain ones, rather than strips of gummed paper of any shape or size.

The paragraph begins with a simple generalization about the main topic of the paragraph—wine bottles and which ones to use. Then it moves back over more specific perceptions, probably ones that the author experienced when he made his own wines. Don't use old bottles or any bottle that happens to be available; use bottles made to hold wine, especially the ones with indentions in the bottom. Use dark bottles for red wines, clear bottles for light wines. Use "decent labels," not "strips of gummed paper."

Bravery might have gone even further. He might have told us specifically *why* we should do these things. Then he would need a paragraph to explain the generalization about bottles and perhaps separate paragraphs to explain the "why" behind each little bottling direction. How far you push your explanations depends upon your subject and upon how much your audience already knows about the subject. Bravery, in the above paragraph, feels that his readers will know by common sense why the supporting directives or perceptions are impor-tant.

Let's look at a piece of descriptive writing, an excerpt from William Faulkner's short story "Go Down Moses." Here we find a narrator describing another character. We perceive the person being described *along with* the narrator who describes him. Notice how the excerpt begins with general details of the face and eyes and moves to more specific qualities—the trimmed black hair, the clothes, the man's voice, the white man who questions the subject.

> The face was black, smooth, impenetrable; the eyes had seen too much. The negroid hair had been treated so that it covered the skull like a cap, in a single neat-ridged sweep, with the appearance of having been lacquered, the part trimmed out with a razor, so that the head resembled a bronze head, imperishable and enduring. He wore one of those sports costumes called ensembles in the men's shop's advertisements, shirt and trousers matching and cut from the same fawn-colored flannel, and they had cost too much and were draped too much, with too many pleats; and he half lay on the steel cot in the steel cubicle just outside which an armed guard had stood for twenty hours now, smoking cigarettes and answering in a voice which was anything under the sun but a southern voice or even a negro voice, the questions of the spectacled white man sitting with a broad census-taker's portfolio on the steel stool opposite. . . .
>
> (From *Go Down Moses* by William Faulkner. Copyright 1942 and renewed 1970 by Estelle Faulkner and Jill Faulkner Summers. Reprinted by permission of Random House, Inc.)

In Faulkner's passage, we find a different writing principle at work. The narrator doesn't offer *any* general interpretation in this paragraph. He assembles the detail, working from general to specific, and leaves the rest to the reader. But the details he chooses to include and the way he emphasizes them practically force us to interpret the evidence in his way. What do you think of the man who is described? How is your impression enforced by the description itself? Is this man overdressed and a bit too showy—expecially for a man about to die? What do you think the narrator thinks of this man? How can you tell?

These two representative passages demonstrate different principles. The wine-making passage is *expository* writing; its main aim is to show the reader how, to explain a process, to demonstrate and teach a skill. In exposition, the writer jumps in and interprets the evidence. He takes a reader down a natural path, shares details and perception, and works toward a final sharing of the entire process. The reader, in exposition, *expects* careful interpretation and explanation. The experience, in this case the experience of wine-making, supports the conception, the under-standing and interpretation.

The Faulkner passage, however, is *narration*; its main purpose is the *sharing of an experience.* The writer tells his story, uses as much detail and sensory appeal as possible, and usually leaves the actual interpretation to the reader. He may organize and present the experience in a way that encourages the reader to feel or interpret a certain way, but he never interrupts with explicitly interpretive remarks. Suppose Faulkner's narrator had interrupted the story by saying that the man he was describing was a phony. We'd feel insulted. We want the experi-ence, the details and perceptions, to speak for itself in narration.

Poems and perception

An entire school of modern poets write what we might call "per-ceptual poetry." They put stimuli together to capture a brief perception. They write about common objects, use a limited and concrete vocabu-lary, and try to capture little things that their readers might otherwise take for granted. These sample, perceptual poems might help you see how everyday perceptions work.

Unbroken

A. R. AMMONS

Evening falls: earth
            divides:
                  insects waken

      as
birds fly to roost:

out there, nothing happens:
                        everything is
the
         same.

Reprinted from A. R. Ammons: *Northfield Poems.* Copyright © 1966 by Cornell University. Used by permission of Cornell University Press.

Thinking Exercise

1. How successful are you in actually seeing the four details that open the poem—evening falls, earth divides, insects waken, birds fly to roost? Are other senses called into action by these images?

2. How does the poet find these conceptions—that "nothing happens," that "everything is the same"—in these brief perceptions? Something does *seem* to happen. Things do *seem* to change.

3. Is it possible to "hear" silence? Are there "sounds of silence" in this poem?

Lying in a Hammock at William Duffy's Farm in Pine Island, Minnesota

JAMES WRIGHT

Over my head, I see the bronze butterfly,
Asleep on the black trunk,
Blowing like a leaf in green shadow.
Down the ravine behind the empty house,
The cowbells follow one another
Into the distances of the afternoon.
To my right,
In a field of sunlight between two pines,
The droppings of last year's horses
Blaze up into golden stones.
I lean back, as the evening darkens and comes on.
A chicken hawk floats over, looking for home.
I have wasted my life.

Thinking Exercise

1. The poet puts only one conceptual statement into this poem—"I have wasted my life." Considering all that he describes and the way he describes it in this poem, why does he say that he has wasted his life?

2. Can you define the poet's attitude toward what he experiences? Does he feel superior to what he sees and hears? Does a man lying in a hammock really *waste* time? Despite his apparent inactivity, would you say this narrator is actually inactive?

3. *Irony* is saying the opposite of what you mean for humorous effect. Irony often occurs when a writer includes a sentence that obviously is contradicted by its context, the other sentences around it. Would you say that "I have wasted my life" is ironic in this poem?

Man

RICHARD BRAUTIGAN

With his hat on
he's about five inches taller
than a taxicab

In a Cafe

RICHARD BRAUTIGAN

I watched a man in a cafe fold a slice of bread
as if he were folding a birth certificate or looking
at the photograph of a dead lover.

November 3

RICHARD BRAUTIGAN

I'm sitting in a cafe,
drinking a coke.

A fly is sleeping
on a paper napkin.

I have to wake him up,
so I can wipe my glasses.

There's a pretty girl
I want to look at.

Thinking Exercise

1. These little poems focus in on brief perceptions. The poet stops time, puts a few connected images into words, and leaves the rest to the reader. What do these little, concrete experiences *mean* to you? Why are they poetry?

2. Can you think of a meaning you could attach to each poem? What do you know about the old man from his action? How about the I-narrator of "November 3"?

3. Can you imagine yourself writing the poem "Man"? Where would you be as you wrote it? For example, might you be standing on a sidewalk and looking across a busy street at a man who has just gotten out of a taxi? Perhaps only his hat shows above the cab as he reaches in to pay the cabbie. Can you imagine another context for this poem? Be specific; construct a fixed point of view and accurate spatial relationships between the narrator/poet and the man getting out of, or standing alongside of, the taxicab.

The Red Wheelbarrow

WILLIAM CARLOS WILLIAMS

So much depends
upon

a red wheel
barrow

glazed with rain
water

beside the white
chickens.

Activity Exercise

1. Try this experiment. Find three or four common objects, and arrange them around you. Observe them for awhile. Associate other objects and thoughts with them and take some notes. Then arrange the objects in words. Use *concrete* nouns, verbs, and adjectives. *Don't* interpret the experience or lapse into a description of other objects.

2. Write an essay in which you tell what you think "depends upon" the objects of your poem or Williams' poem. Be specific. What did you discover about the objects as you observed them and arranged them in words? Would it help a person to observe this carefully more often? How and why? Make your answer to the first question your thesis and your answers to the following questions your main support.

Writing Exercise

You've read a group of poems that fasten on and capture brief perceptions. Sometimes the poets use metaphors to communicate what they see. At other times, they describe literally and factually. Write an essay in which you explain *why* poets believe it worthwhile to capture such brief, passing moments in their poems. Use these poems as examples. Refer to specific lines, images, and words as you proceed. Imagine yourself addressing readers who might respond this way to these poems: "Poems ought to be about something important. Who cares about what a poet sees while he is sitting in a café or looking at a farmyard in the rain?"

Essays

The following essay makes very emphatic use of personal observation. William Styron, a prominent Southern novelist and acknowledged supporter of liberal political policies, offers a personal analysis of the Democratic convention in Chicago, 1968. As you probably recall, the convention demonstrated, probably for the first time in front of a mass television audience, the dramatic split that had occurred in much of American politics. Street confrontations between those who were protesting the war and the police created chaos at the convention site. Dovish delegates attempted to filibuster, to disrupt convention order, to dislodge professional politicians from their places of power. Styron tries to recapture the chaos, the complexity of imagery, and the sensations and perceptions as he experienced them during the convention week. He begins his essay with bits of objective description. The first few pages describe his feelings in afterthought—about politics, political systems, the entire convention. These descriptions of attitude are then supported with objective descriptions: first, a description of a pre-convention meeting in which Styron himself had participated; then a brief description of the jammed Conrad Hilton lobby and the author's feelings as he walked through it. These descriptions, we are told, led Styron to feel an initial feeling of despair, frustration, and cynicism. Finally, Styron describes the Chicago police, focusing in on their physical stature, their dress, their faces, their attitudes.

All these descriptions, however, are climaxed in Styron's impressionistic description of Chicago street-fighting. We see sharp images, glimpses of human bodies, signs, objects—all merged in the mind of the writer/observer as he attempts to share what he remembers. Notice especially the essay's final scene: the author sits at a bar and watches a violent confrontation between police and protestors; he watches in all the comfort of a dark tavern, with music playing, the television going, the bartender serving customers. As he sits in comfort in the bar he sees street-fighting through the bar's plate-glass window. Styron's sensitive observations and his careful attention to selection and arrangement of detail *are* his essay.

In the Jungle

WILLIAM STYRON

It was perhaps unfortunate that Daley, the hoodlum suzerain of the city, became emblematic of all that the young people in their anguish cried out against, even though he plainly deserved it. No one should ever have been surprised that he set loose his battalions against the kids; it was the triumphant end-product of his style, and what else might one expect from this squalid person whose spirit suffused the great city as oppressively as that of some Central American field marshal? And it was no doubt inevitable, moreover, a component of the North American oligarchic manner—one could not imagine a Trujillo so mismanaging his public relations—that after the catastrophe had taken place he should remain so obscenely lodged in the public eye, howling "kike!" at Abe Ribicoff, packing the galleries with his rabble, and muttering hoarse irrelevancies about conspiracy and assassination, about the *Republican* convention ("They had a fence in Miami, too, Walter, nobody ever talks about *that!*") to a discomfited Cronkite, who wobbled in that Oriental presence between deference and fainthearted suggestions that Miami and Chicago just might not be the same sort of thing.

That is what many of us did along about Thursday night in Chicago—retreat to the center, the blissful black interior of some hotel room and turn on the television set. For after four days and nights in the storm outside, after the sleepless, eventually hallucinated connection with so many of the appalling and implausible events of that week, it was a relief to get off the streets and away from the parks and the Amphitheater and the boorish, stinking hotel lobbies and to see it as most Americans had seen it—even if one's last sight was that of the unspeakable Daley, attempting to explain away a shame that most people who witnessed it will feel to their bones for a very long time.

Yet, again, maybe in the immediate aftermath of the convention it was too bad that Daley should have hogged a disproportionate share of

---

the infamy which has fallen upon the Democratic party; for if it is getting him off the hook too easily to call him a scapegoat, nonetheless the execration he has received (even the New York *Daily News*, though partly of course out of civic rivalry, carried jeering stories about him) may obscure the fact that Daley is only the nastiest symbol of stupidity and desuetude in a political party that may die, or perhaps is already dead, because it harbors too many of his breed and mentality. Humphrey, the departed John Bailey, John Connally, Richard Hughes, Muskie—all are merely eminent examples of a rigidity and blindness, a feebleness of thought, that have possessed the party at every level, reaching down to those Grant Wood delegates from North Dakota who spilled out from the elevators into my hotel lobby every morning, looking bright-eyed and war-hungry, or like Republicans, whom they emulated through becoming one of the few delegations that voted against the pacific minority Vietnam plank *en bloc*. It has been said that if various burdensome and antiquated procedural matters—the unit rule, for instance—had been eliminated prior to this convention, the McCarthy forces might have gained a much larger and more significant strength, and this is at least an arguable point of view; for a long while I myself believed it and worked rather hard to see such changes come about (some did), but now in retrospect it seems that the disaster was meant to be.

Recalling those young citizens for Humphrey who camped out downstairs in my hotel, that multitude of square, seersuckered fraternity boys and country club jocks with butch haircuts, from the suburbs of Columbus and Atlanta, who passed out Hubert buttons and Humphrey mints, recalling them and their elders, mothers and fathers, some of them delegates and not all of them creeps or fanatics by any means but an amalgam of everything—simply well-heeled, most of them, entrenched, party hacks tied to the mob or with a pipeline to some state boss, a substantial number hating the war but hating it not enough to risk dumping Hubert in favor of a vague professorial freak who couldn't feel concern over Prague and hung out with Robert Lowell—I think now that the petrification of a party which allowed such apathy and lack of adventurousness and moral inanition to set in had long ago shaped its frozen logic, determined its fatal choice months before McCarthy or, for the matter, Bobby Kennedy had come along to rock, ever so slightly, the colossal dreamboat. And th.'s can only reinforce what appears to me utterly plausible: that whatever the vigor and force of the dissent, whatever one might say about the surprising strength of support that the minority report received on the floor, a bare but crucial majority of Americans still is unwilling to repudiate the filthy war. This is really the worst thought of all.

Right now, only a day or so after the event, it is hard to be sure of anything. A residue of anguish mingles with an impulse toward cynicism, and it all seems more than ever a happening. One usually sympathetic journalist of my acquaintance has argued with some logic but a little too much levity that the violent confrontations, like the show of muscle among the black militants, were at least only a psychological necessity: after all, there were no killings, few serious injuries, had there been no violence the whole affair would have been tumescent, impossibly strained, like *coitus interruptus,* and who would have had a bruise or a laceration to wear home as a hero's badge? As for myself, the image of one young girl no older than sixteen, sobbing bitterly as she was being led away down Balbo Avenue after being brutally cracked by a policeman's club, is not so much a memory as a scene imprinted on the retina—a metaphor of the garish and incomprehensible week—and it cannot be turned off like the Mr. Clean commercial that kept popping up between the scenes of carnage. I prefer to think that the events in Chicago were as momentous and as fateful as they seemed at the time, even amid the phantasmagorical play of smoke and floodlights where they were enacted.

One factor has been generally overlooked: the weather. Chicago was at its bluest and balmiest, and that gorgeous sunshine—almost springlike—could not help but subtly buoy the nastiest spirit and moderate a few tempers. Had the heat been as intense and as suffocating as it was when I first arrived in the city the Tuesday before the convention began, I feel certain that the subsequent mayhem would have become slaughter. I came at that time to the Credentials Committee meeting in the Conrad Hilton as one of four "delegate challengers" from Connecticut, presenting the claim that the popular vote in the state primaries had indicated that 13 delegates out of 44 should be seated for McCarthy, rather than the 9 allowed the McCarthy forces by John Bailey. Although logic and an eloquent legal brief by Dean Louis Pollak of the Yale Law School were on our side, the megalithic party structure could not be budged and it was on that stifling day—when I scrutinized from the floor the faces of the hundred-odd cozy fat cats of the Committee, two from each state plus places like Guam, nearly all of whom were committed to the Politics of Joy and who indeed had so embraced the establishment mythopoeia that each countenance, male or female and including a Negro or two, seemed a burnished replica of Hubert Humphrey—that I became fully aware that McCarthy's cause was irrevocably lost. Nor was I encouraged to hedge on this conviction when, sweating like a pig, I made a brief *ad hominem* plea in summation of our case, finished, and sat down to the voice of the Committee chairman, Governor Hughes of New Jersey, who said: "Thank you, Mr. Michener." Later, the governor's young aide came up to apologize, saying that the governor knew full well who I was, that in the heat and his fatigue he must have been woolgathering and thinking of James Michener, who was a good friend of Mr. Hughes—a baffling explanation which left me with ominous feelings about life in general.

When I returned as an observer to Chicago the following Sunday, the lobby of the Conrad Hilton resembled a fantasy sequence in some Fellini movie, people in vertical ascent and horizontal drift, unimaginable shoals of walleyed human beings packed elbow to elbow, groin to rump, moving sluggishly as if in some paradigmatic tableau of the utter senselessness of existence. It took me fifteen minutes to cross from one side of the hotel to the other, and although I endured many low moments during the convention, I think it was at this early point, amid that indecent crush of ambitious flesh, that my detestation of politics attained an almost religious passion.

The Conrad Hilton is the archetypal convention hotel of the universe, crimson and gold, vast, nearly pure in its efficient service of the demands of power and pelf, hence somehow beyond vulgarity, certainly sexless, as if dollar hustling and politicking were the sole source of its dynamism; even the pseudo-Bunny waitresses in the Haymarket bar, dungeon-dark like most Chicago pubs, only peripherally distract from the atmosphere of computers and credit cards. Into the Hilton lobby later that week—as into the lobbies of several other hotels—the young insurgents threw stink bombs, which the management misguidedly attempted to neutralize with aerosol deodorants; the effect was calamitous—the fetor of methane mingled with hair spray, like a beauty parlor over an open sewer—and several of the adjoining restaurants seemed notably lacking in customers. Not that one needed any incentive to abandon the scene, one fled instinctively from such a maggot heap; besides there was much to study, especially in downtown Chicago on the streets and in the park, where the real action was, not at the convention itself (I only went to the Amphitheater once, for the vote on the minority report), whose incredible atmosphere of chicanery and disdain for justice could best be observed through television's ceaselessly attentive eye.

Since I somehow felt that sooner or later the cops would make their presense felt upon me more directly (a hunch that turned out to be correct) it appeared to me that they deserved closer scrutiny. They were of course everywhere, not only in the streets but in the hotel lobbies and in the dark bars and restaurants, in their baby-blue shirts, so ubiquitous that one would really not be surprised to find one in one's bed; yet it was not their sheer numbers that truly startled, as impressive as this was, but their peculiar personae, characterized by a beery obesity that made them look half again as big as New York policemen (I never thought I might feel what amounted to nostalgia for New York cops, who by comparison suddenly seemed as civilized as London constables) and by a slovenly, brutish, intimidating manner I had never seen outside the guard room of a Marine Corps brig. They obviously had ample reason for this uptight facade, yet it was instantly apparent that in their sight not only the yippies but all civilians were potential miscreants, and as they eyed passersby narrowly I noticed that Daley, or someone, had allowed them to smoke on duty. Constantly stamping out butts, their great beer guts drooping as they gunned their motorcycles, swatting their swollen thighs with their sticks, they gave me a chill, vulnerable feeling, and I winced at the way their necks went scarlet when the hippies yelled "Pigs!"

On Tuesday night I left a party on the Near North Side with a friend, whom I shall call Jason Epstein, in order to see what was going on in nearby Lincoln Park. There had been rumors of some sort of demonstration and when we arrived, at a little before midnight, we saw that in fact a group of young people had gathered there—I estimated 1,000 or so—most of them sitting peacefully on the grass in the dark, illuminated dimly by the light of a single portable floodlamp, and fanning out in a semicircle beneath a ten-foot-high wooden cross. The previous night, testing the 11 P.M. curfew, several thousands had assembled in the park and had been brutally routed by the police who bloodied dozens of demonstrators. Tonight the gathering was a sort of coalition between the yippies and the followers of a group of Near North Side clergymen, who had organized the sit-in in order to claim the right of the people of the neighborhood to use the park without police harassment. "This is our park!" one minister proclaimed over the loudspeaker. "We will not be moved!" Someone was playing a guitar and folk songs were sung; there was considerable restlessness and tension in the air, even though it was hard to believe that the police would actually attack this tranquil assembly which so resembled a Presbyterian prayer meeting rather than any group threatening public decorum and order. Yet in the black sky a helicopter wheeled over us in a watchful ellipse, and word got back to us that the police had indeed formed ranks several hundred yards down the slope to the east, beyond our sight. A few people began to leave and the chant went up: "Sit down! Sit down!" Most of us remained seated and part of the crowd began singing "The Battle Hymn of the Republic." Meanwhile, instructions were being given out by the old campaigners: don't panic, if forced to the street stay away from the walls and blind alleys, if knocked to the ground use your jacket as a cushion against clubs, above all walk, don't run. The time was now about twelve-thirty. Vaseline was offered as a protection against MACE, wet strips of cloth were handed out to muffle the tear gas. The tension was not very pleasant; while it is easy to over-dramatize such a moment, it does contain its element of raw threat, a queasy, visceral suspense that can only be compared to certain remembered episodes during combat training. "They'll be here in two minutes!" the minister announced.

And suddenly they were here, coming over the brow of the slope fifty yards away, a truly stupefying sight—one hundred or more of the police in a phalanx abreast, clubs at the ready, in helmets and gas masks, just behind them a huge perambulating machine with nozzles, like the type used for spraying insecticide, disgorging clouds of yellowish gas, the whole advancing panoply illuminated by batteries of mobile flood-lights. Because of the smoke, and the great cross outlined against it, yet also because of the helmeted and masked figures—resembling nothing so much as those rubberized wind-up automata from a child's playbox of horrors—I had a quick sense of the medieval in juxtaposition with the twenty-first century or, more exactly, a kind of science fiction fantasy, as if a band of primitive Christians on another planet had suddenly found themselves set upon by mechanized legions from Jupiter.

Certainly, whatever the exact metaphor it summoned up, the sight seemed to presage the shape of the world to come, but by now we were up, all of us, off and away—not running, *walking*, fast—toward Clark Street, bleeding tears from the gas. The streets next to the park became a madhouse. The police had not been content to run us out of the park but, charging from the opposite direction, had flanked us, and were harrying people down the streets and up alleys. On a traffic island in the middle of Clark Street a young man was knocked to his knees and beaten senseless. Unsuspecting motorists, caught up in the pandemonium, began to collide with one another up and down the street. The crowd wailed with alarm and split into fragments. I heard the sound of splintering glass as a stone went through the windshield of a police car. Then somehow we disengaged ourselves from the center of the crowd and made our way down Wells Street, relatively deserted where in the dingy nightclubs Go-Go girls oblivious to the rout outside calmly wiggled their asses in silhouette against crimson windows.

It hardly needs mention that Daley might have dealt with these demonstrators without having to resort to such praetorian measures, but violence was the gut and sinew of Chicago during the week, and it was this sort of scene—not the antiseptic convention itself, with its tedium and tawdriness and its bought and paid-for delegates—that makes its claim on my memory. Amid the confusion, I recall certain serene little vignettes: in the lobby of the Pick-Congress Hotel, Senator Tom Dodd flushing beet-red, smiling a frozen smile while being pounded on the back by a burly delegate, steelworker type, with fists the size of cabbages, the man roaring: "I'm a Polack! We know how to ride that greased pig, too!" Or the visit I made—purportedly to win over delegates to McCarthy—to the Virginia delegation, where I was told by at least three members of the group that, while nominally for Humphrey, they would bolt for Teddy Kennedy in a shot (this helped to convince me that he could have won the nomination hands down had he come to Chicago).

But it is mainly that night-scene out of Armageddon that I recollect or, the next day, the tremendous confrontation in front of the Hilton, at the intersection of Michigan and Balbo (named for Italo Balbo, the Italian aviator who first dumped bombs on the Ethiopians) where, half-blinded from the gas I had just caught on the street, I watched the unbelievable melee not from the outside this time but in the surreal shelter of the Haymarket bar, an hermetically sealed igloo whose sound-resistant plate glass windows offered me the dumbshow of cops clubbing people to the concrete, swirling squadrons of police in Panavision blue and polystyrene visors hurling back the crowds, chopping skulls and noses while above me on the invincible TV screen a girl with a fantastic body enacted a comic commercial for BIC ballpoint pens, and the bartender impassively mooned over his Daiquiris (once pausing to inquire of a girl whether she was over 21), and the Muzak in the background whispered "Mood Indigo." Even the dénouement seemed unreal—played out not in the flesh but as part of some animated cartoon where one watches all hell break loose in tolerant boredom—when an explosion of glass at the rear of the bar announced the arrival of half a dozen bystanders who, hurled inward by the crush outside, had shattered the huge window and now sprawled cut and bleeding all over the floor of the place while others, chased by a wedge of cops, fled screaming into the adjacent lobby.

I left Chicago in a hurry—like many others—pursued by an unshakable gloom and by an even profounder sense of irrelevance. If all this anguish, all this naked protest, had yielded nothing but such a primitive impasse—perhaps in the end best symbolized not even by the strife itself but by a "victorious" Hubert Humphrey promising us still another commission to investigate the violence he might have helped circumvent—then the country truly seemed locked, crystallized in its own politics of immobility. There were to be sure some significant changes—removal of the unit rule for one—at least partially brought about by those who worked outside the establishment, including many amateurs in politics; had they been effected in less hysterical circumstances they might have been considered in themselves prodigious achievements.

And there were some bearable moments amid all the dreck: the kids going to bed unblanketed on the cold ground by the fires in Grant Park when I came back just before dawn after our encounter with the police in Lincoln Park, the crowds by the hundreds hemmed in by National Guard troops (themselves Illinois plow boys or young miners from places like Carbondale, most of them abashed and ill-at-ease—quite a contrast to the brutal belly-swagger of the cops—but all of them just as ignorant about the clash of ideologies which had brought them up here from the prairies); or the next night when again there was a vigil in the park and over a thousand people, including protesting delegates from the convention, came bearing candles and sat until dawn beneath the stirring leaves, singing *Where Have All the Young Men Gone?* as they waved their candles, a forest of arms; or the moment in the daylight, totally unexpected, when a busload of children, no more than six or seven years old, rode up from somewhere on the South Side with a gift of sandwiches for the demonstrators and slowly passed by in front of the park, chanting from the windows in voices almost hurtfully young and sweet: "We want peace! We want peace!" But these moments were rare and intermittent and the emotional gloss they provided was unable to alleviate not just the sense of betrayal (which at least carries the idea of promise victimized) but the sorrow of a promise that never really existed.

Activity Exercise

1. If you had to use one sentence in this essay as an explanation of the writer's thesis, which sentence would you choose?

2. Styron does not claim to be a "neutral" interpreter of the Chicago experience. Do you feel that his emotional involvement caused him to ignore certain perceptions and details and to emphasize others? If so, what in the essay gives you that feeling? Can you cite specific places where such biased reporting occurs?

3. Does Styron's descriptive power, his ability to put what he sees and feels into words, convince you that Chicago was not a betrayal of hope "but the sorrow of a promise that never really existed"? Does the essay make you feel cynical about politics?

4. Styron's essay is not organized as most essays are organized. He moves back and forth between idea-sentences and descriptive-sentences, without much attention to patterns of organization. He doesn't, for example, develop formal comparisons; he seldom uses examples as directly related to general attitudes or emotions. Do you feel this lack of formal organization helps or hinders Styron as he tries to get you to share his negative attitude toward politics? If you feel it helps, why? What *does* Styron do to organize his ideas and experiences?

5. Go back over a past experience and try to explain its significance. First, remember as much as you can about the experience. Jot down some notes on significant details, facts, and images. Then, try to work out in your mind the significance of the experience. Finally, plan your essay by deciding on a thesis, on specific details to support the thesis, and on a plan for connecting your thoughts with your remembered experiences.

6. Write an expository essay in reaction to Styron's remark that American politics has always been "a promise that never really existed." Explain the remark by referring to specifics in the essay and by referring to other political events about which you have read. You'll probably need to begin by defining in your own terms what Styron's remark means. Then compare Styron's evidence to your own.

The controlling eye:

III

Finding form
in experience

"And it is only through complete, unswerving devotion to the perfect blending of form and substance; it is only through an unremitting, never discouraged care for the shape and ring of sentences that an approach can be made to plasticity, to colour, and that the light of magic suggestiveness may be brought to play for an evanescent instant over the commonplace surface of words: of the old, old words, worn thin, defaced by ages of careless usage. . . My task which I am trying to achieve is, by the power of the written word to make you hear, to make you feel—it is, before all, to make you see."

—*Joseph Conrad*

EARLY SUNDAY MORNING by Edward Hopper. Courtesy the Whitney Museum of American Art.

To each his own door.

Can this be?

A Volkswagen with a private entrance for everyone?

Yep.

Incredible as it seems, that nice-looking car standing with those nice-looking people is a Volkswagen.

Which we call the Volkswagen 411 Four-Door sedan.

Take any private entrance into our club car and you'll find more luxury than you've ever laid eyes on in a VW.

Big, plush seats. Thick carpeting, door-to-door. And a refreshing amount of room to relax in.

Of course, now that we've surrounded you with all this elegance, we wouldn't think of

asking you to shift for yourself.

So we endowed the 411 with an automatic transmission. (As standard equipment.)

But maybe the best reason for driving a luxury Volkswagen is the most obvious reason:

 Who will ever know you're driving a Volkswagen?

5

To show . . .
and tell

What do we do once we've found something to say, discovered a purpose, and formed supporting details? We select. We arrange. We tell our readers *why*. In other words, we write in ways that bring the specifics of our experiences together into a clear, forceful communication. We *show* our experience as concretely as we can, letting our readers know how and why these facts and experiences make us think as we do.

Too many poor writers summarize. They write down what they think without showing their readers why. They don't carry their readers back over the actual experiences that formed the product of their thoughts.

And other writers often include too much. They record every detail, every bit of random evidence. In other words, they don't accept the writer's responsibility to write with purpose, to shape and arrange materials so that the reader gets the point quickly and clearly.

Recorded facts aren't enough. They don't lead to questions. They never relate experiences to one another to produce *meaning*. A reader interested in the rise of the laboring classes during the last two decades of the nineteenth century wants to know the *whys* and the *whats* of the Haymarket Square riot. Why did it happen when it did? What social and economic forces caused it? What actually happened? What effect did it have on labor organizations? The reader doesn't learn much by hearing only the recorded facts—that it occurred in 1885 and influenced labor relations for decades to come.

Get used to surrounding your telling generalizations with supporting facts, experiences, feelings, and insights. Always suppose your

159

readers want to know why and how. Get used to asking why and how yourself, both as you write and as you revise. You want your readers to use their senses as well as their minds. You want to show and tell.

Control means careful selection. It also means fitting what you select into an order or design that will help the reader understand. Finally, it means putting actual experience and attitudes together in ways that reinforce one another, that clarify and express what you think and what you feel.

Remember, the main purpose of literature, at least to most people, is sharing. Literature lets us in on how others respond to different situations. Usually, it leaves interpretation out; the reader responds, analyzes, and works up a meaning of his own. Then he shares that meaning with others, always refining, questioning, and learning. People who read a great deal have shared in experiences far beyond their own. Yet they are constantly relating what they read to their own experiences. As a result, their attitudes and opinions are based on a wide range of experience, from what they have read to what they have experienced themselves.

In the following poem, Randall Jarrell very briefly describes the thoughts of a gunner in the turret of a bomber. As you read, put yourself in the gunner's place. Try to feel and think what the gunner feels and thinks. Then go back and try to figure out what the poet is saying about the experience. Can you find evidence of his attitudes in certain words? In the way he describes? In what he chooses to include?

The Death of the Ball Turret Gunner

RANDALL JARRELL

From my mother's sleep I fell into the State,
And I hunched in its belly till my wet fur froze.
Six miles from earth, loosed from its dream of life,
I woke to black flak and the nightmare fighters.
When I died they washed me out of the turret with a hose.

Now suppose someone had just asked you to describe your response to "The Death of the Ball Turret Gunner." Your first response might be a general one. You would *tell* the person how you felt as you read the poem, what you believed was happening in the poem. But after you had described your general response, you would be expected to *show* just what words, images, or experiences in the poem combined to produce that response. Whatever your immediate, general feeling about the poem, you would need to go back to the poem to discover what details created the feeling. Then, you would need to select and arrange what you discovered to present a convincing case for your interpretation.

Let's begin by looking at several students' attempts to share their understanding of "The Death of the Ball Turret Gunner."

> A. Heroism means different things to different people. In this poem I think the heroism comes when the "ball turret gunner" realizes that he probably didn't live his life the way he wanted to. In the sentence "I woke to black flak and the nightmare fighters" he realizes that his end is coming and that maybe he didn't live a full life—in his "service" to mankind. I think if he would have lived a full life, he would have gone back home and he would have been a better person—living in the world of reality. I think the heroism is his realization of that fact that he is dying after never really living.

Thinking Exercise

1. Does this paragraph really describe, or show, what the writer *means* by "heroism"?

2. What other words in the paragraph seem undefined to you? What could the writer have done to have shown you what these words represented—both to the person who wrote the paragraph and to any reader of the poem?

3. How would you rate the sentences in this paragraph? Do they read clearly? Are they detailed?

4. Generally, is there too much telling and not enough showing in this paragraph? What improvements would you suggest to the writer?

5. If you had written this paragraph, could you have thought of a personal experience similar to the one in the poem to explain what the poet says about war heroes? Perhaps you recall the glorified portrayals of fighter-pilots and gunners in American war movies and how they contrast to Jarrell's gunner. Perhaps you recall zooming around the school playground after watching *Combat* on television, making wings of your arms, producing guttural sounds with your throat and imagining yourself shooting down every plane in sight. You probably never imagined yourself being "washed out of the turret with a hose."

> B. Heroism I feel is present in nearly every aspect of war. This man I feel is a hero for a number of reasons and the main one is his

willingness to give his life for his country. He is a hero because he is risking his life in the turret, the most vulnerable place in the airplane; as a result, he is the key man in protecting his comrades. Whether he knew it or not, he was a hero. He wasn't doing what came natural; he was making a sacrifice, the supreme sacrifice.

Thinking Exercise

1. Can *you*, as a reader of this paragraph, define "heroism" as it is used in the paragraph?

2. Is *heroism* "risking" your "life in the turret":

3. Do you agree with this writer's implied definition of heroism? If not, why not? Is it too narrow? Does it exclude some kind of heroism that you admire or recognize?

4. If you were to comment upon the writer's use of detail in this paragraph, what would you say? Does he show rather then tell? Does he choose appropriate details to support his interpretations? Does he mention specific images in the poem—the wet fur of the gunner's jacket, for example—to show you *why* the gunner is a hero?

5. Could you cite specific words or lines that contradict what this reader says about the narrator, the "I," of the poem?

C. I think this man will be a hero in the eyes of his family. First of all his family will not realize how insignificant his life is to the country. He will be a hero simply because he gave his life for his country. Another reason he will be a hero to his family is because they think he is fighting for something in which he really believes. In the poem he makes the discovery that maybe he won't be a hero and what he is doing isn't so great. However, he is not able to tell his family about his discovery. As a result, they will remember him as the person they knew in the dream world and not the new person he has become. Nothing about death is really easy, but it helps the people left behind if they think their loved one died for a good reason and not because of something senseless.

Thinking Exercise

1. How would you evaluate each sentence? Is there enough detail to *show* you what in the poem has produced the writer's impressions?

2. Does this writer assume that heroism is created by other people, not by the hero himself?

3. What would you tell the writer to do with sentences such as "As a result they will remember him as the person they knew in the dream world and not the new person he had become"?

4. Is the paragraph really about the poem? Does it really *share* what the writer has experienced in the poem?

5. This writer assumes that the gunner's life has been insignificant. Where do you think he got that idea as he read the poem?

> D. He was secure in his feelings when he entered the war. Here was a big chance to be a hero. He was sure he would get away from his almost "perfect" life at home with the folks. Doesn't everyone look forward to being on his own? But, before he got this chance he was in the grasp of another Force which would determine his life's direction. His dream again was put aside until he broke loose; it was too strong for *one* insignificant life.

Thinking Exercise

1. Do you understand what the writer means when he uses terms such as *force, dream, life's direction, feelings*? If so, define what they mean. If not, what could the reader have done to show what these abstract terms mean? What experiences could he share to produce meanings common to both himself and his readers?

2. Consider the sentence "Doesn't everyone look forward to being on his own?" What does it mean in relation to the poem?

3. This writer tries to get back into the narrator's mind and tell us what he felt before he went to war. What makes the writer feel that the narrator led a protected life before the war? Consider specifically the poem's first line.

4. Is "the State" the "other force" that replaces the mother's sleep as the controlling influence over the narrator's life?

> E. Ordinary everyday situation. You have the gun, or the newspaper, or the vantage point, but right now it is any view or magazine or tool. Then the cards are stacking—you make one random move, a lucky one, mixed with a planned one, add a break and another lucky one; he makes a bad or good move, thinks, and you win or lose. You just pulled the trigger. You win. You are a hero.

Whether you are a known hero depends on where you were when *it* happens. The magnitude of your heroism depends on who got had. Whether you deserve to *be* a hero is not relevant.

Thinking Activity

1. What do you think of the first two sentences? What's the writer trying to do in these sentences?

2. Is this paragraph really *about* the poem? Can you think of any way the writer might have better related his ideas on heroism to the poem itself?

3. Do you think that the line "From my mother's sleep I fell into the State" supports what the writer of this paragraph says about heroism?

4. What do the first two sentences have to do with the final three sentences? How are they related? Could these sentences be made to support one another more clearly?

5. This writer gives what we might call an impressionistic response to the poem. He decides the poem is about war and heroism and then puts on paper his responses, his "reading" of what the poem means, as they come to his mind. How would you say he might support these impressions by referring to specifics in the poem? Could you go back over these random impressions and compose a general, thesis sentence that will say in *telling* language what this writer says by *showing* the thoughts in his mind?

Here are four hints to help you combine showing and telling in whatever you write.

1. You can accomplish a good deal by approaching experience—whether a painting, a poem, a ballgame, or a history assignment—with a writer's eye. Observe with why and how questions. Try to connect the way you feel to specific words, objects, events, or facts.

2. Let your general attitude direct the way you organize and design your experience in writing. If you are trying to convince your readers that a crash-landing in a small airplane is a terrifying experience, or that a certain management strategy will produce better business results, select details that are critical and avoid or deemphasize those that don't relate to your purpose. Statistics on how many people survive air crashes may be less important than the sinking feeling in the pit of your stomach as you describe the air crash; facts and figures, however, may be more important

than how the businessman's office will look once your management plan is adopted.

3. Follow some kind of plan as you write. A writer as well as a professional football player follows a "game plan." But the writer must be sure that his plan is clear to the reader. The football player tries to keep his plan secret. Randall Jarrell certainly didn't follow a chronological or comparison plan when he wrote his poem. He probably just let his mind go, caught it at certain points—for example, when he remembered that the fur on an airman's jacket often froze when the airman was in the turret of a fighter plane—found specific words to capture those important points, and then found a shocking fact to put at the end of the poem. His plan was to go back over the experience itself to select the most important details and then to arrange those details so that the reader understood his meaning. The actual interpretation he leaves to the reader. We do the connecting and figuring. We supply the meaning. Someone putting together a how-to-do-it manual, however, makes connections clear; he relates one technique to another in some kind of clear order.

4. Remember your audience. If you're showing a group of people who have never hunted or taken target practice how to shoot a rifle, you start from the beginning and take a careful, step-by-step approach. But if you're talking to experienced woodsmen, you can select what you think are the important points—those points that will make good shooters better shooters. Fit your plan to your readers.

Showing and telling in exposition

We need to make some distinctions between showing and telling in descriptive or narrative writing and in exposition. Exposition *informs*. You take an idea, usually a thesis or an opinion, and you try to show a reader why he should accept that idea. Or you just help him to understand that idea. The differences, then, between narration (writing that shares experience in story form) and exposition can be summarized in this list.

1. In exposition, the main idea is expressed clearly and openly; the writer directs all his material toward clarifying, explaining, and illustrating that main idea. Usually both the purpose and the thesis (main idea) are clearly expressed in the opening paragraph. In narration, however, the writer usually lets the experience speak for itself; he shows and forms what he shows so that the reader gets the point by suggestion.

2. In exposition, the writer usually develops a main idea and several supporting ideas. The main idea expresses a *general* purpose—"The Haymarket Square Riot influenced labor-corporation relations for several

decades"—and the supporting ideas express more specific aspects of that general purpose—"In 1885, when the riot occurred, the tension among union members and owners was at its most volatile."—Then, the facts and evidence, the illustrations and descriptions of what happened, fill out each of the paragraphs which develop the supporting-idea sentences. A narrative description of the Haymarket Riot, on the other hand, would bring the reader right into the situation without outside interpretation and comment by the writer.

3. As a result, in exposition we *show* in support of what we *tell*. The concrete, specific descriptions follow upon and support the generalizations and supporting ideas. And the concrete supporting experience may come in the form of *statistics*—how many union members were injured in the Haymarket Riot?—or in the form of a long *narrative* about the first day of the Riot. In any case, don't mistakenly assume that showing doesn't apply to writing essays. We show in essays in a different way, with more attention to the development of a main idea through facts, examples, and well-developed illustrations.

Writing Exercise

Write an essay in which you explain the meaning or purpose of "The Death of the Ball Turret Gunner." Read over the poem and the student responses in this book to help you as you develop a thesis. Then, introduce your thesis in an opening paragraph. Develop your essay by formulating three supporting generalizations which you'll use to organize three supporting paragraphs. Use lines and words from the poem to support your thesis and your supporting generalities. Ask yourself these questions as you proceed. Why is "State" capitalized in the first line? What is "mother's sleep"? What in the poem has a "belly" and where is the fur that is mentioned in line two? Why does the speaker call life on earth a "dream" and the fighters that attack his plane "nightmare fighters"? Why did they wash him "out of the turret with a hose"? Your answers to some of these questions might give you support for your main ideas, but don't just cite factual answers as support. Write a full, detailed account of the scene described in the poem—in other words, really *show* your readers what happens in the poem—as you support your thesis.

The rest of this chapter will take you through various methods of putting the right blend of showing and telling in whatever you write. Since most writing builds from the concrete elements of experience to a general impression, opinion, or attitude, we'll begin with showing through sharing concrete experience. Then we'll move progressively through ways of combining concrete showing with telling.

Describing concrete experiences

In Hopper's painting we see a city street on an early Sunday morning. The artist tries to capture the quiet solitude and the emotional calm of a Sunday morning. As you look at the painting, try to go back over the scene as if you were the artist. What did he feel on some far away Sunday morning that made him produce this painting? Look at the painting closely, noticing details the way the artist must have noticed them when he had the actual scene before him. Take notes, record significant details, shades, colors, repeated shapes and objects. Then ask yourself what they mean as they are composed in this painting. What, for example, do the shades and the white curtains in the windows tell you about the people who live there? Here is what several students said of the artist's intention in a panel discussion.

Color figure 5-1
EARLY SUNDAY MORNING
Edward Hopper
follows page 158.

Chris:	"He's trying to catch the quiet before the storm."
Lois:	"Sunday morning makes him feel sad."
Lisa:	"He's trying to show how everyone living in cities lives a conforming life."
Bob:	"Lower middle-class housing in an urban area. I think the artist likes what he paints."

These different reactions need explanation and support. In fact, each one could be the thesis of an entire essay. They are abstract opinions that ought to be based on the concrete experience in the painting. We can decide which responses are strongest only by following the student's thought and receiving processes in detail. Let's ask each student to expand just a bit.

Chris:	"I don't know, I think it's the light and dark, the shadowing, mainly. The grey sky, the soft textures and colors in the buildings and street made me feel like everything's soft and waiting for a storm."
Lois:	"The colors are somber, nothing really bright. Also, the white curtains and yellow shades, slightly parted, the dull green of the store fronts, all combined to make me feel like Sunday morning, even before I knew what the painting was called."
Lisa:	"The way each window follows the next in almost identical form. The monotonous eaves, the dull, shabby colors of the building. These all remind me of

the film *A Thousand Clowns,* where the star (I think it was Jason Robards) stands outside a row of houses like these, early on a Sunday morning and yells 'Everybody out. All you campers up and at em' or something like that. Trying to wake up all those dead people in there.''

Bob: "I've worked in a city in Head Start this past summer. Maybe that's why I right away noticed what I heard so many city officials call 'lower middle-class housing.' But this painter treats the subject with affection, rather than scorn. His colors are soft, the houses, although simple, seem comfortable, useful, and clean. Kind of a quiet pride.''

That, at least, is a beginning. We can begin to see, in these follow-up remarks, where the general interpretations come from. Each student has pointed to some stimuli—some details—and related those stimuli to sensations which they experienced in response to those stimuli. The sharing has begun. But, we might ask our critics to go much further. Why do shadowy backgrounds and soft textures seem to Lisa like the calm before a storm? Why are the colors somber to Lois? (Is there something universally somber in light grey, green, and soft red? Can the colors be described more specifically so that "somberness" would be clear without adjectives?) Why does Lisa perceive monotony in those windows while Lois notices only the yellow shades and white curtains and relates them to Sunday morning? Why does Bob attach what seems to be his own social worker's values to the houses and the entire scene? Every reaction is personal—it depends on the background and experience of the observer; at the same time, every reaction must, if we are to believe it, relate to the painting. Bob connects his personal experience to certain concrete stimuli in the painting (the neatness, the comfortable qualities of the houses). Each student does that to a greater or lesser degree. To communicate what we feel, we can connect our sensations, perceptions and conceptions to concrete experiential stimuli. Then, the reader can really share our feelings.

We don't need to ask our students to go any further in supporting their interpretations. Let's instead apply the four steps of self-discovery—stimuli, sensation, perception and conception—to our own responses before we attempt to communicate them to others. Before you write down your interpretation of the painting, be sure you have gathered together some of the stimuli, sensations, and perceptions that built that interpretation. Be sure you've selected carefully, and related your selections to your general interpretation. Then share them, in as much detail as possible, with your readers. Before you begin, look at three brief student descriptions, mostly objective, of *Early Sunday Morning.*

> 1. A row of red houses sets atop the stores and shops and peers across the little city as the morning sun casts its golden rays upon the silent brick faces of the houses and storefronts. The little shops and businesses reveal an emptiness and a loneliness as they cast a deadly darkness from their inner walls through their windows. But the solitude is decreasing as the morning sun brightens the blue horizon.

> 2. A row of red houses, stoic and glassy-eyed, watched the world move before them. Each house stood attached to its peers, their fates intermingled, their identities inseparable. What each house lacked in motion, it made up for in contemplation, seeking new ways to deteriorate into obscurity.

> 3. A row of red houses neatly lined the deserted city street, like an early Sunday morning as the sun is rising and can be seen by the shadows cast by the barber pole and fire hydrant, introducing the horizontal lines of the shadows which cause a restful effect, a time when we can enjoy the general air of peace and quiet that fills the air. The long, narrow sidewalk lies in front of the buildings, neatly swept and freed of all litter, causing a never-ending picture. The street is peaceful and quiet as an early Sunday morning, looking quite different from weekday mornings on the street.

In Section II, we began to devise a rationale that we can use to analyze these descriptive paragraphs—to analyze all descriptive writing for that matter. Sentences, we said, are built by addition. We find a main clause, even a core phrase, and watch how the writer adds to and modifies that clause or phrase. Every sentence, almost every word, should work to add further detail to the main idea or object.

Each of the three student descriptions begins with the phrase "A row of red houses. . ." Let's apply the addition theory to the paragraphs by listing the detail added by each writer to the core phrase—"A row of red houses. . ." Decide how successful the added detail is in providing an efficient general description of *Early Sunday Morning.*

Paragraph 1: "A row of red houses . . ."

sun's rays
silent brick faces
houses and storefronts
emptiness
loneliness
deadly darkness
inner walls
windows
blue horizon

Paragraph 2: "A row of red houses . . ."

stoic and glassy-eyed
attached to "peers"
contemplation
deteriorating into obscurity

Paragraph 3: "A row of red houses . . ."

neatly lined
deserted city street
shadows (barber pole and fire hydrant)
horizontal shadow lines
restful effect
general air of peace and quiet
long, narrow sidewalk
neatly swept and freed of all litter
peaceful and quiet (as a Sunday morning)

Three students evaluated these descriptive paragraphs, to tell us how they thought the written descriptions measured up to the painting itself.

Mike: "They don't measure up at all. Sure, the list of details looks good for each paragraph, but they're not really concrete details. As description, they stink."

Lisa: "I agree. Look at the details in Paragraph One. They're too general to be descriptive of anything that's really there. Emptiness, loneliness, houses, storefronts, windows. Not much to see or feel there."

Tom: "The nouns and adjectives, the modifiers of the main phrase, are too abstract. I look at it this way. Each writer had a feeling, an impression, that he wanted to convey. The painting made him feel sad, distraught, etc. But, as we said before, you've got to share concrete details, small bits of observation, with your readers before you can expect the total impression to get across. These paragraphs jump right into that total impression without ever sharing the specifics of the experience. Look at Paragraph Three. All we are given are a few rather stiff, abstract details mixed in with numerous attitude statements. The street is "peaceful and quiet." O.K. But couldn't the writer do more than *tell* us that the street was peaceful and quiet? Maybe he could've *shown* us peace and quiet by giving us specific, concrete details that combined to create the general impression."

Lisa: "True. Like in Paragraph Two. The writer could have expanded his description of the windows. He says they're glassy-eyed and stoic. But what physical details related to the windows in the painting combined to create the stoic and glassy-eyed appearance? Was it the sunlight reflected off the glass, the flat, white and green texture and color of the curtains, the plain, square shape of the windows? The writer doesn't really say."

Mike: "Paragraph Three has more detail. But the words related to the general effect (peaceful, quiet, deserted, etc.) aren't connected to the details. The writer hasn't related specific stimuli to specific sensations; he hasn't told us why particular perceptions (the horizontal shadow-lines) produce, for him, a particular conception (a restful effect)."

Tom: "What we are saying is that the details added by these writers just aren't specific enough; they don't *show* us enough. They tell us something about the way the writer feels after seeing the painting, but that's not enough. We want to share the observing process itself; we want to see, in detail, in very close detail, the painting as the writer saw it. Then we might accept his general impression."

These remarks point out two important qualities: first, the writer who really wants to share must include *enough* detail; second, the writer must relate each detail clearly to the overall impression created by his description. If the writer of the first paragraph wishes us to experience solitude, then he should be careful to arrange and relate detail to produce a solitary feeling. His first sentence—*A row of red houses sets atop the stores and shops and peers across the little city as the morning sun casts its golden rays upon the silent brick faces of the houses and storefronts*—has plenty of detail, but the reader has no idea of where the detail is going. The details seem artificially connected; the impression is not a unified or cumulative one.

Writing concrete sentences

We want to fill our sentences with detail, but we also want them to be readable. Otherwise, we'd merely make lists and avoid sentences altogether. The form of the sentence is the writer's means of relating what he thinks—his generalizations, attitudes, and specific opinions—to what he experiences. Everything in a sentence besides the subject, predicate, and complement is a sentence modifier, something that adds detail to the main words. The actor, the acting, and the receiver of the action in the subject, predicate, and object forms are expanded by the adjectives, adverbs, phrases, and clauses.

> *The small boy leaned forward,* his mouth puckered, his hair short, an eagerness pervading his entire body.

The basic elements of the sentence are italicized; the rest is a series of large-constituent (more than a single word) modifiers that add to what we know about the boy as he leans forward.

Apply this kind of analysis to the first sentence in student paragraph one on page 169. The subject—*a row of red houses*—takes two parallel verbs—*sets* and *peers*. If we look at the long sentence modifiers, we find two prepositional phrases and a single clause—*as the morning sun casts its golden rays.* Certainly each phrase and clause adds more specific detail. First we see the houses. Then, the writer chooses two verbs we normally don't associate with houses or inanimate objects, probably because he wants the reader to imagine how he feels about the houses. And *sets* and *peers* describe more accurately his feeling that these houses are almost living presences.

Our difficulty in reading the sentence comes with the final three long sentence modifiers. The houses *peer across the little city*; so far we can follow easily. But then the writer brings in two prepositional phrases telling us where the sun casts its rays—*upon the silent brick faces of the houses and storefronts.* That's too much for one sentence. We've really got *two* main objects—the houses and the sun. Both need separate treatment, either in a compound or complex sentence or in two separate sentences. Give the reader a chance to focus his mind's eye, to *see* clearly the houses and the way they set and peer *and* the sun as it shines across them. At the same time put the sentences together in a way that makes clear to the readers that these actions are occurring simultaneously. Here is a possible revision: *A row of red houses sets atop the stores and shops and peers across the city. Upon the silent brick faces of the houses, the morning sun casts its golden rays.* These sentences allow the reader to follow with his eye because the main objects—the houses and the sun—are separated and the sentence modifiers in each sentence are clearly related to the main objects. Also, the objects and details are placed in a clearer sequence. First we see the houses, where they are located and where they face or "look." Then we focus in on the "silent brick faces of the houses" and watch the morning sun shine across them. The revised sentences demonstrate three important qualities that were missing in the original.

1. A sense of *purpose* to guide the structuring of main objects and supporting detail.

2. A sense of order to help the reader experience the sentences in all their detail as if he were looking himself at the painting.

3. A sense of *arrangement and perspective*: in this example, the writer has to make the reader *see* concrete objects in clear relation to one another.

Finding an organizing purpose

Even when we want to describe *exactly*, we need to have a purpose in mind. For no one can really reproduce an object or scene *exactly*, especially not in writing. We can only get so much detail on the written page. Just a careful written list of the details in Hopper's painting would take up pages. Even objective description is selective; for example, television networks that try to cover the news objectively have to edit and cut their film. When you describe Hopper's painting, you must select according to some purpose and still try to show enough of the painting so that the reader can imagine the entire painting accurately.

Let's propose that the writer of paragraph one follow this procedure as he refines his purpose.

1. Decide to be *objective*. Don't tell the reader what you think; show him the details of the painting.

2. But even as you are objective, find a purpose of your own to organize your description. Suppose you want to emphasize solitude because you feel that it is the main "feeling" represented in the painting. Then slowly build toward that impression.

3. Apply the three principles or qualities—purpose, order, and arrangement—to the detail in your paragraph, always working toward having your reader experience solitude.

The same principles and directions apply to the other student paragraphs.[1]

Narration: Experience in motion

Everyday we go through experiences that are potentially exciting. We usually ignore them, though, because they never break through our consciousness. Sharp observation can help us save those experiences; writing can help us make them permanent.

So far we've studied concrete detail and how to transfer it to writing. Just by looking and analyzing, you can find many interesting objects and connect them to ideas. But the most exciting aspects of our experience are very seldom concrete objects or people, separate from other objects and people, ready to be analyzed as if under a microscope. Experience is interesting because it moves; things and people interact, relate to one another, come together to create meaningful, exciting sequences of experience. In other words, life *is* a story. Actions have beginnings, middles, and ends; events are related to one another; the objects and people we describe are always changing and moving.

Narration is a kind of writing that tells a story. It tries to capture experience in motion and in action. Effective writing usually demonstrates at least a few carefully developed narrative stories, sometimes to

---

[1]Those teachers and students who wish a more detailed and complete discussion of sentence modification should use the first part of Appendix I in which the various kinds of sentence modifiers are explained and applied more specifically to the paragraph discussed here. See Appendix I, page 403.

support an idea, sometimes just to entertain, usually for both reasons. In fact, you may write better by remembering that most good writing is a series of *stories,* taken right from the writer's experience or reading, mixed in with interpreting or generalizing *ideas.* The connections among the ideas and stories are clear, both to the reader and the writer. In your journal, get used to writing your own experiences in little stories and interpreting them for yourself. Then, when you come to the class-room, you won't write dead prose, filled with borrowed feelings and ideas.

Writing effective narrative sentences is a skill. You can learn it. Once you've become accustomed to looking carefully and to using your senses imaginatively, you'll have plenty of material. The next step is finding sentence forms that will help you connect your stories-from-experience with your ideas. Look carefully at "She's Leaving Home," a cartoon version of the popular Beatles' song. Then we'll try composing narrative sentences that capture the action represented in each frame. In the process, we should be able to make some exciting discoveries about how and why this cartoon works, what it says about what.

Here is a student's attempt to transfer the visual action of the cartoon to writing. He tried to take concrete detail and put it in motion, to show it to readers in interaction and relation. As you look the paragraphs over, find the differences between these narrative sentences and the purely descriptive sentences we discussed on pages 167–173. How does the writer capture action and motion?

> The street was quiet and almost dark. The Spanish-styled houses were just beginning to take shape in the first light of dawn. Carefully, a resigned look on her face, a young girl with short hair closed the door behind her. She turned and walked lightly down the hall steps, opened and locked the front door behind her, and entered the street. Her bulky suitcase swung slowly at her side; her black pocketbook snapped in rhythm with her steps.
>
> Later that morning, in the room across the hall from the girl's, her parents began to stir from sleep. Her mother, with rollers in hair and a loosely-fitting robe pulled around her, steps into her daughter's room, reads the note she left behind, her face slowly registering surprise. "Daddy our baby's gone. Why would she treat us so thoughtlessly. How could she do this to me?" Her face wrinkles with sobs. "We never thought of ourselves, never a thought for ourselves. We struggled hard all our lives to get by."
>
> Several days later, the fading light reveals a small cafe on a far-off road. Our heroine methodically bites into a hamburger, chews—her eyes wandering and vacant.

Figure 5-2 She's Leaving Home *by Julian Allen*

Thinking Exercise

1. How successful is the writer in following the action in words? If you hadn't seen the cartoon, would you still be able to follow the action

with your eyes? Does he leave any important visual detail or sequence out? Does he successfully capture the feeling *you* have when you read this cartoon?

2. This little cartoon-story covers three days. Do you think both the cartoonist and the student-writer give you enough of the action to give you an idea of what happened during those three days? In other words, can you imagine the rest from the details and actions you find in the cartoon and narrative?

3. Why do you think the girl left home? Find specifics in the cartoon to support your answer. Do you think this story is repeated in many people's real lives?

4. As you scan the visual material in this cartoon, can you find physical details that tell you about when and where this story is supposed to have happened? Consider the style of the house, the people's dress, the automobile, and any other significant items.

She's leaving home

THE BEATLES, *comment by PAUL McCARTNEY*

"There was a Daily Mirror story about this girl who left home and her father said: 'We gave her everything, I don't know why she left home.' But he didn't give her that much, not what she wanted when she left home."—Paul McCartney.

Wednesday morning at five o'clock as the day begins
silently closing her bedroom door
leaving the note that she hoped would say more
she goes downstairs to the kitchen
clutching her handkerchief
quietly turning the backdoor key
stepping outside she is free.
She (We gave her most of our lives)
is leaving (Sacrificed most of our lives)
home (We gave her everything money could buy)
she's leaving home after living alone
for so many years. Bye, bye.
Father snores as his wife gets into her dressing gown
picks up the letter that's lying there
standing alone at the top of the stairs
she breaks down and cries to her husband
daddy our baby's gone.

Why should she treat us so thoughtlessly
how could she do this to me.
She (We never thought of ourselves)
is leaving (Never a thought for ourselves)
home (We struggled hard all our lives to
get by)
she's leaving home after living alone
for so many years. Bye, bye.
Friday morning at nine o'clock she is far
away
waiting to keep the appointment she
made
meeting a man from the motor trade.
She (What did we do that was wrong)
is leaving (We didn't know it was wrong)
home (Fun is the one thing that money
can't buy)
something inside that was always denied
for so many years. Bye, bye.
She's leaving home bye bye.

Now compare the Beatles' lyrics to the cartoon. Watch the action as it develops. Past and present are often interchanged and mixed. Why? The Beatles narrate the action, moving back and forth from daughter to parents, keeping the main action—the girl as she leaves home—in constant contrast with the minor action—the parents' reaction to their daughter's note. Also, the dialogue of the parents is scattered, almost like a refrain, throughout the song. Here are four important narrative writing principles. Can you see how the Beatles used them in "She's Leaving Home"?

1. Order

Put your material in some kind of order. You may use a traditional beginning, middle, and end sequence—a *chronological* sequence—like the one used in the cartoon. Or you might use a comparing sequence—by flashbacks or by putting two events that happened at different times or places next to each other—as the Beatles do with the parents' dialogue and the girl's actions in their song. There are many other ways of ordering a narrative. Whatever your story, find an order that fits your purpose and have someone else read your narrative to see if they can follow the action.

2. *Symbolic Detail*

When you narrate, choose your details with an eye toward sequence and meaning. Take, for example, the "She's Leaving Home" cartoon. The fact that the girl is clutching her handkerchief as she leaves tells us that she has been crying, that she has probably debated in her mind leaving for a long time and finally made the decision. The conventional responses of the parents—"We never thought of ourselves"—tells us a great deal about them, their values, how they treated their daughter, and what kind of life they lived. When you write an experience, focus on certain details that will tell the reader a great deal about your subject.

3. *Compression*

Develop a sense of how much experience to include and how much to leave out. In "She's Leaving Home," we don't know exactly what happened to the girl between Wednesday, when she left home, and Friday, when we find her on the road. But we can imagine what happened: the girl drove on and on and stopped at cheap restaurants to eat; the parents continued to cry and complain. We imagine such events because the cartoonist has carefully selected visual details that tell us what the girl and her parents are like. If you want to narrate an experience that will cover three or four days, see if you can find just a few actions and details that will carry the story. You don't need to repeat every bit of experience because the reader can use what you've already given him to figure out the rest.

4. *Showing*

Don't come right out and *tell* the reader what your story means. Show. Use the principles we've outlined here to get your meaning across. Reread to find and cut sentences like this: "When I finally got home, I knew that I really had learned what it was like to suffer." Let your experience speak for itself. Control your material; don't preach it.

Activity Exercise

1. The Beatles used a newspaper story as a basis for the song. Obviously, they felt the little news clipping *symbolized* something that was happening over and over again throughout their society. So they put the clipping into a song-story to make their own comment on society.

Read the song carefully and ask yourself these questions. What are the Beatles saying about the parents and the girl? Which side receives their sympathy? What does the cartoon say about home-life, at least as it is represented in the cartoon?

2. In satire, an artist uses exaggeration, understatement, ridicule, and other devices to criticize a particular social or personal flaw. Is the cartoon serious, satiric, or both? How can you tell? If it is at least partly satiric, who or what is satirized—the girl, the parents, the larger society? Is running away from home an answer to the girl's loneliness? Why or why not?

3. Take just one line in the song and write a one-page essay on it. How does it fit with the rest of the song? What does it mean and why? You might use the line Paul McCartney says originally appeared in slightly different words, in the *Daily Mirror* story: "We gave her most of our lives/Sacrificed most of our lives." What does that line tell you about these parents? Where do you think the father works? Do they make much money? How do you know?

4. Find a news article on your own. Make it brief and factual, perhaps one that tells a little story with practically no interpretation by the writer. Make this article the basis for a story, approximately four or five pages long. You'll need to follow all four of the narrative principles outlined on pages 178–179. Above all, be much more specific than your source. Don't be afraid to revise and develop your own narrative order. Add details of your own. In other words, take the story skeleton from the article and make it your own.[2]

5. Discuss the meaning of this song and cartoon with your class-mates. In a workshop, find and refine a thesis that defines the song's purpose. Work from statements about the song's subject—"this song and cartoon make statements about the generation gap"—to more specific statements of purpose—"the song and cartoon argue that young people often find it impossible to communicate with parents because they share very few experiences." Then, go on to find particular evidence to support your thesis. Find evidence in the song or cartoon or draw your support from essays you've read, people you know, or personal experiences. Discuss your evidence with others before you begin to organize it into a paper.

6. Do you feel the Beatles might be criticizing the young girl as well as her parents? Why? Why not? Or is *all* the satire aimed at the misunderstanding parents? Find evidence for an ironic reading of the lyrics. Does anything you read make you feel that the song means the opposite of what it says on the surface? Are there clichés (conventional

---

[2]Again, refer to Appendix I for a grammatical discussion of narrative sentences. See page 413.

phrases or often repeated sentiments) in the song? How are they used? What do they make you feel toward the characters in the story?

The language around you

We are surrounded everyday by language of all kinds. Most of it we take for granted. The television and newspaper give us "news" or information. We listen to the radio, read books and magazines, look at cartoons and advertising signs and slogans. Especially in modern cities, we are literally bombarded with information that comes to us more rapidly and chaotically than ever before. What we often forget is that we get much more than facts from the language around us. Advertisements don't just tell us about products; they also tell us what to believe, what values to hold and often how to think. Newspapers, however objective they may try to be, must edit and revise the news before they write it. Television news programs must cram enormous amounts of information into fifteen or thirty minutes; in the process, they also must select and edit, show this film and cut another—in other words, they *revise* the news.

What does this mean to you as you write? Above all, the language around you can give you ideas and material for writing. Get used to thinking about the language you hear and see around you every day. If you read gossip columns, or political columns and editorials, or a sports column, or straight news articles on important current events, don't just absorb the information. Get used to analyzing how it is presented. Writing can provide you with the skill and opportunity to evaluate and analyze what you see and hear everyday. Does the writer have an attitude? How do you know? Does the way he writes—the words he uses, the sentences he forms—show you the attitude? Can you think of information or attitudes that the writer ignores? Try figuring out how a particular magazine ad or television commercial works. Does it appeal to your reason? Does it give factual information or try to sell you values as well as a specific product?

Paying close attention to the language around you can help you in another important way. You can begin to pick up useful suggestions on how to control your own attitudes as you write. The best ads beat around the bush. You seldom find a Thunderbird ad that comes right out and sells only the car. No, the ad-writers also sell values that they believe their readers will have to hold to buy a Thunderbird. The basic assumption might run something like this: "Luxury and power are good and necessary; every person should strive for them." The ad may be shaped to sell that value as well as the car. The next time you see an ad for a luxury car, be critical. Ask yourself what the ad is really selling and how it does it? How much is really about the kind of life you will live if and when you buy the car? These kinds of questions will help you to know what you are buying and why. But, just as important, they may help you discover persuasive techniques that you can use yourself. And learn to check the assumptions of an ad. Many ads *are* logical. But they often *assume* a basic agreement that isn't really there. Is dry skin always bad? Does everyone *want* power in a car?

The materials on the following pages are brief examples of everyday language. In each, the writer develops an attitude, but he develops it *indirectly*. In other words, the creator of the language—whether a cartoonist, professional writer, or amateur letter-to-the-editor writer—never really comes out and says exactly what he believes. Instead, he puts his material together in a way that the reader knows leads to a certain attitude, perhaps by exaggeration or understatement or by ridicule and sarcasm.

> The great Downtown pot plot . . .
>
> About the gentleman who was convicted for the possession of 1-28th of an ounce of marijuana: What is to keep some enterprising person from climbing to the top of the IDS tower, throwing a couple of kilos of pot to the winds and then going down and arresting all the businessmen, bankers and secretaries of Downtown Minneapolis?
>
> —Minneapolis Tribune, Letter to the Editor

Thinking Exercise

1. Can you imagine what the writer of this letter's attitudes are toward

a. the fact that a person was convicted of possessing 1-28th of an ounce of marijuana?

b. legislation concerning marijuana?

c. the rights of individuals in a mass society?

2. How does the letter work toward the communication of that attitude?

3. Can you find an article in the current issue of your paper that makes you want to write a letter-to-the-editor? If you can, write a letter something like this one. Ask a question that points out the absurdity in your article.

The Shortest Novel of Them All . . .

NORMAN MAILER

At first she thought she could kill him in three days.
        She did nearly. His heart proved nearly
unequal to her compliments.
Then she thought it would take three
weeks. But he survived
So she revised her tables and calculated
        three months.
After three years he was still alive. So
        they got married.
Now they've been married for thirty
        years. People speak warmly of them.
They are known as the best marriage
        in town
It's just that their children keep dying.

Thinking Exercise

1. What does Norman Mailer think of marriage? Domestic life? Courtship? Women?

2. How do you know from *The Shortest Novel of Them All?*

3. What about the punch-line: "It's just that their children keep dying"? Why do they die? Is this "the best marriage in town"?

Thinking Exercise

Try to relate at least one detail from the following cartoon to each of your answers to the following questions.

1. What does Mort Walker think of:

    the games people play?

    relations between blacks and whites?

Figure 5-3   Beetle Bailey *by Mort Walker*

what people with different backgrounds can do to get together?

the Civil Rights movement?

the Black Panthers?

the Army?

2. Why does the general think Lieutenant Flap ignorant of games? Whose games are more accepted? Where?

3. Could you find examples in your experience that would also support what Mort Walker says about social games and human nature? You might want to make those examples the subject of your next paper. Describe the games; tell how they are played and how they influence people's attitudes.

Activity Exercise

1. Many magazine ads depend on visual appeal more than verbal appeal. How does the background in this ad—the green plants, the ornate wicker rocking chair and long windows, the general elegance of the room, and the man seated in the chair—work to provide a context that will reinforce the ad's written appeal?

2. The written material in this ad puts the reader right into the dress. How does that help sell the product?

3. What do you think is the unstated assumption of this ad? Do you think everyone accepts this assumption? Do you also think that many people who would *not* accept the assumption might still like the ad and buy the gown? Why?

4. Write an essay in which you explain why some people would go for this ad. Show how specific objects in the ad would work to convince them. You might imagine yourself the composer of the ad. You're trying

Those fabulous day people are fabulous night people, too.

Nightdressing by Vassarette

Case in point: this bareback nightdress. In the most sensuous, exciting fabric of the year... Vassarette's own Quintessence. Our exclusive way with Antron® III nylon. Just a slinky, shimmering streak in knock-out Vassarette colors, about $12. Only the Vassarette name says color- and-fabric expertise like this. Because only a vertical house like Vassarette can make its own fabrics, dye its own colors and coordinate across product lines for dynamic retail presentations. Fabulous. Day and night. **Vassarette**® Bodydressing

SUGGESTED RETAIL PRICES. VASSARETTE BRAS, GIRDLES, LINGERIE/ROBES/LOUNGEWEAR/SWIMWEAR/VASSARETTE JUNIORSP, DIVISION OF MUNSINGWEAR, INC. 261 MADISON AVENUE, NEW YORK CITY

Figure 5-4

Vasserette ad

to get Vassarette to use it. Show them how the ad works, why it would sell liberated as well as traditional women.

5. Write an essay in which you explain how a particular ad works. First, explain the logic of the ad. What are its assumptions? What is the premise or thesis of the ad? And how does the ad complete or answer the expectations which are set up by that premise? You might want to review the material on logic on pages 30–39. Then analyze the emotional appeal of the ad. How does it appeal to particular senses? Do the logical and emotional appeals work together?

Showing another's experience

In 1940 Richard Wright published *Native Son*, an explosive, exciting novel. The novel tells the story of Bigger Thomas, a young black boy who smothers the daughter of his rich, white employer during a fit of fear and rage. After the smothering, Bigger becomes the object of an enormous manhunt that covers the entire city of Chicago; he also becomes a victim of radical white reaction, which makes him an arch-villain, a representative to many reactionary and prejudiced whites of all that was evil in the black man. The novel has become a famous example, since its publication, of a school of literature which holds that a man is often determined by his environment, especially if that environment is a city ghetto that seems to offer no escape, no chance for a better life. In such a novel, the writer must get his reader to feel with, to *empathize* with, the main character. He's got to get the reader *inside* the character's skin. Without that empathy, the story can seem artificial. The struggles of Bigger Thomas then seem distant and extreme. As you read, ask yourself how Wright gets you to empathize. To what senses does he appeal? What sensations do you feel most intensely? How would you characterize and describe the emotions Bigger experiences?

Richard Wright found the facts of this story in an actual news story—the Robert Nixon case—which occurred in Chicago during the 1930s. He took factual newspaper and court reports of the Nixon case, in which a boy similar in age and social condition to Bigger Thomas killed a white woman and became a famous fugitive, and made it into fiction. By fictionalizing the case, he made his black hero, Bigger Thomas, into a symbol of many young black males. Their frustrations and suffering were shared by many readers, both black and white.

Flight

RICHARD WRIGHT

He lowered the paper; he could read no more. The one fact to remember was that eight thousand men, white men, with guns and gas, were out there in the night looking for him. According to this paper, they were but a few blocks away. Could he get to the roof of this building? If so, maybe he could crouch there until they passed. He thought of burying himself deep in the snow of the roof, but he knew that that was impossible. He pulled the chain again and plunged the room in darkness. Using the flashlight, he went to the door and opened it and looked into the hall. It was empty and a dim light burned at the far end. He put out the flashlight and tiptoed, looking at the ceiling, searching for a trapdoor leading to the roof. Finally, he saw a pair of wooden steps leading upward. Suddenly, his muscles stiffened as though a wire strung through his body had jerked him. A siren shriek entered the hallway. And immediately he heard voices, excited, low, tense. From somewhere down below a man called,

"They's comin'!"

There was nothing to do now but go up; he clutched the wooden steps above him and climbed, wanting to get out of sight before anyone came into the hall. He reached the trapdoor and pushed against it with his head; it opened. He grabbed something solid in the darkness above him and hoisted himself upward, hoping as he did so that it would hold him and not let him go crashing down upon the hall floor. He rested on his knees, his chest heaving. Then he eased the door shut, peering just in time to see a door in the hall opening. That was close! The siren sounded again; it was outside in the street. It seemed to sound a warning that no one could hide from it; that action to escape was futile; that soon the men with guns and gas would come and penetrate where the siren sound had penetrated.

He listened; there were throbs of motors; shouts rose from the streets; there were screams of women and curses of men. He heard footsteps on the stairs. The siren died and began again, on a high, shrill note this time. It made him want to clutch at his throat; as long as it sounded it seemed that he could not breathe. He had to get to the roof! He switched on the flashlight and crawled through a narrow loft till he came to an opening. He put his shoulder to it and heaved; it gave so suddenly and easily that he drew back in fear. He thought that someone had snatched it open from above and in the same instant of its opening he saw an expanse of gleaming white snow against the dark smudge of night and a stretch of luminous sky. A medley of crashing sounds came, louder than he had thought that sound could be: horns, sirens, screams. There was hunger in those sounds as they crashed over the roof-tops and chimneys; but under it, low and distinct, he heard voices of fear: curses of men and cries of children.

Yes; they were looking for him in every building and on every floor and in every room. They wanted him. His eyes jerked upward as a huge, sharp beam of yellow light shot into the sky. Another came, crossing it like a knife. Then another. Soon the sky was full of them. They circled slowly, hemming him in; bars of light forming a prison, a wall between him and the rest of the world; bars weaving a shifting wall of light into which he dared not go. He was in the midst of it now; this was what he had been running from ever since that night Mrs. Dalton had come into the room and had charged him with such fear that his hands had gripped the pillow with fingers of steel and had cut off the air from Mary's lungs.

Below him was a loud, heavy pounding, like a far-away rumble of thunder. He had to get to the roof; he struggled upward, then fell flat, in deep soft snow, his eyes riveted upon a white man across the street upon another roof. Bigger watched the man whirl the beam of a flashlight. Would the man look in his direction? Could the beam of a flashlight make him visible from where the man was? He watched the man walk round awhile and then disappear.

Quickly, he rose and shut the trapdoor. To leave it open would create suspicion. Then he fell flat again, listening. There was the sound of many running feet below him. It seemed that an army was thundering up the stairs. There was nowhere he could run to now; either they caught him or they did not. The thundering grew louder and he knew that the men were nearing the top floor. He lifted his eyes and looked in all directions, watching roofs to the left and right of him. He did not want to be surprised by someone creeping upon him from behind. He saw that the roof to his right was not joined to the one upon which he lay; that meant that no one could steal upon him from that direction. The one to his left was joined to the roof of the building upon which he lay, making it one long icy runway. He lifted his head and looked; there were other roofs joined, too. He could run over those roofs, over the snow and round those chimneys until he came to the building that dropped to the ground. Then that would be all. Would he jump off and kill himself? He did not know. He had an almost mystic feeling that if he were ever cornered something in him would prompt him to act the right way, the right way being the way that would enable him to die without shame.

He heard a noise close by; he looked round just in time to see a white face, a head, then shoulders pull into view upon the roof to the right of him. A man stood up, cut sharply against the background of roving yellow lights. He watched the man twirl a pencil of light over the snow. Bigger raised his gun and trained it upon the man and waited; if the light reached him, he would shoot. What would he do afterwards? He did not know. But the yellow spot never reached him. He watched the man go down, feet first, then shoulders and head; he was gone.

He relaxed a bit; at least the roof to his right was safe now. He waited to hear sounds that would tell him that someone was climbing up through the trapdoor. The rumbling below him rose in volume with the passing seconds, but he could not tell if the men were coming closer or receding. He waited and held his gun. Above his head the sky stretched in a cold, dark-blue oval, cupping the city like an iron palm covered with silk. The wind blew, hard, icy, without ceasing. It seemed to him that he had already frozen, that pieces could be broken off him, as one chips bits from a cake of ice. In order to know that he still had the gun in his hand he had to look at it, for his hand no longer had any feeling.

Then he was stiff with fear. There were pounding feet right below him. They were on the top floor now. Ought he to run to the roof to his left? But he had seen no one search that roof; if he ran he might come face to face with someone coming up out of another trapdoor. He looked round, thinking that maybe someone was creeping upon him; but there was nobody. The sound of feet came louder. He put his ear to the naked ice and listened. Yes; they were walking about in the hallway; there were several of them directly under him, near the trapdoor. He looked again to the roof on his left, wanting to run to it and hide; but was afraid. Were they coming up? He listened; but there were so many voices he could not make out the words. He did not want them to surprise him. Whatever happened, he wanted to go down looking into the faces of those that would kill him. Finally, under the terror-song of the siren, the voices came so close that he could hear words clearly.

"God, but I'm tired!"

"I'm cold!"

"I believe we're just wasting time."

"Say, Jerry! You going to the roof this time?"

"Yeah; I'll go."

"That nigger might be in New York by now."

"Yeah. But we better look."

"Say, did you see that brown gal in there?"

"The one that didn't have much on?"

"Yeah."

"Boy, she was a peach, wasn't she?"

"Yeah; I wonder what on earth a nigger wants to kill a white woman for when he has such good-looking women in his own race. . . ."

"Boy, if she'd let me stay here I'd give up this goddamn hunt."

"Come on. Give a lift. You'd better hold this ladder. It seems rickety."

"O.K."

"Hurry up. Here comes the captain."

Bigger was set. Then he was not set. He clung to a chimney that stood a foot from the trapdoor. Ought he to stay flat or stand up? He stood up, pushing against the chimney, trying to merge with it. He held the gun and waited. Was the man coming up? He looked to the roof to his left; it was still empty. But if he ran to it he might meet someone. He heard footsteps in the passage of the loft. Yes; the man was coming. He waited for the trapdoor to open. He held the gun tightly; he wondered if he was holding it too tightly, so tightly that it would go off before he wanted it to. His fingers were so cold that he could not tell how much pressure he was putting behind the trigger. Then, like a shooting star streaking across a black sky, the fearful thought came to him that maybe his fingers were frozen so stiff that he could not pull the trigger. Quickly, he felt his right hand with his left; but even that did not tell him anything. His right hand was so cold that all he felt was one cold piece of flesh touching another. He had to wait and see. He had to have faith. He had to trust himself; that was all.

The trapdoor opened, slightly at first, then wide. He watched it, his mouth open, staring through the blur of tears which the cold wind had whipped into his eyes. The door came all the way open, cutting off his view for a moment, then it fell back softly upon the snow. He saw the bare head of a white man—the back of the head—framed in the narrow opening, stenciled against the yellow glare of the restless bars of light. Then the head turned slightly and Bigger saw the side of a white face. He watched the man, moving like a figure on the screen in close-up slow motion, come out of the hole and stand with his back to him, flashlight in hand. The idea took hold swiftly. Hit him. Hit him! In the head. Whether it would help or not, he did not know and it did not matter. He had to hit this man before he turned that spot of yellow on him and then yelled for the others. In the split second that he saw the man's head, it seemed that an hour passed, an hour filled with pain and doubt and anguish and suspense, filled with the sharp throb of life lived upon a needle point. He lifted his left hand, caught the gun which he held in his right, took it into the fingers of his left hand, turned it round, caught it again in his right and held it by the barrel: all one motion, swift, silent; done in one breath with eyes staring unblinkingly. *Hit him!* He lifted it, high, by the barrel. Yes. *Hit him!* His lips formed the words as he let it come down with a grunt which was a blending of a curse, a prayer and a groan.

He felt the impact of the blow throughout the length of his arm, jarring his flesh slightly. His hand stopped in midair, at the point where the metal of the gun had met the bone of the skull; stopped, frozen, still, as though again about to lift and descend. In the instant, almost of the blow being struck, the white man emitted something like a soft cough; his flashlight fell into the snow, a fast flick of vanishing light. The man fell away from Bigger, on his face, full length in the cushion of snow, like a man falling soundlessly in a deep dream. Bigger was aware of the clicking sound of the metal against the bone of the skull; it stayed on in his ears, faint but distinct, like a sharp bright point lingering on in front of the eyes when a light has gone out suddenly and darkness is everywhere—so the click of the gun handle against the man's head stayed on in his ears. He had not moved from his tracks; his right hand was still extended, upward, in midair; he lowered it, looking at the man, the sound of the metal against bone fading in his ears like a dying whisper.

The sound of the siren had stopped at some time which he did not remember; then it started again, and the interval in which he had not heard it seemed to hold for him some preciously hidden danger, as though for a dreadful moment he had gone to sleep at his post with an enemy near. He looked through the whirling spokes of light and saw a trapdoor open upon the roof to his left. He stood rigid, holding the gun, watching, waiting. If only the man did not see him when he came up! A head came into view; a white man climbed out of the trapdoor and stood in the snow.

He flinched; someone was crawling in the loft below him. Would he be trapped? A voice, a little afraid, called from the open hole through which the man whom he had struck had climbed.

"Jerry!"

The voice sounded clearly in spite of the siren and the clang of the fire wagons.

"Jerry!"

The voice was a little louder now. It was the man's partner. Bigger looked back to the roof to his left; the man was still standing there, flashing a light round. If he would only leave! He had to get away from this trapdoor here. If that man came up to see about his partner and found him sprawled in the snow he would yell before he got a chance to hit him. He squeezed against the chimney, looking at the man on the roof to his left, holding his breath. The man turned, walked toward the trapdoor and climbed through. He waited to hear the door shut; it did. Now, that roof was clear! He breathed a silent prayer.

"Jeeerry!"

With gun in hand, Bigger crept across the roof. He came to a small mound of brick, where the upjutting ridge of the building's flat top joined that of the other. He paused and looked back. The hole was still empty. If he tried to climb over, would the man come out of the hole just in time to see him? He had to take the chance. He grabbed the ledge, hoisted himself upon it, and lay flat for a moment on the ice, then slid to the other side, rolling over. He felt snow in his face and eyes; his chest heaved. He crawled to another chimney and waited; it was so cold that he had a wild wish to merge into the icy bricks of the chimney and have it all over. He heard the voice again, this time loud, insistent:

"Jerry!"

He looked out from behind the chimney. The hole was still empty. But the next time the voice came he knew that the man was coming out, for he could feel the tremor of the voice, as though it were next to him.

"Jerry!"

Then he saw the man's face come through; it was stuck like a piece of white pasteboard above the top of the hole and when the man's voice sounded again Bigger knew that he had seen his partner in the snow.

"Jerry! *Say!*"

Bigger lifted his gun and waited.

"Jerry. . . ."

The man came out of the hole and stood over his partner, then scrambled in again, screaming:

"Say! Say!"

Yes; the man would spread the word. Ought he to run? Suppose he went down into the trapdoor of another roof? Naw! There would be people standing in the hallways and they would be afraid; they would scream at the sight of him and he would be caught. They would be glad to give him up and put an end to this terror. It would be better to run farther over the roofs. He rose; then, just as he was about to run, he saw a head bob up in the hole. Another man came through and stood over Jerry. He was tall and he stooped over Jerry's form and seemed to be putting his hand upon his face. Then another came through. One of the men centered his flashlight on Jerry's body and Bigger saw one bend and roll the body over. The spotlight lit Jerry's face. One of the men ran to the sheer edge of the roof, overlooking the street; his hand went to his mouth and Bigger heard the sound of a whistle, sharp, thin. The roar in the street died; the siren stopped; but the circling columns of yellow continued to whirl. In the peace and quiet of the sudden calm, the man yelled,

"Surround the block!"

Bigger heard an answering shout.

"You got a line on 'im?"

"I think he's round here!"

A wild yell went up. Yes; they felt that they were near him now. He heard the man's shrill whistle sounding again. It got quiet, but not so quiet as before. There were shouts of wild joy floating up.

"Send up a stretcher and a detail of men!"

"O.K.!"

The man turned and went back to Jerry lying in the snow. Bigger heard snatches of talk.

". . . . how do you suppose it happened?"

"Looks like he was hit. . . ."

". . . . maybe he's about. . . ."

"Quick! Take a look over the roof!"

He saw one of the men rise and flash a light. The circling beams lit the roof to a daylight brightness and he could see that one man held a gun. He would have to cross to other roofs before this man or others came upon him. They were suspicious and would comb every inch of space on top of these houses. On all fours, he scrambled to the next ledge and then turned and looked back; the man was still standing, throwing the spot of yellow about over the snow. Bigger grabbed the icy ledge, hoisted himself flat upon it, and slid over. He did not think now of how much strength was neeeded to climb and run; the fear of capture made him forget even the cold, forget even that he had no strength left. From somewhere in him, out of the depths of flesh and blood and bone, he called up energy to run and dodge with but one impulse: he had to elude these men. He was crawling to the other ledge, over the snow, on his hands and knees, when he heard the man yell.

"There he is!"

The three words made him stop; he had been listening for them all night and when they came he seemed to feel the sky crashing soundlessly about him. What was the use of running? Would it not be better to stop, stand up, and lift his hands high above his head in surrender? Hell, naw! He continued to crawl.

"Stop, *you!*"

A shot rang out, whining past his head. He rose and ran to the ledge, leaped over; ran to the next ledge, leaped over it. He darted among the chimneys so that no one could see him long enough to shoot. He looked ahead and saw something huge and round and white looming up in the dark: a bulk rising up sheer from the snow of the roof and swelling in the night, glittering in the glare of the searching knives of light. Soon he would not be able to go much farther, for he would reach that point where the roof ended and dropped to the street below. He wove among the chimneys, his feet slipping and sliding over snow, keeping in mind that white looming bulk which he had glimpsed ahead of him. Was it something that would help him? Could he get upon it, or behind it, and hold them off? He was listening and expecting more shots as he ran, but none came.

He stopped at a ledge and looked back; he saw in the lurid glare of the slashing lances of light a man stumbling over the snow. Ought he to stop and shoot? Naw! More would be coming in a moment and he would only waste time. He had to find some place to hide, some ambush from which he could fight. He ran to another ledge, past the white looming bulk which now towered directly above him, then stopped, blinking: deep down below was a sea of white faces and he saw himself falling, spinning straight down into that ocean of boiling hate. He gripped the icy ledge with his fingers, thinking that if he had been running any faster he would have gone right off the roof, hurtling four floors.

Dizzily, he drew back. This was the end. There were no more roofs over which to run and dodge. He looked; the man was still coming. Bigger stood up. The siren was louder than before and there were more shouts and screams. Yes; those in the streets knew now that the police and vigilantes had trapped him upon the roofs. He remembered the quick glimpse he had had of the white looming bulk; he looked up. Directly above him, white with snow, was a high water tank with a round flat top. There was a ladder made of iron whose slick rungs were coated with ice that gleamed like neon in the circling blades of yellow. He caught hold and climbed. He did not know where he was going; he knew only that he had to hide.

He reached the top of the tank and three shots sang past his head. He lay flat, on his stomach, in snow. He was high above the roof-tops and chimneys now and he had a wide view. A man was climbing over a near-by ledge, and beyond him was a small knot of men, their faces lit to a distinct whiteness by the swinging pencils of light. Men were coming up out of the trapdoor far in front of him and were moving toward him, dodging behind chimneys. He raised the gun, leveled it, aimed, and shot; the men stopped but no one fell. He had missed. He shot again. No one fell. The knot of men broke up and disappeared behind ledges and chimneys. The noise in the street rose in a flood of strange joy. No doubt the sound of the pistol shots made them think that he was shot, captured, or dead.

He saw a man running toward the water tank in the open; he shot again. The man ducked behind a chimney. He had missed. Perhaps his hands were too cold to shoot straight? Maybe he ought to wait until they were closer? He turned his head just in time to see a man climbing over the edge of the roof, from the street side. The man was mounting a ladder which had been hoisted up the side of the building from the ground. He leveled the gun to shoot, but the man got over and left his line of vision, disappearing under the tank.

Why could he not shoot straight and fast enough? He looked in front of him and saw two men running under the tank. There were three men beneath the tank now. They were surrounding him, but they could not come for him without exposing themselves.

A small black object fell near his head in the snow, hissing, shooting forth a white vapor, like a blowing plume, which was carried away from him by the wind. Tear gas! With a movement of his hand he knocked it off the tank. Another came and he knocked it off. Two more came and he shoved them off. The wind blew strong, from the lake. It carried the gas away from his eyes and nose. He heard a man yell.

"Stop it! The wind's blowing it away! He's throwing 'em back!"

The bedlam in the street rose higher; more men climbed through trapdoors to the roof. He wanted to shoot, but remembered that he had but three bullets left. He would shoot when they were closer and he would save one bullet for himself. They would not take him alive.

"Come on down, boy!"

He did not move; he lay with gun in hand, waiting. Then, directly under his eyes, four white fingers caught hold of the icy edge of the water tank. He gritted his teeth and struck the white fingers with the butt of the gun. They vanished and he heard a thud as a body landed on the snow-covered roof. He lay waiting for more attempts to climb up, but none came.

"It's no use fighting, boy! You're caught! Come on down!"

He knew that they were afraid, and yet he knew that it would soon be over, one way or another: they would either capture or kill him. He was surprised that he was not afraid. Under it all some part of his mind was beginning to stand aside; he was going behind his curtain, his wall, looking out with sullen stares of contempt. He was outside of himself now, looking on; he lay under a winter sky lit with tall gleams of whirling light, hearing thirsty screams and hungry shouts. He clutched his gun, defiant, unafraid.

"Tell 'em to hurry with the hose! The nigger's armed!"

What did that mean? His eyes roved, watching for a moving object to shoot at; but none appeared. He was not conscious of his body now; he could not feel himself at all. He knew only that he was lying here with a gun in his hand, surrounded by men who wanted to kill him. Then he heard a hammering noise near by; he looked. Behind the edge of a chimney he saw a trapdoor open.

"All right, boy!" a hoarse voice called. "We're giving you your last chance. Come on down!"

He lay still. What was coming? He knew that they were not going to shoot, for they could not see him. Then what? And while wondering, he knew: a furious whisper of water, gleaming like silver in the bright lights, streaked above his head with vicious force, passing him high in the air and hitting the roof beyond with a thudding drone. They had turned on the water hose; the fire department had done that. They were trying to drive him into the open. The stream of water was coming from behind the chimney where the trapdoor had opened, but as yet the water had not touched him. Above him the rushing stream jerked this way and that; they were trying to reach him with it. Then the water hit him, in the side; it was like the blow of a pile driver. His breath left and he felt a dull pain in his side that spread, engulfing him. The water was trying to push him off the tank; he gripped the edges hard, feeling his strength ebbing. His chest heaved and he knew from the pain that throbbed in him that he would not be able to hold on much longer with water pounding at his body like this. He felt cold, freezing; his blood turned to ice, it seemed. He gasped, his mouth open. Then the gun loosened in his fingers; he tried to grip it again and found that he could not. The water left him; he lay gasping, spent.

"Throw that gun down, boy!"

He gritted his teeth. The icy water clutched again at his body like a giant hand; the chill of it squeezed him like the circling coils of a monstrous boa constrictor. His arms arched. He was behind his curtain now, looking down at himself freezing under the impact of water in sub-zero winds. Then the stream of water veered from his body.

"Throw that gun down, boy!"

He began to shake all over; he let go of the gun completely. Well, this was all. Why didn't they come for him? He gripped the edges of the tank again, digging his fingers into the snow and ice. His strength left. He gave up. He turned over on his back and looked weakly up into the sky through the high shifting lattices of light. This was all. They could shoot him now. Why didn't they shoot? Why didn't they come for him?"

"Throw that gun down, boy!"

They wanted the gun. He did not have it. He was not afraid any more. He did not have strength enough to be.

"Throw that gun down, boy!"

Yes; take the gun and shoot it at them, shoot it empty. Slowly, he stretched out his hand and tried to pick up the gun, but his fingers were too stiff. Something laughed in him, cold and hard; he was laughing at himself. Why didn't they come for him? They were afraid. He rolled his eyes, looking longingly at the gun. Then, while he was looking at it, the stream of hissing silver struck it and whirled it off the tank, out of sight. . . .

"There it is!"

"Come on down, boy! You're through!"

"Don't go up there! He might have another gun!"

"Come on down, boy!"

He was outside of it all now. He was too weak and cold to hold onto the edges of the tank any longer; he simply lay atop the tank, his mouth and eyes open, listening to the stream of water whir above him. Then the water hit him again, in the side; he felt his body sliding over the slick ice and snow. He wanted to hold on, but could not. His body teetered on the edge; his legs dangled in air. Then he was falling. He landed on the roof, on his face, in snow, dazed.

He opened his eyes and saw a circle of white faces; but he was outside of them, behind his curtain, his wall, looking on. He heard men talking and their voices came to him from far away.

"That's him, all right!"
"Get 'im down to the street!"
"The water did it!"
"He seems half-frozen!"
"All right, get 'im down to the street!"

Activity Exercise

1. Richard Wright involves as many of his reader's senses as he can. Notice the sensory appeal in each of the following excerpts from "Flight."

Touch

He reached the trapdoor and *pushed against it with his head*; it opened. He *grabbed something solid* in the darkness above him and *hoisted*, hoping as he did so that it would hold him and not let him go crashing down upon the hall floor.

Hearing

He listened; there were *throbs* of motors; *shouts* rose from the streets; there were *screams* of women and *curses* of men. He *heard footsteps* on the stairs. The *siren died* and *began again*, on a *high, shrill note* this time.

Sight

The trapdoor *opened*, slightly at first, then *wide*. He *watched* it, his *mouth open, staring* through the blur of tears which the cold wind had whipped into his eyes . . . He *saw* the *bare* head of a *white man*—the back of the head—*framed in the narrow opening, stenciled against the yellow glare of the restless bars of light*. Then the head *turned slightly* and Bigger saw the *side of a white face*. He *watched* the man, moving like a figure on the screen in close-up slow motion, come out of the hole and stand with his back to him, flashlight in hand.

Smell

A small black object fell near his head in the snow, hissing, shooting forth a white vapor, like a blowing plume, which was carried away from him by the wind. Tear gas!

General Feelings

> He *felt* the *impact* of the *blow throughout the length of his arm, jarring his flesh slightly.* His hand stopped in midair at the point where the metal of the gun had met the bone of the skull; *stopped, frozen, still,* as though again about *to lift* and *descend.*

Select a paragraph from the story and outline the sensory appeal. Then go back over the passage and try to describe the emotions you think Wright wants you to feel as you read.

2. Point out and explain the function of the cumulative sentences in this passage.

> The trapdoor opened, slightly at first, then wide. He watched it, his mouth open, staring through the blur of tears which the cold wind had whipped into his eyes. The door came all the way open, cutting off his view for a moment, then it fell back softly upon the snow. He saw the bare head of a white man—the back of the head framed in the narrow opening, stenciled against the yellow glare of the restless bars of night.

Can you show how Wright manipulates action and detail to create suspense? Check his verb forms, the way he connects his sentence modifiers to the main action, the way he works from general action back through specific detail. Finally, can you identify the sentence modifiers? Are there absolutes, participial phrases, adjective and adverb phrases and clauses, relative clauses—all adding detail to the main action? (See Appendix I to review the various sentence modifiers, page 403.)

3. Sometimes a writer will use a physical detail as a symbol. In the final pages of this excerpt, for example, Bigger climbs on top of a water tank, which is itself on top of a four-story building. On the tank—looking down on the crowds, the faces of his pursuers and the city for miles around—Bigger is "free" one of the few times in the novel. Yet he is "trapped" as well. The tank might symbolize his being *above* the rest, his seeing the deeper social meaning of his actions and the actions of the white world clearly for the first time. Can you find more evidence for or against this interpretation? Can you point to other concrete objects that become symbols of something Bigger feels or understands?

4. Write a brief, objective news story in which you report to the public what happens in "Flight." Imagine yourself having taken notes from the ground or roof, or from a news helicopter flying close over the scene. *Don't* interpret or make personal comments. Just give the news, the "facts."

5. Go back over your analysis of the sensory detail in this passage and organize your observations under a general thesis about the story or about Bigger Thomas and his adversaries. Write an essay that supports that thesis. Point to ways in which sensory appeal supports meaning. How, for example, does a particular action or gesture help you to define

Bigger Thomas' character? Or you might decide what particular emotion—fear, frenzy or terror—Wright most wants his readers to experience. Then, define that emotion as specifically as you can and show how the story's experience works to create that emotion. How do the sentences, words, symbols, or details contribute to the reader's experiencing that emotion?

6

Sharing . . .
through perspectives

This book helps you write from experience. To give that help we've moved from a very close discussion of raw experience to a careful consideration of experience in words. Now, give some attention to where you put yourself between the two. In other words, consider the perspective you take, both in relation to your readers and to your experience.

Sometimes, as in the excerpt you just read from Richard Wright's *Native Son*, the writer wants his readers to feel a part of the experience he describes. He uses every device he can to thrust the reader into the midst of his subject, to keep him breathing with the character. Such a close identification between reader, author, and story is usually most important in narrative writing, where the writer's main purpose is to share a story, an experience, a piece of life. But even in storytelling the writer wants his readers to step back occasionally in order to observe and evaluate. Most effective writing, especially essay writing, successfully moves the readers back and forth—sometimes bringing them in close, sometimes forcing them back to analyze.

Perspective involves the writer's position. Where are you as you write? Do you put yourself right in the situation, as if you were the main character in a story? Or, are you *distant* from your subject, standing back as an observer, scrutinizing the relationships among parts of your subject, finding causes and effects, analyzing and judging? Most likely, as you write, you'll shift your perspective, moving in close to show a detail or fact and then backing off to think and put things in order.

The materials in this chapter should help you control distance and perspective. We'll begin by considering physical perspectives—where you are as you describe an object or scene, tell a story, or illustrate an idea in an essay. Then we'll move to the more complex problems, what writers often call problems of "distance," and discuss perspective as it relates to your subject and your reader. Often, you'll find writers taking on several different physical perspectives as they describe, inform, or persuade.

Taking on different physical perspectives

We've already talked about how you can use perspective to organize writing. But you can also use perspective to control your readers as well. On the following pages you'll find a collection of five faces—some from photos, others from paintings and magazine illustrations. Look at them closely. Consider what the artist or photographer is trying to say and connect it to the perspective he takes. How might this subject appear from a different angle? From close range? From further away?

Activity Exercise

Figure 6-1

1. This illustration covered nearly an entire page in front of a lead article in a popular magazine. Can you guess what the article was about from the painting? How?

2. Why does the artist bring you in so close to this face? What is the significance of the tear? From this close perspective you can see the eyes, hair texture, and the shape of the lips. What do these details tell you?

3. Does a particular poem, story, or film come to mind when you look at this picture? If you think of a poem, what is the poet's tone? How does he address his readers? Does the poet's intimate use of language cause you to associate the poem with the picture? Might this be a beginning to a melodramatic love story, a satiric comment on contemporary hairstyles, or a tragic story of unrewarded genius?

Figure 6-2

1. Does this photographer try to *flatter* his subject? How can you tell? Is the photograph too candid for flattery?

2. Imagine yourself fifty or sixty feet away from this girl. What would you see in a real-life situation that you don't see in this photo? Would she be tall? Fat? "Just average"?

3. Can you find details in this girl's appearance that tell you more about her? How about her expression? Does it tell you anything about her personality? Does the way she has her hair tell you something of her "style"—the way she walks and appears in general?

Figure 6-3

1. The photographer caught this boy in the midst of a gesture. Write an objective sketch of the boy as he appears here in which you limit yourself to the perspective in the photograph. Imagine yourself watching the boy from about the same position as the photographer. Perhaps you'll want to imagine this gesture as part of a longer action.

2. Write a brief essay in which you describe this boy's personality and character. You'll want to begin with a general description of the impression you have of the boy from the photograph. If you feel the boy is gentle, delicate, and quiet, then point to physical details that will reinforce that impression.

3. Write a narrative in which you tell a brief story about this boy. Pick an action or series of actions that you feel will capture the boy's character. Find a beginning, middle, and end, and write sentences that follow your subject closely through the actions. Try to vary your physical perspectives. Bring the reader in close to show revealing details: the way his hair lies thinly on his forehead; the full, round bulge of his cheeks; the fine line of his fingers. Then, bring your readers back to watch from a distance as the boy carries out a gesture or action. Be sure, however, that your reader will not be *shocked* by your shifts in perspectives. Carry him along easily.

Figures 6-4 and 6-5

1. Both these figures show people who are expressing attitudes with their bodies. Could you write captions for both photographs that would capture their attitudes? Point to a few facial details to verify your caption.

2. Figure 6-5 shows consumer crusader, Ralph Nader, at a 1973 news conference on the energy crisis. How would you say Nader feels about reporters? About the energy crisis? Why do you think this photographer caught Nader in this position? Why is the photographer's perspective important in capturing Nader's attitude? Imagine yourself writing an interview with Ralph Nader. Compose two opening paragraphs to intro-

duce Nader to your readers and to set a context for the interview. You'll be setting the tone for the entire interview in these paragraphs. Or, you might want to do the same type of interview with a personal friend. Set up the interview in two carefully-drawn descriptive paragraphs.

3. Have another student in your class be the subject for two written sketches. One should be from far away, say, from a second- or third-story window as he or she walks from the building. The second should be from close range, perhaps two or three feet away. Try to rework your notes into a sketch that smoothly combines the distant and close perspectives. You might prepare for both observations by imagining that you're about to take a picture.

The camera's angle

About fifty-five years ago D. W. Griffith made *Birth of a Nation*, a controversial film about the effects of the Civil War and the reconstruction of the South. The film has often been censured for its racist attitudes toward the war and its biased Southern slant on historical events. But very few question Griffith's technical skills. In fact, Griffith has become one of the most influential filmmakers in the history of film.

Griffith's way of showing battles on screen provides an excellent example of how an artist can control physical perspective. During the battle scenes, Griffith would move his camera back and forth, sometimes in close to emphasize how individual soldiers performed and suffered and fought in battle and sometimes from a distance to show the general panorama of battle—the rows of canons firing, the smoke billowing across the fields, infantry charges and countercharges, the sea of men moving this way and that. The result is a film that gives a more complete, more humane view of war than had ever been produced before; some critics feel the effect has never been matched.

You may not write about subjects as grand as the Civil War, but you can learn nonetheless from Griffith. Be conscious of where you are when you write. If you're covering a campus event for the college newspaper, don't just describe from a distance, like an omniscient god who doesn't have the time to bother with the little things. Look around you. Find a few specifics—a person in the crowd at a football game, the way the guitarist prepares for a performance at a rock concert—and mix them in with your general observations. Then, you'll bring your readers into a real-life situation, seen specifically from close range as well as generally from a distance. We've all heard about people who can't see the forest for the trees. A writer must be careful not to limit his scope. Seeing only "forest" or only "trees" produces tired, dull writing.

Activity Exercise

1. Write an essay in which you describe the character of Van Gogh. Look closely at his portrait first. Then write as if you were introducing him as a character in a novel. Describe him as he walks down a street, looks in a shop window, or sits on a park bench. Don't *tell* the reader his character; let him *infer* it from what he sees as he reads.

2. Imagine that you are Van Gogh and that you've just been badly treated by a waitress in a restaurant. Write two descriptions: one in which you describe the scene in the restaurant as it happens, using the first person ("I"); the second in which you describe your thoughts about the waitress's rude behavior. Base your role-playing on the character traits you detect in the portrait of Van Gogh.

3. Describe the portrait from two different perspectives. First, you might imagine yourself watching Van Gogh as he paints in a public park across the street from your front window. Describe his actions and gestures as specifically as you can. Second, you might imagine yourself

Figure 6-6

Self-Portrait
by Van Gogh

Courtesy The National Gallery of Art, Washington, D.C. Chester Dale Collection.

sitting close by him on a park bench. Again, capture as much specific action and detail as possible.

Journal Exercise

Travel about and find a place where you will be able to sit and observe the people around you: a shopping center mall, somewhere on campus, the student union, a park bench, almost any public place that will not attract attention to you as you observe. After you have observed several people, select one person whom you are fairly sure will make an interesting subject. Take notes on his physical characteristics and, as far as you can, on the way those characteristics affect you. Reorganize your materials in order to communicate a dominant impression. You might, for example, go through a list of general, descriptive adjectives until you find the right one for your subject. Then keep the adjective before you as you redesign and elaborate your material.

From physical perspective to expository distance

We write exposition to *inform* readers—to show them why an experience makes us hold a certain opinion, or to explain why or how something is done. Often we use description and narration to support or clarify a thesis or opinion in exposition. The designer or architect, for example, might describe a particular building to illustrate his plan for a new structure. Or a politician might provide an elaborate description of the results of a policy used in another city to convince his constituents to vote against a certain measure.

There are differences between writing that tries only to *share* the subject with others and writing used in an expository essay where the main purpose is to develop an opinion or idea. Primarily, those differences depend upon the writer's intention. The expository writer wants his readers to analyze; he never wants his subject to "take over," to captivate his readers to the degree that they lose their ability to follow his reasoning. The novelist, on the other hand, hopes his readers will "lose themselves" in his novel; he wants them to experience the action intensely, to share the character's emotions, to receive the experience firsthand.

Often, these different aims lead to different distances between the writer and his subject. The expository writer keeps his distance. He always makes sure that what he describes or narrates clearly supports an idea or opinion. He doesn't want to involve his readers entirely. He shows them where and why as he describes.

Writing Exercise

Go back over a recent event. Let it take shape in rough-draft form. Find your subject's intrinsic unity, develop it, illustrate it. Write so that your readers will feel a part of the experience. Then, find and refine a thesis statement about the event. See it as part of a larger whole. Perhaps a bit of classroom dialogue between a man and woman will represent to you part of a general tendency toward the breaking up of traditional sex roles. Now rewrite the experience as an expository essay. Introduce the general problem, state your thesis clearly somewhere in the essay, and be sure the connections between your experience and your thesis are clear. Above all, be sure that your readers "keep their distance." Don't let them become so involved that they miss the point. Let your purpose guide the way your readers receive the experience.

Perspective and audience: Distance in advertising

Ads are meant to sell products. To sell they must entertain *and* inform. Many ads, as the critics of advertising in the mass media tell us, do more entertaining than they do informing. But the best ads do give us information, although admittedly persuasive, and they give us that information without heavy doses of seriousness, often with wit and lightness. Because of advertising's three purposes—to *entertain,* to *inform,* and to *persuade*—specific ads can provide us with useful subjects for analysis. They provide especially useful ways to study *distance*—the perspectives writers take toward their audience.

We've already mentioned that a writer uses two kinds of perspective: a physical perspective (I'll describe this building as if I were standing beside the building across the street); and a mental perspective (I'll describe the fashion show as if I were someone who hated clothes). In other words, we develop perspectives toward both our subjects *and* our readers. Often one influences the other.

Just as we vary physical perspectives to fit our subject and our purpose, so we can vary the way we treat our audiences. There are probably as many potential distances between writers and readers as there are specific writing situations. But such choices are open only to those writers who recognize certain basic principles. Let's assume, for the sake of simplicity, that there are about four possible distances between a writer and his readers:

1. intimate
2. friendly but not too friendly
3. businesslike
4. very serious

(These categories are approximations, not exact descriptions; few writers begin by deciding that they'll be "friendly but not too friendly" with their readers.) As you write, you make decisions. Perhaps you use a contraction. Then you decide to put words in their normal subject-verb order rather than use inversions or fancy word-orders. Then, further along, you avoid a piece of slang—perhaps you replace *creepy* with *weird*. Near the end, you use an exclamation point rather than a simple period. You've probably created, perhaps without realizing it, a "friendly but not too friendly" distance between yourself and your readers.

How might you have created a "very serious" distance with that same piece of writing? You may have avoided contractions, written a few sentences in which you changed normal word order, replaced the exclamation point with a period, and rewritten a sentence in less direct language. Here are some simple definitions of the four distances we've been describing.

Intimate

The writer stays very close to the reader, treats him like an old friend, and uses language he would use only with very close friends. An intimate distance is characterized by very *talky* language and by *ellipsis*—leaving out certain words and phrases, using shortcuts and abbreviated descriptions because you know your reader knows what you are talking about. Intimate distance is also marked by stories that begin in the middle because the reader knows the background.

Friendly But Not Too Friendly

The writer treats his reader like an everyday acquaintance, someone that he doesn't have to talk fancy to, but someone who will need careful information and the whole story. This distance is marked by talky language—contractions, normal word order and plenty of practical examples. But the writer also assumes the reader must be won over by careful support and description, by sincere attempts to share on paper.

Businesslike

The writer's main concern is to give information on how to do something or on the latest sales statistics in his business. A businesslike distance usually assumes that the reader is interested, that he wants to be informed, and that he doesn't need to be motivated. The language itself is usually talky and natural, but precise. The writer may be friendly, but he's very careful to fill his writing with examples, illustrations, and definitions.

Very Serious

The writer writes as if he were speaking to a large group of prestigious people on a very serious subject. He uses no contractions, exclamation points, or very personal pronouns, but he does use many long sentences with carefully worked-out word orders and public figures of speech—"My Fellow Americans . . . ," "I believe that in this country . . . ," "Give me liberty or give me death." Very serious writing usually uses parallelism (repeated sentence structures for different ideas). A very serious distance is absurdly funny when it doesn't fit the situation; it is very effective when it does.

Color figure 6-7
VOLKSWAGEN AD
follows page 158.

Rather than go through numerous complex examples of these distances, let's turn to the way distance is used in advertising. Look at and read the Volkswagen ad. Keep the four approximations of distance before you as you read. Then do some thinking about how the ad works, what it appeals to in its readers, how it treats the product and, most importantly, how it uses distance to persuade.

Most ads combine sensory and intellectual appeals. The viewer/reader is put into a very concrete situation in which he is asked to identify with the picture he sees and then to adopt the pattern of thinking outlined in the written ad.

Here the ad-writers present a family in a conventional scene—in front of a suburban two-car garage, beside a neat, sprawling lawn. On a purely visual level, the viewer shares in the good fortune of the new car owners. He imagines himself in the scene he sees. The ad-writer usually builds directly upon the picture that accompanies what he writes. The picture puts the reader in the right frame of mind; the words provide the clinchers.

Most of us are sophisticated about ads. We often ridicule the worst and enjoy the best. That makes the ad-writer's job difficult. He doesn't really have a clear idea of his audience. If he is too simple, too interested in the hard sell, he might offend his audience, especially those who take pride in feeling superior to ads, those who are insulted by "common" appeals. The writer of this ad, for example, can't assume that all his readers want to be part of the conventional family scene in the picture. He'll want to sell the unconventional buyer as well as the conventional family man. On the other hand, many in his audience will want the security, the quiet suburban comfort they see in the picture. Look at the words in the ad. How does the ad-writer address his audience? What is his distance from his readers? What does he assume they want? How does he treat them?

First, remember the subject—the product. Volkswagens aren't luxury cars. You don't order power windows, brakes, and steering with a Volkswagen. You can't show off the latest gimmick, the widest tailfin. This ad, then, emphasizes practicality. The car is small and cheap, but roomy. It doesn't waste gas, yet offers a good deal of luxury—private entrances for everyone in the family, even plush seats, thick carpeting, and automatic transmission. "Who will ever know you are driving a Volkswagen?"

But more important than what the ad-writer emphasizes in his product is *how* he handles the words. He stays somewhere between *intimate* and *friendly but not too friendly*. He begins with a casual question, as if we all were thinking the same thing as we looked at the picture. Then an elliptical sentence is offered in answer (he leaves the *Is this* out of "A Volkswagen with a private entrance for everyone?"), as if we were still inside his mind thinking along with him, old friends talking over a familiar scene. Then "Yep"—a friendly, even neighborly confirmation.

The casual, intimate opening brings writer and reader together. Now the ad moves to a *friendly but not too friendly* pitch. We get some facts, some concrete and practical descriptions of the car. The words and sentences are still casual, but now the writer mixes in facts and doesn't assume quite as much agreement from his readers. He gives some *showing* facts, but keeps the talky, casual style—"You'll find more luxury than you've ever laid eyes on."

Finally, the clinching line tells us that we can get luxury without even paying for it: "But maybe the best reason for driving a luxury Volkswagen is the most obvious reason: Who will ever know you're driving a Volkswagen?" This is the longest sentence in the ad and the most complex; it contains two parallel thoughts put together with a colon.

What can we say in summary about the writing in this ad? Above all, the writer maintains a consistently friendly, sometimes intimate, distance. He's *close* to his readers, a friend who shares their thoughts and wishes. Still, he knows enough not to ignore all the facts—that would slight even his friends. And he finishes with a more formal, *businesslike* sentence to make his readers feel they've been somewhere, been shown something valuable and true. The person who would feel insulted by an outrightly persuasive ad that said the Volkswagen was better than any other car instead shares the joke of the ad-writer about having luxuries without paying for them. He feels superior to the person who *does* pay for them. Yet the person who does want comfort and luxury gets some detailed descriptions of luxury items. And through it all the language is never too pushy, always friendly.

Activity Exercise

1. Write a step-by-step analysis of an ad found in a newspaper or popular magazine. Begin with a general statement which describes how the ad works. Then analyze the picture and words systematically to support your generalization. Consider the writer's words. How are they supposed to affect the potential buyer? How would you classify the distance between writer and reader?

2. Find a picture in a magazine or newspaper that you can use as background to an ad of your own. Imagine yourself trying to sell one of the items in the picture. Ask yourself what type of buyer you want to reach and what distance you should maintain between yourself and your reader. Then write the ad.

3. Find ads that you think use different distances: one that treats the reader very simply, or uses the brag and hard-sell approach, or tries to be witty and crafty, or tries to flatter the potential buyer by making him feel superior to other people or the product itself. Write a paper in which you compare the ads, making special note of how the distances between writer and reader are different and why.

4. Choose an object that you own and like very much. Or one that you would like to own and can observe closely. Then write an ad that you think will sell the object to someone else. Find the right distance and present the product in a way that highlights what you like about it.

5. *Parody* is writing that imitates in order to ridicule. Sometimes a writer has such a distinctive voice—for example, Twain, Hemingway or

Tom Wolfe—that critics can easily parody his style with only slight exaggeration or a transfer of context. Imagine, for instance, a funeral service conducted in Tom Wolfe's ironic, wise-cracking style. Try to write a parody of the Brut ad that appears below. Or take another cosmetic and use an exaggerated version of the language in the Brut ad to write your own ad.

Thinking Exercise

Do you think a male who lacked self-confidence would actually buy Brut? Does the verbal message suggest more than appears on the surface? Consider especially "For after shave, after shower, after anything!" To what kind of audience is this ad aimed? What makes you feel that it belongs in *Playboy* magazine? Does this ad underestimate its audience? Find reasons in the ad for your answer.

Showing and telling together

Exposition is writing that *informs*. It tells readers how and why. Narration is writing that *shares*. It shows readers what and why. But the best writing usually can't be classified. It is *both* expository *and* narrative. It shows *and* tells.

Bold new Brut for men. By Fabergé.

If you have any doubts about yourself try something else.

Figure 6-8

Brut advertisement

For after shave, after shower, after anything! **Brut.**

We said before that many effective writers link together stories and ideas. The story helps them to share with their readers the details and feelings of an experience. If they are trying to make a point about the sewage facilities where they live, they write a little story about how those facilities affected them one day. That way the readers know in detail what happened and why. They *share* some everyday result of those sewage facilities.

But the story about the local sewage facilities isn't in itself enough. Readers need to know *why* that little story is important. How does it relate to them? What does it suggest should be done about local sewage facilities? And is this little story really about to happen to them as well?

The wise writer combines a showing experience with some telling facts and opinions. He shares an experience and brings the point home with some straightforward, hard-hitting expository sentences. Or he winds up his essay with a few careful, suggestive sentences that lead the reader to his opinion quietly, without pushing too hard.

As you write, think about how you put together experience and opinions. Try always to show *and* tell. And try as well to connect your descriptions and narratives of experience with clear and honest ideas and opinions. When you're finished writing, ask someone else, a neutral third-party, to read your essay. Then ask him if he can follow your writing as it moves from showing to telling, from *what* happened to *why* it happened, from narration to opinion.

Look at the following essays. Both are excellent examples of writing that shows and tells. In the first essay, Henry James describes Chartres Cathedral, a famous and beautiful French church. Notice how he puts together objectively descriptive sentences of *how* and *what* he observed with statements of opinion and idea-sentences. In the second, George Orwell tells a story about a visit he once made to a Welsh coal mine. His very exact narrative is artfully mixed with expository statements which explain how he, and hopefully the reader, feels about coal mines and the hard life of coal miners.

[Description of Chartres Cathedral]

HENRY JAMES

I spent a long time looking at Chartres Cathedral. I revolved around it, like a moth around a candle; I went away and I came back; I chose

---

[Description of Chartres Cathedral] From Henry James, "Chartres Portrayed: Letter from Henry James, Jr.," *New York Daily Tribune,* Vol. XXXVI, No. 10,946 (April 29, 1876), p. 3.

twenty different standpoints; I observed it during the different hours of the day, and saw it in the moonlight as well as the sunshine. I gained, in a word, a certain sense of familiarity with it; and yet I despair of giving any coherent account of it. Like most French cathedrals, it rises straight out of the street, and is without that setting of turf and trees and deaneries and canonries which contribute so largely to the impressiveness of the great English churches. Thirty years ago a row of old houses was glued to its base and made their back walls of its sculptured sides. These have been plucked away, and, relatively speaking, the church is fairly isolated. But the little square that surrounds it is regretfully narrow, and you flatten your back against the opposite houses in the vain attempt to stand off and survey the towers. The proper way to look at the towers would be to go up in a balloon and hang poised, face to face with them, in the blue air. There is, however, perhaps an advantage in being forced to stand so directly under them, for this position gives you an overwhelming impression of their height. I have seen, I suppose, churches as beautiful as this one, but I do not remember ever to have been so touched and fascinated by architectural beauty. The endless upward reach of the great west front, the clear, silvery tone of its surface, the way a few magnificent features are made to occupy its vast serene expanse, its simplicity, majesty, and dignity—these things crowd upon one's sense with a force that makes the act of vision seem for the moment almost all of life. The impressions produced by architecture lend themselves as little to interpretation by another medium as those produced by music. Certainly there is something of the beauty of music in the sublime proportions of the facade of Chartres.

The doors are rather low, as those of the English cathedral are apt to be, but (standing three together) are set in a deep framework of sculpture—rows of arching grooves, filled with admirable little images, standing with their heels on each other's heads. The church, as it now exists, except the northern tower, are full of the grotesqueness of the period. Above the triple portals is a vast round-topped window, in three divisions, of the grandest dimensions and the stateliest effect. Above this window is a circular aperture, of huge circumference, with a double row of sculptured spokes radiating from its centre and looking on its lofty field of stone as expansive and symbolic as if it were the wheel of Time itself. Higher still is a little gallery with a delicate balustrade, supported on a beautiful cornice and stretching across the front from tower to tower; and above this is a range of niched statues of kings—fifteen, I believe, in number. Above the statues is a gable, with an image of the Virgin and Child on its front, and another of Christ on its apex. In the relation of all these parts there is such a spaciousness and harmony that while on the one side the eye rests on a great many broad stretches of naked stone there is no approach on the other to over profusion of detail . . .

The inside of the cathedral corresponds in vastness and grandeur to the outside—it is the perfection of Gothic in its prime. But I looked at it rapidly, the place was so intolerably cold. It seemed to answer one's query of what becomes of the Winter when the Spring chases it away.

Thinking Exercise

1. As he writes his description of the Cathedral, James tells us how he returned many times and observed from many different perspectives. What do these little facts do for the rest of the essay?

2. Can you point to other places in the essay where James varies physical perspective, bringing his readers in close to the church and then back out for a long-range view?

3. James is fairly objective in this description. Can you, however, find places where a word or sentence does communicate an attitude? What do you think James thinks of Chartres? Is he breath-taken by its beauty? Does he find it an interesting historical monument? Or is he always the objective scientist?

4. Is James ever successful in giving you a complete, factual picture of the cathedral? Can you imagine the whole thing visually? Why or why not? Find a picture, perhaps several, of Chartres and compare it to James' written sketch. What does the picture capture that James misses? What does James get across that the picture misses?

from *The Road to Wigan Pier*

GEORGE ORWELL

When you go down a coal mine it is important to try and get to the coal face when the "fillers" are at work. This is not easy, because when the mine is working visitors are a nuisance and are not encouraged, but if you go at any other time, it is possible to come away with a totally wrong impression. On a Sunday, for instance, a mine seems almost peaceful. The time to go there is when the machines are roaring and the air is black with coal dust, and when you can actually see what the miners have to do. At those times the place is like hell, or at any rate like my own mental picture of hell. Most of the things one imagines in hell are there—heat, noise, confusion, darkness, foul air, and, above all, unbearably cramped space. Everything except the fire, for there is no fire down there except the feeble beams of Davy lamps and electric torches which scarcely penetrate the clouds of coal dust.

When you have finally got there—and getting there is a job in itself: I will explain that in a moment—you crawl through the last line of pit props and see opposite you a shiny black wall three or four feet high. This is the coal face. Overhead is the smooth ceiling made by the rock from which the coal has been cut; underneath is the rock again, so that the

From *The Road to Wigan Pier* by George Orwell. Reprinted by permission of Harcourt, Brace Jovanovich Inc.

gallery you are in is only as high as the ledge of coal itself, probably not much more than a yard. The first impression of all, overmastering everything else for a while, is the frightful, deafening din from the conveyor belt which carries the coal away. You cannot see very far, because the fog of coal dust throws back the beam of your lamp, but you can see on either side of you the line of half-naked kneeling men, one to every four or five yards, driving their shovels under the fallen coal and flinging it swiftly over their left shoulders. They are feeding it on to the conveyor belt, a moving rubber belt a couple of feet wide which runs a yard or two behind them. Down this belt a glittering river of coal races constantly. In a big mine it is carrying away several tons of coal every minute. It bears it off to some place in the main roads where it is shot into tubs holding half a ton, and thence dragged to the cages and hoisted to the outer air.

It is impossible to watch the "fillers" at work without feeling a pang of envy for their toughness. It is a dreadful job that they do, an almost superhuman job by the standards of an ordinary person. For they are not only shifting monstrous quantities of coal, they are also doing it in a position that doubles or trebles the work. They have got to remain kneeling all the while—they could hardly rise from their knees without hitting the ceiling—and you can easily see by trying it what a tremendous effort this means. Shoveling is comparatively easy when you are standing up, because you can use your knee and thigh to drive the shovel along; kneeling down, the whole of the strain is thrown upon your arm and belly muscles. And the other conditions do not exactly make things easier. There is the heat—it varies, but in some mines it is suffocating—and the coal dust that stuffs up your throat and nostrils and collects along your eyelids, and the unending rattle of the conveyor belt, which in that confined space is rather like the rattle of a machine gun. . . .

Probably you have to go down several coal mines before you can get much grasp of the processes that are going on round you. This is chiefly because the mere effort of getting from place to place makes it difficult to notice anything else. In some ways it is even disappointing, or at least is unlike what you have expected. You get into the cage, which is a steel box about as wide as a telephone box and two or three times as long. It holds ten men, but they pack it like pilchards in a tin, and a tall man cannot stand upright in it. The steel door shuts upon you, and somebody working the winding gear above drops you into the void. You have the usual momentary qualm in your belly and a bursting sensation in your ears, but not much sensation of movement till you get near the bottom, when the cage slows down so abruptly that you could swear it is going upward again. In the middle of the run the cage probably touches sixty miles an hour; in some of the deeper mines it touches even more. When you crawl out at the bottom you are perhaps four hundred yards under ground. That is to say you have a tolerable-sized mountain on top of you; hundreds of yards of solid rock, bones of extinct beasts, subsoil, flints, roots of growing things, green grass and cows grazing on it—all this suspended over your head and held back only by wooden props as thick as the calf of your leg. But because of the speed at which the cage has brought you down, and the complete blackness through which you have traveled, you hardly feel yourself deeper down than you would at the bottom of the Piccadilly tube.

What *is* surprising, on the other hand, is the immense horizontal distances that have to be traveled underground. Before I had been down a mine I had vaguely imagined the miner stepping out of the cage and getting to work on a ledge of coal a few yards away. I had not realized that before he even gets to his work he may have to creep through passages as long as from London Bridge to Oxford Circus. In the beginning, of course, a mine shaft is sunk somewhere near a seam of coal. But as that seam is worked out and fresh seams are followed up, the workings get farther and farther from the pit bottom. If it is a mile from the pit bottom to the coal face, that is probably an average distance; three miles is a fairly normal one; there are even said to be a few mines where it is as much as five miles. But these distances bear no relation to distances above ground. For in all that mile or three miles as it may be, there is hardly anywhere outside the main road, and not many places even there, where a man can stand upright.

You do not notice the effect of this till you have gone a few hundred yards. You start off, stooping slightly, down the dim-lit gallery, eight or ten feet wide and about five high, with the walls built up with slabs of shale, like the stone walls in Derbyshire. Every yard or two there are wooden props holding up the beams and girders; some of the girders have buckled into fantastic curves under which you have to duck. Usually it is bad going underfoot—thick dust or jagged chunks of shale, and in some mines where there is water it is as mucky as a farmyard. Also there is the track for the coal tubs, like a miniature railway track with sleepers a foot or two apart, which is tiresome to walk on. Everything is gray with shale dust; there is a dusty fiery smell which seems to be the same in all mines. You see mysterious machines of which you never learn the purpose, and bundles of tools slung together on wires, and sometimes mice darting away from the beam of the lamps. They are surprisingly common, especially in mines where there are or have been horses. It would be interesting to know how they got there in the first place; possibly by falling down the shaft—for they say a mouse can fall any distance uninjured, owing to its surface area being so large relative to its weight. You press yourself against the wall to make way for lines of tubs jolting slowly toward the shaft, drawn by an endless steel cable operated from the surface. You creep through sacking curtains and thick wooden doors which, when they are opened, let out fierce blasts of air. These doors are an important part of the ventilation system. The exhausted air is sucked out of one shaft by means of fans, and the fresh air enters the other of its own accord. But if left to itself the air will take the shortest way round, leaving the deeper workings unventilated; so all short-cuts have to be partitioned off.

At the start to walk stooping is rather a joke, but it is a joke that soon wears off. I am handicapped by being exceptionally tall, but when the roof falls to four feet or less if it is a tough job for anybody except a dwarf or a child. You have not only got to bend double, you have also got to keep your head up all the while so as to see the beams and girders and dodge them when they come. You have, therefore, a constant crick in the neck, but this is nothing to the pain in your knees and thighs. After half a mile it becomes (I am not exaggerating) an unbearable agony. You begin to wonder whether you will ever get to the end—still more, how on earth you are going to get back. Your pace grows slower and slower. You come to a stretch of a couple of hundred yards where it is all exceptionally low and you have to work yourself along in a squatting position. Then suddenly the roof opens out to a mysterious height—scene of an old fall of rock, probably—and for twenty whole yards you can stand upright. The relief is overwhelming. But after this there is another low stretch of a hundred yards and then a succession of beams which you have to crawl under. You go down on all fours; even this is a relief after the squatting business. But when you come to the end of the beams and try to get up again, you find that your knees have temporarily struck work and refuse to lift you. You call a halt, ignominiously, and say that you would like to rest for a minute or two. Your guide (a miner) is sympathetic. He knows that your muscles are not the same as his. "Only another four hundred yards," he says encouragingly; you feel that he might as well say another four hundred miles. But finally you do somehow creep as far as the coal face. You have gone a mile and taken the best part of an hour; a miner would do it in not much more than twenty minutes. Having got there, you have to sprawl in the coal dust and get your strength back for several minutes before you can even watch the work in progress with any kind of intelligence.

Coming back is worse than going, not only because you are already tired out but because the journey back to the shaft is probably slightly uphill. You get through the low places at the speed of a tortoise, and you have no shame now about calling a halt when your knees give way. Even the lamp you are carrying becomes a nuisance and probably when you stumble you drop it; whereupon, if it is a Davy lamp, it goes out. Ducking the beams becomes more and more of an effort, and sometimes you forget to duck. You try walking head down as the miners do, and then you bang your backbone. Even the miners bang their backbones fairly often. This is the reason why in very hot mines, where it is necessary to go about half naked, most of the miners have what they call "buttons down the back"—that is, a permanent scab on each vertebra. When the track is downhill the miners sometimes fit their clogs, which are hollow underneath, on to the trolley rails and slide down. In mines where the "traveling" is very bad all the miners carry sticks about two and a half feet long, hollowed out below the handle. In normal places you keep your hand on top of the stick and in the low places you slide your hand down into the hollow. These sticks are a great help, and the wooden crash-helmets—a comparatively recent invention—are a godsend. They look like a French or Italian steel helmet, but they are made of some kind of pith and very light, and so strong that you can take a violent blow on the head without feeling it. When finally you get back to the surface you have been perhaps three hours underground and traveled two miles, and you are more exhausted than you would be by a twenty-five mile walk above ground. For a week afterward your thighs are so stiff that coming downstairs is quite a difficult feat; you have to work your way down in a peculiar sidelong manner, without bending the knees. Your miner friends notice the stiffness of your walk and chaff you about it. ("How'd ta like to work down pit, eh?" etc.) Yet even a miner who has been long away from work—from illness, for instance—when he comes back to the pit, suffers badly for the first few days.

Thinking Exercise

1. Take a very close look at Orwell's opening paragraph. You won't find any thesis statement there, just some introductory facts about coal mines and a few appeals to your senses—how the coal dust is penetrated by the feeble light of Davy lamps and so forth. But can you already imagine what Orwell's thesis is? How does he feel about coal mines, even in this one paragraph? Could you write out the thesis of this paragraph in one sentence? Does it suggest the thesis of the entire essay?

2. Find a single sentence in the essay which you believe comes closest to the general thesis of the entire essay. Then look through the essay to find specifics, especially ones that appeal to your senses, that support that thesis.

3. In the third paragraph Orwell tries to put you inside the skin of a "filler"—the men who shovel coal onto conveyor belts. What devices does he use to accomplish this? Notice, especially, the pronouns he uses. How successful is he in getting you to feel with the fillers and why? Analyze a sentence like this: "They have got to remain kneeling all the while—they could hardly rise from their knees without hitting the ceiling—and you can easily see by trying it what a tremendous effort this means." How does this sentence bring you into the fillers' skin?

4. As you read the essay, make brief sample lists of Orwell's showing and telling sentences. You'll find many more showing than telling sentences. How does Orwell connect the showing parts of his essay—the sentences and paragraphs that share concrete experiences and appeal directly to the senses—with the telling parts—those that develop an opinion or general attitude about coal mines?

Writing distances and perspectives

Painters often experiment with visual perspectives. They move around as they sketch their plans, taking on different angles of vision, different perspectives, just as Henry James experimented with different perspectives as he described Chartres Cathedral.

Paul Klee, in *Slight Danger at Sea,* has sketched in barest detail his visual impression of two small ships in rough seas. As you look over the painting on the following page, ask yourself what Klee tries to capture. What emotions does he emphasize? Do you think he limits himself to a single visual perspective? Or has he combined in one picture the details of many vantage points? Compare Klee's picture with a more realistic picture of a sailing ship in rough seas—say, a Yankee Clipper ship.

Activity Exercise

1. Put yourself in the place of one of the figures in the boats in Klee's sketch. What is he feeling? How can you tell? Try writing a couple of paragraphs of *objective* description of this scene. Then try a few narrative paragraphs, in which you put yourself in the place of one of the human figures and tell a little story. Select and use only a few concrete details; let your imagination go and try to write adventurously. Remember to consider where *you* are as you tell your story and what distance you want from your audience.

2. Imagine yourself flying over the scene in Klee's drawing in a rescue helicopter. The two small boats bob below you. Describe what you see.

3. Now try an expository exercise. Look over the drawing and try to come up with an opinion that you can support—either an opinion on what is actually happening in the painting or some interpretation of what the painting means. Then put together in one essay your telling, expository sentences and your showing, descriptive sentences. Remember to reinforce your opinions with what you see; be sure to relate your sentences to one another.

4. As a class, decide on a common subject for a collage. Then each student should bring in one item—either a picture, a headline from a newspaper, an advertising photo, or a small everyday object—to contribute to a larger collage. Design, compose and arrange the items into a collage, keeping the agreed-upon subject in mind.

5. Either agree or disagree with one of these interpretations of what Paul Klee intended when he created *Slight Danger at Sea.*

Figure 6-9

Slight Danger at Sea
by Paul Klee

Courtesy of the Klee-Stiftung, Berne.

"This painting is a joke. It is meant to fool people into thinking it has meaning when it's just nonsense."

"There are several different perspectives in this painting. The idea is to notice them and see their visual relationships. Then you begin to see what good painting is all about."

Remember to point to specifics in the work for support. You don't have to mention the interpretation you choose in your paper in exact words, but be sure to illustrate and fully explain just what the interpretation means.

6. Write an expository comparison of *Slight Danger at Sea* and another painting in this book. Consider both important similarities and differences. Focus either on what is in the paintings—their content—or on how they are done—their technique.

The generating eye . .

IV

Working from
sentences to paragraphs

generate: 1. to bring into existence; cause to be. 2. to reproduce; procreate. 3. to produce by a chemical process. 4. to create by a vital or natural process. 5. to create and distribute vitally and profusely.

—The Random House Dictionary

"I often don't know what I know until I get it written down and I can see it."

—a Freshman

"The growth of the power of language is not merely a technical development, it implies a growth of vision."

—Henri Bergson

7

From sentences to paragraphs

Writing is being able to recognize and make order out of experience as we receive it. The sensitive, experienced perceiver knows the world around him. For him experience is filled with potential writings. He sees and perceives subjects, theses, and supporting details everywhere.

So far we've found concrete experiences and transformed them into the beginnings of writing—into sentences and parts of sentences. Now we turn to ways of taking those smaller units—the bits and pieces of experience in writing—and using them to produce, or *generate*, larger pieces of writing. At this level of composing we begin to deal directly with the third component of every writing situation: the *audience*. The writer needs a firm base in his subject and a clear idea of his relationship with his subject. He looks closely at experience and finds details and actualities to write about. Then he considers those experiences in relation to one another and himself. He puts, in other words, his ideas, attitudes, feelings, and theses together with carefully described specifics. But as he progresses toward larger units of writing, he begins also to consider the particular needs of the readers, what they will need to share before they accept his message.

In one sense, this chapter concerns ways of getting your words to speak to each other. You're writing, let us say, about a recent meeting you attended in which two people with very different personalities had an argument. The argument isn't so important. For that matter, neither was the purpose of the meeting. What *is* important is how these people's personalities showed up as they argued. What did they say and do, as they fired their words at one another, that betrayed essential differences in character? As you write you mix up various bits of description: some

225

actual dialogue from the argument, some concrete description of the sense of the argument, a very brief account of why the meeting was held and what was discussed. All these experiences you've received by paying close attention at the meeting, by revising your thoughts after the meeting, and by adjusting what you experienced to fit what you thought.

Now you revise again, always considering what you want your readers to get from your writing. As you write, you put a brief piece of remembered dialogue next to one of your own thoughts to show where that thought came from. Perhaps you bring a word spoken by one person along side of a word spoken by another to show a hidden similarity. In other words, you bring experiences together that create tension, that generate complex meanings. For most meanings are sparks that fly from two ideas or objects rubbed together quickly in your writing. You make your words speak to each other. Then they will speak to your readers as well.

Here is an example of a quick piece of writing that described two people arguing a point. Both had seen a recent film. One felt that Ali McGraw, the heroine, had acted well; the other, that she had acted badly. The writer puts together his own words with the words of the arguers. He adds a bit of background. How well do you think he recreates the scene and the characters? What side do you think the writer himself is on?

> Everyone at the table began to trade knowing glances. Bob's forehead wrinkled slightly as he prepared to respond. "You can't," he said, "ignore her awkward smile. It always seems to me that she smiles ten seconds after she's supposed to or whenever the director tells her." There were titters around the table; Diane's ever-loving heroine had been cut down. She screwed up her eyes, made a small sound like a buried gargle deep in her throat, and blurted "You can't say that. She's just so beautiful. And *whenever* she smiles is fine with me." More titters, this time a bit more rushed, a bit less open. Bob smiled slowly and shifted his weight in the chair. "She ought to go back to modelling toothpaste."

Make the elements of your experience speak to each other. Work your sentences to include specific detail. Then work your paragraphs so that your experiences talk to one another from sentence to sentence.

The above narrative is an example of experiences talking to one another in words. In this instance the writer shares an experience of his own. As he writes, he seems to remember and capture experiences as he puts words on the page. That is something like what Henri Bergson means when he says that "language depends on vision." A writer sees more, experiences more, because of words. One word reminds him of another experience and another word.

You can use words that way, especially if you begin by remembering very concrete experiences, finding words to fit those experiences, and then fitting those words into sentences and paragraphs that create tensions and oppositions in the reader's mind.

The student writer of the paragraph on this page loved cycle riding. But he didn't leave it at that. He *showed*. He brought together meaningful, real, honest experiences he had felt while riding. He shows the cycle and how he feels on the cycle. The result, even for the reader who doesn't particularly care for cycles, is real sharing. As you read, notice how very concrete experiences and sensations strike against each other to create oppositions and feelings that really talk to a reader. Watch the headlight beam as it bounces across the road, feel the seat as it thrusts upward under you after a bump, see the white line waver, feel the tension as the rider grasps the handlebars to round off a curve. But beyond the sharing of concrete experiences, notice how the writer indirectly develops an attitude toward cycling. Pick out the elements of the paragraph that show and those that tell. How well do they work together? The rest of this chapter discusses specific ways to plan paragraphs. But remember that good paragraphs come from good sentences. And good sentences are packed with experiences that talk to one another and create lively tensions in readers. This paragraph is extracted from a longer essay. The writer blocks off just enough experience within the paragraph; he knows how to clinch his point with a sentence placed strategically at the end of the paragraph.

> Riding a cycle is a lot like flying through the air with a dull roar slightly behind you. My Honda always seems a few paces behind me when I ride, propelling me, but not really with me; I feel that I'm steering the road rather than the Honda. The wind whips by your ears and face, like paper scratching against glass. But the sensations I feel don't dull my senses. I feel alert, alive, part of the bike. I'm ready for surprises, a sharp rush of wind from the side as a speeding car passes me.

This writer tells us very specifically why and how he feels. But he also very subtly suggests an attitude: "But the sensations I feel don't dull my senses." We get the idea that some people believe cyclists are careless, wild joy-riders out on suicidal trips every time they drive. No, our writer says, he's actually more alert and careful than he would be in a car, shut off from the elements, his senses dulled. The *clincher* sentence tells the point. The rest of the sentences show us why.

There are other effective devices in this paragraph. The experiences *do* speak to each other. Notice the metaphors: "riding a cycle is like flying through the air . . . I feel that I'm steering the road . . . like paper scratching against glass." These metaphors draw two usually different experiences together; they create useful tensions in the reader as he too tries to experience these sensations. The writer's mind is working through comparisons on the mind of the reader. The sparks of meaning come from friction as minds rub together. So we find most of the elements of good paragraphs here: a main thought—that cycle riders are alert, careful, and very much involved in what they do on the road—with a clincher sentence to bring the point home. And we also find concrete experience brought into oppositions and tensions that involve the reader.

Three ways to build on basic experience

Just as sentences are built from base units expanded through modifiers, so paragraphs are formed. Just as separate stimuli are composed into perceptions and finally into whole patterns of thought, so sentences are worked together, rounded off, sanded to smoothness, and put into paragraph patterns. A paragraph signals the end of one building pattern and the beginning of a new, but related, pattern.

Sometimes you need plans to pull together the experience, ideas and theses in your paragraphs. Such plans ought to help you connect experiences and to get words to talk to one another. They ought to be natural plans in that they build meaning from experience to experience and from word to word, just as an electrical generator takes a small source of power and generates more power. Here are three such building plans. All three are based on the idea that writing works from the general to the specific, or the reverse. Every time a good writer picks up his pen he either refines a big idea by showing its parts, expands a little idea by adding to what his readers know about it, or clarifies the idea by comparing it to another.

Building by Qualification
Building by Detail
Building by Comparison[1]

---

[1]Christensen used these three categories to discuss kinds of modifiers in the second chapter of *Notes Toward a New Rhetoric* (New York, 1969). Here the categories have been expanded to include larger units of writing.

Building by qualification

We all have ideas. But the best thinkers have *complex* ideas. They begin with simple ideas. Then their minds start to work and they begin to qualify: to see facets or parts of the idea or object that they didn't see at first. They turn blanket statements like "all long-haired people are rebellious" around and around; they question their own experiences and others' experiences; they find the exception, then another exception, still another exception, until they question the entire rule. By turning the old saying around, they begin to see the forest as well as the trees. They ask questions like "how many 'long-hairs' do I really know?" and "Do the ones I know represent *all* long-haired people?" Hopefully, the finished product is closer to the truth, although it might be less emphatic and less dramatic because it is less absolute.

Here are examples of statements that two students blurted out on the spot. The first deals directly with a concrete experience. The second deals with an opinion. Watch how both are examined and then qualified in the material that follows. Remember, a quality is like a characteristic: it describes *how* something is done, how a person walks, cries, or laughs; it classifies objects and people.

He stood in the ring, still and fixed.

Here are the questions a few classmates asked in order to give the writer an idea of how he might fill in and qualify what he saw as he wrote.

Who stood in the ring?

How did he or she stand in the ring?

What kind of person was it?

What emotions did the person feel?

Now here is the paragraph the student-writer produced after he had heard the questions.

Muhammad Ali, formerly Cassius Clay, strode to the center of the ring, assured, even *arrogant*. The dull brown skin of his back glistened in the intense light and rippled occasionally as he threw short, deadly punches at an imaginary opponent. He was *tall*, like a pillar crowded into a little box. As the announcer grabbed the microphone, Ali bowed and strutted *graciously*, seeming to savor every theatrical moment in a command performance.

The italicized words are physical qualifications of the original. They answer the question *how*. How did Muhammad Ali strut? What qualities can we add to *still* and *fixed* (that he was *tall*, a quality of Ali's physical appearance?) How did he stride to the center of the ring? Most how-questions are answered by qualities. When the subject of a sentence is a person or object, the answers are usually adverbs, adjectives or adverbial and adjectival phrases.

Don't overload a sentence or paragraph with quality-modifiers. If you do, you'll be telling more than you show. Try to find nouns and verbs that carry the weight of qualification, just as in the paragraph above where the verbs *strode*, *glistened*, *rippled*, *bowed* and *strutted* show us some of Ali's qualities. This writer doesn't need too many adverb/adjective qualifiers—and the ones he does need must be specific and streamlined.

Qualifiers are also usually more abstract than other forms of modification. They fit persons and objects into classes. Ali is of the class of arrogant men in this little portrait; he is also of the class of gracious men. But *only* Ali seems "like a pillar crowded into a little box." The first defines a quality by class; the second adds a physical detail that applies only to the subject. Most writers depend on a mix of abstract and concrete modifiers. Your paragraphs should usually have both.

Now let's move to an essay that qualifies an idea rather than an object or person. Here is another big statement.

Baseball is a dying sport.

These are the questions that several classmates asked the writer of this statement.

How is baseball dying?

Why is baseball dying?

Can you prove that baseball is dying?

Is baseball really a sport?

In developing paragraphs around this main idea, the writer decided to use just a few questions. Here is that essay.

introduces main idea →

why baseball is dying; it is a "slow game" →

what baseball is and how that affects the game →

how do we sports fans live our lives? →

how do other professional sports relate to baseball as modern sports of rapid tempo? →

Baseball is in trouble. In many cities attendance is down and many of the most dedicated fans complain about the slow pace of the game. Baseball, of course, has traditionally been a slow game; at the turn of the century fans and participants spent leisurely hours following every pitch, arguing with umpires, heckling and abusing opponents and cheering their own.

But then baseball was a sport; now it is a business. And like most businesses it must keep up with the times. We live fast lives, filled with intense competition and rapid action. And we want the pace and tension of those lives repeated even in leisure—in our sports and social games.

Professional football and basketball provide that rapid action, color, and sense of complete fan-involvement. Baseball must, to compete economically, also provide that color, rapid action, and general excitement. Fans no longer seem to want to sit through a six-to-eight hour Sunday doubleheader, with long breaks between innings, the elaborate pre-game warmups, the long walks that relief pitchers must make as they travel from the bullpen to the pitcher's mound.

This essay went on to elaborate the argument that baseball must provide more immediate and vital entertainment. But even in these three paragraphs we find a complex grouping of ideas. Each paragraph elaborates a question.

Paragraph One: Why is baseball dying?

(The answer can be found in baseball's slow pace and lack of physical action, especially when we consider that it is as much a business as it is a sport and must "sell" its product—question three.)

Paragraph Two: What are fans like now? How do they compare with fans in baseball's early days?

(The answer is that life is more rapid and intense and fans expect the same from a sport.)

Paragraph Three: What is baseball like in comparison with other professional sports?

(The answer is that baseball has far too many delays, especially when compared with football and basketball.)

Well-organized writing is usually a series of specific answers to a set of specific questions. The questions themselves are often left unstated; the writer concentrates on providing answers. But he uses the questions as directions or markers along the way to keep him following the right track. They are a writer's road map.

You probably noticed how the first student example used specific modifiers—adverbs and adjectives. It was adding qualities to Muhammad Ali, a specific person in a specific place. The second example, however, used a variety of long and short modifiers. Every modifier added to what we know of the specific characteristics of baseball as a dying sport. The writer took the main idea—that baseball was dying—and chipped away until he had qualified and defined the subject to give a more complete picture.

Building by detail

There are two ways to build by details. First, you can take an object and add details to it. We've already talked a good deal about describing by detail. But you can also take an idea and show its parts, much in the way the student took his idea about baseball and structured it.

If your purpose is merely to describe, not to change attitudes or make opinions, then you'll need to fill in with details that create a complete physical picture. You might begin with Muhammad Ali's appearance and work back to the muscles that ripple across his shoulders. You select details according to the total impression you want to create in your reader. You want to practice, like a movie director, zooming in and out, flashing details seen from a distance along side of those seen up close, without losing your reader.

Ideas also have small and large parts. Get used to treating your main ideas like you treat important objects. Qualify them, then point to their specific parts. Let readers see them from a distance, as observer, and close up, as if they had produced the idea themselves. Take your main ideas, your glittering generalities, and your very important opinions and tear them apart right before your reader. Watch how this writer works up to a big idea, a clincher, by showing it part by part.

William Butler Yeats very often wrote only two lines of poetry a day, but you'd never think it when you read his poems. And he never told many people about how hard he worked either. The poems seem the result of natural genius, like they flowed right from his pen. Joe Dimaggio made the most difficult catches look easy, but only after years of playing and loving and working at baseball. And he didn't remind people how long it took to make those catches look easy. Nothing good comes easy. But it certainly helps to make it *seem* that what you do well comes naturally. No one really likes the guy who has to try *too* hard.

You may disagree with the sentiments in this paragraph. And some of the ideas could be more clearly related to one another. But that shouldn't stop you from admiring how the writer works up examples and parts to form and support a concept. The big idea—"No one really likes the guy who has to try too hard"—has many smaller ideas working for it. The writer dissected the idea and then put it together again in front of his reader.

Building by comparison

We've talked a good deal about metaphor already. A metaphor compares two objects in order to get some deeper meaning across to a reader. But sometimes writers let the process of comparison direct entire paragraphs, even entire pieces of writing.

You can pick two parts of your general subject and compare them in order to find out more about the subject itself. Or, you can compare something very familiar with something very unfamiliar. The similarities may surprise you, and the differences will strike up sparks of insight in the reader's mind. This paragraph is clearly and effectively based on one important comparison.

Free Schools

JONATHAN KOZOL

To plant a bean seed in a cut-down milk container and to call this 'revolution' is to degrade and undermine the value of one of the sacred words. To show a poor black kid in East St. Louis or in Winston-Salem or in Chicago how to make end runs around the white man's college entrance scores—while never believing that those scores are more than evil digits written on the sky—to do this, in my scale of values, is the starting point of an authentic revolution. It is not to imitate a confrontation, but to engage in one. It is not to speak of doing 'our own thing,' but rather to do one thing that really matters and can make a visible difference in the lives of our own brothers in the streets that stand about our schools. Harlem does not need a new generation of radical basket-weavers. It does need radical, strong, subversive, steadfast, skeptical, rage-minded and power-wielding obstetricians, pediatricians, lab technicians, defense attorneys, Building Code examiners, brain surgeons. Leather and wheat germ may appear to constitute a revolution in the confines of a far-removed and well-protected farm or isolated commune ten miles east of Santa Barbara or sixteen miles south of Sante Fe; but it does not do much good on Blue Hill Avenue in Boston on a Sunday evening if a man's pocket is empty and his child has a fever and the busses have stopped running.

This long paragraph is filled with oppositions and tensions, with objects and ideas taken from one context and compared or transferred to another. But one overriding comparison guides all the other oppositions and tensions in the paragraph: real hard-nosed revolution that successfully changes people's lives is compared with pseudo or fake revolution. Kozol needs something to pull all his oppositions together and he finds it when he compares planting a bean seed—a superficial sign of a return to a natural life—with the "sacred" word *revolution*. The contrast between superficial and real becomes the focus, the unifying concept, of the entire paragraph.

Notice how other comparisons follow it up: the "poor black kid in East St. Louis" versus the "white man's college entrance scores"; not to "imitate," but to "engage in" revolution; "not to do 'our own thing,' but rather to do one thing that really matters." Then we find the tough comparison of "radical basket-weavers" and "strong, subversive, steadfast, skeptical, rage-minded and power-wielding obstetricians" that brings the comparison home to Jonathan Kozol's general subject: how do we bring the right kind of education to the poor so that they can escape the circle of poverty and imposed ignorance. The contrasts in Kozol's mind create useful tensions in our minds as we read. His examples are tough and put flesh on the skeleton of his central concept. By the time the reader has finished the paragraph he or she sees both sides clearly and understands the writer's position.

Qualifying, adding details, and comparing—these three ways help to make your experiences and thinking into words and paragraphs. They help you to control what you write without stopping your mind or your pen.[2]

---

[2]Consult Appendix I for a more complete grammatical analysis of paragraph structure, especially the structure of the experiential paragraph.

Journal Exercise

1. Find an issue in which you see two sides. Try to unravel your position by thinking up contrasts. What objects do you connect with one side or the other? Can you imagine people who would support one side or the other? Try to show them in action, as Kozol shows what he believes are pseudo-revolutionaries going through symbolic actions like basket-weaving, wearing leather or planting bean seeds. Try to think of phrases or words that have become favorites of one side or the other, like Kozol's reference to "doing our own thing."

2. Try a paragraph that mixes at least two of these paragraph-building schemes. Take a common object—a plate, a saucer, a particular fruit, for example—and describe some of its qualities. Then add to what the reader sees of its physical detail. Use the object as the vehicle of a metaphor. (Remember that earlier we discussed and divided metaphors into *vehicles*, the concrete object a writer uses to carry his idea, and *tenor*, the abstract idea or deeper meaning.) First, try it all in one paragraph. If that's too confusing, try spiraling out into new paragraphs whenever you shift to a new approach. Be sure your paragraphs are clearly connected to one another.

3. Write down in free form as many opinions as you can in five minutes. Then, rather than try to narrow them down with more writing, just make a list of concrete objects, phrases, words, and types of people and relate them to one of the opinions. Can you make metaphors out of the objects as they relate to one of your opinions? Can you get the comparisons to work for you as Kozol gets concrete objects and specific phrases to work for him? If you have a hard time finding opinions, watch a national news program and jot down your own reactions to major issues and news items. Keep alert and watch the film clips that go along with the news accounts for concrete examples to use in your metaphors or general comparisons.

Relating ideas and experience

In the last chapter we talked about how good writing brings together opinions, ideas, and actual experience. We saw how George Orwell, in his essay "The Road to Wigan Pier," developed an attitude and carefully worked in a description of a journey through a coal mine to establish that attitude. In the following essay by Norman Podhoretz, the framework of ideas and the main thesis are even more complex than Orwell's. Yet once again the writer very carefully pulls together his concrete past experiences on New York City's streets to illustrate and emphasize his ideas. As you read, follow *both* Podhoretz's ideas and his experiences. The stories in the essay are meant to clarify how the writer feels as he writes.

As you read, you'll notice that Podhoretz begins and ends his essay with discussions of his thesis. He opens with some general remarks about what it is like to grow up in America—whether in one of New York's ghettos or in an isolated North Dakota town—and how all of us form our deepest feelings and opinions by how our senses are affected by our environments. Throughout his introduction Podhoretz mentions his childhood experiences. In his conclusion he tells us what he believes *now* and develops his solution to racial problems in America.

But it is what comes between that conclusion and introduction that makes or destroys this essay. This middle part begins with narratives of three brief examples, all drawn from the author's childhood. Then, from the examples, Podhoretz makes inferences; he draws conclusions that finally lead him to his main thesis. While you read, try to appreciate the design of this essay, how its various parts are connected and made to work together—for just as words must talk to each other in sentences and paragraphs, the parts must talk to each other in an essay. Watch how Podhoretz leads from personal experience to overall opinions, finally to his main thesis. Watch how the experiences he describes early in the essay are carefully made the foundation for what Podhoretz feels very deeply at the end of the essay.

Finally, watch Podhoretz's paragraphs. Some of them tell ideas; others show real experiences. But most are little works of art that compose both. Sometimes his paragraphs take a main idea and qualify it by pointing to its parts. At other times, Podhoretz takes a very concrete experience and works it into an opinion by the paragraph's end. And very often he works by comparison, sometimes comparing how different minority and ethnic groups interact, how they are different as well as similar.

This essay is a good example of how ideas grow—out of other ideas and actual experience. A clear thinker can see relations among parts. But a good writer sees connections and also gets them across to readers. He knows when he needs to make the connections among ideas and examples clear; he also knows when he can depend on the reader's good sense to make those connections. Getting ideas to grow from experience comes first. Controlling the ideas and bringing them into clear relationships—in other words, creating *unity*—is the next step.

My Negro Problem—and Ours

NORMAN PODHORETZ

> If we and . . . I mean the relatively
> conscious whites and the relatively
> conscious blacks, who must, like lovers,
> insist on, or create, the consciousness of
> the others—do not falter in our duty now,
> we may be able, handful that we are, to
> end the racial nightmare, and achieve our
> country, and change the history of the
> world.
>
> —*James Baldwin*

Two ideas puzzled me deeply as a child growing up in Brooklyn during the 1930's in what today would be called an integrated neighborhood. One of them was that all Jews were rich; the other was that all Negroes were persecuted. These ideas had appeared in print; therefore they must be true. My own experience and the evidence of my senses told they were not true, but that only confirmed what a daydreaming boy in the provinces—for the lower-class neighborhoods of New York belong as surely to the provinces as any rural town in North Dakota—discovers very early: *his* experience is unreal and the evidence of his senses is not to be trusted. Yet even a boy with a head full of fantasies incongruously synthesized out of Hollywood movies and English novels cannot altogether deny the reality of his own experience—especially when there is so much deprivation in that experience. Nor can he altogether gainsay the evidence of his own senses—especially such evidence of the senses as comes from being repeatedly beaten up, robbed, and in general hated, terrorized, and humiliated.

And so for a long time I was puzzled to think that Jews were supposed to be rich when the only Jews I knew were poor, and that Negroes were supposed to be persecuted when it was the Negroes who were doing the only persecuting I knew about—and doing it, moreover, to *me*. During the early years of the war, when my older sister joined a left-wing youth organization, I remember my astonishment at hearing her passionately denounce my father for thinking that Jews were worse off than Negroes. To me, at the age of twelve, it seemed very clear that Negroes were better off than Jews—indeed, than *all* whites. A city boy's world is contained within three or four square blocks, and in my world it was the whites, the Italians and Jews, who feared the Negroes, not the other way around. The Negroes were tougher than we were, more ruthless, and on the whole they were better athletes. What could it mean, then, to say that they were badly off and that we were more fortunate? Yet my sister's opinions, like print, were sacred, and when she told me about exploitation and economic forces I believed her. I believed her, but I was still afraid of Negroes. And I still hated them with all my heart.

It had not always been so—that much I can recall from early childhood. When did it start, this fear and this hatred? There was a kindergarten in the local public school, and given the character of the neighborhood, at least half of the children in my class must have been Negroes. Yet I have no memory of being aware of color differences at that age, and I know from observing my own children that they attribute no significance to such differences even when they begin noticing them. I think there was a day—first grade? second grade?—when my best friend Carl hit me on the way home from school and announced that he wouldn't play with me any more because I had killed Jesus. When I ran home to my mother crying for an explanation, she told me not to pay any attention to such foolishness, and then in Yiddish she cursed the goyim and the schwartzes, the schwartzes and the goyim. Carl, it turned out, was a schwartze, and so was added a third to the categories into which people were mysteriously divided.

Sometimes I wonder whether this is a true memory at all. It is blazingly vivid, but perhaps it never happened: can anyone really remember back to the age of six? There is no uncertainty in my mind, however, about the years that followed. Carl and I hardly ever spoke, though we met in school every day up through the eighth or ninth grade. There would be embarrassed moments of catching his eye or of his catching mine—for whatever it was that had attracted us to one another as very small children remained alive in spite of the fantastic barrier of hostility that had grown up between us, suddenly and out of nowhere. Nevertheless, friendship would have been impossible, and even if it had been possible, it would have been unthinkable. About that, there was nothing anyone could do by the time we were eight years old.

Item: The orphanage across the street is torn down, a city housing project begins to rise in its place, and on the marvelous vacant lot next to the old orphanage they are building a playground. Much excitement and anticipation as Opening Day draws near. Mayor LaGuardia himself comes to dedicate this great gesture of public benevolence. He speaks of neighborliness and borrowing cups of sugar, and of the playground he says that children of all races, colors, and creeds will learn to live together in harmony. A week later, some of us are swatting flies on the playground's inadequate little ball field. A gang of Negro kids, pretty much our own age, enter from the other side and order us out of the park. We refuse, proudly and indignantly, with superb masculine fervor. There is a fight, they win, and we retreat, half whimpering, half with bravado. My first nauseating experience of cowardice. And my first appalled realization that there are people in the world who do not seem to be afraid of anything, who act as though they have nothing to lose. Thereafter the playground becomes a battleground, sometimes quiet, sometimes the scene of athletic competition between Them and Us. But rocks are thrown as often as baseballs. Gradually we abandon the place and use the streets instead. The streets are safer, though we do not admit this to ourselves. We are not, after all, sissies—that most dreaded epithet of an American boyhood.

Item: I am standing alone in front of the building in which I live. It is late afternoon and getting dark. That day in school the teacher had asked a surly Negro boy named Quentin a question he was unable to answer. As usual I had waved my arm eagerly ("Be a good boy, get good marks, be smart, go to college, become a doctor") and, the right answer bursting from my lips, I was held up lovingly by the teacher as an example to the class. I had seen Quentin's face—a very dark, very cruel, very Oriental-looking face—harden, and there had been enough threat in his eyes to make me run all the way home for fear that he might catch me outside.

Now, standing idly in front of my own house, I see him approaching from the project accompanied by his little brother who is carrying a baseball bat and wearing a grin of malicious anticipation. As in a nightmare, I am trapped. The surroundings are secure and familiar, but terror is suddenly present and there is no one around to help. I am locked to the spot. I will not cry out or run away like a sissy, and I stand there, my heart wild, my throat clogged. He walks up, hurls the familiar epithet ("Hey, mo'f——r"), and to my surprise only pushes me. It is a violent push, but not a punch. Maybe I can still back out without entirely losing my dignity. Maybe I can still say, "Hey, c'mon Quentin, whaddya wanna do *that* for? I dint do nothin' to *you*," and walk away, not too rapidly. Instead, before I can stop myself, I push him back—a token gesture—and I say, "Cut that out, I don't wanna fight, I ain't got nothin' to fight about." As I turn to walk back into the building, the corner of my eye catches the motion of the bat his little brother has handed him. I try to duck, but the bat crashes colored lights into my head.

The next thing I know, my mother and sister are standing over me, both of them hysterical. My sister—she who was later to join the "progressive" youth organization—is shouting for the police and screaming imprecations at those dirty little black bastards. They take me upstairs, the doctor comes, the police come. I tell them that the boy who did it was a stranger, that he had been trying to get money from me. They do not believe me, but I am too scared to give them Quentin's name. When I return to school a few days later, Quentin avoids my eyes. He knows that I have not squealed, and he is ashamed. I try to feel proud, but in my heart I know that it was fear of what his friends might do to me that had kept me silent, and not the code of the street.

Item: There is an athletic meet in which the whole of our junior high school is participating. I am in one of the seventh-grade rapid-advance classes, and "segregation" has now set in with a vengeance. In the last three or four years of the elementary school from which we have just graduated, each grade had been divided into three classes, according to "intelligence." (In the earlier grades the divisions had either been arbitrary or else unrecognized by us as having anything to do with brains.) These divisions by IQ, or however it was arranged, had resulted in a preponderance of Jews in the "1" classes and a corresponding preponderance of Negroes in the "3's," with the Italians split unevenly along the spectrum. At least a few Negroes had always made the "1's," just as there had always been a few Jewish kids among the "3's" and more among the "2's" (where Italians dominated). But the junior high's rapid-advance class of which I am now a member is overwhelmingly Jewish and entirely white—except for a shy lonely Negro girl with light skin and reddish hair.

The athletic meet takes place in a city-owned stadium far from the school. It is an important event to which a whole day is given over. The winners are to get those precious little medallions stamped with the New York City emblem that can be screwed into a belt and that prove the wearer to be a distinguished personage. I am a fast runner, and so I am assigned the position of anchor man on my class's team in the relay race. There are three other seventh-grade teams in the race, two of them all Negro, as ours is all white. One of the all-Negro teams is very tall—their anchor man waiting silently next to me on the line looks years older than I am, and I do not recognize him. He is the first to get the baton and crosses the finishing line in a walk. Our team comes in second, but a few minutes later we are declared the winners, for it has been discovered that the anchor man on the first-place team is not a member of the class. We are awarded the medallions, and the following day our home-room teacher makes a speech about how proud she is of us for being superior athletes as well as superior students. We want to believe that we deserve the praise, but we know that we could not have won even if the other class had not cheated.

That afternoon walking home, I am waylaid and surrounded by five Negroes, among whom is the anchor man of the disqualified team. "Gimme my medal, mo'f——r," he grunts. I do not have it with me and I tell him so. "Anyway, it ain't yours," I say foolishly. He calls me a liar on both counts and pushes me up against the wall on which we sometimes play handball. "Gimme my mo'f——n' medal," he says again. I repeat that I have left it home. "Le's search the li'l mo'f——r," one of them suggests, "he prolly got it *hid* in his mo'f——n' *pants*." My panic is now unmanageable. (How many times had I been surrounded like this and asked in soft tones, "Len' me a nickel, boy." How many times had I been called a liar for pleading poverty and pushed around, or searched, or beaten up, unless there happened to be someone in the marauding gang like Carl who liked me across that enormous divide of hatred and who would therefore say, "Aaah, c'mon, let's git someone else, *this* boy ain't go no money on 'im.") I scream at them through tears of rage and self-contempt, "Keep your f——n' filthy lousy black hands offa me! I swear I'll get the cops." This is all they need to hear, and the five of them set upon me. They bang me around, mostly in the stomach and on the arms and shoulders, and when several adults loitering near the candy store down the block notice what is going on and begin to shout, they run off and away.

I do not tell my parents about the incident. My team-mates, who have also been waylaid, each by a gang led by the opposite number from the disqualified team, have had their medallions taken from them, and they never squeal either. For days, I walk home in terror, expecting to be caught again, but nothing happens. The medallion is put away into a drawer, never to be worn by anyone.

Obviously experiences like these have always been a common feature of childhood life in working-class and immigrant neighborhoods, and Negroes do not necessarily figure in them. Wherever, and in whatever combination, they have lived together in the cities, kids of different groups have been at war, beating up and being beaten up: micks against kikes against wops against spicks against polacks. And even relatively homogeneous areas have not been spared the warring of the young: one block against another, one gang (called in my day, in a pathetic effort at gentility, an "S.A.C.," or social-athletic club) against another. But the Negro-white conflict had—and no doubt still has—a special intensity and was conducted with a ferocity unmatched by intramural white battling.

In my own neighborhood, a good deal of animosity existed between the Italian kids (most of whose parents were immigrants from Sicily) and the Jewish kids (who came largely from East European immigrant families). Yet everyone had friends, sometimes close friends, in the other "camp," and we often visited one another's strange-smelling houses, if not for meals, then for glasses of milk, and occasionally for some special event like a wedding or a wake. If it happened that we divided into warring factions and did battle, it would invariably be half-hearted and soon patched up. Our parents, to be sure, had nothing to do with one another and were mutually suspicious and hostile. But we, the kids, who all spoke Yiddish or Italian at home, were Americans, or New Yorkers, or Brooklyn boys: we shared a culture, the culture of the street, and at least for a while this culture proved to be more powerful than the opposing cultures of the home.

Why, *why* should it have been so different as between the Negroes and us? How was it borne in upon us so early, white and black alike, that we were enemies beyond any possibility of reconciliation? Why did we hate one another so?

I suppose if I tried, I could answer those questions more or less adequately from the perspective of what I have since learned. I could draw upon James Baldwin—what better witness is there?—to describe the sense of entrapment that poisons the soul of the Negro with hatred for the white man whom he knows to be his jailer. On the other side, if I wanted to understand how the white man comes to hate the Negro, I could call upon the psychologists who have spoken of the guilt that white Americans feel toward Negroes and that turns into hatred for lack of acknowledging itself as guilt. These are plausible answers and certainly there is truth in them. Yet when I think back upon my own experience of the Negro and his of me, I find myself troubled and puzzled, much as I was as a child when I heard that all Jews were rich and all Negroes persecuted. How could the Negroes in my neighborhood have regarded the whites across the street and around the corner as jailers? On the whole, the whites were not so poor as the Negroes, but they were quite poor enough, and the years were years of Depression. As for white hatred of the Negro, how could guilt have had anything to do with it? What share had these Italian and Jewish immigrants in the enslavement of the Negro? What share had they—downtrodden people themselves breaking their own necks to eke out a living—in the exploitation of the Negro?

No, I cannot believe that we hated each other back there in Brooklyn because they thought of us as jailers and we felt guilty toward them. But does it matter, given the fact that we all went through an unrepresentative confrontation? I think it matters profoundly, for if we managed the job of hating each other so well without benefit of the aids to hatred that are supposedly at the root of this madness everywhere else, it must mean that the madness is not yet properly understood. I am far from pretending that I understand it, but I would insist that no view of the problem will begin to approach the truth unless it can account for a case like the one I have been trying to describe. Are the elements of any such view available to us?

At least two, I would say, are. One of them is a point we frequently come upon in the work of James Baldwin, and the other is a related point always stressed by psychologists who have studied the mechanisms of prejudice. Baldwin tells us that one of the reasons Negroes hate the white man is that the white man refuses to *look* at him: the Negro knows that in white eyes all Negroes are alike; they are faceless and therefore not altogether human. The psychologists, in their turn, tell us that the white man hates the Negro because he tends to project those wild impulses that he fears in himself onto an alien group which he then punishes with his contempt. What Baldwin does *not* tell us, however, is that the principle of facelessness is a two-way street and can operate in both directions with no difficulty at all. Thus, in my neighborhood in Brooklyn, I was as faceless to the Negroes as they were to me, and if they hated me because I never looked at them, I must also have hated them for never looking at *me*. To the Negroes, my white skin was enough to define me as the enemy, and in a war it is only the uniform that counts and not the person.

So with the mechanism of projection that the psychologists talk about: it too works in both directions at once. There is no question that the psychologists are right about what the Negro represents symbolically to the white man. For me as a child the life lived on the other side of the playground and down the block on Ralph Avenue seemed the very embodiment of the values of the street—free, independent, reckless, brave, masculine, erotic. I put the word "erotic" last, though it is usually stressed above all others, because in fact it came last, in consciousness as in importance. What mainly counted for me about Negro kids of my own age was that they were "bad boys." There were plenty of bad boys among the whites—this was, after all, a neighborhood with a long tradition of crime as a career open to aspiring talents—but the Negroes were *really* bad, bad in a way that beckoned to one, and made one feel inadequate. We all went home every day for a lunch of spinach-and-potatoes; *they* roamed around during lunch hour, munching on candy bars. In winter *we* had to wear itchy woolen hats and mittens and cumbersome galoshes; *they* were bareheaded and loose as they pleased. *We* rarely played hookey, or got into serious trouble in school, for all our streetcorner bravado; *they* were defiant, forever staying out (to do what delicious things?), forever making disturbances in class and in the halls, forever being sent to the principal and returning uncowed. But most important of all, they were *tough;* beautifully, enviably tough, not giving a damn for anyone or anything. To hell with the teacher, the truant officer, the cop; to hell with the whole of the adult world that held us in its grip and that we never had the courage to rebel against except sporadically and in petty ways.

This is what I saw and envied and feared in the Negro: this is what finally made him faceless to me, though some of it, of course, was actually there. (The psychologists also tell us that the alien group which becomes the object of a projection will tend to respond by trying to live up to what is expected of them.) But what, on his side, did the Negro see in me that made me faceless to *him?* Did he envy me my lunches of spinach-and-potatoes and my itchy woolen caps and my prudent behavior in the face of authority, as I envied him his noon-time candy bars and his bare head in winter and his magnificent rebelliousness? Did those lunches and caps spell for him the prospect of power and riches in the future? Did they mean that there were possibilities open to me that were denied to him? Very likely they did. But if so, one also supposes that he feared the impulses within himself toward submission to authority no less powerfully than I feared the impulses in myself toward defiance. If I represented the jailer to him, it was not because I was oppressing him or keeping him down: it was because I symbolized for him the dangerous and probably pointless temptation toward greater repression, just as he symbolized for me the equally perilous tug toward greater freedom. I personally was to be rewarded for this repression with a new and better life in the future, but how many of my friends paid an even higher price and were given only gall in return.

We have it on the authority of James Baldwin that all Negroes hate whites. I am trying to suggest that on their side all whites—all American whites, that is—are sick in their feelings about Negroes. There are Negroes, no doubt, who would say that Baldwin is wrong, but I suspect them of being less honest than he is, just as I suspect whites of self-deception who tell me they have no special feelings toward Negroes. Special feelings about color are a contagion to which white Americans seem susceptible even when there is nothing in their background to account for the susceptibility. Thus everywhere we look today in the North we find the curious phenomenon of white middle-class liberals with no previous personal experience of Negroes—people to whom Negroes have always been faceless in virtue rather than faceless in vice—discovering that their abstract commitment to the cause of Negro rights will not stand the test of a direct confrontation. We find such people fleeing in droves to the suburbs as the Negro population in the inner city grows; and when they stay in the city we find them sending their children to private school rather than to the "integrated" public school in the neighborhood. We find them resisting the demand that gerrymandered school districts be re-zoned for the purpose of overcoming de facto segregation; we find them judiciously considering whether the Negroes (for their own good, of course) are not perhaps pushing too hard; we find them clucking their tongues over Negro militancy; we find them speculating on the question of whether there may not, after all, be something in the theory that the races are biologically different; we find them saying that it will take a very long time for Negroes to achieve full equality, no matter what anyone does; we find them deploring the rise of black nationalism and expressing the solemn hope that the leaders of the Negro community will discover ways of containing the impatience and incipient violence within the Negro ghettos.*

But that is by no means the whole story; there is also the phenomenon of what Kenneth Rexroth once called "crow-jimism." There are the broken-down white boys like Vivaldo Moore in Baldwin's *Another Country* who go to Harlem in search of sex or simply to brush up against something that looks like primitive vitality, and who are so often punished by the Negroes they meet for crimes that they would have been the last ever to commit and of which they themselves have been as sorry victims as any of the Negroes who take it out on them. There are the writers and intellectuals and artists who romanticize Negroes and pander to them, assuming a guilt that is not properly theirs. And there are all the white liberals who permit Negroes to blackmail them into adopting a double standard of moral judgment, and who lend themselves—again assuming the responsibility for crimes they never committed—to cunning and contemptuous exploitation by Negroes they employ or try to befriend.

And what about me? What kind of feelings do I have about Negroes today? What happened to me, from Brooklyn, who grew up fearing and envying and hating Negroes? Now that Brooklyn is behind me, do I fear them and envy them and hate them still? The answer is yes, but not in the same proportions and certainly not in the same way. I now live on the upper west side of Manhattan, where there are many Negroes and many

---

* For an account of developments like these, see "The White Liberal's Retreat" by Murray Friedman in the January 1963 *Atlantic Monthly*.

Puerto Ricans, and there are nights when I experience the old apprehensiveness again, and there are streets that I avoid when I am walking in the dark, as there were streets that I avoided when I was a child. I find that I am not afraid of Puerto Ricans, but I cannot restrain my nervousness whenever I pass a group of Negroes standing in front of a bar or sauntering down the street. I know now, as I did not know when I was a child, that power is on my side, that the police are working for me and not for them. And knowing this I feel ashamed and guilty, like the good liberal I have grown up to be. Yet the twinges of fear and the resentment they bring and the self-contempt they arouse are not to be gainsaid.

But envy? Why envy? And hatred? Why hatred? Here again the intensities have lessened and everything has been complicated and qualified by the guilts and the resulting over-compensations that are the heritage of the enlightened middle-class world of which I am now a member. Yet just as in childhood I envied Negroes for what seemed to me their superior masculinity, so I envy them today for what seems to me their superior physical grace and beauty. I have come to value physical grace very highly, and I am now capable of aching with all my being when I watch a Negro couple on the dance floor, or a Negro playing baseball or basketball. They are on the kind of terms with their own bodies that I should like to be on with mine, and for that precious quality they seemed blessed to me.

The hatred I still feel for Negroes is the hardest of all the old feelings to face or admit, and it is the most hidden and the most overlarded by the conscious attitudes into which I have succeeded in willing myself. It no longer has, as for me it once did, any cause or justification (except, perhaps, that I am constantly being denied my right to an honest expression of the things I earned the right as a child to feel). How, then, do I know that this hatred has never entirely disappeared? I know it from the insane rage that can stir in me at the thought of Negro anti-Semitism; I know it from the disgusting prurience that can stir in me at the sight of a mixed couple; and I know it from the violence that can stir in me whenever I encounter that special brand of paranoid touchiness to which many Negroes are prone.

This, then, is where I am; it is not exactly where I think all other white liberals are, but it cannot be so very far away either. And it is because I am convinced that we white Americans are—for whatever reason, it no longer matters—so twisted and sick in our feelings about Negroes that I despair of the present push toward integration. If the pace of progress were not a factor here, there would perhaps be no cause for despair: time and the law and even the international political situation are on the side of the Negroes, and ultimately, therefore, victory—of a sort, anyway—must come. But from everything we have learned from observers who ought to know, pace has become as important to the Negroes as substance. They want equality and they want it *now*, and the white world is yielding to their demand only as much and as fast as it is absolutely being compelled to do. The Negroes know this in the most concrete terms imaginable, and it is thus becoming increasingly difficult to buy them off with rhetoric and promises and pious assurances of support. And so within the Negro community we find more and more people declaring —as Harold R. Isaacs recently put it in an article in *Commentary*—that they want *out:* people who say that integration will never come, or that it will take a hundred or a thousand years to come, or that it will come at too high a price in suffering and struggle for the pallid and sodden life of the American middle class that at the very best it may bring.

The most numerous, influential, and dangerous movement that has grown out of Negro despair with the goal of integration is, of course, the Black Muslims. This movement, whatever else we may say about it, must be credited with one enduring achievement: it inspired James Baldwin to write an essay which deserves to be placed among the classics of our language. Everything Baldwin has ever been trying to tell us is distilled in *The Fire Next Time* into a statement of overwhelming persuasiveness and prophetic magnificence. Baldwin's message is and always has been simple. It is this: "Color is not a human or personal reality; it is a political reality." And Baldwin's demand is correspondingly simple: color must be forgotten, lest we all be smited with a vengeance "that does not really depend on, and cannot really be executed by, any person or organization, and that cannot be prevented by any police force or army: historical vengeance, a cosmic vengeance based on the law that we recognize when we say, 'Whatever goes up must come down.' " The Black Muslims Baldwin portrays as a sign and a warning to the intransigent white world. They come to proclaim how deep is the Negro's disaffection with the white world and all its works, and Baldwin implies that no American Negro can fail to respond somewhere in his being to their message: that the white man is the devil, that Allah has doomed him to destruction, and that the black man is about to inherit the earth. Baldwin of course knows that this nightmare inversion of the racism from which the black man has suffered can neither win nor even point to the neighborhood in which victory might be located. For in his view the neighborhood of victory lies in exactly the opposite direction: the transcendence of color through love.

Yet the tragic fact is that love is not the answer to hate—not in the world of politics, at any rate. Color is indeed a political rather than a human or a personal reality and if politics (which is to say power) has made it into a human and personal reality, then only politics (which is to say power) can unmake it once again. But the way of politics is slow and bitter, and as impatience on the one side is matched by a setting of the jaw on the other, we move closer and closer to an explosion and blood may yet run in the streets.

Will this madness in which we are all caught never find a resting-place? Is there never to be an end to it? In thinking about the Jews I have often wondered whether their survival as a distinct group was worth one hair on the head of a single infant. Did the Jews have to survive so that six million innocent people should one day be burned in the ovens of Auschwitz? It is a terrible question and no one, not God himself, could ever answer it to my satifaction. And when I think about the Negroes in America and about the image of integration as a state in which the Negroes would take their rightful place as another of the protected minorities in a pluralistic society, I wonder whether they really believe in their hearts that such a state can actually be attained, and if so why they should wish to survive as a distinct group. I think I know why the Jews once wished to survive (though I am less certain as to why we still do): they not only believed that God had given them no choice, but they were tied to a memory of past glory and a dream of imminent redemption. What does the American Negro have that might correspond to this? His past is a stigma, his color is a stigma, and his vision of the future is the hope of erasing the stigma by making color irrelevant, by making it disappear as a fact of consciousness.

I share this hope, but I cannot see how it will ever be realized unless color does in fact disappear: and that meant not integration, it means assimilation, it means—let the brutal word come out—miscegenation. The Black Muslims, like their racist counterparts in the white world, accuse the "so-called Negro leaders" of secretly pursuing miscegenation as a goal. The racists are wrong, but I wish they were right, for I believe that the wholesale merger of the two races is the most desirable alternative for everyone concerned. I am not claiming that this alternative can be pursued programmatically or that it is immediately feasible as a solution; obviously there are even greater barriers to its achievement than to the achievement of integration. What I am saying, however, is that in my opinion the Negro problem can be solved in this country in no other way.

I have told the story of my own twisted feelings about Negroes here, and of how they conflict with the moral convictions I have since developed, in order to assert that such feelings must be acknowledged as honestly as possible so that they can be controlled and ultimately disregarded in favor of the convictions. It is wrong for a man to suffer because of the color of his skin. Beside that clichéd proposition of liberal thought, what argument can stand and be respected? If the arguments are the arguments of feeling, they must be made to yield; and one's own soul is not the worst place to begin working a huge social transformation. Not so long ago, it used to be asked of white liberals, "Would you like your sister to marry one?" When I was a boy and my sister was still unmarried I would certainly have said no to that question. But now I am a man, my sister is already married, and I have daughters. If I were to be asked today whether I would like a daughter of mine "to marry one," I would have to answer: "No, I wouldn't like it at all. I would rail and rave and rant and tear my hair. And then I hope I would have the courage to curse myself for raving and ranting, and to give her my blessing. How dare I withhold it at the behest of the child I once was and against the man I now have a duty to be?"

Thinking Exercise

1. Podhoretz uses several devices to give the materials of this essay an overall form. One example of these ordering devices is the way Podhoretz uses references to James Baldwin, an important, contemporary black writer and novelist who has published an essay in the form of a sermon called "The Fire Next Time." In that essay, Baldwin argues that love, not hatred, must guide the actions of both whites and blacks and that both races must take at least some of the blame for the existence of extremist groups like the Black Muslims. Go back over the essay and reread Podhoretz's references to Baldwin. One is the headnote of the entire essay; the others follow about in the middle of the essay. How does Podhoretz's proposed solution—interracial marriage—compare with what Baldwin advocates? How does Baldwin's argument for love fit in with Podhoretz's overall solution?

2. How successful is Podhoretz in sharing with you the experiences of growing up in a mixed racial/ethnic neighborhood in New York City? Do you understand better, after reading this essay, why people seem to grow up harboring hatred and distrust for other races and ethnic groups in cities?

3. Why does Podhoretz make separate "items" out of the three past experiences which he narrates? Why does he think it important to separate them from the rest of the essay? Can you point to particular similarities among the three items? Do all of the blacks seem motivated by similar emotions in the three items? Do the whites respond in similar ways to the blacks in each item?

Writing Exercise

1. Write an essay in which you explain how you feel toward a particular group of people—either an ethnic group or a group such as athletes, sorority girls, professional football players, college professors, teachers, and the like. Support and explain your feelings by referring in detail to at least two examples of your relationships with individuals within the group you select.

2. Take one of the key attitude statements in this essay and write an essay in response to it. Establish your own position as you respond; use your own experience either to explain or oppose Podhoretz's sentence. Here are a few key sentences or parts of sentences.

> . . . and I know from observing my own children that they attri-bute no significance to such differences [racial] even when they begin noticing them.

One of them [childhood attitudes] was that all Jews were rich; the other was that all Negroes were persecuted.

The psychologists, in their turn, tell us that the white man hates the Negro because he tends to project those wild impulses that he fears in himself onto an alien group which he then punishes with his contempt.

. . . I believe that the wholesale merger of the two races is the most desirable alternative for everyone concerned.

3. Go back over the paragraphs in this essay and choose two: one that is organized around a main idea that is qualified and narrowed down; and another that takes a concrete action and describes it by developing its parts in detail. Then analyze how these paragraphs tie in with those around them and, finally, how they relate to and develop the main ideas of the essay.

Reading the paragraph that shows and tells

Most paragraphs string together main and subordinate ideas. If the paragraph intends to describe or narrate experience, as in the examples here, we often find a general description that is modified—usually by the addition of details that complete the reader's picture of the event, object, action or person. You can control those paragraphs in which your main aim is to share, describe or narrate concrete experience by following a few of these principles.

Sentences frame our perceptions in writing. They are distinctly perceived bits of experience, spun from the fabric of personal feelings, emotions, and sensations. Our sentences must, of course, run together smoothly or our readers won't see the overall picture. Sometimes we give our sentences direction and transition merely by asking, as we describe, "what comes next?" In other words, we follow a chronological time pattern. But often two actions may occur one after another and not be related at all. Causes and effect often don't come back to back. For example, the toothache that comes immediately after reading a chapter in a murder mystery probably is not related to the reading at all. The ache might have been caused by the candy you ate earlier in the afternoon. We almost always jump time when we write descriptions.

Look at this paragraph from Ambrose Bierce's short story "An Occurrence at Owl Creek Bridge." The writer introduces a young southern civilian about to be hung by the Yankees during the Civil War. Watch how the storyteller mixes together his thoughts—"The liberal military code makes provision for hanging many kinds of persons, and gentlemen are not excluded"—with concrete physical description.

The man who was engaged in being hanged was apparently about thirty-five years of age. He was a civilian, if one might judge from his habit, which was that of a planter. His features were good—a straight nose, firm mouth, broad forehead, from which his long, dark hair was combed straight back, falling behind his ears to the collar of his well-fitting frockcoat. He wore a mustache and pointed beard, but no whiskers; his eyes were large and dark grey, and had a kindly expression which one would hardly have expected in one whose neck was in the hemp. Evidently this was no vulgar assassin. The liberal military code makes provision for hanging many kinds of persons, and gentlemen are not excluded.

What directs the storyteller's selection and placing of facts, details, and ideas? Can we find a unifying structure, perhaps one that only a careful writer would notice?

First, we can point out that two general purposes relate all the sentences to one another. The writer wants to give us a fairly exact portrait of the man's character. He works very simply from a general description in the opening sentence to more elaborate physical details—the nose, the mouth and forehead, the hair—as the paragraph develops.

But the paragraph also includes a few idea-sentences that tell what the storyteller thinks about his subject. These idea-sentences must be clearly supported by what the reader sees. The experience in the paragraph supports its message. The first three sentences link together general and specific details of "the man who was engaged in being hanged." That's easy enough to follow. The writer gives us what we need to define the man's character, not *every* detail.

The fourth sentence, however, marks a shift in the paragraph's direction. Here the paragraph takes on a dual function: the writer wants to tack his own opinions on to the concrete description of his character. The grammar of this sentence signals the dual purpose: a compound sentence with two, balanced independent clauses which continue to add to what the reader sees of the man, then a relative clause which introduces what the writer thinks—"which one would hardly have expected in one whose neck was in the hemp." We begin as readers to fasten along with the writer on physical details that create sympathy. After all, a kindly man is being hanged. There must be some injustice here: "Evidently this was no vulgar assassin"—the storyteller draws the conclusion for us. And then we find the cause of this unjust hanging—"the liberal military code"—in an ironic turn of phrase. The writer uses "liberal" in a way that indicates to us the opposite of what the word usually means. Military law is brutally just; no matter how kindly and refined the criminal, the punishment is just and severe. The code takes in all kinds, vagrants and gentlemen alike.

We find, then, two streams of thought, two paragraph directions, in this simple little paragraph. They might be plotted something like this.

1	2

Main Ideas or Purposes

To describe the man being hanged (opening sentence)	To tell about the "liberal" military code (fourth sentence)

Paragraph Body

Works from general introduction of situation down through specific physical details of the man	Picks up on physical characteristics of man to convince us of severity of military law

Paragraph Summation

Brings together the description of the "victim" and the writer's thoughts about military justice in a final sentence which indirectly criticizes the severity of the military code through play on the word "liberal."

Often our paragraphs have to carry such double loads. They must develop an idea and describe an object or action simultaneously. And such paragraphs are usually the main parts of our writing. After you've introduced your purpose or main idea, you've got to continue developing it, but not by merely repeating the idea in slightly different words. It has to be developed, carried forward, added to, amplified and qualified. You've got to take it apart and show its parts or begin with one of its parts and show where the idea came from. You've got to illustrate, to bring in examples from your own experience, your reading and your thinking. To accomplish these goals writing must show and tell together, naturally, without artificial connections. Getting your words to speak to one another, to create the friction necessary to produce idea-sparks in readers, takes the skill of showing and telling together, of good thinking connected with real, hard-hitting experience. Main ideas, in other words, should *generate* other ideas, supporting examples, concrete actions and details, a whole essay of linking thoughts and experiences.

Here are a few suggestions to help you bring together ideas and experiences in your paragraphs.

1. As you plan the body of your essay, be sure that you have a clear idea of how you will bring together subideas related to your main thesis and supporting experiential evidence. If your essay is brief, say, five or six hundred words, make a plan, similar to the graph we outlined for the Ambrose Bierce paragraph, that shows how each sentence will either carry the idea a step further or add some new supporting evidence.

2. Traditionally we think of papers as having *introductions,* where the thesis or subject is defined and the reader's attention focused; *bodies,* where the thesis or subject is specifically analyzed, developed and illustrated; *conclusions,* where main ideas are either summarized or condensed in crystal-clear form. But there is more to the concept of introduction, body and conclusion than we often realize. The paragraphs within an introduction, for example, are not like paragraphs in conclusions. And paragraphs in the body of an essay differ even more, in both structure and style, from both introductions and conclusions.

Here are descriptions of the types of paragraphs we often find in these three parts of an essay. Remember these are approximations, not rules. Most good pieces of writing offer some reasonable exceptions.

Introductory Paragraphs

Usually introductory paragraphs are more general and less complex in structure than the paragraphs that follow. A writer never includes a tricky word or special reference in an introduction without defining it, or at least planning to define it later in the essay. The ideas and objects of description come in large form, clear to the eye and the mind, so the reader knows the subject. Notice how Norman Podhoretz summarizes more in his introduction than anywhere else: to attract the reader's attention, to give him what he needs to follow the more particular reasoning that comes later, and to lay a foundation for his thesis, which comes much later in the conclusion of the essay.

Body Paragraphs

The body is the flesh on the bones of your essay. So the paragraphs become more specific. Sometimes very particular examples—like the "Items" in Podhoretz's essay—add the meat of experience to the bone of thought and opinion. If the essay is completely expository, the general ideas introduced earlier are picked apart and analyzed in detail. Sometimes several strategies of development work together. Podhoretz recalls childhood experiences as examples of racial interaction, examines important thoughts from different angles, takes general ideas and rips them into parts, dissects and recomposes. Above all, body paragraphs work in specifics and bring together the whats and the whys of the writer's thesis.

Conclusion Paragraphs

Usually return to a more general level of discussion, but in a way that reminds the reader of the specific whys behind the main ideas. Sometimes the clincher depends on repetition of an earlier word or idea; sometimes on a new example that clarifies what has come before, sometimes merely on a rephrasing of important ideas. Never in a short paper make your conclusion a summary. In fact, your reader may not need it; he may even be insulted if you repeat the obvious.

3. The term "topic sentence" is confusing. Most people either mistakenly think it is always the first sentence in the paragraph, or they assume that every paragraph has a topic sentence. A topic sentence is merely the most general sentence in the paragraph. It frames and unifies everything else in the paragraph; it usually relates back to a previous paragraph and forward to the rest of its paragraph. It often comes at the beginning, but it sometimes comes at the end. Occasionally the writer leaves out the topic sentence or main idea, but even then, in the back of both the reader's and the writer's minds, it is there between the lines pulling sentences together, getting words to create friction. Your paragraphs need directing ideas, whether implied, stated openly, or subtly worked in at the paragraph's end.

Developing paragraphs

Sometimes it helps to follow the structures of other writers when you form your own paragraphs. Reread the paragraph from Ambrose Bierce's "An Occurrence at Owl Creek Bridge" on page 250. Then look over this outline of the levels in that paragraph. Notice how meaning and experience grow in the paragraph.

· Level 1: Topic sentence—introduces the main subject of the paragraph in general terms (the man being hanged).
Level 2: Sentences two and three—both of which add to the reader's knowledge of how the hanged man looks and who and

what he is. The grammatical structures of both sentences are both (the man being hanged wears civilian dress; he has fine features) simple and declarative.

Level 3: Sentence four—which introduces, in the final relative clause, a subjective judgment by the narrator and which also demonstrates a change in structure from the second and third sentences (additional facial features and physical characteristics are added to the main subject, the hanged man, in the two opening coordinate clauses divided by the semi-colon; the relative clauses at the end of the sentences tell us that the narrator believes this is not the kind of man most people expect to see with a noose around his neck).

Level 4: Sentence five—adds another level to the subjective interpretation introduced in sentence four. Again, the level is also marked by a change in sentence structure, from the balance of sentence four to the simple, brief structure of sentence five (this was no vulgar assassin).

Level 5: Sentence six—which adds a further level of meaning to the subjective train introduced back in sentence four. Sentence six also marks a change in sentence structure from the simple pattern of sentence five to the balanced, coordinate structure of sentence six (the fact that this was no vulgar assassin leads the narrator to remark about the general qualities of the military code).

Now apply some level-analysis to a few of your own paragraphs, or to the paragraphs in someone else's essay. Do they stagnate or endlessly repeat? Do they die of "eternal structure"—the repetition of similar sentence patterns, especially *is* and *are* sentences, in a single paragraph? Above all, do your ideas and descriptions really get somewhere? As you explain the level of each sentence, are you really finding a new facet of the idea at every level, like a diamond catching the light from different angles? Or are you finding instead the same old general idea repeated in different but dead words?

You might also want to vary the direction of your paragraphs. We've so far talked primarily about developing from general to particular. But just as we discussed many different ways of ordering the parts of your writing in Section One, you can easily find alternate ways of putting together sentences in paragraphs. Invert the general-to-particular order, begin with a question and provide specific examples as answers. Begin by describing an effect and then work back through various causes. Whatever your plan, use the general-to-specific pattern as a guide and work up your own variations, those that fit both your purpose and your subject.

Here is a very brief list of ways of pulling sentences together in paragraphs.

1. *From general to specific:* either an idea stated in a topic sentence and supported by examples, illustrations or analysis by parts or an object described generally and then elaborated in selected details.

2. *From question to answers or effect back through causes:* usually a problem defined in an opening question or stated in a described effect with illustration through reference to several possible answers or causes.

3. *From specific example to controlling generality:* usually a concrete example described in a way that leads naturally and logically to a general attitude or opinion.

4. *From main classification to subclassification:* usually a group of ideas or objects framed in a topic sentence and elaborated part by part in the remainder of the paragraph.

Try to plot the direction and plan of these paragraphs. Use the structures you just read about or make up your own plot interpretations. Whatever you do, find a way of judging how successfully the paragraph moves forward and develops. Learn to expect forward movement, not repetition or needless backtracking, in your own writing.

Sample paragraphs to consider

1. Over to the right of the stage, a tired-looking long-hair stands by a board covered with the buttons and bumper stickers he has for sale. He's a student at Ann Arbor and in the summer covers the bluegrass circuit, having just got it from Bill Monroe's weeklong festival in Beanblossom, Indiana. He digs bluegrass, he says, doesn't know why, he just digs it. The buttons say I LUV BLUE-GRASS, and the bumper stickers invite everyone to GET HIGH ON BLUEGRASS.
—From "Shenandoah Breakdown," by David Standish,
Playboy, November, 1971.

2. The process of learning is essential to our lives. All higher animals seek it deliberately. They are inquisitive and they experiment. An experiment is a soft of harmless trial run of some action which we shall have to make in the real world; and this, whether it is made in the laboratory by scientists or by fox-cubs outside their earth. The scientist experiments and the cub plays; both are learning to correct

their errors of judgment in a setting in which errors are not fatal. Perhaps this is what gives them both their air of happiness and freedom in these activities.

—From J. Bronowski, *The Common Sense of Science*

3. One evening while Farquhar and his wife were sitting on a rustic bench near the entrance to his grounds, a gray-clad soldier rode up to the gate and asked for a drink of water. Mrs. Farquhar was only too glad to serve him with her own white hands. While she was fetching the water her husband approached the dusty horseman and inquired eagerly for news from the front.

—From Ambrose Bierce, "An Occurrence at Owl Creek Bridge"

4. Even more discouraging than this Auschwitz approach to education is that the students take it. They haven't gone through twelve years of public school for nothing. They've learned one thing and perhaps only one thing during those twelve years. They've forgotten their algebra. They're hopelessly vague about chemistry and physics. They've grown to fear and resent literature. They write like they've been lobotomized. But, Jesus, can they follow orders! Freshmen come up to me with an essay and ask if I want it folded and whether their name should be in the upper right hand corner. And I want to cry and kiss them and caress their poor tortured heads.

—Jerry Farber, "The Student As Nigger"

Thinking Exercise

1. The Farber paragraph is the longest and according to the plot, the most complex. Many students, however, find it the easiest to read and understand. Can you explain why?

2. Is there some underlying reason for the way David Standish selects and arranges detail in paragraph one? Why does he tell us that the button and bumper sticker salesman is a student, that he has long hair, that he's tired looking, while he obviously avoids telling us other things? Can you, even from this very brief paragraph, make an educated guess as to what the subject of the entire essay is?

3. Examine closely the various relationships among the sentences in paragraph two. Do any of them repeat or expand upon the previous sentence without also developing a new application of the "process of learning" idea?

4. Does the Ambrose Bierce paragraph include enough detail, sensation and specific description to be called an ideal descriptive paragraph?

Or would you say there is too much summarizing and not enough showing in this paragraph? You might find the paragraph in the entire story (printed on page 275) and describe its overall function. Every writer, even when he is describing physical detail or action, must summarize *and* show, sometimes in separate paragraphs, sometimes in the same paragraph.

5. Go through each paragraph and try to decide on the writer's attitude toward his subject. Is it neutral? Negative? Positive? What, in the language of the paragraph, in the way the writer makes sentences, is your evidence?

Does the writer's way of ordering or designing his paragraph help you to understand his purpose?

Thinking Exercise

All the following paragraphs have been written by students. Read them and then write a response to each in which you apply some of the paragraph analysis that we have been using in this chapter.

Consider questions like these as you read and respond:

1. Do the paragraphs go anywhere or does the meaning or information remain on the same level of generality from sentence to sentence?

2. Are the ideas in each sentence, especially in paragraphs in which every sentence develops a new idea, carefully related to one another? Does the writer use enough transitional devices—words like "but," "however"—to help the reader along?

3. Does the writer in any one of the paragraphs pay much attention to sentence and paragraph structure? For example, is there any attempt in these paragraphs to use parallel, coordinate sentences to emphasize or intensify an argument? Is there enough variety or too much variety in sentence patterns?

4. As you read these paragraphs, can you imagine what type of person is talking? Why or why not?

a. It is generally agreed that today's technology has increased the need for skilled labor and professionalism. The quickening pulse of the society has released insurmountable pressure on the American male. He should no longer be satisfied with a factory job, but he should continue his education to make him capable of doing the work of a professional. Of course, when the actual decision is made, it is his; but he is forever keeping in mind the "virtues" society has thrust upon him. "Virtues" such as materialism, competition, conformity are all synonymous in a technological society.

b. From the age of four or five, little boys are told by their parents and teachers not to cry or show emotion—"Don't cry, big boys don't cry." From that point on, one of the most inhibiting roles in our society is placed on the male. Any boy who cries is a "sissy"; in a few years, a young boy has learned to repress his gentler feelings, probably for life.

c. It is probably because women get pregnant and men do not and because women are often considered psychologically too frail to compete with men, that men are given preference over women in business. Should women, then, be given preference over men until the results of these false attitudes are rectified? Some tests indicate that women may be able to withstand strain better than most men. Again, why are men getting the jobs that women are better prepared for physically and mentally? Because of outdated, evil attitudes which propagate myths. Because it is very literally a man's world.

8

Language +: Unity, coherence, and transitional devices in paragraphs

Good sentences grow from experience that is sensitively felt and well thought out. But once experience has generated basic sentences, we must begin the process of refinement. Usually we begin this process by considering the design, or the overall pattern and form, of our material. In this section we will discuss ways of judging and refining the unity of paragraphs.

Unity

If you've been careful with pre-writing—how you use your senses to control and develop material and how you develop and organize your material before you actually begin writing—your paragraphs should have at least a rough sense of order. You can polish and refine that order by reading your own paragraphs with an editor's eye. When you read and edit to improve paragraph unity, keep in mind this central question:

> Does every sentence and supporting detail in this paragraph relate to some central idea or controlling object?

If you are writing to describe or narrate physical experience, you need some controlling generality to guide every sentence. Usually the generality describes or defines the object or experience and points to some quality of the object or to some class within which the object fits. If you are writing to develop an idea or opinion, you'll need a central idea to pull together every subidea, supporting example, or illustrating sentence in the paragraph. Unity means that every part of a paragraph relates clearly to some central idea or object. You wouldn't expect to read about baseball rules in a paragraph about giraffes. Nor would you expect a description of pink cotton candy in the middle of a paragraph on Spanish olives. Sometimes the unexpected pleases a reader, but only when the writer makes the surprise work toward his central purpose. Readers don't expect cotton candy and Spanish olives together. Yet the writer who makes a clear point by putting them together has both originality and logic on his side. *Eating snow is bad for your health.* Now that sentence just doesn't fit here. Not unless I can use it to develop the main point of this paragraph—unity. And I can by pointing out that sentences like this one destroy unity by moving the reader's attention from the main point.

Read for unity by asking that question—"Does every sentence and supporting detail relate to some main idea or object?"—of every paragraph. Getting the answer to this question is often not as easy as it sounds. Sometimes a paragraph's topic sentence, the one that contains the central idea or object, is hidden between the lines. The writer has perhaps introduced the idea in a previous paragraph and doesn't feel he needs to write it out again. Or perhaps the writer feels he will be more effective if he allows the reader to formulate the idea himself from the evidence he provides in his paragraph. In either case, the writer who doesn't clearly spell out his topic needs to be even clearer in building up to his main idea. If you have had trouble with unity, begin by writing an explicit topic sentence for almost every paragraph. Then you'll become accustomed to making unified paragraphs and can later practice more subtle paragraph techniques. Unity, then, is including no more or less than is absolutely necessary. And unity means designing those essential parts so that the purpose behind them is clear.

Here are three sample paragraphs. All were taken from papers in which the writers tried to relate the "American Dream"—the idea that every individual in America can achieve vast material success no matter how meager his beginnings—to a character in a short story. One of the paragraphs is scrambled and disordered. Another has a clearly defined topic sentence but is not successful in *developing*, adding to, or clarifying that idea in the rest of the paragraph. Some are generally good, clear paragraphs; but all could be improved. Try to paraphrase or describe the main idea in each paragraph. Then evaluate how well each part relates to the whole idea. If you believe the paragraph is weak, explain why by referring to specifics: sentences that don't fit, large gaps in thought, inadequate illustration by example, lack of definition of key terms in the topic or supporting sentences. Finally, try to describe the structure of each paragraph. Where is the topic sentence? Does the paragraph work from examples to general idea or from general to specific? Could the paragraph be rewritten for clearer emphasis? More specific questions follow each paragraph.

> The concept of the "American Dream" has been prevalent in society as long as America has existed. In early times civil strife and religious persecution in Europe prompted people to seek other areas in which to live. They could have easily chosen a number of places to emigrate to yet chose America, as myths surrounding the new country circulated throughout the rest of the world. Unlimited wealth and happiness were here to find; all one needed was the spirit of hard work to carry out one's dreams.

Thinking Exercise

1. Where is the topic sentence in this paragraph? Are all the key terms in the topic sentence clearly defined?

2. Could you extract a clear definition of the American Dream from this paragraph? Why or why not?

3. What topic, subtopic or idea do you think this writer should develop in his next paragraph?

> Every child is nourished with tales of Daniel Boone and Buffalo Bill. The American hero, brave, bold and free-spirited, evolved from the cowboy and the mountain man. The outlaw, such as Billy the Kid and Jesse James, provides a different insight into the character of the American.

Thinking Exercise

1. This paragraph contains three related general ideas. Each one might be the topic of a long paragraph of its own. Where, then, do you think this paragraph might appear in an essay?

2. Can you formulate several particular questions on this paragraph that you would suggest the writer answer? Try to write questions that you believe would help the writer to know where to go next, what details to add and what clarifications to make.

3. Can you write a fairly specific sentence that would define the central idea of this paragraph—a sentence you feel would *unify* the paragraph?

He is hard-working, motivated by a strong sense of recognizing good and evil. This desire to do the right thing motivates him throughout the entire story. He seeks an answer to his grandfather's deathbed phrase—"Keep this nigger boy running." In the end he achieves the truth of the statement although he doesn't realize it until years later. He also attempts to understand all situations so as to gain the most by them. This is shown in the fight where he uses one boy to attract the others to fight another boy.

Thinking Exercise

1. One sentence in this paragraph just doesn't fit. Can you find it? Do you think it might be moved to a later paragraph and developed there?

2. This paragraph tries to work together general interpretations of what the character in the story does with specific evidence from the story. That is a good general technique for a writer interpreting a story to follow. Yet the specific references to the story don't really work very well in this paragraph. Why not? What's wrong with the references to and descriptions of the story?

3. Pronouns are important ways of pulling a paragraph together. What would you say about the way pronouns are used in this paragraph? Do you always know what they refer to? Do they confuse you?

Coherence

Often we have a clear idea in our own minds. And we can bring together the materials of our writing according to that general idea or plan. But there is more to writing than finding a plan you can understand and apply. We must find a way to make that unifying plan simultaneously clear to the reader. That brings us to a consideration of *coherence*: the ability to put your unifying plan to work in a way that is also clear to the reader. When a reader feels that everything in a piece of writing naturally goes together, when he sees a clear order or plan of which every sentence is an integral part, the writer has accomplished coherence. Every part must clearly relate to the topic sentence or main idea for both the reader and the writer. If only the writer has access to his essay's blueprint, chances are he'll lose his readers somewhere along the way.

As you reread your own paragraphs for coherence, focus on these two questions:

What is my unifying plan?

Does my paragraph include devices for making that plan clear to my readers?

The second question ought to lead you naturally to consider possible ways of making your paragraphs coherent, ways of organizing your paragraphs around a central idea and keeping your reader with you as you go.

There are at least four general means of making paragraphs cohere. These four ways involve the use of repetition, pronouns, parallelism, and transitional devices.

Repetition for coherence

Some repetition bores or annoys your readers. But often repetition is the writer's best and most efficient means of clarifying how his paragraph develops a central idea or object. Generally writers use two kinds of repetition. *Explicit* repetition occurs when a writer actually repeats words or phrases to remind a reader that he is referring back to a central idea or object. *Implicit* repetition occurs when a sentence pattern or a particular series is followed without actual repetition of words. Or sometimes a writer uses a synonym for a key word in a previously explained idea to remind the reader that that main idea is still directing the paragraph. Here are two paragraphs that use both kinds of repetition simultaneously. Brief questions follow the paragraphs to point out the kinds of repetition used.

> Since pioneer days, the Wolf has symbolized evil, backwardness, and the need to conquer the wilderness. Although none of these notions is entirely valid, wolves have all but been exterminated throughout the U.S.—and with them has gone the wilderness whose virtues are so needed in the deteriorating national environment.
> —H. Albert Hochbaum

Thinking Exercise

1. Notice how the principal subject—"wolves"—is repeated in both sentences and also referred to in the clause that follows the dash. We learn what the wolf has symbolized, what effects those symbols have had on the wolf and on the land the wolf inhabits. Can you guess what this writer will concentrate on in his next paragraph? Does one of the ideas developed in this paragraph seem to lead to a following paragraph?

2. Other key words are repeated. Why is "wilderness," for example, repeated? How do the two words—"wolves" and "wilderness"—come together under one main idea?

> Scientists are the most confused and irresponsible people. They are all egg-laying hens sitting on their technology nests in glass and tile henhouses. The eggs they lay are taken out from under them and all they do is crow and cackle about the lack of wisdom in their use.
> —R. Buckminster Fuller from *I Seem to Be a Verb*

Thinking Exercise

1. Notice how some of the words in the topic sentence are repeated, either explicitly or implicitly, in the sentences that follow the topic sentence. As you follow out these repetitions, what do they tell you about the message of the paragraph? Should scientists stop crowing and cackling or stop laying eggs?

2. Point to *every* instance of a repeated word, synonym, idea or sentence pattern in this paragraph.

Pronouns and coherence

We've already shown in the discussion of repetition how pronouns bring the reader back to a main idea or object. Be sure, when you use pronouns, that the reader can clearly relate the pronoun to its antecedent. Can you point out the unclear pronouns in contrast to useful pronouns in this paragraph? Also, how do the pronouns keep the main subject before the reader and why do the effective pronouns sound better than the nouns they represent?

> Ligget, described by *his* roommate as a 'smelly, fat slob,' is the opposite of *his* classmates' hero, Sammy, *whose* experiences in reform school were quite impressive. *We* hear *his* confident speech

to arouse *his* spirits. When Herbie says, "Did you say 'nigger-Lip' to *him*," only once do the boys barely see that Liggett has feelings; "Shaking *his* head slowly," he denied the charge. *He* was incapable of expressing *himself*, or maybe even, incapable of wanting to express *himself*. *He* only "stood stock still, *his* hidden eyes gleaming."

Thinking Exercise

1. Can you figure which pronouns refer to whom. Where would you substitute proper names for pronouns?

2. Could a few of these sentences be re-written to avoid overuse of pronouns or proper names?

Parallelism and coherence

Writers often use similar word orders, sentence patterns or grammatical structures to signal the way their ideas are related. Some of you might feel that parallel structure is too showy a way to create coherence. And sometimes it is. But the most effective parallelisms usually don't draw attention to themselves; they just naturally work ideas into parallel clauses or phrases so that the reader finds it easier to follow the paragraph's direction. Notice how literary critic Ray B. West, Jr., in this brief paragraph on Ernest Hemingway, begins with a general assertion about Hemingway's critics and then makes the connection between that general assertion and the remaining three sentences clear through parallelism.

Too often critics have been content to accept Ernest Hemingway's attitudes at their face value. Thus, *when he writes* that all men die like animals, *he is* put down as a materialist or a naturalist. *When he says,* as *he does* through the character of Jake Barnes in *The Sun Also Rises, that all love* becomes finally a matter of sex, or through Frederick Henry in *A Farewell to Arms that the life of man* is no more than the struggle of ants on the burning log of a campfire, the inference is only too plain: *he is* indeed the spokesman for the lost generation. *When he says* that morals are what you feel good after, *he is* put down as an impressionist and a pragmatist.

Notice how the pronoun *he* is followed in both the introductory subordinate when-clauses and in the main clauses by an active verb. And every sentence after the first follows the subordinate clause/main clause introduced by *he* structure. Yet these parallels are neither forced or showy; they function as natural ways of patterning West's ideas about Hemingway's critics.

Transitional devices and coherence

Of course there are more obvious ways to pull together the parts of your paragraphs. Perhaps the most obvious are transitional words and phrases. Watch how this paragraph, by means of specific transitional devices (shown in italics), links ideas and sentences.

> A careful comparison of these two outlines should suggest *two conclusions. First,* unless a writer seeks a logical progression, he can drift into a plan which does not organize, but merely ties material into bundles without regard to why things are put into one bundle rather than another, or even why the bundles were made up in the first place. *Second,* if the progression of ideas or materials is confused in the outline, it will be worse in the essay. The writer *then* simply passes his confusion along to the reader.
> —James M. McCrimmon, *Writing With a Purpose*

You won't find many transitional words here, but there are enough to keep the reader abreast of the unity of ideas in the paragraph. The paragraph has a very simple one, two structure pointed out by a *first* and *second,* topped off by a *then* that signals a final assertion which develops directly from ideas one and two. Don't overuse specific transitional expressions; they can make a paragraph seem overwritten and often insult a reader by pretending to set out in clear terms a structure that is already very obvious. Here is a paragraph that suffers severely from transitionalitis.

> *Of course, on the one hand,* the narrator tells his own story. *But, on the other hand, when* the story gets finally to its main part, we know who is really talking. *Then, when* everything seems in order, the writer, *however* serious he tries to be, is *nonetheless* comically dishonest.

This writer bores us with signals of where he is going. He needs to show us more naturally, by separating his ideas into clear sentences that are related logically. Then he wouldn't need to worry so much about explicit transitions. When you manage to arrange your events, descriptions, or ideas in clear, logical orders, you won't need to depend on so many obvious connecting words. The ones you do use will that much more effectively direct your readers. (Consult the Appendix I, page 414 for a more specific outline of the functions of common transitional devices.)

Unifying perspectives and paragraphs

We begin to organize experience in writing by working on language itself, by pulling ideas and experiences together through key repetitions, by pronoun consistency, by structural devices such as parallelism. But to organize our materials into whole essays, we often need to discover ways of categorizing our material, of sifting and classifying evidence, that will produce a unity that our readers can follow easily and will also produce new evidence and a more complex understanding of our material. Often you can achieve those objectives by finding the right perspective on your material. In the last chapter, we discussed how writers control their perspectives on physical objects or scenes; we'll focus here on developing perspectives on ideas.

We can generally say that specific experiences and ideas are seen in three ways:

1. As a single element separate from others

2. As an element in a larger network of elements, but separable from one another for purposes of analysis

3. As an element in a *process* in which specific elements cannot be singled out and in which the process is *dynamic*—that is, all elements are in constant motion and interaction

As you prepare to write, consider how you plan to analyze your material. Will you separate it from its context, as if you were putting it under a microscope separate from its usual environment, the way a biologist puts a blood cell under his microscope separate from other cells? Or will you consider your subject in relation to other similar subjects, all contained in one larger network of subjects, the way a sports writer might consider Willie Mays in relation to other major league centerfielders? You might, finally, look at your subject as an ongoing process, one that you have to describe in motion and action, just as a good film critic considers all the frames and shots in a film as one item of evaluation, or just as a good literary critic considers all the parts of a short story as one artistic whole. Or perhaps you will use all three perspectives at various times in your essay—a single-element perspective in one paragraph, a network perspective in another, a process perspective in a third paragraph.

Here are a series of discussions and exercises that demonstrate how these perspectives—single-element, network, and process—might be used to organize writing about the following Associated Press news photograph.

Suppose you wanted to develop some organizing strategy for a brief paragraph on this news photo. How would you use the single-element, network, and process perspectives to generate something to say?

First, you would need to decide on your general purpose. Would you be writing to describe the entire photo or some particular aspect of the photo? Would you want to relate the action in the photo to some larger theme—say violence in our society or in the media—or would you describe the action objectively and avoid interpretation? Let's suppose your purpose is to describe in objective terms the impact this photo would have on the newspaper readers who first saw it. You would want, then, to use the three perspectives to help you locate details in the photo which you might then use to support your interpretation and to organize your material.

To apply a single-element perspective, you would have to scan the photo item by item. Perhaps a list of details, in no particular order, would be a first step: the signs overhead, the faces set in different expressions in the background, the camera held high over the heads of others in the upper right-hand corner, the top of the automobile parked by the curb, the "1965" tag on the rear of the automobile in the foreground and, of course, the four human figures who are most involved in the action in the foreground.

You would more than likely treat several of these details as isolated units of experience, separating them from their immediate context and examining them closely, perhaps relating one to another only when you summarized what you thought was the general effect of the photo. Or you might treat the photo itself as an isolated unit.

A commission formed to investigate the entire situation, however, might first apply a single-element perspective to examine and discover every implication in the photo. Then, they would probably move to a network perspective to form an idea of the entire incident, to see this photo as one unit in an over-all network of activity.

How would you go about applying the network perspective? You would consider the field of action within the boundaries of the photo, how the man screaming over the top of the auto relates visually to the gun held in the air and fired by one of the four main figures, or how the buildings and faces in the background form a spatial network that serves as a background to the automobile and four figures in the foreground. Then, depending on your purpose and space, you would go on to consider, as would the investigating commission that we mentioned above, how the action represented in the photo related to the entire sequence of actions in the completed event. A newsman, for example, would have observed more than he was able to capture in this photo; his

Figure 8-1

complete news story would probably deal with the photo as one unit of action within a network of related actions.

Finally, how might you apply a process perspective? Such a perspective would include a description of the way one action developed into another. You would not be able to isolate units of experience for close analysis, nor would you be able to view the elements of the photo as distinct units combined into an over-all network or system of units. You would have to consider how the particles of experience came together, how they combined into an entire interrelated process. The firing of the gun, the scream of the man, the lifting and aiming of the camera in the background all happened almost simultaneously. Some actions are caused by others; all the actions in the various places work together to provide the total experience. An observer who uses this perspective is like the film critic who moves from one specific action to a consideration of action in motion and change in the entire film. The photograph is dramatized, brought to life, and seen as an interrelated piece of action.

In most cases, you will need to apply all three perspectives. Certainly, a newsman covering the event represented in this photo would probably use all three. He'd want to be precise and discuss details, to be dramatic and discuss the action as an integrated experience, to develop an overview by showing how the particular event in the photograph related to others that occurred almost simultaneously. The important thing, however, is to be able to decide what perspective to emphasize and why. Usually, your perspective will depend upon your purpose. What perspectives do you think should be emphasized if your purpose were one of the following?

1. You want to describe what happened to the man in plainclothes who is being helped by the policeman.

2. You want to support the interpretation that this photo portrays a violent racial conflict in a large city.

3. You want to write a paragraph that analyzes the structure of the photo itself, how the various portions of the photo are related and unified.

4. You want to use an analysis of this photo to convince your readers that the news media can make the public feel that it has participated in the news event itself.

The following paragraphs demonstrate a mixture of perspectives; but usually one perspective is dominant. As you read, try to identify both major and minor perspectives as they appear in the paragraphs. Consider how the perspective works and why the writer chose it.

The signs in the background create a context for the action in this photo. One sign is marked with foreign lettering, another has a dark fire-escape superimposed over it. The store windows are dark and framed with dirtied concrete. Altogether, I'd say the background in this photo is urban; it makes the dramatic action in the foreground seem almost natural.

Everything happened so fast. The gunshot rang out, a puff of smoke hovered above the crowd, floating above the taunting bystanders, the automobiles and the four main figures. The crowd, moving forward rapidly, filled the spot where the shooting had occurred, closing in behind the wounded man and those assisting him. Every word, every gesture, seemed blended into one, enormous roar.

If you look over the photo carefully, expecially the human figures in it, you will notice that several figures seem calm, almost "matter-of-fact." The man who is firing the pistol above his head and the heads of the crowd has a bland, disinterested look, as does the white face with glasses which appears immediately beyond the top of the automobile. We might say the same of the camera men who are studiously taking pictures along the right-hand margin of the photo. These people are all calm and businesslike.

Writing Exercise

1. Imagine yourself walking along this street and coming upon the situation portrayed in the photo. Of course, you can't really tell just what is going on because you are in the immediate vicinity of the action, perhaps right behind some of the bystanders who line the sidewalk in the photo. Write a narrative in which you describe your sensations as you approach the scene of action. You'd probably want to show how you were confused, how various stimuli impressed themselves on your consciousness, how you tried to sort out and form some over-all impression of what was going on. Since you'd be narrating an experience as if it were actually happening, you'd probably emphasize a process perspective more than any other.

2. Imagine yourself observing the action in this photo from a fifth-story window in an apartment building across the street. Unlike the writer in the first exercise, you would be "above" the action and able to observe it carefully without the emotional involvement of someone actually in the scene. Also, you'd be able to see actions and people from a position that would enable you to judge their relationships, how they influence one another, how one action causes another. Limiting yourself to what you see in this photo, write a short essay describing the situation. Show cause and effect relations, what happened as the four

main figures came into view and disappeared. In this exercise, in contrast to the first, you'd probably pay more attention to transitions to clarify the relationships among various actions. With such a general "above-the-action" view, you'd probably use a network perspective.

3. Imagine yourself a news reporter. You are on the scene, perhaps in the position of one of the picture-takers on the sidewalk. Build a complete news story using the evidence you have in the photo. You'll have to imagine what happened immediately before and after the action you find in the photo. After you have sketched out the details of your story, write an "on-the-spot" article for the late edition of your newspaper. Dramatize the situation to make it come alive for your readers while still providing some order. You might, to prepare for such an exercise, find some similar articles in your local newspapers. How are they written? How are the sentences and paragraphs formed? How do they "sound"?

Journal Exercise

Take your journal and walk through a crowded city street. The more varied the people and background the better. Begin by finding a good vantage point, one that takes in a fairly wide range of action but still provides some boundaries to what you see. Then, take quick notes—some objective and concrete and others that record how you feel as you observe. After you've taken notes for a while, find an action, a brief one, that you can follow from beginning to end—someone buying popcorn from a vending machine or street vendor. As you write, use all three perspectives, sometimes scanning the entire scene, sometimes zooming in, as if with a movie camera, on particular details, sometimes analyzing relationships among various details and actions. Create some sparks as you write. Rub objects, words, and ideas together; create some tension and drama.

Finding unity in the paragraph of experience

When you read a story, you read first to understand what happens. You take part in the story much in the same way you would take part in a play. This section should help you find your way into a story and, at the same time, help you develop a few techniques for bringing *your* readers into *your* writing.

We usually don't find many of the common transitional devices —especially words like *however, therefore, because,* or *likewise*—in the paragraph of experience. These words appear more often in idea paragraphs where the writer wants to direct a reader through the various parts and extensions of an opinion or idea. But descriptive writers, storytellers, and writers of experience paragraphs have their own ways of creating unity and coherence.

A writer can unify the experience he shares by controlling his narrator or storyteller and his point of view. Point of view is not the same as physical perspective; it is the way a writer controls how his readers *receive* their information, what his readers hear and see. Remember, a narrator is *not* the writer of a story. Rather, he is a mouthpiece, a spokesman, for the writer; he is someone the writer can control to get the effects he wants from his readers.

In fiction we usually find four common kinds of narrators:

1. *Third person observer:* the storyteller refers to the main character in the story as *he* or *she* (the third person pronoun) and remains a distant observer from what he describes, always judging and evaluating his story. A third person observing narrator reshapes the experience of the story so that the reader sees it his way.

2. *Third person dramatic:* the storyteller or narrator refers to the main character in the story in the third person (*he* or *she*), but in a way that is dramatic and puts the narrator himself *into* the action of the story. A third person dramatic narrator does *not* judge or evaluate the characters or actions in his story; he acts as if he were doing the action himself.

3. *First person observer:* the storyteller refers to the main character in the story as "I," (the first person pronoun). But the "I" remains *apart* from the action, as if judging himself as he acts. The first person observer can, of course, judge himself and his story as he writes.

4. *First person dramatic:* the storyteller tells his story as if he were going through the experience as he writes it down. The "I," in other words, cannot evaluate, judge, or reorder the experience because he wants you to feel that it is actually happening as you read.

These points of view help writers control and unify the experiences they relate. They put a frame on the experience of the story; they help you, as readers, to see the experience of the story from the inside, as if you were in the position of the narrator. The first person narrators bring you into the story—you are the "I" along with the narrator. But the observing narrators, whether first or third person, keep you distant from the action, able to sort out details, evaluate actions, and make a general sense of the experiences as you read. The dramatic narrators, however, put you in the place of characters in the story; events and actions whirl around you as if you were actually in the situation yourself and were unable to judge or analyze because of the immediacy of the story's action.

Ambrose Bierce uses several of these points of view in "An Occurrence at Owl Creek Bridge" on pages 275–282. In fact, his most obvious and important unifying technique is point of view. He sets up a particular kind of narrator and then lets the way that narrator sees the experience organize each paragraph. The point of view brings into a unified frame what otherwise would be disconnected stimuli and sensations. We see the experience through the eyes of a narrator who organizes the experience for us. Almost every paragraph begins with a general object or action, as it is seen by the narrator, and then works back to specific details which complete our picture of the object or action.

As you read, notice how the narration is controlled. We begin by getting the story from a third person observer—a narrator who might be standing on a nearby hill and overlooking the entire scene. He gives us a piece-by-piece description of what he sees; he remains distant and objective, almost like a scientist who analyzes what he sees bit by bit without making judgments. Mostly he keeps to concrete, physical descriptions. Yet, occasionally, he draws inferences from what he sees—for example, when he says that the hanged man's dress indicates that he was a gentleman and when he tells us that the military code is strict and just. This third person observer sets the scene for the entire story. We receive an overview of the scene from him, as if we were watching a panoramic opening shot in a film.

In section II of the story, we find an even more distant third person observer telling the story. This narrator fills us in on the events that lead up to the scene we saw in detail in section I. He also gives us some background on the main character. To fill in this way, he stays out of the present situation, the main action of the story—the hanging of the man, his "escape," and the final resolution. Notice how the narrator in section II uses the past tense, intersperses a bit of dialogue from a past incident, and generally lets you know what characters think and why they act.

In section III, the point of view shifts back to Peyton Farquhar, the man about to be hanged and the main character. We observe him through the eyes and words of a third person dramatic storyteller. This narrator limits himself to describing only what Farquhar would see and observe—in other words, he stays within the dramatic limits of the action, never straying into observations or judgments that could not be made by the character himself as he goes through the action. Occasionally we hear Farquhar's thoughts; we focus in and out following *his* eyes—we see a tree from a distance, then zoom in close to see the veins and the insects on the leaves.

Finally, at the story's end, we are taken abruptly back to the factual, distant narrator of section I. We see the dead body swinging beneath the timbers from a distance again, taking in the whole scene with this narrator who, as we said before, writes as if he were standing on a nearby hillside.

An Occurrence at
Owl Creek Bridge

AMBROSE BIERCE

I

A man stood upon a railroad bridge in northern Alabama, looking down into the swift water twenty feet below. The man's hands were behind his back, the wrists bound with a cord. A rope loosely encircled his neck. It was attached to a stout cross-timber above his head, and the slack fell to the level of his knees. Some loose boards laid upon the sleepers supporting the metals of the railway supplied a footing for him and his executioners—two private soldiers of the Federal army, directed by a sergeant who in civil life may have been a deputy sheriff. At a short remove upon the same temporary platform was an officer in the uniform of his rank, armed. He was a captain. A sentinel at each end of the bridge stood with his rifle in the position known as "support," that is to say, vertical in front of the left shoulder, the hammer resting on the forearm thrown straight across the chest—a formal and unnatural position, enforcing an erect carriage of the body. It did not appear to be the duty of these two men to know what was occurring at the center of the bridge; they merely blockaded the two ends of the foot plank which traversed it.

Beyond one of the sentinels, nobody was in sight; the railroad ran straight away into a forest for a hundred yards, then, curving, was lost to view. Doubtless there was an outpost farther along. The other bank of the stream was open ground—a gentle acclivity topped with a stockade of vertical tree trunks, loopholed for rifles, with a single embrasure through which protruded the muzzle of a brass cannon commanding the bridge. Midway of the slope between bridge and fort were the spectators—a single company of infantry in line, at "parade rest," the butts of the rifles on the ground, the barrels inclining slightly backward against the right shoulder, the hands crossed upon the stock. A lieutenant stood at the right of the line, the point of his sword upon the ground, his left hand

Reprinted from *In the Midst of Life and Other Tales* by Ambrose Bierce.

resting upon his right. Excepting the group of four at the center of the bridge, not a man moved. The company faced the bridge, staring stonily, motionless. The sentinels, facing the banks of the stream, might have been statues to adorn the bridge. The captain stood with folded arms, silent, observing the work of his subordinates, but making no sign. Death is a dignitary who when he comes announced is to be received with formal manifestations of respect, even by those most familiar with him. In the code of military etiquette silence and fixity are forms of deference.

The man who was engaged in being hanged was apparently about thirty-five years of age. He was a civilian, if one might judge from his habit, which was that of a planter. His features were good—a straight nose, firm mouth, broad forehead, from which his long, dark hair was combed straight back, falling behind his ears to the collar of his well-fitting frockcoat. He wore a mustache and pointed beard, but no whiskers; his eyes were large and dark gray, and had a kindly expression which one would hardly have expected in one whose neck was in the hemp. Evidently this was no vulgar assassin. The liberal military code makes provision for hanging many kinds of persons, and gentlemen are not excluded.

The preparations being complete, the two private soldiers stepped aside and each drew away the plank upon which he had been standing. The sergeant turned to the captain, saluted, and placed himself immediately behind that officer, who in turn moved apart one pace. These movements left the condemned man and the sergeant standing on the two ends of the same plank, which spanned three of the crossties of the bridge. The end upon which the civilian stood almost, but not quiet, reached a fourth. This plank had been held in place by the weight of the captain; it was now held by that of the sergeant. At a signal from the former, the latter would step aside, the plank would tilt, and the condemned man go down between two ties. The arrangement commended itself to his judgment as simple and effective. His face had not been covered nor his eyes bandaged. He looked a moment at his "unsteadfast footing," then let his gaze wander to the swirling water of the stream racing madly beneath his feet. A piece of dancing driftwood caught his attention and his eyes followed it down the current. How slowly it appeared to move! What a sluggish stream!

He closed his eyes in order to fix his last thoughts upon his wife and children. The water, touched to gold by the early sun, the brooding mists under the banks at some distance down the stream, the fort, the soldiers, the piece of driftwood—all had distracted him. And now he became conscious of a new disturbance. Striking through the thought of his dear ones was a sound which he could neither ignore nor understand, a sharp, distinct, metallic percussion like the stroke of a blacksmith's hammer upon the anvil; it had the same ringing quality. He wondered what it was, and whether immeasurably distant or near by—it seemed both. Its recurrence was regular, but as slow as the tolling of a death knell. He awaited each stroke with impatience and—he knew not why—apprehension. The intervals of silence grew progressively longer; the delays became maddening. With their greater infrequency the sounds increased in strength and sharpness. They hurt his ear like the thrust of a knife; he feared he would shriek. What he heard was the ticking of his watch.

He unclosed his eyes and saw again the water below him. "If I could free my hands," he thought, "I might throw off the noose and spring into the stream. By diving I could evade the bullets and, swimming vigorously, reach the bank, take to the woods, and get away home. My home, thank God, is as yet outside their lines; my wife and little ones are still beyond the invader's farthest advance."

As these thoughts, which have here to be set down in words, were flashed into the doomed man's brain rather than evolved from it, the captain nodded to the sergeant. The sergeant stepped aside.

II

Peyton Farquhar was a well-to-do planter, of an old and highly respected Alabama family. Being a slave owner and, like other slave owners, a politician, he was naturally an original seccessionist and ardently devoted to the southern cause. Circumstances of an imperious nature, which it is unnecessary to relate here, had prevented him from taking service with the gallant army which had fought the disastrous campaigns ending with the fall of Corinth, and he chafed under the inglorious restraint, longing for the release of his energies, the larger life of the soldier, the opportunity for distinction. That opportunity, he felt, would come, as it comes to all in war time. Meanwhile he did what he could. No service was too humble for him to perform in aid of the South, no adventure too perilous for him to undertake if consistent with the character of a civilian who was at heart a soldier, and who in good faith and without too much qualification assented to at least a part of the frankly villainous dictum that all is fair in love and war.

One evening while Farquhar and his wife were sitting on a rustic bench near the entrance to his grounds, a gray-clad soldier rode up to the gate and asked for a drink of water. Mrs. Farquhar was only too happy to serve him with her own white hands. While she was fetching the water her husband approached the dusty horseman and inquired eagerly for news from the front.

"The Yanks are repairing the railroads," said the man, "and are getting ready for another advance. They have reached the Owl Creek Bridge, put it in order and built a stockade on the north bank. The commandant has issued an order, which is posted everywhere, declaring that any civilian caught interfering with the railroad, its bridges, tunnels, or trains will be summarily hanged. I saw the order."

"How far is it to the Owl Creek Bridge?" Farquhar asked.

"About thirty miles."

"Is there no force on this side the creek?"

"Only a picket post half a mile out, on the railroad, and a single sentinel at this end of the bridge."

"Suppose a man—a civilian and student of hanging—should elude the picket post and perhaps get the better of the sentinel," said Farquhar, smiling, "what could he accomplish?"

The soldier reflected. "I was there a month ago," he replied. "I observed that the flood of last winter had lodged a great quantity of driftwood against the wooden pier at this end of the bridge. It is now dry and would burn like tow."

The lady had now brought the water, which the soldier drank. He thanked her ceremoniously, bowed to her husband, and rode away. An hour later, after nightfall, he repassed the plantation, going northward in the direction from which he had come. He was a Federal scout.

III

As Peyton Farquhar fell straight downward through the bridge he lost consciousness and was as one already dead. From this state he was awakened—ages later, it seemed to him—by the pain of a sharp pressure upon his throat, followed by a sense of suffocation. Keen, poignant agonies seemed to shoot from his neck downward through every fiber of his body and limbs. These pains appeared to flash along well-defined lines of ramification and to beat with an inconceivably rapid periodicity. They seemed like streams of pulsating fire heating him to an intolerable temperature. As to his head, he was conscious of nothing but a feeling of fullness—of congestion. These sensations were unaccompanied by thought. The intellectual part of his nature was already effaced; he had power only to feel, and feeling was torment. He was conscious of motion. Encompassed in a luminous cloud, of which he was now merely the fiery heart, without material substance, he swung through unthinkable arcs of oscillation, like a vast pendulum.

Then all at once, with terrible suddenness, the light about him shot upward with the noise of a loud plash; a frightful roaring was in his ears, and all was cold and dark. The power of thought was restored; he knew that the rope had broken and he had fallen into the stream. There was no additional strangulation; the noose about his neck was already suffocating him and kept the water from his lungs. To die of hanging at the bottom of a river!—the idea seemed to him ludicrous. He opened his eyes in the darkness and saw above him a gleam of light, but how distant, how inaccessible! He was still sinking, for the light became fainter and fainter until it was a mere glimmer. Then it began to grow and brighten, and he knew that he was rising toward the surface—knew it with reluctance, for he was now very comfortable. "To be hanged and drowned," he thought, "that is not so bad; but I do not wish to be shot. No; I will not be shot; that is not fair."

He was not conscious of an effort, but a sharp pain in his wrist apprised him that he was trying to free his hands. He gave the struggle his attention, as an idler might observe the feat of a juggler, without interest in the outcome. What splendid effort! What magnificent, what superhuman strength! Ah, that was a fine endeavor! Bravo! The cord fell away; his arms parted and floated upward, the hands dimly seen on each side in the growing light. He watched them with a new interest as first one and then the other pounced upon the noose at his neck. They tore it away and thrust it fiercely aside, its undulations resembling those of a water snake. "Put it back, put it back!" He thought he shouted these words to his hands, for the undoing of the noose had been succeeded by the direst pang that he had yet experienced. His neck ached horribly; his brain was on fire; his heart, which had been fluttering faintly, gave a great leap, trying to force itself out at his mouth. His whole body was racked and wrenched with an insupportable anguish! But his disobedient hands gave no heed to the command. They beat the water vigorously with quick, downward strokes, forcing him to the surface. He felt his head emerge; his eyes were blinded by the sunlight; his chest expanded convulsively, and with a supreme and crowning agony his lungs engulfed a great draught of air, which instantly he expelled in a shriek!

He was now in full possession of his physical senses. They were, indeed, preternaturally keen and alert. Something in the awful disturbance of his organic system had so exalted and refined them that they made record of things never before perceived. He felt the ripples upon his face and heard their separate sounds as they struck. He looked at the forest on the bank of the stream, saw the individual trees, the leaves and the veining of each leaf—saw the very insects upon them: the locusts, the brilliant-bodied flies, the gray spiders stretching their webs from twig to twig. He noted the prismatic colors in all the dewdrops upon a million blades of grass. The humming of the gnats that danced above the eddies of the stream, the beating of the dragonflies' wings, the strokes of the water spiders' legs, like oars which had lifted their boat—all these made audible music. A fish slid along beneath his eyes and he heard the rush of its body parting the water.

He had come to the surface facing down the stream; in a moment the visible world seemed to wheel slowly round, himself the pivotal point, and he saw the bridge, the fort, the soldiers upon the bridge, the captain, the sergeant, the two privates, his executioners. They were in silhouette against the blue sky. They shouted and gesticulated, pointing at him. The captain had drawn his pistol, but did not fire; the others were unarmed. Their movements were grotesque and horrible, their forms gigantic.

Suddenly he heard a sharp report and something struck the water smartly within a few inches of his head, spattering his face with spray. He heard a second report, and saw one of the sentinels with his rifle at his shoulder, a light cloud of blue smoke rising from the muzzle. The man in the water saw the eye of the man on the bridge gazing into his own through the sights of the rifle. He observed that it was a gray eye and remembered having read that gray eyes were keenest, and that all famous markmen had them. Nevertheless, this one had missed.

A counterswirl had caught Farquhar and turned him half round; he was again looking into the forest on the bank opposite the fort. The sound of a clear, high voice in a monotonous singsong now rang out behind him and came across the water with a distinctness that pierced and subdued all other sounds, even the beating of the ripples in his ears. Although no soldier, he had frequented cramps enough to know the dread significance of that deliberate drawling, aspiration chant; the lieutenant on shore was taking a part in the morning's work. How coldly and pitilessly—with what an even, calm intonation, presaging and enforcing tranquillity in the men—with what accurately measured intervals fell those cruel words!

"Attention, company! . . . Shoulder arms! . . . Ready! . . . Aim! . . . Fire!"

Farquhar dived—dived as deeply as he could. The water roared in his ears like the voice of Niagara, yet he heard the dulled thunder of the volley and, rising again toward the surface, met shining bits of metal, singularly flattened, oscillating slowly downward. Some of them touched him on the face and hands, then fell away, continuing their descent. One lodged between his collar and neck; it was uncomfortably warm and he snatched it out.

As he rose to the surface, gasping for breath, he saw that he had been a long time under water; he was perceptibly farther downstream—nearer to safety. The soldiers had almost finished reloading; the metal ramrods flashed all at once in the sunshine as they were drawn from the barrels, turned in the air, and thrust into their sockets. The two sentinels fired again, independently and ineffectually.

The hunted man saw all this over his shoulder; he was now swimming vigorously with the current. His brain was as energetic as his arms and legs; he thought with the rapidity of lightning.

"The officer," he reasoned, "will not make that martinet's error a second time. It is as easy to dodge a volley as a single shot. He has probably already given the command to fire at will. God help me, I cannot dodge them all!"

An appalling plash within two yards of him was followed by a loud, rushing sound, *diminuendo*, which seemed to travel back through the air to the fort and died in an explosion which stirred the very river to its deeps! A rising sheet of water curved over him, fell down upon him, blinded him, strangled him! The cannon had taken a hand in the game. As he shook his head free from the commotion of the smitten water, he heard the deflected shot humming through the air ahead, and in an instant it was cracking and smashing the branches in the forest beyond.

"They will not do that again," he thought, "the next time they will use a charge of grape. I must keep my eye upon the gun; the smoke will apprise me—the report arrives too late; it lags behind the missile. That is a good gun."

Suddenly he felt himself whirled round and round—spinning like a top. The water, the banks, the forests, the now distant bridge, fort and men—all were commingled and blurred. Objects were represented by their colors only; circular horizontal streaks of color—that was all he saw. He had been caught in a vortex and was being whirled on with a velocity of advance and gyration which made him giddy and sick. In a few moments he was flung upon the gravel at the foot of the left bank of the stream—the southern bank—and behind a projecting point which concealed him from his enemies. The sudden arrest of his motion, the abrasion of one of his hands on the gravel, restored him, and he wept with delight. He dug his fingers into the sand, threw it over himself in handfuls, and audibly blessed it. It looked like diamonds, rubies, emeralds; he could think of nothing beautiful which it did not resemble. The trees upon the bank were giant garden plants; he noted a definite order in their arrangement, inhaled the fragrance of their blooms. A strange, roseate light shone through the spaces among their trunks and the wind made in their branches the music of aeolian harps. He had no wish to perfect his escape—was content to remain in that enchanting spot until retaken.

A whiz and rattle of grapeshot among the branches high above his head roused him from his dream. The baffled cannoneer had fired him a random farewell. He sprang to his feet, rushed up the sloping bank, and plunged into the forest.

All that day he traveled, laying his course by the rounding sun. The forest seemed interminable; nowhere did he discover a break in it, not even a woodman's road. He had not known that he lived in so wild a region. There was something uncanny in the revelation.

By nightfall he was fatigued, footsore, famishing. The thought of his wife and children urged him on. At last he found a road which led him in what he knew to be the right direction. It was a wide and straight as a city street, yet it seemed untraveled. No fields bordered it, no dwelling anywhere. Not so much as the barking of a dog suggested human habitation. The black bodies of the trees formed a straight wall on both sides, terminating on the horizon in a point, like a diagram in a lesson in perspective. Overhead, as he looked up through this rift in the wood, shone great golden stars looking unfamiliar and grouped in strange constellations. He was sure they were arranged in some order which had a secret and malign significance. The wood on either side was full of singular noises, among which—once, twice, and again—he distinctly heard whispers in an unknown tongue.

His neck was in pain and lifting his hand to it he found it horribly swollen. He knew that it had a circle of black where the rope had bruised it. His eyes felt congested; he could no longer close them. His tongue was swollen with thirst; he relieved its fever by thrusting it forward from between his teeth into the cold air. How softly the turf had carpeted the untraveled avenue—he could no longer feel the roadway beneath his feet!

Doubtless, despite his suffering, he had fallen asleep while walking, for now he sees another scene—perhaps he has merely recovered from a delirum. He stands at the gate of his own home. All is as he left it and all bright and beautiful in the morning sunshine. He must have traveled the entire night. As he pushes open the gate and passes up the wide white walk, he sees a flutter of female garments; his wife, looking fresh and cool and sweet, steps down from the veranda to meet him. At the bottom of the steps she stands waiting, with a smile of ineffable joy, an attitude of matchless grace and dignity. Ah, how beautiful she is! He springs forward with extended arms. As he is about to clasp her, he feels a stunning blow upon the back of the neck; a blinding white light blazes all about him with a sound like the shock of a cannon—then all is darkness and silence!

Peyton Farquhar was dead; his body, with a broken neck, swung gently from side to side beneath the timbers of the Owl Creek Bridge.

Writing Exercise

1. Omit the final two paragraphs of the story and compose an alternate ending, one that you believe would be consistent with the narrative technique and content of the story. Discuss how the alternate endings change the meaning of the story.

2. A student, in discussing this story, remarked that the second section serves a summarizing purpose in the factual background leading up to the main focus of the story, the hanging. Omit the second section and write a few paragraphs which would alter the context of the story—the family background of the main character—without being inconsistent with sections I and III.

3. As a journal exercise, find a place where you can observe an action through its completion. Then compose a series of four or five paragraphs in which you describe that action from the third person (*he, she,* etc.). Describe as if you were a close observer that would see only what would occur in the immediate environment. Follow some of the descriptive techniques used by Bierce to arrange and organize stimuli and sensations. Remember, your main purpose will be to describe so that the reader will experience *with* the character. Make each paragraph develop new material, but be sure they all are unified by point of view.

4. Write an essay in which you interpret and support what you think is the purpose of this story. You might begin by writing out four or five main topic sentences, beginning with the very general and moving to more specific statements of purpose. These sentences would become topic sentences for your paragraphs and provide an organizational pattern for your opinions and their support. An example pattern of head sentences might be:

Ambrose Bierce's "An Occurrence at Owl Creek Bridge" demonstrates how individuals become objects in many institutions.

Peyton Farquhar, the "hero" of the story, is a pawn in a military chess game.

Bierce narrates the story so that we, the readers, share Farquhar's experience first-hand, as if we were Farquhar ourselves.

Partially because we do share Farquhar's experience first-hand, we are ready to empathize with the individual, not with the "system," in the story.

These sentences are topic or head sentences because they are relatively general and need support and explanation to be convincing. As the essay develops, the head or topic sentence becomes increasingly specific, as do the supporting sentences in each paragraph. That support comes in the form of more specific example and analysis in the rest of the paragraph. Of course, you will want to make smooth transitions between opinion and support and among paragraphs.

5. Imagine yourself with Peyton Farquhar or one of the characters in the story (perhaps the wife or the lieutenant who commands the hanging). Write a four- or five-paragraph letter in which you summarize the events of the story for a newspaper or to a personal friend. Of course, you'll want to select a few specifics to support your summary.

Finding unity in media

A comic strip reproduces life in small, separated segments that the reader perceives one by one. The structure of the action is somewhat like a movie without motion or sound. The reader contributes the motion as he perceives by imaginatively connecting the actions portrayed in separate frames; the "sound" is added in the form of bits of dialogue by the cartoonist. The cartoonist sets up his own guidelines. For example, he cannot leave too large a gap between the action in each frame. Otherwise the viewer cannot meaningfully connect the actions. The dialogue must also follow certain rules. All the verbal material appears in the form of dialogue. The dialogue must also fit the character; Beetle Bailey would seem incredible if he were speaking elegant English. At the same time, the dialogue must naturally provide the viewer with an indication of what is going on in the visual frame, what characters are saying or thinking, how their minds and emotions are developing along with their physical actions and gestures.

Activity Exercise

Writing paragraphs from comic strips can help combine visual and verbal language. Try the following exercises, using "Doonesbury" as your subject.

1. "Doonesbury" has eight frames. The two characters don't really move around or do very much; most of the "action" in the cartoon is limited to the facial expressions and a few gestures. Compose a paragraph for each frame. Describe the situation as closely as possible; include the dialogue for each frame within your paragraph. When you are finished, you'll have a six paragraph narrative based upon the visual material and dialogue in the cartoon.

2. Nichole's article is an excellent example of irony, of saying the opposite of what you mean in order to ridicule your subject. Rewrite her article changing the *he* to *she* and making the few adjustments in wording that would be necessary to make this a "straight" article. Then write a paragraph in which you define the "point" that Nichole was trying to make in her article.

3. Could you write a paragraph that defined *stereotype* using the material of this cartoon as support? Begin with a topic sentence that defines the term generally. Then apply your definition to Trudeau's ironic treatment of the sexual stereotyping of women in "Doonesbury."

4. Plan a satiric cartoon of your own. First, find some contemporary issue, like women's liberation, that you would enjoy commenting upon. Explain the issue and your purpose in a paragraph. Plan out a sequence of frames by composing a series of frame sentences. These frame sentences should also describe the visual material to be included in each frame. Then write a paragraph describing the characters to appear in the cartoon. Finally, compose bits of dialogue for each frame, perhaps with some final analysis of how the cartoon is to achieve your overall purpose. These plans might be passed about and discussed in small workshops as a preliminary to a final analysis of some of the cartoon plans.

Finding unity in the idea paragraph

Idea paragraphs usually need more transitional devices than other types of paragraphs. The writer must find a unified pattern to develop his central idea. Sometimes he develops by illustration, referring to or describing examples. At other times he takes his idea and analyzes it part by part—applying logic to expand and qualify a general idea. But whatever the strategy of development, the parts of an idea paragraph, or

Figure 8-2 Doonesbury by G. B. Trudeau

the parts of an entire essay, must be clearly related or *coherent*. The reader has to be able to follow the writer's plan.

Experienced essay writers are usually able to make their work coherent by using less obvious transitional devices. Too many transitional words and phrases make for a dull paragraph or essay. As you read "Who Are Who?" by Stephen Birmingham, notice how the sentences are pulled together into paragraphs by repetition of key ideas and words, by sentences that are often parallel both in structure and meaning, and by the careful use of pronouns. There aren't many *on the other hands* or *in like manners*. Birmingham also makes effective use of simple connecting words, especially *and* and *but*. Contemporary American prose writers rely on *and* and *but* more than ever before. These words show where an idea is going simply and naturally, without disturbing the natural rhythm and flow of ideas.

Who Are Who?

STEPHEN BIRMINGHAM

In America, there is Society. Then there is Real Society. Real Society is a part of Society—the upper part. Everybody who is in Society knows who the people in Real Society are. But the people in Real Society do not necessarily know who the other Society people are. The two groups seldom mix. Real Society is composed of older people. It is composed of older families. Older families are better people. Better people are nicer people. Newer people may be richer people than older people. That doesn't matter. Ordinary Society people may get to be Real Society people one day only if they work at it. It sounds confusing, but it is really very simple. Cream rises to the top.

Once, in my extreme youth, I had the difference between Society and Real Society demonstrated to me rather vividly. I was perhaps fifteen, and I was at a dinner party in New York in a very grand—or so it seemed to me—town house in the East Sixties. (The house seemed grand because it had one room, called "the music room," which contained no furniture whatever except a huge golden cello in a glass case.) The party was a children's party before one of the "junior dances," I forget which, and we were offered our choice (it seemed a grand choice, too) of sauterne or tomato juice. It was the first party to which I had worn a black tie. My clothes were new, my shave was new and I, too, was very new. I was so new that I made the mistake of offering to carry the plate of the young lady I was escorting, along with my own plate, back to the buffet table for seconds of creamed chicken in timbales and petits pois.

And, in the process of carrying the two laden plates back to our seats, my cummerbund, newly acquired and only dimly understood, became undone. I was in the center of the room when I felt it begin to slip, and I clapped my elbows tight against my sides to stop it. But it continued to slide down about my hips. Lowering myself to a half-crouch, and jabbing my right elbow into my upper thigh, I became aware that the plate I held in my left hand had emptied itself of peas and chicken, and I felt this warm, moist mass flowing along my arm, inside the sleeve of my dinner jacket.

This was not a Real Society dinner party. I know because, a few days later, when I told this story in all its detail to a lady who *was* a member of Real Society, she said, "Do you mean they served *Sauterne* and not Dubonnet? How dreadful!" She might have added, too, that no young gentleman of Real Society would have found himself in such a predicament. He would have not carried a young lady's plate to the serving table. He would have let her take care of herself.

Real Society people, I once thought, do not listen to what other people are saying. But I was wrong. They listen, but their ears are attuned to different sounds; they respond to different cues. It is not that they miss ordinary conversations, but they pick up different drifts. It is as though most people were on AM and they were on FM. Once, at a Saltonstall wedding in the 1940's, one guest was overheard whispering to another, "Did you know that she was for Wallace?" There was a pause, and then the other guest said thoughtfully, "Really? Wallace *Who*?"

In Philadelphia recently, a matron was exclaiming to a visitor over the great supply of books and plays that have been written about the Philadelphia social scene—*Kitty Foyle, The Philadelphia Story*, and more recently, Richard Powell's *The Philadelphian*. The visitor commented that he, personally—as an outsider—had found parts of Mr. Powell's novel hard to credit. "Oh, really?" said the lady eagerly. "So did *I*. Tell me what it was that bothered you." The visitor cited the opening section of the book, which centers about a Philadelphia Society wedding. As readers of the novel will remember, when the fictional bride and groom have settled in their wedding-night rooms at the Bellevue-Stratford, the bride makes the belated discovery that her husband is impotent. In her distress, she runs out of the hotel into Broad Street where, walking in the opposite direction, she encounters a burly construction worker whom she has eyed admiringly in the past. He is drunk, and walking arm in arm with a prostitute. In the convenient darkness, the young bride pays off the prostitute and takes the arm of the construction worker, who does not notice the artful substitution. The bride and her new beau now proceed to a handy shed where the union is consummated. (And, in the best tradition of modern fiction, where one encounter guarantees a pregnancy, the young woman nine months later gives birth to the child who becomes the novel's hero.) Meanwhile, back at the Bellevue-Stratford, the young bridegroom is so distraught at his wife's discovery that he, too, races off into the night in a fast sports car and is killed in a hideous accident, thereby easing things considerably for his wife's future. All this, said the visitor, "I simply found impossible to believe." "I completely agree," said the Philadelphia lady quickly. "It's absurd. *Nobody* would ever spend their wedding night at the Bellevue-Stratford."

An Englishman, who has made a hobby of studying American Society, feels that Real Society people are indeed different from you and me. "You can spot them immediately," he says. "They have a special way of talking, a special way of thinking, and a special look. They even smell a special way. I love the way they smell."

Though I am still unable to identify Real Society people by their odor, his other points of difference seem perfectly valid. And these differences provide the most formidable obstacles to the social climber. Such is the nature of Society that a person can live his whole life, quite happily and quite successfully, without being aware of Society, or feeling its effect in any way. Only when he attempts to move into it does he discover that it was there all along, like a wall, stern and unscalable, a wall with a small grilled door in it—locked.

Perhaps a better image than a wall with a door in it would be a series of walls, arranged in a crazy-quilt pattern like a bit of New Hampshire farm country seen from the air. Social climbing is like a game. You play it by climbing the walls and crossing the little squares between, one after another. Progress is slow and arduous, and often you must rely on guesswork. Through it all, your goal is *Real* Society, and as you approach its fringes, the going becomes harder. You must learn to recognize, even though you may have not yet seen one, a Real Society person. And one way to do this is to remember a few things a Real Society person is not.

People who go regularly to charity balls, who have been photographed dancing with the Duke of Windsor, who have played poker on the yacht of a Greek shipping magnate, are not necessarily all members of Real Society. Some may be, but most are the other kind. There are Real Society people who have never set foot on a yacht of any sort and who, if the Duke of Windsor walked into the room, would fail to identify him. Sheer splash has nothing to do with Real Society. There were few Real Society people in attendance, for instance, at the wedding of Luci Johnson. ("An August wedding in *Washington?*" people murmured.) Nor were there Real Society people at the wedding of Grace Kelly and Prince Rainier of Monaco. ("I hear that they met," said a Philadelphia Society woman at the time, "at the home of a mutual friend in Ocean City, New Jersey. But how can that be? No one has gone to Ocean City for years.") To this day, the best Philadelphia people make a point of explaining that they did not attend these nuptials; there are a number of princesses in Real Society, but Grace is not one of them. When a splash does occur at a Real Society function, it occurs by coincidence or by accident more often than by design. The wedding of Janet Jennings Auchincloss, a Real Society occasion, generated a good deal of inadvertent splash—and upset the bride so much that she burst into tears.

The *Social Register* is no longer—if it ever was—a reliable guide to who is Real Society and who is not. The little black and red "stud book" has always been published for profit, and has depended on its listees' willingness to be listed, as well as on their subscriptions. The *Social Register* grows thicker in times of economic boom, and shrinks when the economic pendulum falls the other way. The number of *Social Register* families may wax and wane, but the size of *Real Society* remains constant. Many Real Society families ridicule the *Register* now, and make the familiar comment, "It's just a telephone book." In New York, for instance, it is still smaller and more wieldy than the Manhattan directory. As often as not, however, when an entrant is "dropped" from the *Register,* he has simply neglected to—or chosen not to—fill out the necessary annual forms. Still, many Society people feel as the writer Louis Auchincloss does. "The *Social Register* has gotten so enormous," he says, "that it looks rather peculiar if you're *not* in it."

One can frequently recognize a woman of Real Society by the way she dresses. Real Society women's clothes have a way of staying in style longer than other peoples' because Real Society fashions do not change markedly from year to year. Neither the junior-cut mink coat nor the beaver jacket has gone through many transitions since the introduction of the designs, nor has the cut of the classic camel's hair topper. The short-sleeved, round-collared McMullen blouse is ageless, and the hemline of the Bermuda short has hardly been known to fluctuate. What is more classic than a double strand of good pearls? The poplin raincoat is as suited to suburban shopping today as it was to the Smith campus in 1953. It has been said that were it not for the tastes of the young Society woman, the great firm of Peck & Peck would soon go out of business, and all the knitwear on the second floor of Abercrombie & Fitch would quickly fall prey to the moth.

The look is easy, tweedy. Hair is a blond mixture, streaked from the sun, of middle length, and is often caught at the back of the neck in a little net bag. This style is as much at home on the back of a horse as it is with a full-length dinner dress; it has also been with us since the 1920's. Real Society women are often tanned the year round—from riding and playing golf and tennis wherever the sun shines—and a perpetual tan may lead to a leathery look, with crinkled squint lines about the eyes. It is a look exemplified in both the Mrs. Nelson Rockefellers, who had identically impeccable Real Society origins. It is a look that is instantly recognizable but, because of its particular composition, quite difficult for the outsider to simulate.

Then there is the Society voice. Trying to duplicate the American Society accent has provided the greatest stumbling block for the parvenu. Some say you must be born with it to speak it properly and convincingly, but it is safe to say that graduates of such private schools as St. Paul's, Foxcroft, and Madeira, who may not have had the accent to begin with, can emerge with a reasonably close facsimile of it. It is a social accent that is virtually the same in all American cities, and it is actually a blend of several accents. There is much more to it than the well-known broad A. Its components are a certain New England flatness, a trace of Southern drawl, and a surprising touch of the New York City accent that many people consider Brooklynese. Therefore, in the social voice, the word "shirt" comes out halfway between "shirt" and "shoit." Another key word is "pretty," which, in the social voice, emerges sounding something like "prutty." There is also the word "circle," the first syllable of which is almost whistled through pursed lips, whereas the greeting, "Hi," is nearly always heavily diphthonged as "Haoy." This speech has been nicknamed "the Massachusetts malocclusion," since much of it is accomplished with the lower jaw thrust forward and rigid, and in a number of upper-class private schools, children are taught to speak correctly by practicing with pencils clenched between their teeth.

Accent and appearance help Real Society people to recognize one another quickly, but other factors also weld them into a recognizable unit. The school, college, and clubs are just as important considerations as how much money one has to spend, or where one lives. Addresses have become of minor importance to members of Real Society. They may own estates on Long Island which they call places, palaces in Newport which they call cottages, duplexes on Fifth Avenue which they call houses. A number simply own houses which they call houses. Though, for the most part, Real Society lives on the better streets of America's larger cities, and in the more affluent of these cities' suburbs, Real Society can still be encountered on beachheads along the Carolina coast, in tiny hamlets in Vermont, or in the Mojave Desert.

Society has always had a matriarchal cast—particularly in the United States. But in Real Society the male reigns over his own preserve. Real Society wives have no need to be pushy. The male has his club, even though a number of the most exclusive clubs have been forced to admit ladies at the dinner hour. And, if the men's club has become less important than it used to be, this is not blamed upon women but on urban economics and, of course, newcomers. New money has been inexorably pushing the old money out of the leather club chair, and the result is that men of Real Society have retreated to their homes again. Here, their position is secure. Their wives would never think of accepting an invitation or planning a party without consulting them. And the man may even, provided he is able to afford it, be permitted to keep a mistress.

In Real Society it is less a matter of which club, which school, which street, and what clothes, than it is a matter of *who. Who* will always count more than how, or how much. One does *not* ask, "Where are you from?" or "Where did you go to school?" or "What do you do?"

Such questions are considered as tactless as "How much did it cost?" If you have to ask such questions, you have no right to the answers. On the other hand; you may ask without fear of rebuke, "Who . . . ?" "Who is she?" as a question may mean, "What was her maiden name?" It may also mean what was her mother's maiden name, and what was her grandmother's maiden name, and so on. The members of the family are the family's most precious family jewels. Grandfather may have been Ambassador to The Hague or an alcoholic suicide; it doesn't matter, if he belongs. Family talk is a favorite cocktail-hour diversion wherever Real Society gathers. Each genealogical fact is brought out lovingly and tenderly, examined meticulously, then carefully put away. To talk family properly, you never need a reference book or printed family tree, or any other aid; the facts are at your fingertips with dates, with snippets of incidental history, with little anecdotes. Done well, family talk is a beautiful and bewildering thing to listen to—a concerto of whos. Done poorly—by the poseur or dissembler—it can be disastrous. A social climber can sometimes fake an ancestor, but he had better examine his company carefully before he tries it. "All we Van Rensselaers," says a Van Rensselaer significantly, *"know* our Van Rensselaers." And the parvenu had better be prepared to let family values dominate all other values. Not long ago in Philadelphia the talk turned to art and, parochially enough, to Philadelphia's two most prominent woman painters, Mary Cassatt and Cecilia Beaux—both of whom were members of distinguished families. In the middle of a debate on their relative artistic merits, with Miss Cassatt seemingly favored, someone commented sharply, "But the Cassatts weren't anybody!"

People named Vanderbilt are not necessarily in Real Society, but people named Vanderlip are. In Real Society, the name Morris means somewhat more than Belmont. Rockefellers now are safely in Real Society, though they didn't use to be, and Astors, who used to be, are pretty much out. Roosevelts always were and always will be of Real Society, despite the political affiliations of one of the family's branches. Other impeccable Society names are, in New York: Aldrich, Auchincloss, Blagden, Burden, French, Stillman, Wickes, and Woodward; in Boston you are safe with Sedgwicks and Gardners and Fiskes, as well as with Adamses, Cabots, Lowells, and Saltonstalls. In Philadelphia, there are Drinkers and Ingersolls and Chews and Robertses. There are Biddles, but there are also other Biddles. There are Cadwaladers. It is said that a true Philadelphian can distinguish between single-*l* Cadwaladers, who are Real Society, and double-*l* Cadwalladers, who are not, simply by the way the name is pronounced.

There are, furthermore, in every American city, families who might be called *local* Real Society. Thus the Fords, who are Real Society in Detroit, lose a bit of their Reality in Philadelphia or Boston. The Uihlein family and their beer may have made Milwaukee famous, but their name does not carry imposing social weight in New York. The phenomenon also works in reverse. The Kennedys, who are *from* Boston, are closer to

Real Society elsewhere than they were—or ever will be—on their native soil.

Certain social critics have claimed that Society has been "killed" by publicity. This is rather like saying that Dacron has killed the fashion industry. There has always been a small but colorful segment of Real Society that has labored to see that its name and picture got in the papers, just as there has always been an element more fond of going to clubs and bars and bistros than of staying home. Café Society, whether by that label or any other, is no new phenomenon, and the spiritual descendants of C. K. G. Billings's famous dinner-on-horseback at Sherry's dance today at the Electric Circus. Publicity filled out the "image" of American Society in the eighteenth and nineteenth centuries, just as it does today, providing it with gaudy accents. The only difference is that the outlets for publicity, thanks to modern mass communications, have escalated. It should never be assumed that publicity and Society are alien concepts, and that one can flourish only at the expense of the other. On the contrary, Society enjoys—and is grateful for—its publicity-seeking members. They, the few, in many ways protect a facade and a showcase—a deceptively glossy showcase, to be sure—for what has become an enduring structure in America, the Social Establishment. Behind the facade and the showcase, the others of the Establishment like to feel they are being given a little peace. It is not *they* who will be asked to give the interviews.

Publicity, by making Society appear glamorous and celebrated, also provides the greatest lure for social climbers. And Society could not exist without its climbers.

When a person says, with a little sigh, that Real Society is dead and gone, it is reasonably safe to assume that that person is not a member. People in Real Society know that their world is very much alive. But they don't think it is quite polite to say so.

Activity Exercise

1. Throughout this essay certain key words are repeated. Follow one of these words—the words *real* and *society* are two obvious examples—through the essay and explain how it is defined and clarified by the essay's end. Could you write a brief definition of "Real Society" after reading this essay?

2. This essay, like most of the essays in this book, uses descriptions of personal experience to illustrate the central idea. Notice how specific experiences combine with ideas, sometimes within single paragraphs, at other times in separate but related paragraphs. How clearly is the supporting experience related to the ideas?

3. At times Birmingham leaves an example undeveloped. For example, he never really explains why the Englishman said about Real Society, "They even smell a special way." Can you explain why some examples or bits of dialogue and anecdotes are left unexplained?

4. Taken generally, how serious would you say Birmingham is in this essay? Does he really believe that there is a Real Society? If you think he does, what does he think of it? How do you know?

5. Look around you. Can the society in which you travel be categorized and defined in the way Birmingham defines American Society? Do you hear the social click in the way some of your friends talk, do you find the high social sign in the way some of them dress, use gestures, in their actions? Write an essay in which you classify the people around you and point to their habits and customs. Be specific, refer to the way they talk and act to support your classifications. Don't be afraid to adopt a tongue-in-cheek approach.

6. Write an expository essay in which you apply one of Birmingham's key terms to people you know. Introduce and explain the concept—perhaps a kind of social behavior described by Birmingham as part of the social clique—and describe particular actions that you have observed that fit under the concept.

Some guidelines for rewriting paragraphs

Every paragraph should have a central idea, and in the course of the paragraph something should happen to that idea. As you go over your paragraphs, ask yourself whether you've *developed* your central idea. Do you feel that your reader will actually know more about the idea when he finishes the paragraph than he did when he began? Or do you merely rephrase or repeat without really developing? In every paper you write, select a few paragraphs and ask yourself the following questions. The answers should help you develop some operational guidelines.

1. Can you describe the central idea or object of the paragraph in a single, simple sentence? You may not find that sentence in the paragraph itself, but you ought to be able to reproduce the idea in a single sentence even if it is not stated openly in your paragraph. When you feel you have the right sentence, refine its wording carefully and see whether you can improve the wording of your original paragraph.

2. Is your *topic* sentence, which is the sentence in your paragraph that comes closest to describing your central idea, in the right position? Can the reader easily tell that it is the most important sentence? Does the paragraph seem to build up to or lead from your central idea?

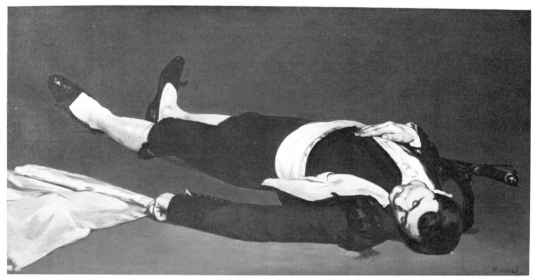

Courtesy the National Gallery of Art, Washington, D.C. Widner Collection.

Figure 8-3   The Dead Toreador *by Edouard Manet*

3. Are your supporting sentences clearly related to your central idea? Can you add transitions that will clarify the direction of the paragraph? Go back over your paragraph and number sentences consecutively according to their importance. Then show your numbered sentences to someone else and ask him if he can explain why they are numbered as they are.

Writing Exercise

1. What do you know about this man from what you see in Manet's *The Dead Toreador?* Write a paragraph in which you objectively describe the man—his face, clothing, the way he is posed even in death. Work out some plan before you actually write. Begin with the most general observation and work back to specifics, or begin with a detail that fits your general impression and work up to more general descriptions. Then write an interpretive paragraph. Judge the man's character, name his occupation or the time when he lived, and provide specific supporting evidence.

2. Write a paragraph in which you explain one of this man's characteristics when he lived. You'll have to draw references from what you see in the painting. He is a bullfighter, but can you tell from the

painting whether he was brave? Graceful? Charming? Adventurous? Make that characteristic the main idea in a paragraph and provide specific support and illustration.

3. Write a series of paragraphs in which you follow the toreador through a brief sequence of action. You may, for example, describe him as he walks slowly to the center of the bull ring. Follow his actions closely, filling in visual detail as you go, and *suggest* what you feel is the toreador's character in the process. Visualize the action you describe and make transitions smoothly from one action to another. Again, you'll need to draw inferences for your essay from what you see in this painting.

4. Write an expository interpretation of the painting. Your thesis might answer the question: "What was the painter trying to say about toreadors?" Shape a question of your own and make your answer your thesis. Then refer to details in the painting to support your thesis.

From eye to thou . . .

V

Self-discovery to public expression

I should not talk so much about myself if there were anybody else I knew as well.

—*Henry Thoreau*

When one individual enters the presence of others, he will want to discover the facts of the situation . . . To uncover fully the factual nature of the situation, it would be necessary for the individual to know the actual outcome or end product of the activity of the others during the interaction, as well as their innermost feelings concerning him. Full information of this order is rarely available; in its absence the individual tends to employ substitutes—cues, tests, hints, expressive gestures, status symbols, etc.

—*Erving Goffman*

Conversation gives force to writing and cuts down on Explainery. In a dialogue the writer doesn't constantly say how the speakers feel as they respond to each other. Frequently they say the opposite of what they feel. The reader has to figure out whether one man's words are striking sparks with the others' . . .

—Ken Macrorie

INTRODUCTION

The first four sections of this book talk mostly about you, your experience, and the ways you can turn your talents and experience into effective writing. But good writing is usually more than thoughts and feelings transcribed on paper. Writing, like living, must be dramatic, filled with the oppositions, frictions, and tensions that make everyday life interesting. And you have to write as if you are alive, sending your own sparks out to kindle the interest of your readers.

In essence, this entire section is about style. We've all heard about "style"; people develop different "life-styles," different styles of dressing and acting. We know a person's life-style by observing his actions—how he dresses, where he goes for entertainment, the car he drives, the friends he keeps. More sensitive people look to a person's values, his opinions, ideas, and general attitudes to discover life-style.

We know a writer's style by his words, by how he makes sentences, by his sense of humor or lack of one, by what he chooses to write about, and by how he chooses to treat his readers. Words are a writer's actions. They do more than convey information; they also convey an image of the writer. Whenever we write, we tell our readers who we are as well as what we think or feel.

There is, however, a value to writing that we don't usually have when we talk or act in everyday life. We often can't control what we say and do in actual experience; the impulse to say exactly what we think the other person wants, or the impulse to oppose what the other person wishes, often cuts into our real feelings. But we can control words. And the more we learn control the more we can create the right image of ourselves as we write. The three chapters in Section V deal specifically with ways writers can control style—by considering the three basic elements of any writing situation: the speaker, the subject, and the audience or readers. Once we learn to shape words to fit the relationships among these elements, we have learned to control style.

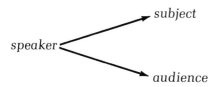

Before we begin with specific discussions of these elements, let's consider a definition of a writer's style. We've described how style can be recognized. But what is it? *Style* is choice. Everytime you write a word you make a choice, whether consciously or unconsciously. Style is the result of those choices. If you choose to use *ain't* over *isn't*, you are making a choice in style. If you choose to use the pronoun *one* rather than *you*, you've made another style choice. Once you've made a large number of these decisions, from single words on through the way you phrase whole sentences, you've established your own style. And that style will work either for or against your message. It will create an image of you on paper—perhaps the only image your reader will ever receive. These chapters should help you make the right impression—depending on the situation, your audience, your subject, and you. Between *you* and *they*, between *I* and *thou*, comes style. And style often makes or breaks the message.

9

Voice: Your personality on paper

If you listen carefully, you'll hear lively words everywhere. The housewife lectures the garbage collector who has dumped her garbage cans on the front lawn; the traffic cop directs a sarcastic remark at a motorist who has missed his signal; the girl down the hall argues with a librarian about an overdue book fine. The words we hear people talking in everyday life are usually always dramatic; questions, answers, and quick retorts swing back and forth with tension and opposition. Whenever two people talk we have drama, especially if they are talking without thinking about subjects that really interest them.

When you write, you want to capture some of the liveliness and drama of everyday talk. You'll need to listen more carefully to the language you hear around you. Make your mind a tape recorder. Listen to what the fellow at the next table says and try to capture the personality that you hear in his voice. Follow people's gestures as they talk and you'll be able to write dialogue and support it with remembered actions or little details that will bring entire conversations alive.

We walked along slowly. Everytime Tom spoke he brought his hand slowly across his forehead as if delivering a very grave thought.

"I wouldn't want to tell him right away, though. He might never really get over it."

I kept him talking about his father, revealing his fears and opening himself to someone else. The more he talked the faster the cracks in the pavement slipped by underfoot.

"And even if he did, I wonder if he'd ever treat me the same again. I don't know."

That's a dramatic moment. We feel the tension and drama of a coming revelation, even though we don't know the speaker or even what he's worried about. The words strike sparks and talk to one another; the brief pieces of action, the hand across the forehead, give the scene just enough reality.

The trouble with most of our school writing, however, is that it doesn't grow from such dramatic moments. You are told what to write about and even how to write it. But once you've developed an attentive ear, you can inject everyday drama into even school writing. And you can do it without sacrificing the sharpness, accuracy, or seriousness of what you have to say. You can use *style* to strike up sparks between you, your material, and your audience.

Activity Exercise

1. Go to a busy place and spend some time just listening. Listen long enough so that you can find one or two personalities in what you hear. Then go to a quiet place and record a dialogue in which you try to recreate those personalities as they talk to one another. Try to recall exact catch phrases, words and passing remarks from what you actually heard. Add a few pieces of background detail to give the scene reality.

2. Go visit a friend. Get your friend talking on a subject you know he or she will enjoy discussing and one that you know he or she is interested in. Listen carefully. Then go back and write a dialogue of the conversation in as much detail as you can. Again, try to capture your friend's personality, his or her *style* of talking and acting.

3. Take a ride on a crowded elevator. In the middle of your ride, make some kind of surprising remark, perhaps just the comment "My, this ceiling is blue" will be enough. Then record in your memory the reactions and remarks of others, along with your own feelings as you observe. Why don't people expect such remarks on elevators? Notice how the closer together people are in public places the more uncomfortable they feel when someone speaks directly to them or does something unexpected. Why?

4. Try writing a note to a friend in an unconventional or unexpected style. For example, leave your roommate, wife, or husband a note about some everyday item. But write it in extremely formal language. Or, better yet, try speaking very formally in a familiar, everyday situation—say, at a basketball game, at a dorm meeting, or while walking across campus to your next class. What responses do you get? Why?

As Erving Goffman suggests in one of the epigraphs to this section, we seldom say exactly what we mean. In speaking, we use gestures, cues, body movements, and actions to let our listeners know how to take our words. In writing, however, we don't have the benefit of physical actions. But we do have *style*. By choosing our words and forming our sentences we present an image of who we are, at least of who we are in a particular piece of writing. In a sense, we have a chance to make over our personalities whenever we write. Both these writers talk about the same subject. Yet they are decidedly different people. Why? Can you point to words, sentences, and phrases that make these writers different?

> Sports figures are very often heroes before they really understand what heroism is. The result of this lack of understanding is often immature behavior and failure to create a successful public image.

> Lots of sports heroes are bums off the field. They're little kids having a tantrum or big kids bullying the others. I feel like socking the TV screen every time I see some brainless prima donna trying to sell me hair tonic.

For our purposes, we can subdivide style into three separate qualities—voice, tone, and attitude. In this chapter we'll discuss the writer's voice.

What is your writing voice?

Voice is the sound of you on paper; it is the impression of your personality that your words give to your readers. Your voice should support your message. You should sound like the type of person a reader can know and like, one that fits the occasion, isn't too stuffy or formal or too chummy and casual. To discover and control your own voice, you need to do two things.

First, learn that you do have a voice. Listen to yourself. At least once in a while, let yourself write as you would talk. Copy down some of your everyday talk. Notice how you repeat certain terms or phrases; remember how you spoke the last time you got a rise out of your listeners. Everyone speaks a language native to his country. He also speaks a dialect—a language fitted to a certain region or group of people. Everyone also shares some special bits of language with people he or she works with or socializes with: fraternity brothers share jargon (a special vocabulary shared by groups with common interests); the psychologist shares jargon with his fellow workers. But all of us also speak a *personal* language—a particular way of putting key words together, the way we repeat certain common expressions and ignore others, the particular way our voice rises and falls as we grow excited or involved. Voice depends primarily on our being able to transfer those personal characteristics to writing, without sacrificing the general significance and accuracy of our message.

Second, learn to appreciate voice in others—either in what you hear in the talk of your friends or in what you hear in the language of what you read. Ask yourself what attracts you to the way certain friends speak. Ask yourself why you enjoy reading a certain sports columnist, fashion writer, or feature writer. Look for specific language devices that create their voices.

Here are three voices from a daily newspaper. What do you think of them? Why? What kind of person is talking? How do you know? Do you think the voices you hear are appropriate to the subjects?

> Johnny Bench's Mark IV hums along I-75 North a little bit faster than the speed limit. His primary destination is Dayton, where he will tape the Phil Donahue Show.
>
> "Got to stop," he says. And indeed he does. He's stopping to pick up Debbie Woodward, a blond model, tall and slender and sharp of tongue.
>
> It is then, when Bench announces the upcoming stop, that you think of the rumor you've heard and you ask Johnny Bench if he is, indeed, engaged.
>
> He laughs and admits that he, too, has heard the rumor, even though it has been just a couple of days since he returned from Florida.
>
> —Bob Hertzel from "Who'd Want to Be Engaged to You," an article on Cincinnati Reds ballplayer Johnny Bench from the *Cincinnati Enquirer,* Monday, January 29, 1973

> True, some of them had to be pushed in chairs, some were carried by college volunteers, some made it on their own . . .
>
> But the entire student body of Redwood School for Cerebral Palsy in Ft. Mitchell, Ky. (all 90 of them) produced a variety show last week. And they had a ball doing it.
>
> So did the audience—the Women's Guild.
>
> —From "Heart's Just Part" from the *Cincinnati Enquirer,* Monday, January 29, 1973

> But the playfulness was only on the surface. Underneath was a masterful mix of old Ellington favorites like "Perdido," "Take the A Train," and "Creole Love Call" with new works, the finest of which was the aforementioned "Togo Brava."

—From "Aged Ellington Shows His Old Vigor," by Jerry Carter, the *Cincinnati Enquirer*, Monday, January 29, 1973

The newspaper is a good place to find many different voices. Turn to the front page for straight, objective news reporting, to the amusement pages for clever, witty reviews and opinions on movies and television shows, and to the sports pages for hard-hitting opinions on contemporary sports figures as well as factual game reports. Every writer has a voice of his own *and* a voice that fits the situation. You won't find much wit in the article describing a very serious fire, but you will find a voice—probably one that is serious and objective. And you will find humor and tough talk in Dear Abby's answers to many letter-writers. Try looking over the many voices you find in letters-to-the-editor columns. Ask yourself what kind of person probably wrote the letter and why.

Hopefully, such practices will make you more attentive to voice as a writer's way of putting himself into any writing situation. If your subject is solemn and serious, your voice should be also, but it should also be *you*, with your particular way of talking captured in the words.

Activity Exercise

If your class has access to a tape recorder, use it to capture voice-in-action. Do this by working up an interesting subject for discussion. When the talk becomes lively and animated, have your teacher switch on the recorder—to catch people's voices without their realizing they are being taped. At the discussion's end, play back the tape and discuss the voices you hear. Could they be captured and transferred to writing? What would have to be done to the spoken words in the process?

Voice and the writer's "distance"

Voice is usually influenced by the distance you take from your readers. When you speak to someone in your immediate family, you often leave much background information out because you rely on his familiarity. The person you are speaking to knows you well enough to fill in background. You use familiar expressions, and you let the way you really feel and think show in your words. But when you speak to a stranger, your voice changes; you may be more courteous and careful to fill in background. You may decide to sound more sweet than tough;

in other words, you adjust the way you really feel and are to meet the needs of a listener who *doesn't* know you.

Your readers will almost always be strangers. They'll know only the you they see on the page, not the you that acts, speaks, and lives day by day. When you create a voice on paper, then, you want to create the right distance between yourself and your readers. Otherwise you'll sound tough when you should sound courteous or you'll sound too polite when more direct, "tell 'em like it is" language would be more effective.

Consider the way you treat strangers in public places. You don't stare too long at someone on the sidewalk unless you want to get their attention. It's impolite. Never catch the eye of a stranger for too long a time unless you want his or her embarrassed attention. A quick look, a glance, a brushing of the eyes in passing is all that we are allowed when we pass people on the sidewalk. Otherwise we invade a person's privacy, his private space, with our eyes, and that makes him or her uncomfortable. In fact, if you notice some particular physical characteristic of a person—say his long hair, a particularly revealing dress, or an outlandish outfit—you will probably make a point of turning away immediately to prove you *haven't* noticed. If you continue to stare, that person will probably think you disapprove of him.

Consider how your voice fits a writing situation in the same way you would consider physical behavior appropriate or inappropriate when you first meet or pass a person on a street corner.

Look at these two excerpts from contemporary essays. Imagine the speakers of these paragraphs standing before you. How would they address you? What gestures or voice inflections would accompany the words? How do you know? Are there hints in the paragraphs? Read the pieces using several different kinds of inflections. Do the words change their meaning when you emphasize different syllables and sounds?

> I'm not sure why teachers are so chicken. It could be that academic training itself forces a split between thought and action. It might also be that the tenured security of a teaching job attracts timid persons who need weapons and the other external trappings of authority.
>
> —Jerry Farber, "The Student as Nigger"

> We know through painful experience that freedom is never voluntarily given by the oppressor; it must be demanded by the oppressed.

Frankly, I have yet to engage in a direct-action campaign that was "well-timed" in the view of those who have not suffered unduly from the disease of segregation. For years now I have heard the word "wait!" It rings in the ear of every Negro with piercing familiarity. This "wait" has almost always meant "never." We must come to see, with one of our distinguished jurists, that "justice too long delayed is justice denied."

—Martin Luther King, Jr. "Letter from Birmingham Jail"

Thinking Exercise

1. The first paragraph follows a common plan. The writer begins with a question and then follows with a specific answer in the rest of the paragraph. How would the writer change his voice as he moved from the question to the answer, finally through to the specific reasons?

2. The speaker in the first passage is at least partially sarcastic. How would sarcasm influence the way sentences are spoken? What specific devices are used to create sarcasm—the parallel structures of each sentence, the way the speaker uses "might," "not sure," and other words to tell us he is suggesting, not actually accusing? Could you explain what sarcasm is by using this paragraph and other examples from your own experience?

3. Have another student read these paragraphs aloud. Which one is most suited to public address? How do you know? Can you point to specific devices that make the paragraph seem more like a speech or public letter? Find particular phrases which you feel would work well in a speech.

Writing Exercise

1. In your journal, compose some careful observations of people as they speak in informal situations—on a streetcorner, in the student union, in front of a store.

2. In your journal, compose a few careful observations of television personalities. You might turn the sound off and observe only visual

action, expressions and gestures. Remember the techniques of descriptive writing that you practiced in the first section.

3. Observe television personalities with the sound shut off and write a fictional dialogue for what you see.

4. Have some members of the class compose several carefully described dramatic situations—a quiet conversation in a small restaurant or an interview between student and teacher in the teacher's office. These sketches should be described in as much physical detail as possible, but without dialogue. Other members of the class can improvise dialogue.

5. Write an analysis of the various voices of your local newspaper. Compare, say, a sports column or article, a gossip column, a political editorial, a straight news article, and a feature article. Emphasize how the writers create voices individualized yet suited to the particular context. For example, as you read a passage mark down what you can find as evidence that the writer is using a particular voice—a talky or colloquial voice, a formal or informal voice, a tough, pushy voice, whatever. Does he use contractions or slang? Does he use words that are usually associated with particular professions, like "politicos" for shrewd politicians or "fan" for a baseball spectator? How long are the sentences? Or, more importantly, how *complicated* are the sentences? Do they follow a simple subject-verb order? Are there many subordinate phrases or clauses? What pronouns does the writer use—the relatively formal *one* or the informal *we*? Are the sentences ever parallel? Are similar structures repeated in different words in several sentences?

The voices of advertising and cartoons

Ads and cartoons often put words and actions together. The pictures and illustrations work together to create a voice behind the ad or cartoon.

Activity Exercise

1. In the cartoon by Barsotti, the cartoonist takes special baseball jargon and puts it into the mouth of a hermit or prophet. Whenever we find someone using language that we don't expect them to use, the results are usually funny. Reverse the situation that you find in the cartoon. Can you imagine the ballplayer talking like a Biblical prophet? What would he sound like? Compose some prophetlike dialogue for him. Can you translate the prophet's advice to the ballplayer into common language? Is

Figure 9-1

"Perhaps if you choked up on your bat a little more and just tried for clothesliners into short outfield, instead of those long rides that send the apple out of the park, you wouldn't whiff so often, and would be rewarded with a modest rise in your batting average."

Drawing by C. Barsotti; copyright © 1972 by The New Yorker Magazine, Inc.

Figure 9-2

Parker Pen ad

A pen can't tell you everything about a man. But it can tell a lot.
The Parker 75 Classic Ball Pen.

Courtesy of the Parker Pen Company.

anything lost in the translation? If you can remember someone who recently used jargon that really wasn't natural to him, write up a brief sketch, with some actual dialogue, that recaptures that situation.

2. What kind of person would find the Parker Pen ad appealing? How can you tell? Parker makes relatively expensive pens; not everyone wants to spend much money on ballpoint pens. Do you think this ad takes that fact into consideration? Does the voice and language of the ad seem to fit the product? How would you describe the voice of this ad? Does it sound elegant and cool or practical and common? Could you physically describe the man who holds the pen in the Parker ad? How would you expect him to dress? What kind of car might he drive? What books and newspapers might he read? Find a few other ads with particular voices—perfume ads that appeal to the sensuous woman, automobile ads that present an executive or practical voice.

3. Find another common object and write an ad that you think suits it. Create a voice that sounds just right for the product—not too elegant or cheap, not condescending or insulting. Use the Parker ad as a model if you wish. You'll need to think out your voice before you begin. Decide on a few general adjectives to define your voice. If you want to write an "elegant and superior" ad, then begin to find words and phrases you might use to create the sound of elegance and superiority. Remember, the ad should create a voice *and* describe the object or product. As you write, keep your eye on the object or product and your ear on the sound of the words, the shape of the sentences, and the catchiness of the phrases.

Finding voices in what you read

The final step in understanding voice in writing is to analyze it in what you read. Ask yourself what kind of person you hear talking as you read. Very often we form unconscious impressions of writers as they speak to us on paper. Once we begin to understand how and why those impressions are created, we're on the way to recognizing and appreciating voice.

Mark Twain had a talent for creating real people talking on paper. Anyone who reads *Huckleberry Finn* gets to know Huck as if he were a personal friend. Yet all a reader knows of Huck comes through words on paper. Look at the opening passage of the novel. Right away you know an uncommon person is talking. Even if you haven't read the novel, form an impression of Huck just from what you read here. Jot down a few adjectives you think describe Huck's character. Then look over the passage and try to point to particulars in the language that create Huck's particular voice. What about his vocabulary, his particular dialect, the figures of speech he uses ("with some stretchers"), the way he puts words together?

> You don't know about me, without you have read a book by the name of *The Adventures of Tom Sawyer*, but that ain't no matter. That book was made by Mr. Mark Twain, and he told the truth, mainly. There were things which he stretched, but mainly he told the truth. That is nothing. I never seen anybody but lied, one time or another, without it was Aunt Polly, or the widow, or maybe Mary. Aunt Polly—Tom's Aunt Polly, she is—and Mary, and the Widow Douglas, is all told about in that book—which is mostly a true book; with some stretchers, as I said before.

A writer of fiction almost always speaks through another character, someone *in* the story who the writer has tell the story, as Huck Finn tells the story for Mark Twain. In a sense, the storyteller is the writer's dramatic mask, concealing the real author behind his dramatic character. Most often you will be writing essays. And in essays you won't have to create a dramatic mask like Huck Finn to do your talking for you. But, even in essays where you write more directly to your readers without a dramatic mask, you'll need to present the best side of yourself to your readers. That means you'll have to create a voice that works for you, dramatizes your message or information, and makes the right impression on the reader. If you sound too snooty or imperious when you are discussing a humorous or fairly common subject, chances are your readers will be put off, if not by what you say, by how you say it. In other words, you'll want your words to carry your personality along with your message.

Here is a brief letter-essay that Cesar Chavez, the well-known leader of the California grape and lettuce boycotts during the past few years, published in a local newspaper during the worst moments of the grape-pickers' strike in 1969. In the letter, Chavez tries to convince the general public of the sincerity of those conducting the grape strike. He doesn't, on the one hand, want to sound too self-righteous or condescending or his readers will feel put out even if they agree with his cause. And they would probably discredit his words and believe the company representatives. On the other hand, Chavez must sound serious and sincere or his readers will think that he jokes, that he wants only personal attention. As you read, analyze the prose to see how Chavez' voice works. Do you think he is successful in drawing that fine line between moral pomposity and moral flippancy? Do you believe him? Why? What do you like or dislike about Chavez' voice? Does he sound like a man of sincere convictions?

Letter from Delano

CESAR E. CHAVEZ

The following statement on nonviolence was issued on Good Friday by Cesar Chavez, leader in the struggle to obtain justice for those who have labored in California's vineyards; it is in the form of an open letter to the head of the growers' league which has opposed unionization of the grape pickers. . . .

Good Friday 1969

I am sad to hear about your accusations in the press that our union movement and table grape boycott have been successful because we have used violence and terror tactics. If what you say is true, I have been a failure and should withdraw from the struggle; but you are left with the awesome moral responsibility, before God and man, to come forward with whatever information you have so that corrective action can begin at once. If for any reason you fail to come forth to substantiate your charges, then you must be held responsible for committing violence against us, albeit violence of the tongue. I am convinced that you as a human being did not mean what you said but rather acted hastily under pressure from the public relations firm that has been hired to try to counteract the tremendous moral force of our movement. How many times we ourselves have felt the need to lash out in anger and bitterness.

Today on Good Friday 1969 we remember the life and the sacrifice of Martin Luther King, Jr., who gave himself totally to the nonviolent struggle for peace and justice. In his "Letter from Birmingham Jail" Dr. King describes better than I could our hopes for the strike and boycott: "Injustice must be exposed, with all the tension its exposure creates, to the light of human conscience and the air of national opinion before it can be cured." For our part I admit that we have seized upon every tactic and strategy consistent with the morality of our cause to expose that injustice and thus to heighten the sensitivity of the American conscience so that farm workers will have without bloodshed their own union and the dignity of bargaining with their agribusiness employers. By lying about the nature of our movement, . . . you are working against non-violent social change. Unwittingly perhaps, you may unleash that other force which our union by discipline and deed, censure and education has sought to avoid, that panacean shortcut: that senseless violence which honors no color, class or neighborhood.

You must understand—I must make you understand—that our membership and the hopes and aspirations of the hundreds of thousands of the poor and dispossessed that have been raised on our account are, above all, human beings, no better and no worse than any other cross-section of human society; we are not saints because we are poor, but by the same measure neither are we immoral. We are men and women who have suffered and endured much, and not only because of our abject poverty but because we have been kept poor. The colors of our skins, the languages of our cultural and native origins, the lack of formal education, the exclusion from the democratic process, the numbers of our slain in recent wars—all these burdens generation after generation have sought to demoralize us, to break our human spirit. But God knows that we are not beasts of burden, agricultural implements or rented slaves; we are men. And mark this well, . . . we are men locked in a death struggle against man's inhumanity to man in the industry that you represent. And this struggle itself gives meaning to our life and ennobles our dying.

As your industry has experienced, our strikers here in Delano and those who represent us throughout the world are well trained for this struggle. They have been under the gun, they have been kicked and beaten and herded by dogs, they have been cursed and ridiculed, they have been stripped and chained and jailed, they have been sprayed with the poisons used in the vineyards; but they have been taught not to lie down and die nor to flee in shame, but to resist with every ounce of human endurance and spirit. To resist not with retaliation in kind but to overcome with love and compassion, with ingenuity and creativity, with hard work and longer hours, with stamina and patient tenacity, with truth and public appeal, with friends and allies, with mobility and discipline, with politics and law, and with prayer and fasting. They were not trained in a month or even a year; after all, this new harvest season will mark our fourth full year of strike and even now we continue to plan and prepare for the years to come. Time accomplishes for the poor what money does for the rich.

This is not to pretend that we have everywhere been successful enough or that we have not made mistakes. And while we do not belittle or underestimate our adversaries—for they are the rich and the powerful and they possess the land—we are not afraid nor do we cringe from the confrontation. We welcome it! We have planned for it. We know that our cause is just, that history is a story of social revolution, and that the poor shall inherit the land.

Once again, I appeal to you as the representative of your industry and as a man. I ask you to recognize and bargain with our union before the economic pressure of the boycott and strike takes an irrevocable toll; but if not, I ask you to at least sit down with us to discuss the safeguards necessary to keep our historical struggle free of violence. I make this appeal because as one of the leaders of our nonviolent movement, I know and accept my responsibility for preventing, if possible, the destruction of human life and property. For these reasons and knowing of Gandhi's admonition that fasting is the last resort in place of the sword, during a most critical time in our movement last February 1968 I undertook a 25-day fast. I repeat to you the principle enunciated to the membership at the start of the fast: if to build our union required the deliberate taking of life, either the life of a grower or his child, or the life of a farm worker or his child, then I choose not to see the union built.

. . . Let me be painfully honest with you. You must understand these things. We advocate militant nonviolence as our means for social revolution and to achieve justice for our people, but we are not blind or deaf to the desperate and moody winds of human frustration, impatience and rage that blow among us. Gandhi himself admitted that if his only choice were cowardice or violence, he would choose violence. Men are not angels, and time and tide wait for no man. Precisely because of these powerful human emotions, we have tried to involve masses of people in their own struggle. Participation and self-determination remain the best experience of freedom, and free men instinctively prefer democratic change and even protect the rights guaranteed to seek it. Only the enslaved in despair have need of violent overthrow.

This letter does not express all that is in my heart. . . . But if it says nothing else it says that we do not hate you or rejoice to see your industry destroyed; we hate the agribusiness system that seeks to keep us enslaved, and we shall overcome and change it not by retaliation or bloodshed but by a determined nonviolent struggle carried on by those masses of farm workers who intend to be free and human.

Sincerely yours,
CESAR E. CHAVEZ
United Farm Workers Organizing
    Committee, A.F.L.-C.I.O.
Delano, California

Activity Exercise

1. At several points in the letter, Chavez takes pains to point out that he does not wish the destruction or suffering of his opponents. How does this contribute to our impression of his moral character?

2. Look closely at Chavez' sentences. How would you describe them? Are they the sentences of a rational, calm man or an excited and emotional man? How can you tell? Take, for example, this sentence:

You must understand—I must make you understand—that our membership and the hopes and aspirations of the hundreds of thousands of the poor and dispossessed that have been raised on our account are, above all, human beings, no better and no worse than any other cross-section of human society; we are not saints because we are poor, but by the same measure neither are we immoral.

3. This letter follows a simple logic elaborated in several complex ways. The logic goes something like this: If you who hold power don't provide access to ways out of suffering and hardship for the poor, then *you*, not *we*, will be responsible for the violence that follows. Can you think of any way that logic might be refuted? Does Chavez mention any? Does Chavez write what you would consider an emotional or logical letter?

4. Take just one paragraph in this letter and rewrite it in a different voice. A good way to get started is to imagine someone very different from Cesar Chavez talking. How would an irate militant labor unionist talk? Keep the message the same.

More voice to analyze

Read the following selections with special attention to the voice used in each.

If I am out of my mind, it's all right with me, thought Moses Herzog.

Some people thought he was cracked and for a time he himself had doubted that he was all there. He had fallen under a spell and was writing letters to everyone under the sun. He was so stirred by these letters that from the end of June he moved from place to place with a valise full of papers. He had carried this valise from New York to Martha's Vineyard, but returned from the Vineyard immediately; two days later he flew to Chicago, and from Chicago he went to a village in western Massachusetts. Hidden in the country, he wrote endlessly, fanatically, to the newspapers, to people in public life, to friends and relatives and at last to the dead, his own obscure dead, and finally the famous dead.

It was the peak of summer in the Berkshires. Herzog was alone in the big old house. Normally particular about food, he now ate Silvercup bread from the paper package, beans from the can, and American cheese. Now and then he picked raspberries in the overgrown garden, lifting up the thorny canes with absent-minded caution. As for sleep, he slept on a mattress without sheets—it was his abandoned marriage bed—or in the hammock, covered by his coat.

You deplore the demonstrations taking place in Birmingham. But your statement, I am sorry to say, fails to express a similar concern for the conditions that brought about the demonstrations. I am sure that none of you would want to rest content with the superficial kind of social analysis that deals merely with effects and does not grapple with underlying causes. It is unfortunate that demonstrations are taking place in Birmingham, but it is even more unfortunate that the city's white power structure left the Negro community with no alternative.

In any nonviolent campaign there are four basic steps: collection of the facts to determine whether injustices exist; negotiation; self-purification; and direct action. We have gone through all these steps in Birmingham. There can be no gainsaying the fact that racial injustice engulfs this community. Birmingham is probably the most thoroughly segregated city in the United States. Its ugly record of brutality is widely known. Negroes have experienced grossly unjust treatment in the courts. There have been more unsolved bombings of Negro homes and churches in Birmingham than in any other city in the nation. These are the hard, brutal facts of the case. On the basis of these conditions, Negro leaders sought to negotiate with the city fathers. But the latter consistently refused to engage in good-faith negotiation.

Then, last September, came the opportunity to talk with leaders of Birmingham's economic community. In the course of the negotiations, certain promises were made by the merchants—for example, to remove the stores' humiliating racial signs. On the basis of these promises, the Reverend Fred Shuttlesworth and the leaders of the Alabama Christian Movement for Human Rights agreed to a moratorium on all demonstrations. As the weeks and months went by, we realized that we were the victims of a broken promise. A few signs, briefly removed, returned; the others remained.

        —Martin Luther King, Jr. "Letter from Birmingham Jail"

I like to folk dance. Like other novices, I've gone to the Intersection or to the Museum and laid out good money in order to learn how to dance. No grades, no prerequisites, no separate dining rooms; they just turn you on to dancing. That's education. Now look at what happens in college. A friend of mine, Milt, recently finished a folk dance class. For his final he had to learn things like this: "The Irish are known for their wit and imagination, qualities reflected in their dances, which include the jig, the reel and the hornpipe." And then the teacher graded him A, B, C, D, or F, while he danced in front of her. That's not education. That's not even training. That's an abomination on the face of the earth. It's especially ironic because Milt took that dance class trying to get out of the academic rut. He took crafts for the same reason. Great, right? Get your hands in some clay? Make something? Then the teacher announced that a 20-page term paper would be required—with footnotes.

—Jerry Farber, "The Student as Nigger"

I am an invisible man. No, I am not a spook like those who haunted Edgar Allan Poe; nor am I one of your Hollywood-movie ectoplasms. I am a man of substance, of flesh and bone, fiber and liquids—and I might even be said to possess a mind. I am invisible, understand, simply because people refuse to see me. Like the bodiless heads you see sometimes in circus sideshows, it is as though I have been surrounded by mirrors of hard, distorting glass. When they approach me they see only my surroundings, themselves, or figments of their imagination—indeed, everything and anything except me.

Nor is my invisibility exactly a matter of a bio-chemical accident to my epidermis. That invisibility to which I refer occurs because of a peculiar disposition of the eyes of those with whom I come in contact. A matter of the construction of their *inner* eyes, those eyes with which they look through their physical eyes upon reality. I am not complaining, nor am I protesting either. It is sometimes advantageous to be unseen, although it is most often rather wearing on the nerves. Then too, you're constantly being bumped against by those of poor vision. Or again, you often doubt if you really exist. You wonder whether you aren't simply a phantom in other people's minds. Say, a figure in a nightmare which the sleeper tries with all his strength to destroy. It's when you feel like this that, out of resentment, you begin to bump people back. And, let me confess, you feel that way most of the time. You ache with the need to convince yourself that you do exist in the real world, that you're a part of all the sound and anguish, and you strike out with your fists, you curse and you swear to make them recognize you. And, alas, it's seldom successful.

Activity Exercise

1. Recall some public person—a visiting lecturer, writer, actor or actress, political figure—preferably someone who had something controversial to say—or some public occasion you witnessed during the past three or four months. Begin by remembering as much as you can about the person, his voice or actions, physical appearance, any particular speech characteristics, some phrase or gesture he repeated. Then remember, as accurately as you can, how you felt about the person. Were you repulsed or attracted? Why? Then, write a letter describing the

person or event in detail and make your feelings clear. Shape your voice to fit your feelings. If you were attracted, then show that attraction by your choice of words, by the verbs you use to show his walk—did he *trudge* or *amble* or *plod along*—and by the shape of your sentences. If you write short, choppy sentences, for example, you may make your subject seem silly or childish. And long, balanced sentences might make your subject seem refined. You might also write the letter to a particular person, someone you can be yourself with, a personal friend, a parent or a girl or boy friend. Let your voice say as much or more than your message. In other words, say what you remember specifically and let your attitude come to your reader through the sound of your words.

2. Select a product you use often that you feel is not a good one. Then write a letter to the manufacturer to express your dissatisfaction with the product. Be specific and keep your tongue in your cheek. Take on what you think will be an effective voice. Imagine yourself creating a particular image, perhaps a polite and intelligent consumer courteously annoyed by the product or a blunt tough guy ready to express your dissatisfaction and anger openly. Again, you'll need to consider matters of style, word choice, syntax, and design.

3. Spend some time observing a person carefully in a public place. Jot down details rapidly; then try to describe your over-all impression of the person. Finally, imagine your subject meeting someone on the street and engaging in a lengthy conversation about some common subject—taxes, a particular kind of automobile, a well-known television show. Write up a fifteen- or twenty-minute dialogue that captures the conversation.

4. *Irony* is the ability to say the opposite of what you really mean in order to emphasize or clarify. In speech we often call irony *sarcasm.* Someone, for example, who has just seen what he feels is a terrible movie might answer *great* in a sarcastic tone of voice to someone who asks him how the movie was. The listener then knows by the way *great* is spoken that the movie was terrible, a bore, not worth even talking about. Try to compose some ironic or sarcastic voices in response to these suggestions. Then read your responses aloud to the class, being sure to use the right sarcastic pronunciations.

a. Change the voice of a straight news article to irony. You might use exaggeration or understatement (put a very serious or important news item in very unemotional or everyday language).

b. Find a very serious public speech or announcement and read it to the class ironically. What do you do with your voice and the language of the item to make it sarcastic?

c. Find some distinctive voices around you. Find a disc-jockey on the radio, perhaps one you hear every time you drive your car. Or analyze the language and style of your favorite television news-caster. If you can, tape one of the subject's performances. Then play it back and point out any instance in which you think the speaker uses language indirectly, where his or her meaning seems to be hidden or "below the surface" of the words.

Three common voices

Whenever we talk about voices in writing, we must not categorize too broadly, for then we oversimplify the many individual voices we hear and read everyday. Yet it does help to be able to recognize a few common "styles" or voices that are generally used to fit a variety of situations. Don't take these descriptions as rules to follow. They are more norms to use in judging your own writing voices, to pinpoint the appropriateness of your own style. Any voice must, of course, fit a specific writing situation more than it fits any general description. Analyze the situation, the needs of your audience and subject; then adopt some general attitude toward the voice you will use according to one of the following broad categories. Then let *your* own voice take over as you write.

Formal

Formal language is usually relegated to ceremonious or public situations, where the voice and tone are of the public person speaking on public matters to a large and varied audience. In such writing, the sentences are usually carefully formed and balanced in structure—the words are carefully chosen to meet public decorum and the audience is addressed from a distance in rhetoric that suits public ceremony. The following paragraph from Martin Luther King's "Letter from Birmingham Jail" is an excellent example of formal rhetoric. Notice the parallel sentence structure, the direct and formal address to the reader, and the carefully placed figurative language ("dark clouds of racial prejudice"). Figurative language uses metaphor and analogy; it relies on objects to define ideas or emotions by comparison. The "dark clouds" of an imminent storm are like the "racial prejudice" of an impending race riot. Can you point to other common devices of style in this passage, to places where particular words and syntax (sentence structure) indicate the writer's attitude?

I hope this letter finds you strong in the faith. I also hope that circumstances will soon make it possible for me to meet each of you, not as an integrationist or a civil rights leader but as a fellow clergyman and a Christian brother. Let us all hope that the dark clouds of racial prejudice will soon pass away and the deep fog of misunderstanding will be lifted from our fear-drenched communities, and in some not too distant tomorrow the radiant stars of love and brotherhood will shine over our great nation with all their scintillating beauty.

Informal

Informal language is used in situations in which the speaker or writer does not wish to establish the seriousness and sobriety of the ceremonious occasion, but also does not wish to create an intimate or casual relationship with his audience. The informal writer would not resort to the figurative language of King's letter, for that would seem out of place or stuffy; he would also avoid the slang and talky rhythms and words of Jerry Farber's "The Student as Nigger." Academic writing, objective newspaper articles, and essays on current events in large circulation magazines are all examples of informal writing contexts. The following paragraph from Pauline Kael's *Kiss Kiss Bang Bang*, a collection of movie reviews, is informal. Notice the contractions, phrases such as "kind of," the relatively natural and straightforward sentence structure, and the somewhat casual—but not too intimate—address to the reader.

It's obvious that there's a kind of noninvolvement among youth, but we can't get at what that's all about by Antonioni's terms. He is apparently unable to respond to or to convey the new sense of community among youth, or the humor and fervor and astonishing speed in their rejections of older values; he sees only the emptiness of pop culture.

Colloquial

Colloquial language reproduces the rhythm and sound of everyday speech, usually to create a casual and intimate relationship between reader and writer. Colloquial language is especially suited to satire— where the writer and reader want to be on intimate terms in order to share the ridicule and criticism of some institution, group of people, or values. It is also suitable for any context in which the writer hopes to get a familiar response from his reader. For example, the experienced sports columnist usually treats his readers as if they were old friends or cronies; he writes as if he were talking to his readers over coffee about an old and familiar subject. Notice the slang, the direct but intimate form of address to the audience, and the natural sentence order in this paragraph from *Kiss Kiss Bang Bang*.

Those who enjoy seeing this turned-on city of youth, those who say of *Blow-Up* that it's the trip, it's where we are now in consciousness and that Antonioni is in it, part of it, ahead of it like Warhol, may have a better sense of what Antonioni is about than the laudatory critics. Despite Antonioni's negativism, the world he presents looks harmless, and for many in the audience, and not just the youthful ones, sex without "connecting" doesn't really seem so bad—naughty, maybe, but nice. Even the smoke at the pot party is enough to turn on some of the audience. And there's all that pretty color which delights the critics, though it undercuts their reasons for praising the movie because it's that bright, cleaned-up big-city color of "I-have-seen-the-future-and-it's-fun." Antonioni, like his fashion-photographer hero, is more interested in getting pretty pictures than in what they mean. But for reasons I can't quite fathom, what is taken to be shallow in his hero is taken to be profound in him. Maybe it's because of the symbols: do pretty pictures plus symbols equal art?

Thinking Exercise

1. The words in this paragraph are everyday words, except perhaps for "laudatory" and "negativism." Yet this paragraph also reads as if it were, as it actually is, written by a sophisticated, experienced movie critic. What gives Kael's voice that sense of sophistication, if it's not her vocabulary? What would you say about the way her sentences are formed?

2. Pauline Kael uses several compound words (two words functioning as one word and connected by a hyphen) in this paragraph— "turned-on," "fashion-photographer," "big-city," "cleaned-up," and "I-have-seen-the-future-and-it's-fun." What do these contribute to her voice? Do they make her sound more natural, an everyday talker, or more formal and sophisticated? Or both? Why?

Writing Exercise

1. Go over a film you have recently seen, preferably one to which you responded strongly. Write a brief expository essay in which you explain *why* you experienced such a response. First, get your response into a clear thesis sentence. Then go back over the film to recall specific actions, scenes or characters that contributed to that response. Once

you've planned your essay, you can then plan your voice as well. Will you be informal or talky? Why? And, more importantly, how? Will you use cumulative, natural-ordered sentences and everyday words? Will you ask rhetorical questions and then provide your own surprising answers? (Rhetorical questions are asked to clarify the speaker or writer's point, not to get an answer.)

2. Recall a character from a movie you have recently seen. Then make a statement something like the one Pauline Kael made about a character in *Blow-Up:* "Antonioni, like his fashion-photographer hero, is more interested in getting pretty pictures than in what they mean." Compose a brief essay to illustrate by examples from the film how you formed your reaction to that character. What specific actions, bits of dialogue, gestures and mannerisms led to your general observation of the character? This time try to imitate Kael's voice as you write. She often moves quickly from point to point, addresses the reader directly and relies on the quick-wit of her readers. She draws quick contrasts, repeats words and phrases in catchy ways and generally gives the impression of being an "in-the-know," snappy and sarcastic movie expert.

10

Attitude and tone:
You and your readers

So far we've talked about the sound of a writer in his words or the personality a writer projects through what he writes. Voice brings a sense of *you* into your writing. But there are other important elements of you at work on your audience whenever you write. First, you must demonstrate to your audience some clear opinion of your subject. Even a writer who decides to be objective has an opinion, but he may choose not to reveal his own feelings on the subject. His writing opinion, in other words, is neutral.

Second, you have to decide how you will address your readers themselves. Will you, for example, write as if your readers are not there, in a style that never talks to them directly? Or will you try to treat your readers as old friends to win them over? Questions like these bring us from considerations of voice to those of *tone* and *attitude*. You'll find a working definition of these terms in the following diagram.

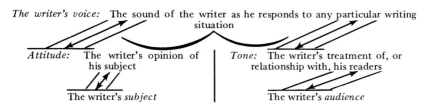

Dramatic Context

The writer's voice: The sound of the writer as he responds to any particular writing situation

Attitude: The writer's opinion of his subject

The writer's *subject*

Tone: The writer's treatment of, or relationship with, his readers

The writer's *audience*

In a sense, every writer is an actor in words. Critics of classical Greek theater often refer to the word *persona*, which means *mask*. Every actor on the Greek stage wore a mask that indicated to the large audiences of Greek theater what kind of character the actor was portraying. A tragic villain wore a tragic mask; the comic character wore the traditional comic mask. As the theater developed, the masks became more and more sophisticated; the audiences became better able to make subtle character distinctions from the masks the actors wore.

In a sense, you wear a mask whenever you write. You try to project the right part of you into the writing situation. Just as Erving Goffmann points out at the beginning of this section, we *act out* our communications in words. The speaker in conversation uses his body as well as his words to communicate. He is an actor in a scene that includes his message or subject, his listeners, and himself. The writer finds himself in a similar dramatic context; the interactions between himself and his subjects and readers are the main parts in his communication. But the writer doesn't have the benefit of gestures, inflections, or eye movement; he resorts to choice and word-order to project himself into the situation. The diagram subdivides the writer's mask, his persona, into three major elements: voice, tone, and attitude. *Tone* is the way a writer treats his readers; *attitude* is the particular opinion a writer develops toward his subject. All three elements can be controlled. The writer who does control them controls the dramatic context of the situation. And all three elements affect one another. Your voice, for example, may affect the attitude you take toward your subject. Or tone, the way you treat your audience, might well influence your voice—the way you sound as you write.

Voice, tone, and attitude together

Learning to recognize the relationships between voice and attitude in what you read is the first step toward developing control over those elements in your own writing.

Often we allow our attitudes, our opinions on the subject about which we are writing, to dictate our voice. The results are often disastrous. Take, for example, the following excerpt from a student newspaper editorial on intercollegiate athletics.

> We pay a heckuva lot out of our Incidental Fees for the football and basketball programs and we don't get much back in the way of services or academic returns. I like football as well as the next guy, but is it worth it? Being 'objective' is easy when you don't want to study or learn in the first place.

We feel uneasy with this writer's voice. He sounds unsure of himself;

his voice is inconsistent and a bit awkward. He doesn't seem to know just how he wants to treat his audience, nor does he seem sure of his attitude toward his subject. Where and how does this writer fail?

As readers, we can easily tell what the writer's basic attitude is: he'd like the intercollegiate athletic budget cut or revised. But he hasn't really decided on how to sound as he argues his position. Sometimes he is pushy, sounding like a raging critic—"We pay a heckuva lot out of our incidental fees . . ." At other times he pleads, playing the role of the nice guy forced to make a just but unpopular decision—"I like football as well as the next guy . . ." Then he becomes sarcastic—"Being 'objective' is easy when you don't want to study or learn . . ." Such inconsistencies in tone make readers feel uneasy. Unconsciously, the readers feel as unsure of the writer as he does of them.

Read this revision of the editorial.

> We pay a great deal for our intercollegiate program. Do we get enough in return? These programs bring in less than they cost year after year. Certainly I enjoy our athletic program as much as anyone, but I still believe that the entire campus would benefit from a thorough reevaluation of funding priorities, especially the relationship between academic and athletic spending.

This version isn't remarkable for its display of flashy skills, but the voice is consistent, calm, and evenly directed toward presenting an attitude and making a request. The tone is firm without being pushy. We might suppose that even those firmly opposed to any cut in the athletic budget might be moved by the appeal for a careful re-evaluation. The writer here is in control; he knows just where he wants to place himself in his relationship toward his readers.

A writer's mask or persona usually depends on three qualities: how he arranges and forms his ideas; how he uses words and sentences to project a suitable personality; and how carefully he analyzes his subject and develops his opinions. Most readers will credit, even if they decide not to adopt, arguments which effectively control these qualities.

Before you go on to analyze the relationships among voice, tone, and attitude in a few other examples of student writing, look over these analyses of the original student newspaper editorial and the revised version. You'll find the writer's tone charted by a spatial diagram which demonstrates the distance between the writer and his audience.

Consider this analysis of the original editorial:

Voice: a tough and angry writer
Tone: sarcastic and pushy toward other students
Attitude: totally negative toward the football program

In the original editorial, we might describe the distances in this way:

Tone: speaker   audience
             └─────────────────┘

Speaker and audience are close together as if the writer knows his readers well enough to jump right in and tell them what to think and do. A more rational or formal tone would look something like this:

speaker   audience
└──────────────────────────┘

The writer would keep his distance and evaluate the subject before he'd tell his readers what to do.

Attitude: speaker   subject
                └──────────────────────────┘

Speaker and subject are far apart because the writer is consistently negative and doesn't really analyze the subject that closely. A slight change occurs when the writer mentions that he likes the sport. But the clearly negative attitude returns in the sarcasm of the final line, where the writer really means the opposite of what he says.

Consider these statements concerning the revised editorial:

Voice: a quiet, sober writer who appeals to facts
Tone: moderately concerned in his appeal to other student's attitude: generally negative, but willing to listen

Here are the spatial graphs for the second excerpt:

Tone: speaker   audience
             └──────────────────────────┘

Speaker and audience are more distant and formal than in the first passage. Here the writer wants to attract other students with facts and reasons before he tells them what to do.

Attitude: speaker   subject
             └────────────────────┘

Speaker and subject are closer together here than in the first passage. The writer still has a negative attitude toward the football program but he seems

less decided and more willing to listen to counterar-
guments. He resorts less to slang, his sentences are
more balanced, and his vocabulary is generally more
formal. These stylistic qualities help the writer
maintain some distance between himself and his
readers.

Some paragraphs for analysis

The student paragraphs on page 329 are taken from essays on the
American dream. In each example the writer clarifies his attitude toward
the American dream—the idea that every American can find his or her
particular form of happiness through hard work. These are not paragraphs
of proof, illustration, or support; they are rather introductory paragraphs
in which the writer sets up his attitude, establishes the tone he will take
with his readers, and develops the voice he will use throughout the paper.
As you read, analyze how each writer establishes his dramatic relationships. In other words, how do these writers create the right (or wrong)
frictions, tensions, and oppositions among themselves, their personas and
voices, their subjects and readers? Keep the diagram of dramatic context
before you as you read.

Thinking Exercise

Ask yourself these questions about the selections:

1. What kind of person is talking? Would you enjoy having a
conversation with him? Why or why not? What specific language
qualities combine to create his voice? Is the writer too tough or pushy?
How might he or she improve in personality?

2. Sometimes a writer presents an obviously artificial voice. Can you
find any paragraphs in which the writer's voice seems different from his
"real" self? What gives you that feeeling? Does he or she use a phrase, a
few words, or a particular metaphor that seems inconsistent with the rest
of the paragraph? Do you feel "put on" by the writer, in the sense that
what you read sounds like an "act," an obvious attempt to fool you?

3. What is the writer's attitude toward the American dream? Does the
writer tell you his attitude directly or indirectly, with irony or sarcasm?
How would you diagram the writer's attitude? Is it totally negative and
distant? Very positive and close? Perhaps most important, does the writer

present his attitude in a way you find effective? Or is he or she too pushy, too emotional, or too "neutral"? Can you find specific language devices—the way sentences are formed or the particular vocabulary the writer uses—that indicate or suggest the writer's bias toward his subject?

4. Now analyze the writer's tone. Does he seem to ignore you because he is more interested in his own opinions? Or does the writer want to cozy up too close to you to win you over? Notice, especially, how the writers use pronouns. The first person (I), the third person plural (they), and the second person (you) are all used by one writer or another. Each writer picks a particular pronoun, stays with it, and lets the pronouns contribute to his tone. One writer avoids pronouns completely. What effect does that have on you as you read?

5. Try adding any one of these devices to one of the paragraphs. How does it affect the voice, tone, and attitude of the paragraph?

a. *Rhetorical questions* are statements that a writer really doesn't want answered because he has already suggested the answer. For example, you might begin an essay on taxes with the question, "Should our taxes be lowered?" and then go on to suggest an answer indirectly later in the essay. Such questions are usually used to focus the argument or subject. Look back at the Jerry Farber excerpt (p. 306) in the previous chapter. He uses a series of short rhetorical questions to point out the expected answer. Then he goes on to show how the expected answer isn't the answer you really get.

b. *Contractions* usually add informality to your voice and tone. Sometimes a very serious subject can be pleasantly lightened by contractions. But used indiscriminately, they can damage your credibility and voice, especially for readers who expect formality.

c. *Sentence inversions,* or reversals of word order, occasionally used, can add variety and sophistication to a writer's voice and make his tone more formal and elegant. Be careful, however. Too many inversions can sound awkward and silly; they create a "show-off" voice that calls too much attention to itself and detracts from the writer's subject.

d. *Pronoun shifts* can help or hinder writing effectiveness. Most times you need to keep consistently to one type of pronoun (first, second, or third person) in order not to confuse your readers. But sometimes a shift in pronouns helps create emphasis, if used sparingly and carefully. Try shifting the pronoun in one of these paragraphs at a point that you think requires more emphasis. Take, for example, a third person pronoun and shift to the first or second person pronoun (I or you) near the end of the paragraph to emphasize an important sentence or idea. Also, be careful to change the verb tense to fit the pronoun shift.

e. *Changes in sentence length and structure* can also be effective. Rewrite the sentences in one of these paragraphs in ways that change the voice of the writer. You might, for example, make shorter sentences out of longer. Or change the verbs from active to passive, or the reverse. Try altering punctuation, either by bringing two simple sentences together and connecting them by *and, but,* or some other connecting word, or by taking a sentence connected by such words and adding a semicolon to replace the connecting word. Then look the paragraph over and try to describe the change in voice. Is the speaker's personality changed by the new sentence forms? How? Does he sound more moderate or formal?

Paragraphs on the American dream

1. The next time you get sick of American society, stop and take a look at other countries. Stop and realize how many more freedoms you as an American have and how proud you should be to be an American. Then, if you are still sick of it and don't want to improve it, go somewhere else. Remember, no one is forcing you to stay.

2. Our forefathers said that all men were created equal and had certain inalienable rights. It therefore follows that all men have the right to share in the American dream. What our forefathers really should have said, however, was that "some," not "all" Americans had those rights. All Americans don't have equal opportunity. All Americans don't share "inalienable rights" and most certainly all Americans have *not* been allowed equal access to the American dream.

3. When I was in seventh grade the ultimate in a girl's life was "popularity." You had popularity if you had a bright smile, school spirit, pretty legs and, above all, "personality." You didn't have to be a raving beauty, just pleasant looking, not *too* fashionable, not *too* dull, not *too* swinging, not *too* anything. Above average, but not superior grades also made you popular. In other words, you conformed or sacrificed your "popularity."

4. Fever. Hellish fever. A feeling of temperatures beyond control and producing madness unmatched by any virus disease. A madness that blocks out all humanistic ideas from the mind of its victims and replaces those ideas with an uncontrollable lust for power. A tyrannical desire that sticks hard in your craw like cheese sticks to the pan when left on the stove to burn.

"Seeing" tone

We are very accustomed to visual forms of persuasion, especially in an age of mass communication. But we sometimes forget that what we see functions by persuasive techniques that are similar to those we find in writing. The dramatic context in both media are similar—the communicator, his subject, and his audience. And the visual communicator, like the writer, tries to control the relationships among those three components.

Analyze the voice and tone of the Seagram's ad on this page. The attitude is obviously positive—Seagram's wants to sell their product. But the ad-writers create a definite tone, one they feel will sell and will appeal to the tastes and values of the liquor-buying public.

First, what about the caption, "Thank you, America, for making our whiskey your whiskey"? Visually, it's practically in a position to be the cap on the bottle. It's in large print and has high-sounding parallel phrasing—". . . our whiskey . . . your whiskey." The two tempting drinks rest side-by-side next to the Seagram's bottle, and the panoramic view of an American mountain range makes an elegant background. As you look over these specifics, how would you describe the advertisement's voice and tone? Is the ad-writer trying to establish the product's noble American tradition? Is his voice an attempt to sound

Figure 10-1

Seagram's ad

properly noble and elegant, properly "American" in a patriotic and grand way? Does the picture fit the words?

Perhaps most importantly, how is the ad-writer addressing his audience? Would you say the tone is distant and formal? Why? And is the tone right for the product? Why would drinkers of Seagram's be apt to enjoy this ad?

On a more complex level, just how serious is the ad-writer here? Is this a little joke the ad-writer and the manufacturers of Seagram's share with a sophisticated audience? Or, perhaps, the appeal works both ways—a straight and serious appeal for people who want to drink an elegant, grand whiskey; a "put-on" or tongue-in-cheek appeal for people who feel that talking about grand whiskey is hogwash. If the advertisement is *both* put-on and straight, then we have two tones working at once—the formal, serious, elegant tone we find on the surface and the lighter, self-mocking tone that we find or feel below the surface.

Attitude in forms

Anyone who tries to express himself, whether in serious art, painting, cartoons, ads, or essays, develops an attitude toward his subject. Sometimes attitude is easy to define—we know, for example, that most advertisements take on a positive attitude because they want to sell a product by pointing out its strongpoints. A few, however, try reverse psychology; they seem to poke fun at their products, but usually to sell to an audience that is too sophisticated to buy straight flattery. Volkswagen advertisements, for example, have for years ridiculed their product. The car is called a "bug" and belittled for its bad looks, low horsepower, even occasionally berated for its low pricetag, which doesn't compare favorably with the status pricetags of luxury cars. Underneath the mockery, however, we know that Volkswagen is really ridiculing the big American cars—their fins, horsepower, and lack of economy are frills for which only the uninitiated or foolish would pay extra money.

Cartoons treat their subjects humorously, often ridiculing or exaggerating weaknesses or absurdities in everyday life. As a result, a cartoonist's attitude is usually clear; we know how he feels about his subject by figuring out why he wants us to laugh at weaknesses and absurdities in his cartoon.

Attitude is often less obvious in painting. Take a few minutes to study de Kooning's *Woman I.* Ask yourself what the painter feels toward

Figure 10-2

Woman I
by Willem de Kooning

Collection. The Museum of Modern Art. New York.

the woman. How do you know? What details in the painting indicate the painter's attitude? What specific shapes, lines, or strokes indicate to you how the painter felt about the woman? What kind of woman is this? How do you think she makes the painter feel? What character qualities is the painting trying to capture?

Activity Exercise

Each class member should observe another member of the class. As you observe, write a very specific and objective description of your subject. Don't judge your subject. Remember the descriptive skills you practiced in the earlier chapters of this book. Begin with specific observations and then work up to a description of your general impression (not your general opinion) of your subject. Then pass the rough draft of your description to your subject and ask him or her to evaluate it. Does your subject find a hidden attitude? Do you seem to emphasize certain characteristics more than others? Are there any glaring inaccuracies in the description? Do these emphases and inaccuracies indicate a hidden attitude toward the subject? Does your subject learn as much about you as he does about himself by reading your sketch? Finally, write your description on ditto paper so that your instructor can reproduce a few examples for class discussion. Your subject's responses can be included in the margins and between the lines of your descriptions so that the entire class can see what both the observer and the observed had to say.

After discussing the descriptions as a class, each student should rewrite his description, openly and clearly developing his attitude and working it directly into his subjective impression.

Dramatic context and the critical essay

A critical essay examines a subject very closely and passes on the writer's evaluation and analysis to the reader. Usually critical essays work by one or more of these three methods:

1. *Internal analysis:* the writer examines the subject itself part by part, trying to measure effects by their causes, to classify the parts as they relate to the whole, or to point out relationships between main ideas and evidence.

2. *Comparison:* the writer compares his subject with others in the same class, pointing out similarities as well as differences and demonstrating the degrees of similarity or difference.

3. *Definition or description:* the writer tries to pinpoint just what the subject is by defining its essential nature, or he or she clarifies the form and content of the subject by exact physical description.

All these methods work simultaneously in Pauline Kael's essay on the movie *Blow-Up*. The marginal notes point out how the writer develops her arguments by using internal analysis, definition, and comparison. But Kael's use of these techniques contributes also to her development of tone. She selects particular comparisons that not only develop her attitude toward *Blow-Up*, but also show us what she feels about many of her more superficial, modish readers who like any film that others have told them is sophisticated and "in." Her methods of developing her argument about the film also contribute to her witty and wise-cracking relationship with her readers.

Tourist in the City of Youth

PAULINE KAEL

Some years ago I attended an evening of mime by Marcel Marceau, an elaborate exercise in aesthetic purification during which the audience kept applauding its own appreciation of culture and beauty, i.e., every time they thought they recognized what was supposed to be going on. It had been bad enough when Chaplin or Harpo Marx pulled this beauty-of-pathos stuff, and a whole evening of it was truly intolerable. But afterwards, when friends were acclaiming Marceau's artistry, it just wouldn't do to say something like "I prefer the Ritz Brothers" (though I do, I passionately do). They would think I was being deliberately lowbrow, and if I tried to talk in terms of Marceau's artistry versus Harry Ritz's artistry, it would be stupid, because "artist" is already too pretentious a term for Harry Ritz and so I would be falsifying what I love him for. I don't want to push this quite so far as to say that Marceau is to comedians I like as Antonioni's *Blow-Up* is to movies I like, but the comparison may be suggestive. And it may also be relevant that Antonioni pulls a Marceau-like expressionist finale in this picture, one of those fancy finishes that seems to say so much (but what?) and reminds one of so many naïvely bad experimental films.

Will *Blow-Up* be taken seriously in 1968 only by the same sort of cultural diehards who are still sending out five-page single-spaced letters on their interpretation of *Marienbad*?[1] (No two are alike, no one interesting.) It has some of the *Marienbad* appeal: a friend phones for your opinion and when you tell him you didn't much care for it, he says, "You'd better see it again. I was at a swinging party the other night and it's all anybody talked about!" (Was there ever a good movie that everybody was talking about?) It probably won't blow over because it also has the *Morgan!– Georgy Girl* appeal; people identify with it so strongly, they get *upset* if you don't like it—as if you were rejecting not just the movie but *them*. And in a way they're right, because if you don't accept the peculiarly slugged consciousness of *Blow-Up*, you *are* rejecting something in them. Antonioni's new mixture of suspense with vagueness and confusion seems to have a kind of numbing fascination for them that they associate with art and

introduction through an analogy: *Blow-Up* compared to the mime of Marcel Marceau

comparison of movies that belong to one class: movies that people identify with strongly

---

[1]*Last Year at Marienbad* is a French film directed by Alain Resnais. Foreign film lovers have fastened on it as an "in" film, one that every connoisseur should know and love. Kael finds their fascination superficial.

intellectuality, and they are responding to it as *their* film—and hence as a masterpiece.

definition of Antonioni's perspective

Antonioni's off-screen conversation, as reported to us, is full of impeccable literary references, but the white-faced clowns who open and close *Blow-Up* suggest that inside his beautifully fitted dinner jacket he carries—next to his heart—a gilt-edged gift edition of Kahlil Gibran. From the way people talk about the profundity of *Blow-Up*, that's probably what they're responding to. What would we think of a man who stopped at a newsstand to cluck at the cover girls of *Vogue* and *Harper's Bazaar* as tragic symbols of emptiness and sterility, as evidence that modern life isn't "real," and then went ahead and bought the magazines? Or, to be more exact, what would we think of a man who conducted a leisurely tour of "swinging" London, lingering along the flashiest routes and dawdling over a pot party and mini-orgy, while ponderously explaining that although the mod scene appears to be hip and sexy, it represents a condition of spiritual malaise in which people live only for the sensations of the moment? Is he a foolish old hypocrite or is he, despite his tiresome moralizing, a man who knows he's hooked?

definition of "new noninvolvement" and application of phrase to Antonioni

It's obvious that there's a new kind of noninvolvement among youth, but we can't get at what that's all about by Antonioni's terms. He is apparently unable to respond to or to convey the new sense of community among youth, or the humor and fervor and astonishing speed in their rejections of older values; he sees only the emptiness of pop culture.

description of scenes in film as related to the previously defined noninvolvement theme

Those who enjoy seeing this turned-on city of youth, those who say of *Blow-Up* that it's the trip, it's where we are now in consciousness and that Antonioni is in it, part of it, ahead of it like Warhol, may have a better sense of what Antonioni is about than the laudatory critics. Despite Antonioni's negativism, the world he presents looks harmless, and for many in the audience, and not just the youthful ones, sex without "connecting" doesn't really seem so bad—naughty, maybe, but nice. Even the smoke at the pot party is enough to turn on some of the audience. And there's all that pretty color which delights the critics, though it undercuts their reasons for praising the movie because it's that bright, cleaned-up big-city color of I-have-seen-the-future-and-it's-fun. Antonioni, like his fashion-photographer hero, is more interested in getting pretty pictures than in what they mean. But for reasons I can't quite fathom, what is taken to be shallow in his hero is taken to be profound in him. Maybe it's because of the symbols: do pretty pictures plus symbols equal art?

description of how critics fasten on noninvolvement symbols in film

There are the revelers who won't make room on the sidewalk for the nuns (spirit? soul? God? love?) and jostle them aside; an old airplane propeller is found in an antique shop; the hero considers buying the antique shop; two homosexuals walk their poodle, etc. Antonioni could point out that the poodle is castrated, and he'd probably be acclaimed for that, too—one more bitter detail of modern existential agony. There is a mock copulation with camera and subject that made me laugh (as the planes fornicating at the beginning of *Strangelove* did). But from the reviews of *Blow-Up* I learn that this was "tragic" and "a superbly realized comment on the values of our time" and all that. People seem awfully eager to abandon sense and perspective and humor and put on the newest fashion in hair shirts; New York critics who are just settling into their upper East Side apartments write as if they're leaving for a monastery in the morning.

Hecht and MacArthur used to write light satirical comedies about shallow people living venal lives that said most of what Antonioni does and more, and were entertaining besides; they even managed to convey that they were in love with the corrupt milieu and were part of it without getting bogged down. And Odets, even in late work like his dialogue for *Sweet Smell of Success*, also managed to convey both hate and infatuation. Love-hate is what makes drama not only exciting but possible, and it certainly isn't necessary for Antonioni to resolve his conflicting feelings. But in *Blow-Up* he smothers this conflict in the kind of platitudes the press loves to designate as proper to "mature," "adult," "sober" art. Who the hell goes to movies for mature, adult, sober art, anyway? Yes, we want more from movies than we get from the usual commercial entertainments, but would anybody use terms like mature, adult, and sober for *The Rules of the Game* or *Breathless* or *Citizen Kane* or *Jules and Jim*?

The best part of *Blow-Up* is a well-conceived and ingeniously edited sequence in which the hero blows up a series of photographs and discovers that he has inadvertently photographed a murder. It's a good murder mystery sequence. But does it symbolize (as one reviewer says) "the futility of seeking the hidden meanings of life through purely technological means"? I thought the hero did rather well in uncovering the murder. But this kind of symbolic interpretation is not irrelevant to the appeal of the picture: Antonioni loads his atmosphere with so much confused symbolism and such a heavy sense of importance that the viewers use the movie as a Disposall for intellectual refuse. We get the stock phrases about "the cold death of the heart," "the eroticism is chilling in its bleakness," a "world so cluttered with synthetic stimulations that natural feelings are overwhelmed," etc., because Antonioni *inspires* this jargon.

When the photographer loses the photographic record of the murder, he loses interest in it. According to *Time*, "Antonioni's anti-hero"—who is said to be a "little snake" and "a grincingly accurate portrait of the sort of squiggly little fungus that is apt to

comparison to light satirical comedies also based on noninvolvement theme and to Clifford Odets' love-hate theme; finally to other movies

internal analysis of film sequences as related to superficial symbolism

internal analysis and symbols—discussion continued through analysis of main character in the film

grow in a decaying society"—"holds in his possession, if only for an instant, the alexin of his cure: the saving grace of the spirit." (My Webster doesn't yield a clue to "grincingly"; an "alexin" is "a defensive substance, found normally in the body, capable of destroying bacteria.") In other words, if he did something about the murder, like going to the police, he would be accepting an involvement with the life or death of others, and he would find his humanity and become an OK guy to *Time*. (Would he then not be a representative of a decaying society, or would the society not then decay? Only *Time* can tell.)

definition of what
happens in *Blow-Up*
through a comparison
with Kitty Genovese case

This review, and many others, turn the murder into something like what the press and TV did with the Kitty Genovese case: use it as an excuse for another of those what-are-we-coming-to editorials about alienation and indifference to human suffering.[2] What was upsetting about the Genovese case was not those among the "witnesses" who didn't want to get involved even to the degree of calling the police (cowardice is not a new phenomenon), but our recognition that in a big city we don't know when our help is needed, and others may not know when we need help. This isn't a new phenomenon, either; what is new is that it goes against the grain of modern social consciousness, *i.e.*, we feel responsible even though we don't know how to act responsibly. The press turned it into one more chance to cluck, and people went around feeling very superior to those thirty-eight witnesses because they were sure *they* would have called the police.

definition of
noninvolvement by
comparisons with other
cases

The moral satisfaction of feeling indignant that people take away from these cases (though I'm not sure that *Time*'s moral is what Antonioni intended; probably not) is simple and offensive. Do all the times that the police are called when they are or aren't needed prove how humanly involved with each other we are? The editorial writers don't tell us. And they couldn't do much with the West Coast case of the young academic beaten, tied to his bed, moaning and crying for help for days before he died. His friends and neighbors heard him all right, but as that's how he customarily took his pleasure, they smiled sympathetically and went about their own affairs, not knowing that this time the rough trade he had picked up to beat him had been insanely earnest.

definition of "cool" hero
and analysis of critic's
responses to him

The quick rise to celebrity status of young fashion photographers, like the quick success of pop singers, makes them ideal "cool" heroes, because they don't come up the slow, backbreaking Horatio Alger route. And the glamour of the rich and famous and

---

[2]Kitty Genovese was murdered by an attacker who drove away and returned to finish the job while Kitty screamed for help before thirty-eight silent witnesses. No one called for help until the murder was completed—a two-hour duration. After her murder, the case was used to point out how people had stopped caring for one another in large cities in America.

beautiful rubs off on the photographer who shoots them, making him one of them. Antonioni uses David Hemmings in the role very prettily—with his Billy Budd hair-do, he's like a Pre-Raphaelite Paul McCartney. But if we're supposed to get upset because this young man got rich quick—the way some people get morally outraged at the salaries movie stars make—that's the moral outrage television personalities specialize in and it's hardly worth the consideration of art-house audiences. Yet a surprising lot of people seem willing to accept assumptions such as: the fashion photographer is symbolic of life in our society and time; he turns to easy sex because his life and ours are empty, etc. Mightn't people like easy sex even if their lives were reasonably full? And is sex necessarily empty just because the people are strangers to each other, or is it just different? And what's so terrible about fast, easy success? Don't most of the people who cluck their condemnation wish they'd had it?

rhetorical questions

Vanessa Redgrave, despite an odd mod outfit, has a tense and lovely presence, and because she has been allowed to act in this film (in which almost no one else is allowed to project) she stands out. However, someone has arranged her in a wholly gratuitous mood—laughing with her head back and teeth showing in a blatant imitation of Garbo. It's almost a subliminal trailer for *Camelot* in which, according to advance publicity, she will be "the Garbo of the sixties." This little deformation does not stick out as it might in another movie because this movie is so ill-formed anyway. The exigencies of the plot force Antonioni to alter his typical "open" construction (famous partly because it was the most painstakingly planned openness in movie history). In *Blow-Up* he prepares for events and plants characters for reappearances when they will be needed, but limply, clumsily; and he finds poor excuses for getting into places like the discotheque and the pot party, which "use" London to tell us about dehumanization. In some terrible way that I suppose could be called Antonioni's genius, he complains of dehumanization in a dehumanized way, and it becomes part of noninvolvement to accept a movie like this as "a chronicle of our time."

internal analysis of Vanessa Redgrave's performance

Just as *Marienbad* was said to be about "time" and/or "memory," *Blow-Up* is said (by Antonioni and the critics following his lead) to be about "illusion and reality." They seem to think they are really saying something, and something impressive at that, though the same thing can be said about almost any movie. In what sense is a movie "about" an abstract concept? Probably what Antonioni and the approving critics mean is that high fashion, mod celebrity, rock and roll, and drugs are part of a sterile or frenetic existence, and they take this to mean that the life represented in the film is not "real" but illusory. What seems to be implicit in the prattle about illusion and reality is the notion that

definition of "illusion and reality" in movies and Blow-Up

the photographer's life is based on "illusion" and that when he discovers the murder, he is somehow face to face with "reality." Of course this notion that murder is more real than, say, driving in a Rolls-Royce convertible, is nonsensical (it's more shocking, though, and when combined with a Rolls-Royce it gives a movie a bit of box office—it's practical). They're not talking about a concept of reality but what used to be called "the real things in life," the solid values they approve of versus the "false values" of "the young people today."

definition of Antonioni as director

Antonioni is the kind of thinker who can say that there are "no social or moral judgments in the picture": he is merely showing us the people who have discarded "all discipline," for whom freedom means "marijuana, sexual perversion, anything," and who live in "decadence without any visible future." I'd hate to be around when he's making judgments. Yet in some sense Antonioni is right: because he doesn't *connect* what he's showing to judgment. And that dislocation of sensibility is probably why kids don't notice the moralizing, why they say *Blow-Up* is hip.

description of specific critical responses to *Blow-Up* with a final definition of how these responses show the superficiality of the film's popularity

The cultural ambience of a film like this becomes mixed with the experience of the film: one critic says Antonioni's "vision" is that "the further we draw away from reality, the closer we get to the truth," another that Antonioni means "we must learn to live with the invisible." All this can sound great to those who don't mind not knowing what it's about, for whom the ineffable seems most important. "It's about the limits of visual experience. The photographer can't go beyond make-believe," a lady lawyer who loved the movie explained to me. "But," I protested, "visual experience is hardly make-believe any more than your practice is—perhaps less." Without pausing for breath she shifted to, "Why does it have to mean anything?" That's the game that's being played at parties this year at Marienbad. They feel they understand *Blow-Up,* but when they can't explain it, or why they feel as they do, they use that as the grounds for saying the movie is a work of art. *Blow-Up* is the perfect movie for the kind of people who say, "now that films have become an art form . . ." and don't expect to understand art.

internal analysis of the picture sequence as it relates to the film's intention

Because the hero is a *photographer* and the blow-up sequence tells a story in pictures, the movie is also said to be about Antonioni's view of himself as an artist (though even his worst enemies could hardly accuse him of "telling stories" in pictures). Possibly it is, but those who see *Blow-Up* as Antonioni's version of *8½*—as making a movie about making a movie—seem to value that much more than just making a movie, probably because it puts the film in a class with the self-conscious autobiographical material so many young novelists struggle with (the story that ends with their becoming writers . . .) and is thus easy to mistake for the highest point of the artist process.

There is the usual post-*Marienbad* arguing about whether the murder is "real" or "hallucinatory." There seems to be an assumption that if a movie can be interpreted as wholly or partially a dream or fantasy, it is more artistic, and I have been hearing that there is no murder, it's all in the photographer's head. But then the movie makes even less sense because there are no indications of anything in his character that relate to such fantasies. Bosley Crowther has come up with the marvelously involuted suggestion that as the little teeny-bopper orgy wasn't "real" but just the hero's "juvenile fantasy," the Production Code people shouldn't have thought they were seeing real titbits on the screen.

another specific description of critical responses as superficial

What is it about the symbolic use of characters and details that impress so many educated people? It's not very hard to do: almost any detail or person or event in our lives can be pressed into symbolic service, but to what end? I take my dogs for a walk in New York City in January and see examples of "alienation." An old Negro woman is crooning, "The world out here is lonely and cold." A shuffling old man mutters, "Never did and never will, never again and never will." And there's a crazy lady who glowers at my dogs and shouts, "They're not fit to shine my canary's shoes!" Do they tell us anything about a "decaying society"? No, but if you had some banal polemical, social, or moral point to make, you could turn them into cardboard figures marked with arrows. In so doing I think you would diminish their individuality and their range of meaning, but you would probably increase your chances of being acclaimed as a deep thinker.

comparison of symbolism in film to "symbolism" in everyday life

When journalistic details are used symbolically—and that is how Antonioni uses "swinging" London—the artist does not create a frame of reference that gives meaning to the details; he simply exploits the ready-made symbolic meanings people attach to certain details and leaves us in a profound mess. (The middle-brow moralists think it's profound and the hippies enjoy the mess.) And when he tosses in a theatrical convention like a mimed tennis game without a ball—which connects with the journalistic data only in that it, too, is symbolic—he throws the movie game away. It becomes ah-sweet-mystery-of-life we-are-all-fools, which, pitched too high for human ears, might seem like great music beyond our grasp.

a summing up paragraph in which the writer defines just what Antonioni is doing

Activity Exercise

1. Write a paragraph in which you describe Pauline Kael's voice. Does her voice fit the movie review style especially well? What is a common movie review style? If you don't know, look up some movie

reviews in several newspapers and decide whether you can find similarities in their styles.

2. Pauline Kael doesn't like *Blow-Up*. Can you write a specific definition of *why* she doesn't like the film? Keep your definition to a sentence or two. Refer to specific parts of the essay to support your interpretation.

3. To whom is Kael speaking? Does she address her essay primarily to those who *like* the film? And how does she address her audience? Is she critical of them as well as the film? Does she occasionally ridicule them? What about the tone in this sentence? *"Blow-Up* is the perfect movie for the kind of people who say, 'now that films have become an art form . . .' and don't expect to understand art"? Can you cite specific words and sentences that clearly indicate the essay's tone?

4. Reread the marginal notes on the essay. Can you point to specific organizational techniques, such as comparison, definition or description, internal analysis, that also contributes to the essay's tone? For example, does a specific comparison, aside from helping to explain Kael's attitude toward *Blow-Up,* also contribute to her ridicule of those readers who like the film? Try to show how the structure you find in the essay affects the reader.

5. One of the purposes of any persuasive essay is identification. The writer presents his material in a way that helps the reader to momentarily become the writer, by sharing particular experiences concretely, by getting the reader to take on another perspective as he or she reads. How does Pauline Kael get you to identify with her as she criticizes *Blow-Up*? Are you as a reader included with those who were fooled by *Blow-Up*'s tricky devices, or are you included by Pauline Kael with those, like herself, who saw through the movie's superficial sophistication to what she calls its overworked "noninvolvement" theme? Do you *identify* with Kael's wit, her tongue-in-cheek criticism of all those "who enjoy seeing this turned-on city of youth"?

Sentence style, attitude, and tone

Consider this rather simple sentence from George Orwell's "The Road to Wigan Pier."

> When you go down a coal mine it is important to try and get to the coal face when the 'fillers' are at work.

What is most important in that sentence? Orwell tells us it is that you need to "get to the coal face when the 'fillers' (the men who throw coal onto conveyor belts to carry it out) are at work." Yet the sentence begins with a subordinate clause that leads naturally to the main idea—"When you go down a coal mine." Try this:

> It is important to try and get to the coal face when the 'fillers' are at work, when you go down a coal mine.

Essentially the sentence says the same thing. But the two "when" clauses follow each other awkwardly and the whole purpose of the sentence—to tell us when to visit a coal mine—seems less important, probably because it comes *first* when the most emphatic position in most sentences is *toward the end*. Sentences often build, like this one, from the least to the most important idea. This next sentence also comes from Orwell's essay.

> When you have finally got there—and getting there is a job in itself: I will explain that in a moment—you crawl through the last line of pit props and see opposite you a shiny black wall three or four feet high.

This sentence begins with the least important information in an opening subordinate clause (a clause that is grammatically connected to some independent clause in the sentence and is usually introduced by a subordinating word such as *when, who, if* and others). Then we find a bit of related but not yet important information—"and getting there is a job in itself: I will explain that in a moment"—and finally we move to the "shiny black wall" which makes up the main part of the sentence. Orwell brings us up sharply against that wall by placing it in the emphatic, final position in the sentence. Each part of the sentence leads up, step-by-step, to the "shiny black wall."

But emphasis is not always the main purpose of a sentence. In fact, *most* of our sentences are shaped according to natural, grammatical order, having a subject/verb/object sequence. If the sentence has a main clause with added clauses and phrases, the "normal" order usually has the main clause first with the added clauses following. Look at this sentence, taken again from Orwell's essay.

> It is impossible to watch the 'fillers' at work without feeling a pang of envy for their toughness.

Here a series of prepositional phrases ends the sentence, all relating to *fillers* in the main clause. Yet the writer also tries a bit of inversion. He might have written "Watching the 'fillers' at work is impossible without feeling a pang of envy for their toughness." The slight inversion of the subject into an object position adds just a bit of emphasis before the final string of phrases appears.

So far we've introduced two general sentence patterns.

Loose: when a sentence follows normal word order (subject, verb, object; subordinate clauses and phrases following the main clause). *Loose,* when used to describe a sentence pattern, is *not* a negative word. It merely means that the writer puts down his ideas in the order in which they come to his mind and according to the natural ways of speaking and writing sentences.

Periodic: when a writer reshapes a sentence so that the most important idea comes at the most emphatic place in the sentence—usually at the end. Normal word order is inverted or changed to give emphasis to a main idea. Periodic sentences usually occur less frequently than loose sentences in the prose of professional writers, probably because too many inverted or changed word-orders sound artificial and false. Use periodic sentences as exceptions to emphasize a particularly important idea. Let your everyday voice dictate the rest of your sentence patterns.

There is yet another general sentence pattern. A *balanced* sentence puts two equal main ideas together in one sentence. They are often set side-by-side and separated by a semicolon or colon, as in this example from Orwell's "The Road to Wigan Pier."

In the middle of the run the cage probably touches sixty miles an hour; in some of the deeper mines it touches even more.

A balanced sentence shows a poised mind, one that has already sorted out the tensions in an idea and set them up for the reader. Such sentences show a mind that cuts an idea into equal halves and serves it up ready to swallow. Still, balanced sentences shouldn't be overused; they can give an essay a too formal, too "already-thought-out" effect. Use the balanced sentence when you want to round-off two complex ideas in a single sentence or, as Orwell does in this example, when you want to show yet another possibility alongside the one you've already expressed.

In most cases we form sentences according to our normal speech patterns. But occasionally we want a sentence to jolt the reader, to call his attention to an important idea, or just to remind him by the variety in sentence patterns that as writers we are alive and speaking. Even our most colloquial voice is capable of an occasional balanced idea or an ironic twist. Sentence variety, if used carefully and without exaggeration and pretense, makes more exciting reading because it makes you a more interesting writer. It helps your reader to see you as a writer with style, one who is capable of a surprising sentence.

Look over this paragraph from "The Road to Wigan Pier." Find examples of all three sentence patterns and show how they work. Are they used to give emphasis to a particular idea? Or are the patterns used to contribute some kind of sophistication or quality to the writer's voice or tone? Finally, try to decide how the patterns of the sentences contribute to the writer's voice. Does the writer sound like someone you might overhear talking over a recent visit to a coal mine in an everyday style? Would you say his tone is forceful and directed toward supporting a particular attitude toward what he sees?

> What *is* surprising, on the other hand, is the immense horizontal distances that have to be traveled underground. Before I had been down a mine I had vaguely imagined the miner stepping out of the cage and getting to work on a ledge of coal a few yards away. I had not realized that before he even gets to his work he may have to creep through passages as long as from London Bridge to Oxford Circus. In the beginning, of course, a mine shaft is sunk somewhere near a seam of coal. But as that seam is worked out and fresh seams are followed up, the workings get farther and farther from the pit bottom. If it is a mile from the pit bottom to the coal face, that is probably an average distance; three miles is a fairly normal one; there are even said to be a few mines where the average distance is five miles. But these distances bear no relation to distances above ground. For in all that mile or three miles as it may be, there is hardly anywhere outside the main road, and not many places even there, where a man can stand upright.

Writing Exercise

1. Take one of your earlier papers and rework just a few of the sentences. Select sentences that you believe are critical to meaning and rewrite them to put clearer emphasis on the important idea. You might want to shift natural word-order so that you make a periodic sentence out of a loose one. Or perhaps you'll find the need to change some awkwardly complex sentences back to a more natural, loose form. Whatever the case, don't overuse any one pattern. Make your revisions fit meaning without distracting from your everyday voice.

2. Take your journal into a crowded place. Listen carefully for some conversation and copy it down in rough form in your journal, paying close attention to the speaker's words and style. Then rewrite the passage,

putting it in more formal language and revising both the vocabulary and the word-order. Does the person's meaning change when you change the style? Which passage is clearer and more emphatic?

3. Find the lyrics to one of your favorite popular songs. Usually song lyrics are closer to poetry than prose. Rewrite your chosen lyrics in prose. Try to explain the emotion and message of the lyrics in more detail, keeping the general voice and tone, but filling in more detail and elaborating on meaning. You might also try rewriting the lyrics in extremely formal language.

4. Imagine yourself arguing with a friend about some current event, perhaps the Watergate hearings or some domestic problem such as inflation. Transfer your imagined argument to paper. And use some of Orwell's techniques as you do. For example, support your contentions by referring to specifics, to testimony by specific individuals during the hearings, to the way the national newspapers and syndicated columns responded to Watergate, to a television interview on the subject. Explain how these items led to your thesis. Develop a personal voice; sound like you would if you were really arguing.

Reading for tone

Tone is the stance a writer takes toward his readers. If we're angry about a recent tax increase and we write to the local newspaper about that anger, we might also be angry toward our readers in the letter. Or perhaps we'd find a more rational argument, one in which we ask the reader to reason quietly with us. Or perhaps we'd be most effective with an ironic tone, one in which we'd criticize the politicians who passed the higher tax law by praising them for their outrageous actions. With consistent and careful application, all three tones might prove successful.

Here are three brief excerpts from student essays on "the American character." First try to describe the writer's tone. Then make some comment on how effective you think the tone is and tell why.

> The American is naturally hard-working and ambitious. He wants to pull himself up by the bootstraps to a successful position in society. He can be crafty, even dangerous, in his desire to get ahead.

> I have no idea what Americans are really like, although I'm one of them. After all, what's a twenty-year-old innocent young man like me doing writing about a complex subject like America? If I knew what Americans were really like, I'd leave the country.

America—'God shed his grace on thee.' Has He? Some say 'no'; some say 'yes'; some 'maybe.' But whatever the answer, this is an interesting, explosive and sometimes exciting country to live in.

In each passage, we find some variation in tone. We can use a spatial metaphor to begin our analyses of tone. When the writer assumes a formal, rational style, we can say that he develops a distant tone. He keeps the reader at a proper distance by avoiding the colloquial, by using pronouns such as "one," by maintaining an objective stance toward his subject through the avoidance of subjective adjectives and words with highly emotional meanings. On the other hand, a writer who uses the colloquial, who addresses his readers in the first person, who uses familiar words and an everyday speaking rhythm uses what we might call an *intimate* tone; he leaves very little distance between himself and his audience.

The distinction between intimate and distant tones is clear when we compare the first excerpt with the second and third. The first speaker addresses what seems to be a general audience. He does not use any of the forms of direct address we find in the second and third excerpts—the direct questions, the contractions (which indicate a kind of informality and intimacy between writer and reader). The first speaker is objective, general, even conventional. He uses a few phrases—"pull himself up by the bootstraps," ". . . to get ahead"—that have been used by many writers. The first speaker seems to avoid his readers, to write as if they weren't there, in order to maintain some formality and objectivity in his writing.

What is more important than the distance or lack of distance between writer and reader in all these excerpts, however, is the impression the reader gets of the writer. We see no indication that anything new, interesting, or informative will be presented in the first excerpt. This writer seems competent; he can write the general and obvious, but he also seems a little bit too conventional.

The speakers in the second and third passages do seem to involve their readers, primarily because they create a lively, forceful tone that comes right at the reader with a message. The writer of the second excerpt adopts a humorous tone. He knows that writing about Americans is at least partially absurd—because no one really knows enough to write in a completely authoritative way about every American. He admits his fallibility and, as a result, has a better chance of having his readers on his side. He's able to develop a friendly, joking voice that keeps the reader following the quickness of his mind rather than arguing with his opinions. The contractions, the simple, colloquial vocabulary, and the loose sentence structure combine to tell us that what is to follow will not be dull. Here, no matter what the message, we have an interesting mind at work on an interesting subject.

You might find the third writer a bit too friendly, almost to the point of seeming frivolous. The quick questions, the sarcastic reference to a patriotic song, and the rough, almost "pushy" sentences might be too much for even the good-humored reader to handle. You might be tempted to reply, "Now wait a minute, we're really not *that* friendly, are we?" You might feel the sentence fragments are too intimate and tricky to be effective.

In each excerpt, we find that the writer plays a role which he feels is suited to both his subject and his audience. Readers might honestly disagree about the relative successes of these projected roles, but, in each case, the created personality must come to work in balance with the particular audience. Some audiences might prefer the conventional language of the first excerpt, whereas others would find it terribly corny or monotonous. The sarcasm and intimacy of the second excerpt might be successful with a relatively sophisticated reader; it might, however, fail miserably with readers who lacked a sense of humor or with readers who were very serious about their subject. The third excerpt might be very successful if delivered orally to an intimate group of people who might appreciate the jokes and the informal style. But it would almost surely fail to please most history professors on an exam.

Activity Exercise

Discuss what you feel would be an effective tone for papers on the following controversial subjects. Ask yourself how the writer ought to treat his readers. Should he come on strong and push the reader around a bit? Should he be moderate and rational? Mention any specific combination of tones you think would be effective.

1. an argument *against* the woman's role in the traditional family as mother, housewife, and domestic guide for her children

2. an argument that intercollegiate sports should be de-emphasized and more emphasis placed on intramural sports

3. an argument that explicit sex should or should not be represented on television

4. an argument that freshmen should *not* have to take required courses

5. an argument that a liberal arts student should not have to take any science requirements

11

Irony:
Writing indirectly

Have you ever sat through or even participated in a conversation like this?

John: Hi Ted, How're you?

Ted: Oh, *as good as can be expected.* I went to that chem lecture last night but it was *over my head.* My girl has been giving me a *rough time* so everything hasn't been *sunny* in the ol' *love life.*

John: Well, my life's been *dead as a doornail* lately. I went with Tom, who is as *strong as an ox,* to the wrestling match yesterday. After the match, he insisted on our testing out a few of the holds we saw. I can tell you, I'm no better off for it. Then my mother said I was *living the life of Riley* and that I was *getting soft,* so I'm helping the guy next door nail shingles on his garage roof. *When it rains, it pours.*

Ted: Yeah, my life hasn't been a blast recently either. I *rang up* my sister yesterday and found out that my old car, which I left back home, is just *not what it used to be.* So I'm thinking of just *copping out* for a while and resting the ol' *think-tank.*

John: Maybe that's a good idea. *Why fight it?* I just don't feel like *hanging in there* any longer myself.

349

And we, as listeners, don't want to "hang in there" any longer either. Our everyday talk is often lively and dramatic because it is rooted in our concrete experiences. But because we usually speak without having time to think out and plan what we say, we often rely on conventional words, phrases, and sentences.

Overworked words and limping language

Dull words can make even the most interesting idea seem tired, lifeless, and boring. The effective conversationalist usually avoids sounding too conventional. When he does use a cliché, he makes sure that he uses it in a fresh context or in an original way. Here are the most common symptoms of a most common disease called "overworked words," or "limping language."

Clichés: an expression that closes the possibility of further thought because of its dull familiarity. In the conversation between John and Ted, the italicized words and phrases are all clichés. They don't really make a listener *think* because he's heard them so many times. Avoid clichés *like the plague* if you want your listeners or readers not to avoid you.

Platitudes: clichés that are pronounced as if they have high moral or philosophic truth. A platitude is above all dull, however serious. For example, someone who had just read a highly romantic novel about the distressing circumstances of coal-miners in Eastern Kentucky might close the book with the remark: "Ah, me. Life is difficult." Platitudes, like clichés, close the possibility of further thought or effort. The speaker doesn't *do* anything for coal-miners; he just sighs.

Dead and dying metaphors: we already know that a metaphor is a comparison between two objects that works to clarify an idea. Some metaphors have been around too long, however, and we don't really think when we hear or read them. Such metaphors are either dying or dead. They *stop* rather than carry forward the main idea. Consider "think-tank" in the above dialogue. People have been saying that difficult ideas are "rough on the old think-tank" for years. The first person to use the phrase made a fresh comparison; the last person you've heard say it threw yet another weed on the grave of what was once fresh and lively.

Activity Exercise

1. Listen to your own talk. How many of your own phrases have you heard before? In what context did you hear them? Sometimes a cliché or dead metaphor can be revitalized by being thrust into a fresh context. Robert Burns said that his love reminded him of a red, red rose. Over the years that's become a very dead metaphor. You might freshen it up a bit by pointing out that roses, like lovers, have thorns.

2. Reread some of the papers you've already written. Jot down your favorite clichés (the ones you use the most). Then include each one in a new paragraph in which you apply the cliché in a fresh context. For example, you might apply the phrase "love is a many splendored thing" to two people who constantly argue over their wedding plans. Or you might apply a phrase like "living the life of Riley" to a person who *seems* to live an easy life but really works very hard and has to withstand much hardship.

Sarcasm and irony

Students use *sarcasm*. Teachers use *irony*. Both words mean essentially the same thing; both refer to the ability to use language *indirectly*, to say the opposite of what you really mean. Sarcasm, however, is usually more personal and blunt than irony. Also, sarcasm refers to using language indirectly in speech; irony usually applies to saying the opposite of what you mean in writing.

Suppose you decide late on a Friday night that you would like a pizza. You and one other person are the only ones willing to leave the house or dormitory to get the pizza. The weather is wet, snowy, and blowing. You trudge a mile and a half through the snow to the local pizza parlor and a mile and a half back. When you return, another person innocently asks, "How's the weather?" You look slowly down at your drenched feet, your rumpled, saggy trousers, your dripping overcoat and say, "Great!" That's sarcasm. Your friend knows you're not serious. He has only to look at your condition to see that you mean the opposite of what you say. He feels ridiculed by your answer, both for asking a silly question and maybe for not going with you to get the pizza.

Sarcasm transferred to writing usually becomes irony. Irony is less personal than sarcasm. Spoken sarcasm ridicules a flesh-and-blood person who is usually standing right in front of you. In writing, however, unless you are writing a personal letter, your reader is not someone you can visualize standing before you. Automatically, then the ridicule and humor become less personal and more general. Irony is usually directed toward the flaw or error the writer finds *in* the person, rather than *at* the person himself.

Why use irony? The answers are many. Above all, writers use irony because they want to overcome the dulling effects of overworked words, to avoid the disease of limping language. They want, in other words, to say what they believe in a way that is interesting, fresh, and entertaining. We've already established that every writer creates his own voice and projects part of himself into every writing situation. Irony, because it relies on indirection and humor to persuade a reader to take on an attitude or opinion, helps a writer to avoid the more commonplace and preachy styles of persuasion.

Take, for example, a writer who wants to say something about the yearly talks between baseball owners and players over contracts. Every year strikes and "lock-outs" are threatened. Every year the newspapers are filled with columns and features that tell us how the game is being ruined by these unsportsmanlike arguments, how baseball isn't what it used to be when both owners and players were dedicated to the great national pastime, not money. Someone who writes in a straight and serious style about these yearly arguments takes the chance of being just another contributor to the mountain of very serious, very important newsprint already produced. If he wants to persuade his readers to take action against the yearly baseball contract fights, he might effectively resort to irony. He might copy the highly serious tone of both owners and players in order to ridicule; he might exaggerate a particular part of the problem to clarify its absurdity, always saying the opposite of what he really means. He might pretend, on the surface, to agree with the exaggerated demands of either the players or owners and leave it to the reader to figure out that their arguments are absurd and deserving of censure.

On the following pages you'll find specific devices you can use to write irony. Above all, remember that irony is the practice of saying the opposite of what you mean. The more subtle and clever you become at saying one thing and suggesting another, the more impact your irony will have on your readers. Dictionaries define *sarcasm* as "a sneering or cutting remark." Superficial irony, like sarcasm, can often be reduced to sneering or cutting remarks. But truly effective and useful irony doesn't just cut down a person; it points, with humor and a fair critical eye, at human folly and absurdity, whether it's found in one or a group of persons, in an institution, a nation, or a government. The true and fair ironist always remembers to include himself among those who fall prey to the follies he exposes. Then his irony goes beyond the personal to reveal universal error.

Irony by exaggeration

Perhaps the most common form of irony is exaggeration. The writer selects the most obvious characteristics, qualities, or ideas of the attitude which he is opposing and enlarges them to make their absurdity more obvious. An educational traditionalist, for example, might take the common qualities of an educational innovator—his enthusiasm for new ideas, his idealistic belief in each student's abilities and worth—and exaggerate them so that they become absurd. The educational innovator, then, becomes someone who never questions anything that is new, never shows the least bit of critical perception; in short, he becomes someone that almost any reasonably intelligent person would find incredible.

When you use exaggeration, remember that there must be *some* truth to justify your exaggeration. Ironic exaggeration works by extending a smaller flaw or weakness into a larger one. The writer says, in effect, here's what will happen in the future if we don't see the folly of what we are doing now. Aldous Huxley in *Brave New World* showed us by exaggeration what might happen if we depended too exclusively on science and technology to run our society. People become machines put together and controlled by other, more complicated machines and systems. The idea of freedom in *Brave New World* vanished and was replaced by "canned happiness," which consisted of people developing certain physical appetites that could be satisfied only by the State. In any exaggerated situation, the writer must be sure that the reader can understand how the exaggeration might logically develop from the actual circumstance. Otherwise, the irony seems more like pure selfishness, exaggeration motivated only by a desire to ridicule your opponent and not by a logical desire to reveal a weakness.

As you plan to write irony by exaggeration, focus your exaggeration on some specific aspect of your subject. Begin by writing down a description of the weakness you want to expose. Get it into as specific a language as you can. Then pick out a theme, person, object, or idea on which you can focus your irony. If your general purpose, for example, is to point out the dangers of the socialization of medicine, pick out a potential patient and show how socialized medicine would affect him in his everyday affairs. Exaggerate, but stay within the boundaries of possibility.

Take a close look at Gahan Wilson's cartoon on this page. Wilson, in all his cartoons, shows us character exaggerations. He takes the tendency toward cruelty and the love of the grotesque that we all share to at least a small degree and exaggerates it in his cartoon characters. Here we find a middle-aged man feeding his fiendish garbage can with a satisfied grin on his face. His wife cowers behind begging him to "get rid of that thing." Why is the cartoon funny? Probably because we recognize in Irwin, who is probably an otherwise civilized and gentle man, a universal tendency toward cruelty and a fascination with the macabre. Most times we hold back such feelings, at least in civilized company. But Irwin, at least in his kitchen, openly displays his grotesque side every time he uses his sinister garbage disposal. Wilson uses Irwin to identify, by exaggeration, a universal human trait.

Figure 11-1

Cartoon by Gahan Wilson

"Oh, Irwin, I wish to God you'd get rid of that thing!"

Reproduced by special permission of *Playboy* magazine; copyright © 1972 by *Playboy*.

Activity Exercise

1. Find another cartoon that you believe makes an ironic comment on human nature by exaggeration. What is the general purpose of the irony? How does the particular exaggeration work to suggest that purpose?

2. Look around and try to find a person whom you think is a particularly good example of some kind of absurd behavior. Don't exclude yourself from the field of possibility. Then fasten on those physical and psychological characteristics which you feel are clearly related to the absurd behavior and exaggerate them. Remember you can't come right out and say what you mean. Let the exaggeration speak for itself. Use plenty of concrete detail and try to keep your exaggeration at least within the realm of possibility.

3. Read several of the "Dear Abby" columns in your local newspaper. Select one in which you feel a letter-writer has been particularly melodramatic and corny—say, someone who has undergone a preposterous series of illnesses, lover's rebukes, mishaps, job hardships, personal slights, and general bad luck. Then write your own answer to the letter, using exaggeration similar to what you find in the letter to ridicule its melodramatic sentimentality. Again, remember that you don't want to come right out and say what you think. Write indirectly.

Irony by understatement

Understatement is the reverse of exaggeration. It ridicules or criticizes by saying less than a reader expects. Suppose you want to stir people up about the recently soaring percentages of people killed or injured on American highways. Safety organizations across the country use these percentages over and over again to warn people; they reproduce photographs and make films of major accidents, all without having much effect on the rising percentages. Scare tactics don't seem to work, perhaps because the general public has grown used to high traffic death counts, sensational accident photographs, and ultimate warnings. Faced with such a situation, you might decide to write up a recent horrible accident in everyday language, as if it really *were* an everyday incident in everybody's life. At first, your readers might be startled by your inhumane attitude. But they'd soon get your real point. Your understated article might have more effect than fifty loud outcries about highway safety.

Understatement proves most useful when the reader expects overstatement, exaggeration, or at least high seriousness. Like most irony, it works by surprise, shocking the reader to attention with an unconventionally quiet or sober response in a context that would usually demand direct and open concern. Jonathan Swift in his essay "A Modest Proposal," which is included later in this chapter, makes an absurd and openly uncivilized proposal that the British and Irish eat the children of the Irish poor in order to solve the country's economic problems. But the proposal is presented in a rational tone, with careful reference to statistics and evidence, so that very many *civilized* readers took it seriously and were outraged both by the essay's proposal and its matter-of-fact style. Swift, by understating his case, made his proposal more effectively ironic; his intended satire of the inhumanity of those who cruelly did nothing about poverty was more effectively pointed out when he did them one better. He came up with a proposal even they considered inhumane, offered it in a sober and serious tone, and caught his opponents in their own trap. Once his opponents had committed themselves to opposing the "modest proposal," they had also shown up their own lack of concern. For they had done nothing, while he had at least made a proposal, however crude and absurd.

Most advertising works by straight exaggeration. All the good points

Figure 11-2

Yamaha ad

of a product are often elevated into absolute values while weak points are ignored. Look at this following interpretation of the message implied by the Yamaha advertisement on page 356.

> Here we have it. The ideal escape machine for the modern woman. She becomes a part of the male world through a motorcycle. The advertisement promises her freedom, practicality, perhaps even greater sexual attractiveness. Someday we will all own a Yamaha. All this we should take with a grain of salt. The good life might not be assured, even for a thoroughly modern woman, by a Yamaha.

Writing Exercise

Now try writing advertising copy to accompany the Yamaha advertisement. Appeal to what you believe the woman in the advertisement would want to hear. Be straightforward; imagine yourself a Yamaha adman.

Later, you may want to write a parody of your advertising copy. Somehow, in your parody, you will need to let your readers know that you are only half-serious. Your imitation of the adman's style and message, in other words, must be clearly meant to ridicule rather than sell.

Irony by parody and burlesque

Parody is criticism or ridicule by imitation. Burlesque, like parody, also imitates, but usually for a more directly humorous effect. The most common form of parody either uses a high, formal style to describe common, vulgar events or an informal style to describe events that normally merit a serious style.

During the eighteenth century Alexander Pope wanted to write a satiric poem about the quibbles and absurd social behavior of the aristocracy. He had seen ladies stunned by the most insignificant slight or social cut. His poem, "The Rape of the Lock," was his answer, a piece of social criticism that has endured for several hundred years. In "The Rape of the Lock" Pope imitated the style of heroic literature—a style usually reserved for descriptions of grave battles and important events between important countries. Yet his poem was actually about the cutting off of a lock of a lady's hair by an aristocratic gentleman during a card party. The ironic contrast between the heroic style of the poem and its very unheroic subject still provides entertainment and criticism of human vanity for readers today.

Mark Twain reversed Pope's use of parody in a little story called "Buck Fanshaw's Funeral," taken from the novel *Roughing It.* In "Buck Fanshaw's Funeral," Twain had a frontier character, Scotty, explain a funeral in crude, everyday slang. The result is humorous, but it also points up how we usually try to cover up the bare facts of death with wordy descriptions and high-sounding clichés. In fact, Twain's irony is made even more effective because Scotty is describing the funeral to an Eastern dude minister who actually uses pompous, exaggerated language in his description of the funeral. The clash of languages is double-parody, two imitations for the purpose of ironic criticism going on simultaneously.

Look at the Doonesbury cartoon on this page. In it you'll find an obvious bit of parody. The combat reporter writes an article on B.D., our common, everyday soldier. In the article, he uses the melodramatic style we usually associate with romantic war novels and second- and third-rate war movies—"The brave private, B.D., sits by his machine gun. . . ." The contrast between the romantic, melodramatic style and the comic characters we see in the cartoon makes for irony; we feel the cartoonist saying the opposite of what the words mean. Somehow B.D.'s "bravery" isn't bravery—he's too much in love with his work. Can you find a general comment on heroism in Trudeau's cartoon? Try to define the cartoon's thesis.

Activity Exercise

1. Turn on one of the television soap operas. Follow the outlines of the story and the dialogue as closely as you can, recording catch phrases,

Figure 11-3 Doonesbury *by G. B. Trudeau*

particularly trite or conventional phrases, clichés, dead and dying metaphors. Jot down the outlines of any particularly melodramatic and clichéd situations—say, a secret conversation between two lovers during a chance meeting at a party or the hysterics of a wife who has just found out that her husband has a lover. Turn your notes into a brief parody of soap operas. Ridicule by imitation, using soap-opera content and style.

2. Read several examples of sports writing. Select sports columns from your local papers along with a few nationally syndicated columnists like Red Smith of the *New York Times*. Pick out any common sportswriter's jargon—words like "four-bagger" or "homer" or "grand slam." Describe some of the common qualities in a sportswriter's voice—do they usually sound tough or wise-cracking, sarcastic or straight? Then write up a parody of sports writing style. Exaggerate the qualities of other sportswriters a bit. Pick a local sports event or issue as your content, but remember your parody will be of the typical sportswriter's lingo. You might also turn to the society page and pick up on the clichés that are used to describe a recent garden-party, wedding, or dance. Write a parody on this writing style.

3. Select your favorite television talk show personality or a favorite disc-jockey on radio. Listen carefully for at least fifteen minutes, recording key phrases. Then write a parody of your subject, trying to capture the sound of his or her voice in the form of a radio monologue or television interview. Exaggerate if you feel the need. Be as concrete as you can in reproducing your subject's performance; use specific words and phrases, and describe particular gestures and actions. Then write a separate paragraph in which you explain what you wanted to say about your subject through the parody.

4. Write an essay in which you classify different kinds of clichés or dead metaphors. Find your means of classification. You might classify according to language context, field of interest, profession, or physical sitaution (in the student union, at the refreshment stand at a ball game, during the intermission of a play). Write a general definition of the clichés you include under each classification and then analyze a few sample clichés closely.

A note on irony and humor

Not all irony is humorous. In fact, some forms of irony are far more serious than standard exposition. Swift's "A Modest Proposal" is certainly very serious; it has the serious intention of pointing out indirectly but very emphatically the cruel treatment of the Irish poor by their British overseers early in the eighteenth century. Swift uses irony to go beyond direct criticism. The exaggeration of his narrator's solution points up the critical state of affairs in Ireland. Bitter irony usually grows out of a state of near-despair in the writer. If you feel that you've reached the end of your patience, that there's nothing further you can do about a situation, irony may well be your last resort. In such cases, the laughter, if there is any, is dark, bitter, and terribly cynical.

Reserve the bitterest irony for the truly bitter situation. Most irony is more effective when it is laced with lightness, when you and a reader can laugh and still work to right a bad situation. The best irony usually combines a sense of humor with a sense of absurdity. It is the result of a critical mind and a sharp wit. Above, all, it excludes no one, including the writer, from the exposed folly. Yet it also maintains critical balance. No one is much interested in the criticisms of a chronic complainer.

From irony to satire

Throughout his life Jonathan Swift was aware of the wide gap between things as they were and things as they should be. That recognition made him a premier satirist. Irony is a group of verbal devices that ridicule or criticize by saying the opposite of what seems intended in the actual words. Swift used irony to build his general satire on the obvious differences between the actual and the ideal. Often he would exaggerate or understate in order to point out a deeper, more complex evil in society. Satire is a general system of writing that holds up to ridicule widespread human folly of any kind; it incorporates irony within its system along with other techniques. Almost always, as with Swift, a satirist points out the gap between things as they are and as they should be.

Later in his career as writer and churchman Swift became the champion of the Irish cause against the British. He levelled his satire against the British exploitation of Ireland in a *Proposal for the Universal Use of Irish Manufacture* (1720), in which he suggested that the Irish boycott English goods. In *Drapier's Letters* (1724) Swift attacked the British system of coinage which he felt exploited the Irish currency. His satire of British exploitation of Ireland climaxed in *A Modest Proposal,* first published in 1729.

Keep in mind the historical context within which the pamphlet was written. Ireland had been beset by famine, by economic ills of every kind, and by British exploitation of what little in the way of material goods the Irish were able to produce. Swift, himself an Anglican Protestant and an educated minister in a largely Catholic and uneducated country, was bitter for two reasons. First, he was thoroughly disenchanted because the Anglican church in Britain had given him a relatively minor appointment as Bishop of St. Patrick's Cathedral in Dublin when he had hoped for an appointment in England, away from the poverty of Ireland. Second, since he himself felt mistreated by the British, his understanding of the resentment, frustration, and suffering of the Irish people doubled. He felt more than compassion as he watched the poor in Dublin starve; he felt personal outrage.

Within the context of his own bitter feelings and the outrageous condition of the people around him, Swift had to find a way to criticize the British without becoming the victim of their reaction. He naturally turned to satire and irony as a way of levelling the gravest ridicule without being held responsible for his words. So Swift created an anonymous British narrator who, with a very straight face, recommends that the rich eat the children of the poor. And he supported his outrageous proposal with numerous facts, statistics, and rational arguments. The conditions of the poor are revealed, and the solution, however horrible in itself, actually begins to seem sensible when compared to the suffering that already existed. Perhaps it's not surprising that more than a few British readers took Swift seriously and supported his proposal.

Find examples of exaggeration, understatement and parody in the essay. More importantly, consider Swift's persona in this essay. Remember persona is the mask a writer wears, the personality he takes on in a given writing situation. In this essay Swift's persona had to be believable; otherwise the satiric proposal would have lost a good deal of its effect. What does Swift do to make his British persona seem believable, even while he makes an absurd proposal? What about the essay's tone—would you say it is moderate and rational? Enthusiastic and emotional? What about the facts and statistics cited by the persona? Do they give the persona an air of credibility he wouldn't otherwise have? Is the modest proposal actually as absurd as it first seems when you compare it to the actual conditions of the poor in Ireland? In a sense, the essay says to the British that some form of mercy killing put to good use would be far better than the brutality presently shown toward the Irish.

A Modest Proposal

JONATHAN SWIFT

FOR PREVENTING THE CHILDREN OF POOR PEOPLE IN IRELAND FROM BEING A BURDEN TO THEIR PARENTS OR COUNTRY, AND FOR MAKING THEM BENEFICIAL TO THE PUBLIC.

It is a melancholy object to those who walk through this great town, or travel in the country, when they see the streets, the roads, and cabin-doors crowded with beggars of the female sex, followed by three, four, or six children, *all in rags*, and importuning every passenger for an

---

Reprinted from *Eighteenth Century Poetry and Prose*, ed. by Louis I. Bredvold, Alan D. McKillop, Lois Whitney, The Ronald Press Company, New York, 1939.

alms. These mothers instead of being able to work for their honest livelihood, are forced to employ all their time in strolling, to beg sustenance for their helpless infants, who, as they grow up, either turn thieves for want of work, or leave their dear Native Country to fight for the Pretender[1] in Spain, or sell themselves to the Barbardoes.

I think it is agreed by all parties, that this prodigious number of children, in the arms, or on the backs, or at the heels of their mothers, and frequently of their fathers, is in the present deplorable state of the kingdom a very great additional grievance; and therefore whoever could find out a fair, cheap and easy method of making these children sound useful members of the commonwealth would deserve so well of the public, as to have his statue set up for a preserver of the nation.

But my intention is very far from being confined to provide only for the children of professed beggars, it is of a much greater extent, and shall take in the whole number of infants at a certain age, who are born of parents in effect as little able to support them, as those who demand our charity in the streets.

As to my own part, having turned my thoughts, for many years, upon this important subject, and maturely weighed the several schemes of other projectors, I have always found them grossly mistaken in their computation. It is true a child, just dropped from its dam, may be supported by her milk for a solar year with little other nourishment, at most not above the value of two shillings, which the mother may certainly get, or the value in scraps, by her lawful occupation of begging, and it is exactly at one year old that I propose to provide for them, in such a manner, as, instead of being a charge upon their parents, or the parish, or wanting food and raiment for the rest of their lives, they shall, on the contrary, contribute to the feeding and partly to the clothing of many thousands.

There is likewise another great advantage in my scheme, that it will prevent those voluntary abortions, and that horrid practice of women murdering their bastard children, alas, too frequent among us, sacrificing the poor innocent babes, I doubt, more to avoid the expense, than the shame, which would move tears and pity in the most savage and inhuman breast.

The number of souls in this kingdom being usually reckoned one million and a half, of those I calculate there may be about two hundred thousand couple whose wives are breeders, from which number I subtract thirty thousand couple, who are able to maintain their own children, although I apprehend there cannot be so many under the present distresses of the kingdom, but this being granted, there will remain an hundred and seventy thousand breeders. I again subtract fifty thousand

---

[1]*The Pretender* was James Stuart, son of James II, King of England, both Catholics. James II had fled to France when the "revolution" of 1688 placed William and Mary on the throne. In 1715 the Pretender unsuccessfully tried to regain the throne, and some of his followers still tried.

for those women who miscarry, or whose children die by accident, or disease within the year. There only remain an hundred and twenty thousand children of poor parents annually born: the question therefore is, how this number shall be reared, and provided for, which, as I have already said, under the present situation of affairs, is utterly impossible by all the methods hitherto proposed, for we can neither employ them in handicraft, or agriculture; we neither build houses, (I mean in the country) nor cultivate land: they can very seldom pick up a livelihood by stealing till they arrive at six years old, except where they are of towardly parts,[2] although, I confess they learn the rudiments much earlier, during which time, they can however be properly looked upon only as *probationers*, as I have been informed by a principal gentleman in the County of Cavan,[3] who protested to me, that he never knew above one or two instances under the age of six, even in a part of the kingdom so renowned for the quickest proficiency in that art.

I am assured by our merchants, that a boy or a girl, before twelve years old, is no saleable commodity, and even when they come to this age, they will not yield above three pounds, or three pounds and half-a-crown at most on the Exchange, which cannot turn to account either to the parents or kingdom, the charge of nutriment and rags having been at least four times that value.

I shall now therefore humbly propose my own thoughts, which I hope will not be liable to the least objection.

I have been assured by a very knowing American of my acquaintance in London, that a young healthy child well nursed is at a year old a most delicious, nourishing, and wholesome food, whether stewed, roasted, baked, or boiled, and I make no doubt that it will equally serve in a fricassee, or ragout.

I do therefore humbly offer it to public consideration, that of the hundred and twenty thousand children, already computed, twenty thousand may be reserved for breed, whereof only one fourth part to be males, which is more than we allow to sheep, black-cattle, or swine, and my reason is that these children are seldom the fruits of marriage, a circumstance not much regarded by our savages, therefore one male will be sufficient to serve four females. That the remaining hundred thousand may at a year old be offered in sale to the persons of quality, and fortune, through the kingdom, always advising the mother to let them suck plentifully in the last month, so as to render them plump, and fat for a good table. A child will make two dishes at an entertainment for friends, and when the family dines alone, the fore or hind quarter will make a reasonable dish, and seasoned with a little pepper or salt will be very good boiled on the fourth day, especially in winter.

I have reckoned upon a medium, that a child just born will weigh

---

[2]*towardly parts:* natural ability.

[3]*Cavan:* a county of Northern Ireland.

12 pounds, and in a solar year if tolerably nursed increaseth to 28 pounds.

I grant this food will be somewhat dear, and therefore very proper for landlords, who, as they have already devoured most of the parents, seem to have the best title to the children.

Infants' flesh will be in season throughout the year, but more plentiful in March, and a little before and after, for we are told by a grave author, an eminent French Physician, that fish being a prolific diet, there are more children born in Roman Catholic countries about nine months after Lent, than at any other season; therefore reckoning a year after Lent, the markets will be more glutted than usual, because the number of Popish infants is at least three to one in this kingdom, and therefore it will have one other collateral advantage by lessening the number of Papists[4] among us.

I have already computed the charge of nursing a beggar's child (in which list I reckon all cottagers, labourers, and four-fifths of the farmers) to be about two shillings *per annum*, rags included, and I believe no gentleman would repine to give ten shillings for the carcass of a good fat child, which, as I have said, will make four dishes of excellent nutritive meat, when he hath only some particular friend, or his own family to dine with him. Thus the Squire will learn to be a good landlord, and grow popular among his tenants, the mother will have eight shillings net profit, and be fit for work till she produces another child.

Those who are more thrifty (as I must confess the times require) may flay the carcass; the skin of which, artificially dressed, will make admirable gloves for ladies, and summer boots for fine gentlemen.

As to our City of Dublin, shambles[5] may be appointed for this purpose, in the most convenient parts of it, and butchers we may be assured will not be wanting, although I rather recommend buying the children alive, and dressing them hot from the knife, as we do roasting pigs.

A very worthy person, a true lover of his country, and whose virtues I highly esteem, was lately pleased, in discoursing on this matter, to offer a refinement upon my scheme. He said, that many gentlemen of this kingdom, having of late destroyed their deer, he conceived that the want of venison might be well supplied by the bodies of young lads and maidens, not exceeding fourteen years of age, nor under twelve, so great a number of both sexes in every country being now ready to starve, for want of work and service: and these to be disposed of by their parents if alive, or otherwise by their nearest relations. But with due deference to so excellent a friend, and so deserving a patriot, I cannot be altogether in his sentiments; for as to the males, my American acquaintance assured me from frequent experience, that their flesh was generally tough and

---

[4]*Papists:* Catholics.

[5]*Shambles:* a place for slaughtering or marketing animals.

lean, like that of our schoolboys, by continual exercise, and their taste disagreeable, and to fatten them would not answer the charge. Then as to the females, it would, I think with humble submission, be a loss to the public, because they soon would become breeders themselves: and besides, it is not improbable that some scrupulous people might be apt to censure such a practice, (although indeed very unjustly) as a little bordering upon cruelty, which, I confess, hath always been with me the strongest objection against any project, however so well intended.

But in order to justify my friend, he confessed that this expedient was put into his head by the famous Psalmanazar,[6] a native of the island of Formosa, who came from thence to London, about twenty years ago, and in conversation told my friend, that in his country when any young person happened to be put to death, the excutioner sold the carcass to persons of quality, as a prime dainty, and that, in his time, the body of a plump girl of fifteen, who was crucified for an attempt to poison the emperor, was sold to his Imperial Majesty's Prime Minister of State, and other great Mandarins of the Court, in joints from the gibbet, at four hundred crowns. Neither indeed can I deny, that if the same use were made of several plump young girls in this town, who, without one single groat to their fortunes, cannot stir abroad without a chair, and appear at the playhouse, and assemblies in foreign fineries, which they never will pay for, the kingdom would not be the worse.

Some persons of a desponding spirit are in great concern about that vast number of poor people, who are aged, diseased, or maimed, and I have been desired to employ my thoughts what course may be taken, to ease the nation of so grievous an encumbrance. But I am not in the least pain upon that matter, because it is very well known, that they are every day dying, and rotting, by cold, and famine, and filth, and vermin, as fast as can be reasonably expected. And as to the younger labourers they are now in almost as hopeful a condition. They cannot get work, and consequently pine away for want of nourishment, to a degree, that if at any time they are accidentally hired to common labour, they have not strength to perform it; and thus the country and themselves are in a fair way of being soon delivered from the evils to come.

I have too long digressed, and therefore shall return to my subject. I think the advantages by the proposal which I have made are obvious and many, as well as of the highest importance.

For first, as I have already observed, it would greatly lessen the number of Papists, with whom we are yearly over-run, being the principal breeders of the nation, as well as our most dangerous enemies, and who stay at home on purpose with a design to deliver the kingdom to the Pretender, hoping to take their advantage by the absence of so many good Protestants, who have chosen rather to leave their country, than

---

[6]*Psalmanazar:* an impostor who had passed himself off as a native of exotic Formosa and published a book about the island.

stay at home, and pay tithes against their conscience, to an Episcopal curate.

Secondly, The poorer tenants will have something valuable of their own, which by law may be made liable to distress, and help to pay their landlords rent, their corn and cattle being already seized, and *money a thing unknown.*

Thirdly, Whereas the maintenance of an hundred thousand children, from two years old, and upwards, cannot be computed at less than ten shillings a piece *per annum,* the nation's stock will be thereby increased fifty thousand pounds *per annum,* besides the profit of a new dish, introduced to the tables of all gentlemen of fortune in the kingdom, who have any refinement in taste, and the money will circulate among ourselves, the goods being entirely of our own growth and manufacture.

Fourthly, The constant breeders, besides the gain of eight shillings sterling *per annum,* by the sale of their children, will be rid of the charge of maintaining them after the first year.

Fifthly, This food would likewise bring great custom to taverns, where the vintners will certainly be so prudent as to procure the best receipts for dressing it to perfection, and consequently have their houses frequented by all the fine gentlemen, who justly value themselves upon their knowledge in good eating; and a skilful cook, who understands how to oblige his guests will contrive to make it as expensive as they please.

Sixthly, This would be a great inducement to marriage, which all wise nations have either encouraged by rewards, or enforced by laws and penalties. It would increase the care and tenderness of mothers toward their children, when they were sure of a settlement for life, to the poor babes, provided in some sort by the public to their annual profit instead of expense. We should see an honest emulation among the married women, which of them could bring the fattest child to the market; men would become as fond of their wives, during the time of their pregnancy, as they are now of their mares in foal, their cows in calf, or sows when they are ready to farrow, nor offer to beat or kick them (as it is too frequent a practice) for fear of a miscarriage.

Many other advantages might be enumerated: For instance, the addition of some thousand carcasses in our exportation of barrelled beef; the propagation of swine's flesh, and improvement in the art of making good bacon, so much wanted among us by the great destruction of pigs, too frequent at our tables, which are no way comparable in taste, or magnificence to a well-grown fat yearling child, which roasted whole will make a considerable figure at a Lord Mayor's feast, or any other public entertainment. But this, and many others I omit, being studious[7] of brevity.

---

[7]*Studious:* desirous.

Supposing that one thousand families in this city, would be constant customers for infants' flesh, besides others who might have it at merry-meetings, particularly weddings and christenings, I compute that Dublin would take off annually about twenty thousand carcasses, and the rest of the kingdom (where probably they will be sold somewhat cheaper) the remaining eighty thousand.

I can think of no one objection, that will possibly be raised against this proposal, unless it should be urged that the number of people will be thereby much lessened in the kingdom. This I freely own, and was indeed one principal design in offering it to the world. I desire the reader will observe, that I calculate my remedy *for this one individual Kingdom of Ireland, and for no other that ever was, is, or, I think, ever can be upon earth.* Therefore let no man talk to me of other expedients: *Of taxing our absentees at five shillings a pound: Of using neither clothes, nor household furniture, except what is of our own growth and manufacutre: Of utterly rejecting the materials and instruments that promote foreign luxury: Of curing the expensiveness of pride, vanity, idleness, and gaming in our women: Of introducing a vein of parsimony, prudence and temperance: Of learning to love our Country, wherein we differ even from Laplanders, and the inhabitants of Topinamboo.*[8] *Of quitting our animosities and factions, nor act any longer like the Jews, who were murdering one another at the very moment their city was taken: Of being a little cautious not to sell our country and consciences for nothing: Of teaching landlords to have at least one degree of mercy toward their tenants. Lastly, of putting a spirit of honesty, industry, and skill into our shopkeepers, who, if a resolution could now be taken to buy our native goods, would immediately unite to cheat and exact upon us in the price, the measure, and the goodness, nor could ever yet be brought to make one fair proposal of just dealing, though often and earnestly invited to it.*

Therefore I repeat, let no man talk to me of these and the like expedients, till he hath at least some glimpse of hope that there will ever be some hearty and sincere attempt to put them in practice.

But as to myself, having been wearied out for many years with offering vain, idle, visionary thoughts, and at length utterly despairing of success, I fortunately fell upon this proposal, which as it is wholly new, so it hath something solid and real, of no expense and little trouble, full in our own power, and whereby we can incur no danger in disobliging ENGLAND. For this kind of commodity will not bear exportation, the flesh being of too tender a consistence, to admit a long continuance in salt, *although perhaps I could name a country, which would be glad to eat up our whole nation without it.*

After all I am not so violently bent upon my own opinion, as to

---

[8]*Topinamboo:* a supposedly savage district of Brazil.

reject any offer, proposed by wise men, which shall be found equally innocent, cheap, easy and effectual. But before something of that kind shall be advanced in contradiction to my scheme, and offering a better, I desire the author, or authors will be pleased maturely to consider two points. First, as things now stand, how they will be able to find food and raiment for an hundred thousand useless mouths and backs. And secondly, there being a round million of creatures in human figure, throughout this kingdom, whose whole subsistence put into a common stock would leave them in debt two millions of pounds sterling; adding those who are beggars by profession to the bulk of farmers, cottagers, and labourers with their wives and children, who are beggars in effect; I desire those politicians who dislike my overture, and may perhaps be so bold to attempt an answer, that they will first ask the parents of these mortals, whether they would not at this day think it a great happiness to have been sold for food at a year old, in the manner I prescribe, and thereby have avoided such a perpetual scene of misfortunes, as they have since gone through, by the oppression of landlords, the impossibility of paying rent without money or trade, the want of common sustenance, with neither house nor clothes to cover them from the inclemencies of the weather, and the most inevitable prospect of entailing the like, or greater miseries upon their breed for ever.

I profess in the sincerity of my heart that I have not the least personal interest in endeavouring to promote this necessary work, having no other motive than the *public good of my country, by advancing our trade, providing for infants, relieving the poor, and giving some pleasure to the rich*. I have no children, by which I can propose to get a single penny; the youngest being nine years old, and my wife past childbearing.

Activity Exercise

1. Why does the narrator constantly refer to other "experts" in offering his proposal—merchants, lawyers, an American, a "lover of his country"? What do these "authorities" lend to the essay?

2. How would you go about writing an ironic response to this proposal, say, in the form of a letter to a Dublin newspaper in 1729? Discuss the possibilities with the class and mention specific techniques you would use as well as what you would say.

3. Are you concerned about some issue on your campus or some injustice in your city? Are the parking regulations, for example, unfair to students on your campus? Try some Swiftian irony on the people who enforce the unjust practice. Write a letter to the editor of your local or campus paper in which you modestly propose some absurd solution to the injustice. Aside from the obvious absurdity of your solution, be as

moderate and rational as you can. Exaggerate your solution, but use understated language. Find as many pseudo-statistics and facts as you can to support your absurd proposal.

4. Take one of Swift's paragraphs and write a "straight" paragraph to correspond with it. In other words, define what Swift is *really* criticizing. Begin with a general sentence that defines the paragraph's satiric purpose and move on to show, by referring to specifics in the paragraph, how the purpose is developed.

Irony and the "put-on"

There is a distinct difference between what people call the "put-on" and irony. In irony, the speaker or writer *always* has a clear underlying purpose or truth in mind. Swift, for example, has his persona suggest that the rich eat the babies of the poor. But the reader who understands the irony knows that Swift's real purpose, his ironic purpose, is to ridicule the cruelty of the British as they exploit the Irish and keep them in severe poverty.

But in the put-on, the real, or underlying, purpose of the speaker or writer is never clear. The whole purpose of the communication is to make the listener or reader uncomfortable and awkward, to "put him on." Almost everyone has seen the put-on in action. Have you ever been to a party in which two "with-it" people converse in a way that a third person can't follow? The two talk in half-sentences and special words so that the third person is confused and disoriented and finally made a fool of. Usually there is awkward, knowing laughter from the people who watch. They feel at least a little sorry for the victim. Yet they also feel a grudging admiration for the two who work the put-on.

Bob Dylan was a master of the put-on. Once, while being interviewed by a very straight reporter from *Time* magazine, Dylan made up an absurd and totally false story about his background, saying he had grown up on the streets of Philadelphia under severe hardship, had been raised by an old, sickly grandmother, and had fought his way through the jungle of the city. Actually, Dylan was raised in Hibbing, Minnesota, a relatively small midwestern town far from the city environment of the East coast, by parents who were middle-class rather than poor. The *Time* reporter was completely confused. He knew something of Dylan's true background yet didn't really want to discredit Dylan's story. Dylan, probably sick of numerous interviews, decided to put-on this interviewer, to give a fictional account of his background in an otherwise straight situation.

The put-on can be fun, as long as the victim goes along with the

**Next to you I like
Green Stripe
best**

GREEN
STRIPE

USHER'S
GREEN STRIPE

USHER'S GREEN STRIPE
Since 1853, the original light Scotch

Figure 11-4

Usher's Scotch ad

game and isn't mistreated in the process. Although it aims at no deep
truth or serious message, it is especially effective at relieving the tension
in very serious situations. And when tried in good spirit, the put-on can
help us to understand how language works indirectly.

Ads often contain half put-on and half serious message. Usually an
ad can be taken both ways—as serious message *and* as exaggerated
put-on. The Usher's Green Stripe ad is exaggerated spoof—"Next to you I
like Green Stripe best"—as well as a real attempt to sell Scotch. Perhaps
the Green Stripe will sell *because* the ad-writers were clever enough to
spoof, to put-on their readers. What other details tell you this ad is a
put-on? Can you find other ads that work the same way?

Activity Exercise

Work up some put-on skits in class. Have two people work up a give-and-take conversation and a third person play the bystander who tries to catch on but can't. In a sense, the verbal put-on is something like the child's game "Keep Away," in which two children grab a third child's hat or gloves and throw them back and forth while the third child scrambles to retrieve them. In the put-on, two people fire words back and forth while a third person scrambles to retrieve the meaning.

12

Shaping an overall design: Clarifying your purpose

Plans and designs for longer pieces of writing must grow naturally from the writer's situation. They are the results of continual give-and-take between you, your subject, and your readers. They begin to take shape when you first look for something to say; they are crystallized and developed from momentary perceptions and insights which you catch, form and, shape into larger and larger patterns as you write. Effective essays grow from experience; they are not planned from outlines.

Later in the process of writing, however, you do need to impose order and to find a unifying design for the ideas and experiences in your essay. Order is essential especially when you write exposition—essays to inform your readers, to give them a working knowledge of a subject and some practical clarification of that subject in the form of examples and evidence. Usually, such clarification of design must be worked into the *process* of revision: you capture ordering strategies after you've immersed yourself in your subject, tried sentences and paragraphs written from experience, found a main idea and supporting evidence, and experimented with your preliminary efforts by reading aloud to interested, critical readers and listening to their criticisms. If you have engaged honestly in the activities of this book, you should now be ready to benefit from the imitation of some commonly used, overall organizing strategies.

In the pages that follow, you'll find four basic designs or organizing strategies. They can be used to present numerous expository theses and to develop numerous opinions and general ideas. You should discover how these designs can be applied to your material *as* you revise. In fact, you'll often already have produced the beginnings of a particular design in your rough drafts. Each model plan should help you to see more clearly the *order* of your ideas and the clearest means of *structuring* those ideas for your readers. Each organizing strategy answers one of these four questions.

1. *Illustration:* How can you *show* your readers where your thesis idea or opinion came from? What examples and evidence—drawn from personal experience or from readings and outside sources—can you use to develop your thesis?

2. *Definition and Description:* How can you provide your readers with a clear idea of the limits and qualities of your subject?

3. *Comparison:* Can you compare your thesis to another idea, or one of your examples to other examples, in order to clarify your purpose?

4. *Classification:* How can you divide your subject or main idea into parts to explain it? How can you clarify the relationships between those parts for your readers?

In essence, these questions accomplish two purposes: they should help you to define the purpose of an essay; and they should provide the means of achieving that purpose. You may, for example, have begun an essay on the role of women in contemporary America without realizing that you were illustrating with examples and drawing inferences from the roles played by particular women. Your job at this point is to recognize the plan you may have already suggested and to build a clear, unified essay around that plan. Or you may write a general draft of an essay on progressive education and come to realize in rereading it that you had yet to *define* progressive education. Your entire essay might then provide that key definition. The real purpose of your essay often won't emerge until you begin to revise. Go back over a few of the rough drafts you've already written. Ask yourself the above questions as you read them. Use the questions to clarify your purpose *and* to plan a subsequent design to achieve that purpose.

Here are four essays that follow our four essential plans— illustration, definition and description, comparison, and classification. Each essay is preceded by a general discussion of its organiz- ing principles. As you read, you'll also find marginal notations which point to specific sentences and paragraphs to show how the **organizing principle develops.** Finally, each essay is followed by a series of activity exercises which should help you clarify your understanding of the essay's organization and should also suggest ways in which these organizational designs can be applied to your own essays. As you read further, you'll discover that all four organizational patterns overlap. Writers use what they need, what fits their subjects and purposes. Someone whose main purpose is to define may occasionally use comparison. But usually, the well-made essay has one dominating organizational pattern. In this chapter our purpose is to find the dominating or controlling patterns and to understand how they give longer essays clarity and unity.

The illustrative essay

A person stands in front of a class to talk about "middle America." He begins with a socioeconomic *definition,* telling how much the "middle American" usually makes and what his comparative status is in society. Income and status are explained by facts: the middle American makes between $7,500 and $15,000 a year; he sends his children to public schools and state colleges or universities. But, along with the facts, the listeners might want some concrete account of what middle Americans actually do, how they act, what they think. Of course, the speaker doesn't have information on all this. Who really knows what the "silent majority," as the media often refer to the middle class, is thinking? And does a social group ever really think collectively? What, then, can the speaker do to develop his talk?

The most obvious answer is that he can *illustrate* with examples. Illustration clarifies a subject or thesis by providing examples from personal experience, from reading, from authoritative sources such as reference books, articles, experiments, television, and the newspaper. The speech on middle America might include several descriptions of contemporary ranch houses on Long Island, or it might provide a running description of the automobiles owned by the speaker's middle class friends. An illustrative paragraph takes a general idea or thesis and explains it by referring to examples. But the speaker on middle America would have to provide clear definitions of terms, in his case terms supported by some sociological facts, *before* he presented his examples. Otherwise his listeners might feel his examples were not representative.

If you, for example, write an essay that defines the mystery story, you would probably refer to particular stories as you proceed. But your examples would have to follow clearly from your definitions of all mystery stories, and they would need to be clearly related to one another. How does Mike Hammer's toughness compare with Perry Mason's or Ironsides' cool rationality? How does the mystery that holds to the end the revelation of who is guilty compare with the story in which all the mystery is centered on *when* the guilty one will be apprehended? These questions need clear definition linked with detailed illustration.

Remember these three principles when you write illustrative essays:

1. *Before* you begin to illustrate, be sure that your key terms are clearly defined and that you understand where you are going. Select your examples according to your purpose.

2. Be sure that you relate your examples clearly to your thesis or statement of purpose. Don't let the reader wonder why you chose a particular example. Some readers or listeners, for example, wouldn't understand why a description of a particular house would contribute to an understanding of the middle class American? *Show* them why.

3. Be sure that you know how your examples relate to one another. Do they show contrast? Are they all illustrative of one idea? Can they be arranged in order of importance?

In this excerpt from Betty Friedan's *The Feminine Mystique,* we see illustration used in several ways. Ms. Friedan begins with a general statement about the "nameless, aching dissatisfaction" felt by many American housewives. Then she provides three examples of statements made by women in Ohio, Texas, and Connecticut to substantiate her opening statement.

Later, in the main part of her essay, Friedan uses the Table of Contents from a leading women's magazine to illustrate her claim that women are provided a certain "feminine" image by the popular media. Then she winds up by contrasting the material in that women's magazine to the major issues in the world at that time to show how out of touch most women's magazines were with international current events.

Read this brief essay once to find its purpose. Then read it more carefully a second time, consulting the marginal notes to discover how Ms. Friedan mixes definition and illustration to develop her purpose.

The Happy Housewife Heroine

BETTY FRIEDAN

Why have so many American wives suffered this nameless aching dissatisfaction for so many years, each one thinking she

rhetorical question used to set up main purpose

was alone? "I've got tears in my eyes with sheer relief that my own inner turmoil is shared with other women," a young Connecticut mother wrote me when I first began to put this problem into words. A woman from a town in Ohio wrote: "The times when I felt that the only answer was to consult a psychiatrist, times of anger, bitterness and general frustration too numerous to even mention, I had no idea that hundreds of other women were feeling the same way. I felt so completely alone." A Houston, Texas, housewife wrote: "It has been the feeling of being almost alone with my problem that has made it so hard. I thank God for my family, home and chance to care for them, but my life couldn't stop there. It is an awakening to know that I'm not an oddity and can stop being ashamed of wanting something more."

three illustrative examples of housewives' remarks on the problem ("this nameless, aching dissatisfaction")

That painful guilty silence, and that tremendous relief when a feeling is finally out in the open, are familiar psychological signs. What need, what part of themselves, could so many women today be repressing? In this age after Freud, sex is immediately suspect. But this new stirring in women does not seem to be sex; it is, in fact, much harder for women to talk about than sex. Could there be another need, a part of themselves they have buried as deeply as the Victorian women buried sex?

examples of types of women used to answer the questions of whether the image of modern women leaves something out

If there is, a woman might not know what it was, any more than the Victorian woman knew she had sexual needs. The image of a good woman by which Victorian ladies lived simply left out sex. Does the image by which modern American women live also leave something out, the proud and public image of the high-school girl going steady, the college girl in love, the suburban housewife with an up-and-coming husband and a station wagon full of children? This image—created by the women's magazines, by advertisements, television, movies, novels, columns and books by experts on marriage and the family, child psychology, sexual adjustment and by the popularizers of sociology and psychoanalysis—shapes women's lives today and mirrors their dreams. It may give a clue to the problem that has no name, as a dream gives a clue to a wish unnamed by the dreamer. In the mind's ear, a geiger counter clicks when the image shows too sharp a discrepancy from reality. A geiger counter clicked in my own inner ear when I could not fit the quiet desperation of so many women into the picture of the modern American housewife that I myself was helping to create, writing for the women's magazines. What is missing from the image that mirrors and creates the identity of women in America today?

examples drawn from the writer's own experience to illustrate what happens to other women

In the early 1960s *McCall's* has been the fastest growing of the women's magazines. Its contents are a fairly accurate representation of the image of the American woman presented, and in part created, by the large-circulation magazines. Here are the complete editorial contents of a typical issue of *McCall's* (July, 1960):

1. A lead article on "increasing baldness in women," caused by too much brushing and dyeing.

2. A long poem in primer-size type about a child, called "A Boy Is A Boy."

3. A short story about how a teenager who doesn't go to college gets a man away from a bright college girl.

4. A short story about the minute sensations of a baby throwing his bottle out of the crib.

5. The first of a two-part intimate "up-to-date" account of the Duke of Windsor on "How the Duchess and I now live and spend our time. The influence of clothes on me and vice versa."

6. A short story about a nineteen-year-old girl sent to a charm school to learn how to bat her eyelashes and lose at tennis. ("You're nineteen, and by normal American standards, I now am entitled to have you taken off my hands, legally and financially, by some beardless youth who will spirit you away to a one-and-a-half-room apartment in the Village while he learns the chicanery of selling bonds. And no beardless youth is going to do that as long as you volley to his backhand.")

7. The story of a honeymoon couple commuting between separate bedrooms after an argument over gambling at Las Vegas.

8. An article on "how to overcome an inferiority complex."

9. A story called "Wedding Day."

10. The story of a teenager's mother who learns how to dance rock-and-roll.

11. Six pages of glamorous pictures of models in maternity clothes.

12. Four glamorous pages on "reduce the way the models do."

13. An article on airline delays.

14. Patterns for home sewing.

15. Patterns with which to make "Folding Screens—Bewitching Magic."

16. An article called "An Encyclopedic Approach to Finding a Second Husband."

17. A "barbecue bonanza," dedicated "to the Great American Mister who stands, chef's cap on head, fork in hand, on terrace or back porch, in patio or backyard anywhere in the land, watching his roast turning on the spit. And to his wife, without whom (sometimes) the barbecue could never be the smashing summer success it undoubtedly is . . . ."

table of contents from *McCall's* used to illustrate what leading women's magazines often provide for women

Friedan defines the image
of the woman that evolves
from magazines like
McCall's

There were also the regular front-of-the book "service" columns on new drug and medicine developments, childcare facts, columns by Clare Luce and by Eleanor Roosevelt, and "Pots and Pans," a column of readers' letters.

The image of woman that emerges from this big, pretty magazine is young and frivolous, almost childlike; fluffy and feminine; passive; gaily content in a world of bedroom and kitchen, sex, babies, and home. The magazine surely does not leave out sex; the only passion, the only pursuit, the only goal a woman is permitted is the pursuit of a man. It is crammed full of food, clothing, cosmetics, furniture, and the physical bodies of young women, but where is the world of thought and ideas, the life of the mind and spirit? In the magazine image, women do not work except housework and work to keep their bodies beautiful and to get and keep a man.

Friedan compares what
the woman was reading to
what was happening
world-wide to support her
thesis that women are
secluded, protected, and
treated as children.

This was the image of the American woman in the year Castro led a revolution in Cuba and men were trained to travel into outer space; the year that the African continent brought forth new nations, and a plane whose speed is greater than the speed of sound broke up a Summit Conference; the year artists picketed a great museum in protest against the hegemony of abstract art; physicists explored the concept of anti-matter; astronomers, because of new radio telescopes, had to alter their concepts of the expanding universe; biologists made a breakthrough in the fundamental chemistry of life; and Negro youth in Southern schools forced the United States, for the first time since the Civil War, to face a moment of democratic truth. But this magazine, published for over 5,000,000 American women, almost all of whom have been through high school and nearly half to college, contained almost no mention of the world beyond the home. In the second half of the twentieth century in America, woman's world was confined to her own body and beauty, the charming of man, the bearing of babies, and the physical care and serving of husband, children, and home. And this was no anomaly of a single issue of a single women's magazine.

Activity Exercise

1. Define Friedan's purpose in a single sentence. Then go through the essay and find three or four sentences or brief passages to illustrate how she develops that thesis. Be sure to connect your examples to one another and to Friedan's purpose.

2. Take a commonly held opinion and work on developing your attitude toward it. Think of examples from your experience or something

you've read or looked at to support your thesis on that opinion. Consider opinions such as these:

    a. Professional football has replaced baseball as the number one spectator sport.

    b. Conservatives usually vote for the Republican candidates.

    c. Most college women *do* want to get married.

    d. Television programs offer very little intellectual stimulation.

    e. People that are blind tend to have lively inner lives.

You don't have to agree with these statements. Just illustrate your reactions to one of them by citing examples.

3. Take Friedan's statement that "The image of woman that emerges from this big, pretty magazine is young and frivolous, almost childlike; fluffy and feminine; passive; gaily content in a world of bedroom and kitchen, sex, babies, and home." Do you know women that fit parts or all of this description? Could you select a few and describe them in ways that would illustrate Friedan's remark? Or could you give illustrative examples of women who don't fit her categories? Again, be sure to develop your own thesis and to show the reader how your examples either support or oppose Friedan's.

4. Look through various popular magazines, some for women and some for men. Then develop a thesis that explains the important differences between the two. Write an essay that illustrates that thesis by referring to examples from the magazines. You might want to contrast two ads, one from a "male" magazine (*Esquire, Playboy, Sports Illustrated,* or *Penthouse*), another from a women's magazine (*Cosmopolitan, McCall's, Ladies Home Journal,* or *Redbook*). Or you might work your essay around a comparison of the Tables of Contents in men's and women's magazines, as Friedan in her article uses the Table of Contents of *McCall's.*

The defining and describing essay

Almost every expository essay includes some definition. To define is to *set limits*—the limits of your key words and ideas as well as the limits of key parts of your entire subject. As you write, you define your ideas and material by the words you choose and by the types and kinds of modifiers you add to your sentences. (See the discussion of sentence modification in Chapters 5–8 and in the grammatical appendix if you wish to review sentence and paragraph definition.) In this chapter, we shall deal with definition and description as ways of organizing entire essays.

In general, brief essays include a main idea or thesis, a series of supporting general ideas which are related to the thesis, and specific analysis or examples to support and clarify the general ideas. The process

of definition can help you develop your materials at all three levels—
thesis, supporting ideas, and specifics. The process of definition can be
divided into three related categories.

1. *Lexical* defining: the kind of definition you find in a dictionary,
which usually includes the word itself, a copula like *is* or *means,* and
other words that define a part of the concept represented in the word
being defined. Usually lexical definitions include a *generic* term to place
the word being defined into a general class (a *rocker* belongs to the class
category *chairs)* and a *qualifying* term to add detail to what we know of
the word in its class. The added detail usually places the defined word
within the general class.

> A *rocker* is a *chair* (generic term) that is placed on runners or springs
> in order to allow the sitter to sway back and forth as he or she sits.

Of course this definition could be expanded into an entire essay. Here is
an expanded paragraph.

> A rocker is a chair that is placed on runners or springs in order to
> allow the sitter to sway back and forth as he or she sits. There are
> several kinds of rockers, some going back many years to colonial
> times. Two of the most popular antique rockers are the Boston and
> Salem types, both high-backed favorites of the founding fathers.

That paragraph provided an effective opening for an essay on Boston
and Salem rockers. Notice how the limits of the subject are progressively
defined—the paragraph moves from general subject (rockers) to qualifying detail (the purpose of rockers) to the more specific fact that there are
several kinds of rockers and, finally, to the specific subjects of a potential
essay, the Boston and Salem rockers. This student used the processes of
lexical definition to introduce and define an entire subject. There are, of
course, dangers to such an approach. Don't start with lexical definitions
just to pad or add filler. Most readers would already know the purpose of
a rocker. The writer of this introductory paragraph would need to refer to
his opening lexical definition later in the essay. Otherwise, he'd be better
off beginning with his specific definitions of the Boston and Salem
rockers.

There are other dangers to lexical defining. Often a dictionary
definition doesn't provide *exact* information. Consider this definition.

> *expressway*—a highspeed divided highway for through traffic with
> access partially or fully controlled and grade separations at impor-

tant intersections with other roads. *(Webster's Third New International Dictionary)*

The reader might ask the writer to define "highspeed" more succinctly, to clarify the meaning of "through traffic" and "access," and to explain more clearly "partially or fully controlled," "grade separations," "important intersections." The answers to all these questions might provide a basis for a brief essay that uses general definitions, works back to more specific definitions of key terms, and adds examples and descriptions.

2. *Descriptive* defining: most lexical or general definitions tell what something *is* or *is not.* Once the general limits of a subject or idea are set, you may wish to describe the idea or subject in more detail. You may want to enumerate physical qualities such as size, shape, color, degree, and the like. A writer working from a general, lexical definition of a freeway might want to describe two or three intersections in detail, with charts and illustrations, to clarify "grade separations at important intersections." Read the following definition of *horse*. Notice how it works from a general definition of class and purpose into a detailed physical description.

A large solid-hoofed herbivorous mammal domesticated by man since a prehistoric period and used as a beast of burden, a draft animal, or for riding, and distinguished from the other existing members of the genus *Equus* and family *Equidae* by the long hair of the mane and tail, the usual presence of a callosity on the inside of the hind leg below the hock and other less constant characters (as the larger size, larger hooves, more arched neck, small head, short ears). *(Webster's Third New International Dictionary)*

3. *Stipulative* defining: you can stipulate a definition by devising a personal meaning clearly connected to the context within which you use a concept or word. Betty Friedan, in her essay on women included in the previous section, coins a phrase—"the problem that has no name"—to capture the general dissatisfaction and unhappiness of many women in American culture. You may wish to take one of the several possible lexical definitions of a word and use it in your essay. Stipulative defining can be especially useful when you want to make a very abstract word—say *freedom*—the subject of an essay. You can then stipulate just what the word means to you by focusing on one of its numerous possible lexical definitions or by coining a definition of your own. Decide which of the following sentences is a stipulative definition:

a. freedom means controlling your actions within a relatively limited sphere of possible action;

b. you have experienced freedom only when you've been in chains and been released;

c. a free spirit makes a man free even when his body is imprisoned.

Principles of definition

1. Organize an entire essay around definition only when the subject requires defining. Don't define the obvious, unless you intend to provide new insights or information.

2. Make a practice of applying the processes of lexical definition to your subject as you define your subject or thesis. If you are writing an essay on automobiles, consider giving a general definition of characteristics and purpose as a means of setting up and developing your personal thesis. You might mention that automobiles have always provided transportation *and* pleasure and have always had four wheels. Then you might use these given facts to set up a projection into the future. What might be done to alter our attitudes toward automobiles? How? In any case, setting the limits of your subject by telling what it *is* and *is not* can help control the overall design of your essay.

3. Consider, as you revise your essays, whether your subject will benefit from definition by description. If your main purpose is to define expressways in your city or town, you might consider how you can work in a specific description of a particular intersection or stretch of highway to illustrate your general definition.

4. Consider working in imaginative stipulative definitions. Perhaps you've seen ads that make similar appeals for different products: a cigarette ad that appeals to the "independent man," a beer slogan for the "American sportsman," or an automobile ad which tells you that only the brave and independent would buy a convertible. Can you develop your own definition of these related ads, working from a stipulative name for the category back into specific details and description? Be sure to show the reader *how* the illustrative examples support the categorical definition.

5. As you revise an essay, ask yourself whether your key terms are clearly defined. Begin by considering the key words in your thesis. Even if your thesis is implied, write it out on a separate piece of paper and check the clarity of each important word in it. Apply the same process to your supporting general ideas. And be sure that your descriptions and examples or contrasts are clearly related to your general ideas.

Notice how Alice Rossi, in the following essay, uses the processes of definition to organize "Visions of the Future." The entire essay tells what the woman of the future *will* and *will not* be. And Ms. Rossi further unifies her definition by using a contrasting structure. What the girl of the future *will be* is consistently contrasted to what she *is* now.

> She *will be* reared, as her brother will be reared, with a combination of loving warmth, firm discipline, household responsibility and encouragement of independence and self-reliance. She will not be pampered and indulged, subtly taught to achieve her ends through coquetry and tears, *as so many girls are taught today.*

Also notice how Ms. Rossi provides working definitions of subordinate ideas—"Marriage for our hypothetical woman will not mark a withdrawal from the life and work pattern that she has established . . ."

Visions For the Future

ALICE S. ROSSI

She will be reared, as her brother will be reared, with a combination of loving warmth, firm discipline, household responsibility and encouragement of independence and self-reliance. She will not be pampered and indulged, subtly taught to achieve her ends through coquetry and tears, as so many girls are taught today. She will view domestic skills as useful tools to acquire, some of which, like fine cooking or needlework, having their own intrinsic pleasures but most of which are necessary repetitive work best gotten done as quickly and efficiently as possible. She will be able to handle minor mechanical breakdowns in the home as well as her brother can, and he will be able to tend a child, press, sew, and cook with the same easy skills and comfortable feeling his sister has.

During their school years, both sister and brother will increasingly assume responsibility for their own decisions, freely experiment with numerous possible fields of study, gradually narrowing to a choice that best suits their interests and abilities rather than what is considered appropriate or prestigeful work for men and women. They will be encouraged by parents and teachers alike to think ahead to a whole life span, viewing marriage and parenthood as one strand among many which will constitute their lives. The girl will not feel the pressure to belittle her accomplishments, lower her aspirations, learn to be a receptive listener in her relations with boys, but will be as true to her growing sense of self as her brother and male friends are. She will not marry before her adolescence and schooling are completed, but will be willing and able to view the college years as a "moratorium" from deeply intense cross-sex

From "Equality Between the Sexes: An Immodest Proposal." Reprinted by permission of *Daedalus*, Journal of the American Academy of Arts and Sciences, Boston, Mass. Spring 1964, *The Woman in America*.

commitments, a period of life during which her identity can be "at large and open and various." Her intellectual aggressiveness as well as her brother's tender sentiments will be welcomed and accepted as *human* characteristics, without the self-questioning doubt of latent homosexuality that troubles many college-age men and women in our era when these qualities are sex-linked. She will not cling to her parents, nor they to her, but will establish an increasingly larger sphere of her own independent world in which she moves and works, loves and thinks, as a maturing young person. She will learn to take pleasure in her own body and a man's body and to view sex as a good and wonderful experience, but not as an exclusive basis for an ultimate commitment to another person, and not as a test of her competence as a female or her partner's competence as a male. Because she will have a many-faceted conception of her self and its worth, she will be free to merge and lose herself in the sex act with a lover or a husband.

Marriage for our hypothetical woman will not mark a withdrawal from the life and work pattern that she has established, just as there will be no sharp discontinuity between her early childhood and youthful adult years. Marriage will be an enlargement of her life experiences, the addition of a new dimension to an already established pattern, rather than an abrupt withdrawal to the home and a turning in upon the marital relationship. Marriage will be a "looking outward in the same direction" for both the woman and her husband. She will marry and bear children only if she deeply desires a mate and children, and will not be judged a failure as a person if she decides against either. She will have few children if she does have them, and will view her pregnancies, childbirth and early months of motherhood as one among many equally important highlights in her life, experienced intensely and with joy but not as the exclusive basis for a sense of self-fulfillment and purpose in life. With planning and foresight, her early years of child bearing and rearing can fit a long-range view of all sides of herself. If her children are not to suffer from "paternal deprivation," her husband will also anticipate that the assumption of parenthood will involve a weeding out of nonessential activities either in work, civic or social participation. Both the woman and the man will feel that unless a man can make room in his life for parenthood, he should not become a father. The woman will make sure, even if she remains at home during her child's infancy, that he has ample experience of being with and cared for by other adults besides herself, so that her return to a full-time position in her field will not constitute a drastic change in the life of the child, but a gradual pattern of increasing supplementation by others of the mother. The children will have a less intense involvement with their mother, and she with them, and they will all be the better for it. When they are grown and establish adult lives of their own, our woman will face no retirement twenty years before her husband, for her own independent activities will continue and expand. She will be neither an embittered wife, an interfering mother-in-law nor an idle parasite, but together with her husband she will be able to live an independent, purposeful and satisfying third act in life.

Activity Exercise

1. Go through "Visions for the Future" and pull together all the defining statements into one general statement about the woman of the future. You might think of yourself providing an organizing thesis for all the remarks in the essay.

2. Take one of Rossi's sentences and make it the topic sentence of a paragraph of your own. Then develop the paragraph by providing an extended description of how the woman of the future described in the topic sentence would act in a typical situation. For example, you might take the sentence "She will not cling to her parents, nor they to her, but will establish an increasingly larger sphere of her own independent world in which she moves and works, loves and thinks, as a maturing young person." Then, in the rest of the paragraph and perhaps a few added paragraphs, you can write a description of how the young woman would actually demonstrate her independence in her relations with her parents. You might describe a scene in which the young woman of the future reaches a personal decision with her parent's help. Or you might summarize specific decisions the young girl would have to make for herself that might in the present be made for her. Be specific and relate the description clearly to the topic sentence.

3. Compare the image of the woman that is presented in Betty Friedan's essay, to the image of the future woman that Alice Rossi presents. Describe examples of both images and develop some account of where you think most women are now. Are they between the extremes of the women's magazine image and Ms. Rossi's woman of the future? Give examples and illustrations.

4. Take another idea, object, or type of person and project it into the future. Define how it will be different and how it will be similar to what it is now. Work from general, lexical statements back to specific descriptions, examples and illustrations. You might use subjects such as automobiles of the future, *lawnmowers* of the future, *fashion models* of the future, *college professors* of the future, or *classrooms of the future.* Follow Alice Rossi's example in developing your essay.

5. Find a collective noun (a noun that names a group of people or objects related under one heading or class) and write an essay in which you define the noun in the three ways outlined in this chapter. Begin with a *lexical* definition that includes a listing of general purposes and some elaboration of common details. Then move on to more detailed *descriptions* of common examples of the noun. Choose an example that you have seen many times and describe it closely. Then close with a personal (stipulated) definition of the noun, one that draws from your own experience and wouldn't fit in the first two sections of your essay. *Expressway,* the example of a collective noun used in this section, is an example of the kind of word for which you should look.

The essay of comparison and contrast

Comparison brings together two objects, ideas or subjects in order to reveal a thesis or main idea. Like all the other organizing patterns which are included in this chapter, comparison can be used to design an entire essay. Essentially, there are three general ways to develop an extended comparison.

1. Compare a *known* to an *unknown* in order to clarify the unknown in your reader's mind. For a reader who has never seen an ocelot you might develop comparisons between the ocelot and a common housecat—comparisons of size, headshape, paws, coat, markings, and diet—pointing out similarities as well as differences.

2. Compare two objects or concepts that are similar in one important way but different in most other ways. Actually, this process applies the technique of *analogy* to an entire essay, for analogies show an important and striking similarity between otherwise very different objects.

John Williams moves with the grace of a well-bred racehorse.

You could take this analogy and organize an entire descriptive essay around it, describing John Williams' actions by comparing them with those of a racehorse.

3. Compare two objects or ideas that are usually considered to be completely similar and point out a few previously unrecognized differences. Or take two objects or ideas usually considered similar and point out some important dissimilarities. Often you can use comparison in order to point out the differences between items in the same general class, as Ira Shor does in the following paragraph on the differences between two-year college students and elite, four-year college students. The similarities are easy to recognize—both types of students are of similar ages, both contain similar distributions of men and women, both attend college to learn, both receive instruction in classroom situations and under curriculum which are similar. Shor suggests, however, that these similarities are not as important as the following differences.

> On elite campuses in the years of the Vietnam escalation, college proved itself to be an important arena for unfreezing consciousness and history. The situation at a community college is more difficult, for obvious reasons—the students are here for only two years, they still live in the patriarchal family, and commute lengthy distances, their attention and energy are drained by long hours on

(Reprinted from "Anne Sexton's 'For My Lover . . .': Feminism in the Classroom," by Ira Shor, which appeared in *College English*, XXXIV, viii (May 1973), 1082-1093.)

part-time jobs. Further, a purely intellectual or theoretical attack on politics and sexuality is hampered by our students' suspicion of education and intellectualism. Twelve years of pre-college school has managed to instill deep dislike for mental work. Our students read little, and disregard High Culture. TV, movies, pop magazines, radio, rock music, and concerts have dominated the culture presented to them. Their major energy focuses on visceral things (sex, dancing, fast cars, sports) or on the great American pastime, consumerism. To provoke their radical intelligence means to combat the ideology trying to neutralize their minds. To expose the consequences of their ideology, or even to make it apparent that systematic ideology exists in their minds, takes some ingenuity in an English course, as well as the conviction that the form no less than the content of a course is in question. The very atmosphere of a classroom is an irresistible invitation more often than not for students to put their energies asleep. In school, they train for the discipline and boredom of their future jobs, and begin dreaming of the only tangible liberation—money and a Florida vacation.

Shor wants his readers to understand the very different atmospheres in, say, an elite Ivy League college classroom and a community college classroom. He begins his paragraph by telling us that, during the escalation of the Vietnam War, the elite college often became a place to question rather than blandly receive information. The consciousnesses of many students were "unfrozen," were liberated to see the reasoning behind what was happening around them. Not so, Shor suggests, in community colleges where students tend to accept the *status quo*, to resign themselves to society the way it is and to receive rather than question information. Then Shor proceeds to list reasons behind the differences in community college students as well as to pinpoint the results of those differences in the classroom.

In Shor's paragraph, the differences between the subjects are highlighted because they suit his purposes more than the similarities. Another writer, arguing against Shor's suggestion that community college students must be taught differently than elite university students, might emphasize the similarities between both types of students. When you choose to develop an essay through comparison, be sure to consider these three aspects of any comparison.

1. Similarity *and* Difference—Have you considered *both* similarities and differences as you planned your essay? Have you ignored an important difference between the two sides of an analogy? For example, there may be many important and interesting similarities between the Watergate scandal of 1972-73 and the Teapot Dome scandal of the early 1920's. But there are important differences as well. You must consider both to write a competent comparative essay.

2. What You Choose to Compare—You may often want to compare two ideas or objects according to their effects. Often you can accomplish such a comparison by analyzing those effects according to their greater or lesser impact on people. Has Watergate involved more people than the Teapot Dome Scandal? If so, does that make it a more important scandal? Are state colleges and universities more important to American education because they serve more students? Is a volunteer army better because fewer people complain about the random selection of recruits? Whenever you compare according to more or less, be sure that you also refer to other means of comparison. Numbers are not the only means of considering comparative degree. Some people might argue, for example, that small private colleges provide a better education than larger, public universities *precisely because* they educate fewer people and do a better job with those people. Consider quality as well as quantity. Also, be sure that you integrate a consideration of numbers with considerations of other criteria—with overall consequences and ends and means.

3. Evaluation of the Terms or Subjects Being Compared—Have you carefully evaluated the similarities and differences you have chosen to emphasize in your comparison? Are they the important similarities or differences? Does your analogy break down because your reader can easily think of a difference that will cancel out the similarity you point out? Are all guilty prisoners like rats in a cage? Perhaps not, for men possess reason while rats act mostly on instinct and stimulus-response reactions. Are all base-stealers in baseball like tightrope walkers in circuses? Perhaps not, since many ballplayers are not graceful and speedy; the slugger hits homeruns, but he often makes an awkward base-runner.

Developing the comparative essay

There are two general ways of comparing through an entire essay: by block and alternating structures.

Block comparison occurs when you set up your comparison in an opening paragraph, develop one side of your comparison in the first half of your essay and the second side of your comparison in the second half of your essay. Block comparisons are easier for the writer than they are for the reader. You can deal with one side in one place, the other side in another place, and conclude with a summary statement of the similarities and differences between the objects or ideas compared. Because you can concentrate on one idea or object at a time, you won't have to make rapid transitions and difficult cross-references.

For readers, however, the block method is often less efficient. You read about one side of the comparison separate from the other. As a reader, *you* have to make the specific comparisons between the two subjects. You must remember what the writer said about A when, later on, you read about B. Often, you'll find it difficult to keep both A and B in mind at once.

Alternating structure takes up the characteristics of both subjects at once and takes the reader through a point by point analysis. A comparative essay on *Vantage Point* and *Easy Rider* might consider the two movies in alternating pattern by analyzing both according to similarities in theme, then by considering point of view in both films and, finally, by contrasting the heroes in both films.

Because the alternating pattern of comparison is usually more difficult to organize, you'll usually need to divide your comparison into clearly defined parts. An essay comparing two contemporary novels might be subdivided into point of view, theme, plot, and character. Then you could discuss both novels simultaneously according to the particular purpose of the subdivision. Such subdivisions will help you unify as you write as well as provide your readers with yet another way of following your design through to an understanding of your purpose.

When should you use the block or alternating structures? Generally, less complex subjects can easily and clearly be dealt with in block structures. If you are, for example, comparing radial and bias ply automobile tires, you can simply introduce the subject of your comparison in the opening paragraph and consider the radial tire in the first three or four paragraphs of the body of your essay and the bias ply tire in the final three or four paragraphs. With a conclusion that clearly summarizes the characteristics of both tires, your reader should have no trouble combining both sides of your analysis.

If, however, you are dealing with a more complex subject, especially with complex ideas rather than concrete objects, you may have to use alternating structure to make your points and overall purpose clear to the reader. A point-by-point comparison of the Supreme Court under Presidents Franklin D. Roosevelt and Richard Nixon is complex enough to warrant alternating treatment, with perhaps one sentence dealing with Roosevelt's Supreme Court, the next with Nixon's, or at least with alternating paragraphs on each.

When you design an alternating structure for a comparative essay, remember these important points:

1. Begin to plan by dividing your essay into parts. The proposed essay on Supreme Courts under Roosevelt and Nixon might first consider how the members of the respective courts were selected. Then it might consider both courts' attitudes toward a common type of case—say, toward civil right's cases or toward constitutional questions such as whether the death penalty is justified. And, finally, such an essay might evaluate the respective courts' relations with the Presidency. With the

subject of comparison divided into three parts, the writer ought to be able to analyze both courts simultaneously without losing focus or unity.

2. Decide before you begin writing whether you plan to alternate within paragraphs or from paragraph to paragraph. If you've divided your essay into three or four basic categories or approaches, you can probably treat both sides of your comparison in alternate paragraphs. If you are writing a brief essay, you may have to alternate your comparison within the paragraph unit, from sentence to sentence.

In the following brief essay, Arthur Schlesinger, a noted historian who was associated with John F. Kennedy's administration and has written numerous books on contemporary events, offers an at least partial solution to the problem of violence in America. Schlesinger was one of the few social critics to make comparisons between violence in America and other nations to support his suggestions.

As you read, remember that the sixties in America produced three major assassinations—John F. Kennedy, Robert Kennedy, and Martin Luther King, Jr.—as well as several mass murders and a general rise in crime rates throughout the country. Schlesinger's essay speaks to people's concern with those events.

Many critics blamed the rise in crime on the loss of faith in traditional moral values, others on a permissive society and educational system, still others on the pressures and tensions that result when people find themselves jammed together in cities as they live highly competitive lives. Some critics also pointed to racial tension and prejudice as a cause of growing violence.

Schlesinger uses a comparison–contrast technique to develop his own attitude toward violence in America. Some critics, for example, had argued that the frontier tradition encouraged violence in America. People modelled their actions on gun-slinging frontier heroes and pioneers who could not and would not rely on generally accepted laws and customs. We, in other words, still enjoy "taking the law into our own hands," vigilante style. We forget, or ignore, these critics say, that we now live in a more complex, civilized society.

But, says Schlesinger, comparison shows us that other nations with frontier traditions do not produce as much violence as America. Why? Schlesinger goes on to argue against other possible explanations, using statistical comparisons of America and other nations and demonstrating major counter-arguments. Then he proceeds to develop *his* proposed solution—stricter gun laws.

"Shooting: The American Dream" works by *both* alternating and block comparison: Schlesinger alternates his analysis of violence in America as contrasted to other nations in order to counter the suggestions of other social critics; he then proceeds to develop an overall block comparison between the statistics he cites on comparative violence in the first half of his essay and his gun control solution developed in the second half of the essay. Also, notice how Schlesinger always considers similarity and difference as he compares. In some ways Australia and America are similar: they share a frontier tradition. In other important ways they are different: there is more violence in America than in Australia.

Shooting: The American Dream

ARTHUR SCHLESINGER, Jr.

Now in the third quarter of the twentieth century violence has broken out with new ferocity in our country. What has given our old propensity new life? Why does the fabric of American civility no longer exert restraint? What now incites crazy individuals to act out their murderous dreams? What is it about the climate of this decade that suddenly encourages—that for some evidently legitimatizes—the relish for hate and the resort to violence? Why, according to the Federal Bureau of Investigation, have assaults with a gun increased 77 percent in the four years from 1964 through 1967?

introduces the problem in a series of specifically worded questions

We talk about a legacy of the frontier. No doubt the frontier has bequeathed us a set of romantic obsessions about six-shooters and gunfighters. But why should this legacy suddenly reassert itself in the nineteen sixties? Moreover, Canada and Australia were also frontier societies. Canadians and Australians too have robust, brawling traditions; they too like to strike virile poses. Indeed, the Australians exterminated their aboriginies more efficiently than we did our Indians. But Canadians and Australians do not feel the need today to prove themselves by killing people. The homicide rate in Canada and Australia is one quarter that of the United States.

introduces the first in a series of possible solutions; also introduces first of a series of comparisons of America and foreign nations on violence

We talk about the tensions of industrial society. No doubt industrial society generates awful tensions. No doubt the ever-quickening pace of social change depletes and destroys the institutions which make for social stability. But this does not explain why Americans shoot and kill so many more Americans than Englishmen kill Englishmen or Japanese kill Japanese. England, Japan and West Germany are, next to the United States, the most heavily industrialized countries in the world. Together they have a population of 214 million people. Among these 214

second in series of possible explanations; second in series of nation comparisons to counter the possible explanation

million, there are 135 gun murders a year. Among the 200 million people of the United States there are 6,500 gun murders a year—about *forty-eight times* as many. Philadelphia alone has about the same number of criminal homicides as England, Scotland and Wales combined—as many in a city of two million (and a city of brotherly love, at that) as in a nation of 45 million.

third in series of possible explanations; points to internal inadequacy of this explanation

We talk about the fears and antagonisms generated by racial conflict. Unquestionably this has contributed to the recent increase in violence. The murders of Dr. King and Senator Kennedy seem directly traceable to ethnic hatreds. Whites and blacks alike are laying in arms, both sides invoking the needs of self-defense. Yet this explanation still does not tell us why in America today we are tending to convert political problems into military problems—problems of adjustment into problems of force.

introduces fourth in the series of possible explanations; counters this explanation with nation comparisons and a contrasting fact

The New Left tells us that we are a violent society because we are a capitalist society—that capitalism is itself institutionalized violence; and that life under capitalism inevitably deforms relations among men. This view would be more impressive if the greatest violence of man against man in this century had not taken place in non-capitalist societies—in Nazi Germany, in Stalinist Russia, in pre-capitalist Indonesia. The fact is that every form of society is in some sense institutionalized violence; man in society always gives up a measure of "liberty" and accepts a measure of authority. Competition for power, moreover, takes place in every community; and it is obviously more healthy to have that competition relatively legitimate, open and routine, as it is in a capitalist democracy, than to deny it all channels and outlets save those of violence.

cities statistics on firearm ownership to support his introduction of more gun laws as thesis

No, we cannot escape that easily. It is not just that we were a frontier society or have become an industrial society or are a racist or a capitalist society; it is something more specific than that. Nor can we blame the situation on our gun laws, or the lack of them; though here possibly we are getting closer. There is no question, of course, that we need adequate federal gun laws. In 1967, according to the Criminal Division of the Department of Justice, 4,585,000 firearms were sold in the United States for individual use. An estimated 42.5 million Americans—more than a fifth of the population of the country—own firearms; and the estimates of the number of firearms in private hands range from 50 to 200 million. A recent city gun registration ordinance in Chicago produced 357,598 guns—enough, according to Major General Francis P. Kane, to "to equip more than twenty full-strength army divisions with hand weapons." The citizens of Chicago, General Kane said, "probably have more equipment in their hands than the entire active strength of the United States Army."

specifically describes gun law legislation which he sees as partial solution

President Johnson is everlastingly right in calling for an end to what he has properly described as "the insane traffic in guns";

and he set forth the essentials of the program in his message to Congress on June 24, 1968:

> A national registration of all firearms, both those already in private hands and those acquired in the future.
>
> Federal licensing of all possessors of firearms in those states whose laws fail to meet minimum federal standards.

The success of the National Rifle Association in blocking gun controls demanded by the great majority of the American people (by 71 to 23 percent, according to a Harris poll in April, 1968) is a national scandal. And the hysteria expressed by some at the thought that guns should be licensed, like automobiles,dogs and marriages, only strengthens the psychiatric suspicion that men doubtful of their own virility cling to the gun (like Clyde in *Bonnie and Clyde*) as a symbolic phallus and unconsciously fear gun control as the equivalent of castration. There seems wisdom in Attorney General Homer Cummings' remark of thirty years ago: "Show me the man who doesn't want his gun registered, and I will show you a man who shouldn't have a gun."

an opinion on reasons behind anti-gun registration movement

Statistics make it evident that gun controls have some effect. Sixty percent of all murders in the United States are by firearms; and states with adequate laws—New Jersey, New York, Massachusetts, Rhode Island—have much lower rates of gun murder than states with no laws or weak ones—Texas, Mississippi, Louisiana, Nevada. The same is true among countries. The American rate of homicide by gunfire is 3.5 murders per 100,000 population. Compare this to countries with strong gun laws: the rate is .04 per 100,000 in Japan, .05 in Britain, .52 in Canada.

statistics supporting his proposed solutions: comparison of homicide rates in states with and without gun laws

The National Rifle Association suggests that, if a person wants to commit a murder and does not have a gun, he will find some other way to do it. This proposition is at best dubious, and it does not apply at all to the murder of political leaders. No one has ever tried to assassinate a President with a bow and arrow. Every assassination and attempted assassination has been by gun; and, if we could reduce that, we would at least gain something. Still, however useful in making it harder for potential murderers to get guns, federal gun legislation deals with the symptoms and not with the causes of our trouble. We must go farther to account for the resurgence in recent years of our historical propensity toward violence.

concluding summary of his position

concludes with a qualification of his thesis

Activity Exercise

1. Do you think Schlesinger writes too argumentively? Does he admit the complexity of his subject? Does he admit the limitations of his own solution? Is he, on the other hand, too weak, unwilling to take a rigid and

clear stand on any issue? Cite evidence in the language of the essay for your answers.

2. Arthur Schlesinger is considered by most experts a "liberal" on social and political issues. He usually argues for relaxation of laws and for faith in the individual's ability to run his own life. Why, then, does he argue for more restrictive laws when it comes to guns?

3. Make an outline of the heirarchy of ideas in Schlesinger's essay. Begin with your idea of the thesis of the essay (phrase it as accurately as you can); then work back through the essay's supporting ideas and examples. Show how specifics relate to your approximation of Schlesinger's thesis. As you proceed, show as well how ideas, examples and facts are related. Be especially careful to relate minor comparisons to the dominating thesis of the essay.

4. Point out where Schlesinger uses alternating comparison and where he uses block comparison. Which do you prefer and why? Does Schlesinger seem to have specific reasons for using various methods of comparison? For example, why does he compare different state and national gun laws *within* paragraphs while he compares different explanations of the problem of violence in alternating paragraphs?

5. What are Schlesinger's basic assumptions? What does he, for example, take for granted about violence? What does he assume about his readers? Are there assumptions that should have been questioned and explained?

6. Take a local incidence of violence, perhaps a hold-up or an assault that occurred nearby, and discuss it within the context of Schlesinger's essay. How would his proposed solution apply? Would any of the explanations which he dismissed apply? Can you apply your own analysis of the causes and effects of the violence, drawn from your memory, your immediate experience or your reading?

7. Take one of the following subjects and plan a comparison essay around it. First, decide on what specific points—including similarities as well as differences—you'll use to develop your comparison. Be specific and use examples to illustrate points of comparison. Then decide whether you will use alternating or block patterns of organization and be ready to tell why. What in your subject makes you choose one or the other? Finally, define the purpose of your comparison. Will you be trying to persuade your readers to agree that one side of the comparison is superior to another or will you want only to provide information, to compare and contrast in order to clarify the relationship between the sides of your subject? You might also want to list examples, anecdotes and analogies which you'll use to illustrate the various points in your comparison. Be sure you don't ignore significant points of comparions.

a. *Music* (rock and classical, rock and roll and blues or jazz, the styles of two current performers or rock groups)
b. *People* (regional types, campus types, different professional types—teachers, doctors, dentists, or lawyers)

c. *Styles of Dress* (the dress of two different groups of people, airline stewardesses and policewomen, or the relationship between the way a person dresses and his general attitudes)
d. *Different Types of Warfare* (wars of the past, land wars, sea wars, limited wars, nuclear wars)
e. *Magazines* (women's magazines, men's magazines, sports magazines, car magazines, literary magazines, trade journals)
f. *Different Attitudes* (educational progressives and conservatives, democratic and aristocratic types, elitists and egalitarians)

The essay of classification

Just about everything we write involves dividing large subjects into smaller parts. We often develop main ideas by referring to specific examples. Or we describe an object by referring to its physical details. We begin this process when we compose sentences, by shifting from general summaries, interpretations and analyses of ideas down to illustrative examples, descriptive details, by including anything that will develop and clarify the general points of our essays.

Classification is merely a means of organizing an entire essay around the process of dividing a larger subject into smaller parts. Usually, we classify according to *likeness*. College women might be classified into these categories by a college placement office:

career women

potential housewives

part-time career women

potential professional women (lawyers, doctors, dentists, and college teachers)

Someone writing an essay on feminist attitudes toward contemporary women might produce this categorical outline:
unliberated women

moderate feminist

"fem-libbers"

radical feminists

traditional moderates

In other words, the way you divide your subject into parts will depend on your purpose.

Usually, you'll use classification to help your readers understand your subject better. A general essay on feminism, for example, might classify in order to explain, to help the uninformed reader comprehend a complex subject. Often, however, you'll use classification to persuade or argue that your reader should take a new perspective on your subject. A moderate feminist, for example, might classify the different types of feminism to convince her readers that *all* feminists can't be stereotyped according to one, two, or three types. In the process, the writer may also convince readers to alter their attitudes toward the feminist movement.

Develop categorical classifications for the following subjects:

movie actresses	writing assignments
movie actors	magazines
types of nuts	newspapers
baseball players	comic strips
novels you have read	presidents that you have observed
families you have known	mothers
music	teachers
fruits you enjoy eating	
noses	

Classification imposes order on otherwise chaotic materials. You should remember five points as you organize and develop a classifying essay.

1. Be sure to form categories that add something to the reader's understanding of your subject. For example, you wouldn't be doing much for an informed reader if you divided baseball players according to the positions they play. Most reasonably informed readers already know these classifications. But even an avid fan might be interested in categories explaining how different centerfielders play their positions. Are there *daring* centerfielders who are apt to make the occasional sensational catch as well as an occasional error; are there *steady* centerfielders who make very few errors and very few sensational catches; are there *erratic* centerfielders who play superbly one day and poorly the next? In any case, be sure that your categorical divisions are directed to your audience. Informed readers usually want more specific and more complex classification than general readers, who often learn a good deal from less specific classifications. A European, for example, might find a classification of movie actors into lead, support and spot roles interesting. But an American, who has watched several Academy Award shows on television, would probably find such classifications redundant. He'd probably be more interested in character typing.

2. Classes of data can be developed in two ways. You can limit your categories to only those parts of a class which you have personally

observed. If you have read two kinds of comic novels—black humor and political satire—you may limit your classification to those two types. You should, however, make clear that you are writing from personal observation and that the main class or subject will not be covered in all its subdivisions or categories. If you are writing on a class whose data can be developed and illustrated completely in a single essay, then you must include analysis of every category.

3. Be sure to define the premises upon which your subdivisions are formed. A classification essay on the types of families you have observed might, for example, form categories according to family size, income, organization of authority, or living conditions. Let your reader know exactly what the basis of your categories are. Point out how the examples which you include in a category are similar and how they differ from those in other categories.

4. When we use classification, we often create artificial subdivisions to give unity to our subject. An essay on different types of college teachers, for example, might use the categories *game-players, straight lecturers, free-discussion types, outliners* and *paraphrasers.* Of course, most college teachers combine some characteristics of all these types. For the purpose of your essay you may create "types" who would be difficult to find in real life. That's acceptable, as long as you point out that you are aware of your oversimplifications.

5. Once you've defined a class subject and divided it into categories, don't *cross* categories unless you explain why a particular object is included in two or more categories. If you, for example, divide popular music into folk, hard rock, rock and roll, country, and jazz, be sure that you explain *why* and *how* a particular song or performer fits into more than one category—as Bob Dylan might fit into folk, rock, and country. Otherwise your categories will ultimately become meaningless and useless. Also, be sure to recognize when a particular category should be divided into subdivisions of its own. Should country music be subdivided into the "Nashville" sound, black country music, and Bluegrass? Can the same type of question be asked of the other categories?

Can People Be Judged by Their Appearance?

ERIC BERNE

Everyone knows that a human being, like a chicken, comes   the embryo's structure
from an egg. At a very early stage, the human embryo forms a
three-layered tube, the inside layer of which grows into the
stomach and lungs, the middle layer into bones, muscles, joints,

Reprinted from *A Layman's Guide to Psychiatry and Psychoanalysis* (New York: Grove Press, 1962), pp. 3–5. Copyright © 1947, 1957, 1968 by Eric Berne M.D. Reprinted by permission of Simon and Schuster, Inc.

and blood vessels, and the outside layer into the skin and nervous system.

sets the limits of this essay

Usually these three grow about equally, so that the average human being is a fair mixture of brains, muscles, and inward organs. In some eggs, however, one layer grows more than the others, and when the angels have finished putting the child together, he may have more gut than brain, or more brain than muscle. When this happens, the individual's activities will often be mostly with the overgrown layer.

the purpose of this essay introduced

We can thus say that while the average human being is a mixture, some people are mainly "digestion-minded," some "muscle-minded," and some "brain-minded," and correspondingly digestion-bodied, muscle-bodied, or brain-bodied. The digestion-bodied people look thick; the muscle-bodied people look wide; and the brain-bodied people look long. This does not mean the taller a man is the brainier he will be. It means that if a man, even a short man, looks long rather than wide or thick, he will often be more concerned about what goes on in his mind than about what he does or what he eats; but the key factor is slenderness and not height. On the other hand, a man who gives the impression of being thick rather than long or wide will usually be more interested in a good steak than in a good idea or a good long walk.

characteristic results of exaggeration

Medical men use Greek words to describe these types of bodybuild. For the man whose body shape mostly depends on the inside layer of the egg, they use the word *endomorph*. If it depnds mostly upon the middle layer, they call him a *mesomorph*. If it depends upon the outside layer, they call him an *ectomorph*. We can see the same roots in our English words "enter," "medium," and "exit," which might just as easily have been spelled "ender," "mesium," and "ectit."

further definition of each category in the classification

Since the inside skin of the human egg, or endoderm, forms the inner organs of the belly, the viscera, the endomorph is usually belly-minded; since the middle skin forms the body tissues, or soma, the mesomorph is usually muscle-minded; and since the outside skin forms the brain, or cerebrum, the ectomorph is usually brain-minded. Translating this into Greek, we have the viscerotonic endomorph, the somatatonic mesomorph, and the cerebrotonic ectomorph.

further defines terminology

Words are beautiful things to a cerebrotonic, but a viscerotonic knows you cannot eat a menu no matter what language it is printed in, and a somatotonic knows you cannot increase your chest expansion by reading a dictionary. So it is advisable to leave these words and see what kinds of people they actually apply to, remembering again that most individuals are fairly equal mixtures and that what we have to say concerns only the extremes. Up to the present, these types have been thoroughly studied only in the male sex.

limits of categories

Viscerotonic endomorph. If a man is definitely a thick type rather than a broad or long type, he is likely to be round and soft, with a big chest but a bigger belly. He would rather eat than breathe comfortably. He is likely to have a wide face, short, thick neck, big thighs and upper arms, and small hands and feet. He has overdeveloped breasts and looks as though he were blown up a little like a balloon. His skin is soft and smooth, and when he gets bald, as he does usually quite early, he loses the hair in the middle of his head first.

The short, jolly, thickset, red-faced politician with a cigar in his mouth, who always looks as though he were about to have a stroke, is the best example of this type. The reason he often makes a good politician is that he likes people, banquets, baths, and sleep; he is easygoing, soothing, and his feelings are easy to understand.

His abdomen is big because he has lots of intestines. He likes to take in things. He likes to take in food, and affection and approval as well. Going to a banquet with people who like him is his idea of a fine time. It is important for a psychiatrist to understand the natures of such men when they come to him for advice.

Somatotonic mesomorph. If a man is definitely a broad type rather than a thick or long type, he is likely to be rugged and have lots of muscle. He is apt to have big forearms and legs, and his chest and belly are well formed and firm, with the chest bigger than the belly. He would rather breathe than eat. He has a bony head, big shoulders, and a square jaw. His skin is thick, coarse, and elastic, and tans easily. If he gets bald, it usually starts on the front of the head.

Dick Tracy, Li'l Abner, and other men of action belong to this type. Such people make good lifeguards and construction workers. They like to put out energy. They have lots of muscles and they like to use them. They go in for adventure, exercise, fighting, and getting the upper hand. They are bold and unrestrained, and love to master the people and things around them. If the psychiatrist knows the things which give such people satisfaction, he is able to understand why they may be unhappy in certain situations.

Cerebrotonic ectomorph. The man who is definitely a long type is likely to have thin bones and muscles. His shoulders are apt to sag and he has a flat belly with a dropped stomach, and long, weak legs. His neck and fingers are long, and his face is shaped like a long egg. His skin is thin, dry, and pale, and he rarely gets bald. He looks like an absent-minded professor and often is one.

Though such people are jumpy, they like to keep their energy and don't fancy moving around much. They would rather sit

---

elaboration of the characteristics of each type

the politician-endomorph as example

defines characteristics of the "broad" type

examples of the "broad" type

characteristics defined

example-type

characteristics contrasted

quietly by themselves and keep out of difficulties. Trouble upsets them, and they run away from it. Their friends don't understand them very well. They move jerkily and feel jerkily. The psychiatrist who understands how easily they become anxious is often able to help them get along better in the sociable and aggressive world of endomorphs and mesomorphs.

how the classifications can be applied

In the special cases where people definitely belong to one type or another, then, one can tell a good deal about their personalities from their appearance. When the human mind is engaged in one of its struggles with itself or with the world outside, the individual's way of handling the struggle will be partly determined by this type. If he is a viscerotonic he will often want to go to a party where he can eat and drink and be in good company at a time when he might be better off attending to business; the somatotonic will want to go out and do something about it, master the situation, even if what he does is foolish and not properly figured out, while the cerebrotonic will go off by himself and think it over, when perhaps he would be better off doing something about it or seeking good company to try to forget it.

why knowledge is useful

Since these personality characteristics depend on the growth of the layers of the little egg from which the person developed, they are very difficult to change. Nevertheless, it is important for the individual to know about these types, so that he can have at least an inkling of what to expect from those around him, and can make allowances for the different kinds of human nature, and so that he can become aware of and learn to control his own natural tendencies, which may sometimes guide him into making the same mistakes over and over again in handling his difficulties.

Activity Exercise

1. Take Berne's classification of physical types and apply them to two or three people you know. You might compare and contrast your subjects in the three categories according to their manifestations of characteristics. Be specific; describe closely and observe carefully.

2. Take any one of the broad subjects listed on page 397. First, limit your essay to one part or aspect of your subject. You might, for example, limit a paper on noses to a description of male or female noses or to only the types of noses which draw attention to themselves. Then subdivide your subcategory and write a classification of these further subdivisions.

3. Write a satire of what you believe are the major types of college students. Classify them and then exaggerate the characteristics of each general type. You might want to organize your type-descriptions around

the attitudes the students hold, their family backgrounds, whether they come from small towns, suburbs, or large cities, their major interests and activities, their academic performances or special interests. Introduce your categories and suggest your satiric purpose in an opening paragraph; then use an alternating comparison structure to illustrate your categories. Compare examples from several categories. Go through all your categories and develop your examples in as much exaggerated detail as you can. Remember, satire works best when you don't come right out and *tell* your reader what you think of your subject. *Show* and *suggest.*

4. Do you think Berne's essay is as useful as he suggests? Is he serious, half-serious, or satiric? Can you tell from this brief essay? How? Might such classifications as Berne's lead to oversimplification of people, despite his warnings that most people contain characteristics of several types? Can you think of other classifications, say, of social or racial types, that might also lead to oversimplification?

Appendix I

The writer's eye for grammar: On applying grammatical principles

Chapter 5, Reference 1

A few people write better when they don't really know what they're doing. They study and know the subject they will write about; they know their readers; and they know what they want to say. Then, they just write and everything comes out fine. Such writers can avoid this appendix.

Others, however, work best knowing exactly what they're doing. They know themselves, their subjects, and their readers. But they also want to know just how the words they put on paper fit together and function. They want to be *conscious* of what they are doing so that they can more effectively control every word. This appendix is meant for these writers.

Generally, there are three kinds of sentence modifiers. They are explained in the following outline. Study the outline and we will apply its principles to the student paragraph that we have already begun to analyze in Chapter 5. Ask your teacher to explain grammatical terms you may not understand.

1. *Adjectival modifiers* modify *nouns;* they may be single word or large constituent modifiers (phrases and clauses), according to the following outline:

a. one word modifiers   b. large constituent modifiers

participle

adjective   infinitive   phrase   clause

c. Examples:

(1) The boy carried a *large case.* (one word *adjective* modifier)
(2) The players *remaining* on the field shook hands and talked. (one word *present participle* modifier)
(3) The *tested* veteran was sent to the front lines. (one word *past participle* modifier)
(4) Give him the book *of proverbs.* (large constituent *prepositional phrase* modifier)
(5) The quarterback, *who had played an outstanding game,* sat in the corner of the locker room talking with reporters. (large constituent *adjective clause* modifier)

d. Remember that there are many kinds of phrases. At this point, you need only familiarize yourself with the general possibilities in adjectival modification.

2. *Adverbial modifiers* modify *verbs, adjectives* or other *adverbs;* they may also be one word or large constituent (phrase or clause) modifiers, according to the following outline:

a. one word modifiers   b. large constituent modifiers

adverb   phrase   clause

c. One word adverbial modifiers of verbs usually define the following qualities of verbs: time, place, manner, frequency, certainty. Some examples:

(1) The guest speaker will arrive *soon.* (time)
(2) Put the tablecloth *here* before we set the table. (place)
(3) That car engine runs *smoothly.* (manner)
(4) *Occasionally,* the young man crossed the street, recrossed it, and looked nervously about. (frequency)
(5) More than *likely* the child will rebel. (certainty)

d. Both prepositional and infinitive phrases can be used as large constituent adverbial modifiers of verbs. Examples:

(1) He cut the string with a *knife.* (prepositional phrase)
(2) The detective spoke, in a clipped voice, *to frighten the suspect.* (infinitive phrase)

Some examples of adverb clauses:

(1) *Before Tom got home,* the sun had set and darkness had begun to cover the city.
(2) *If the phone rings,* don't answer it.

e. One word adverbial modifiers *of adjectives* take two forms: the intensifying adverb and the infinitive. Most one word adverbial modifiers of adjectives *intensify* the quality described in the adjective.

Examples:

    (1) Tom is *very* worried; his task is *rather* challenging.
    (2) Any task is easy *to do* when you have had much experience. (infinitive)

f. Large constituent adverbial modifiers *of adjectives* take the forms of phrases and clauses. The phrases are usually *infinitive phrases:*

    (1) The quarterback was ready *to release the pass.*
    (2) Some people think a long walk is pleasant *to take after dinner.*

Adverb clauses can also be used to modify adjectives, as in this sentence:

    (3) Fred's musical abilities are better *than my abilities* (are).

g. One word adverbial modifiers *of adverbs* usually function to intensify the adverb being modified; they take the form of *single adverbs* and *infinitives.*

Examples:

    (1) Celeste plays the violin *very* well.
    (2) Tom knows *extremely* well how I feel.
    (3) He was too excited *to speak* or even to stop for breath. (infinitive; the adverb modified is *too*)

h. Large constituent adverbial modifiers *of adverbs* also take the form of phrases and clauses. As in adverbial clauses that modify adjectives, the kind of phrase often used is the *infinitive phrase.*

Examples:

    (1) As he entered the classroom fairly late, he was courteous enough to make very little noise. (infinitive phrase)
    (2) When he finally did get home, he was so excited *that he practically ran through the door.* (relative clause modifying *so*)

    3. *Absolute clause sentence modifiers* do not modify any particular word outside their own structure. They are set off by commas from the main clause and relate to the *idea* that is being presented in the main clause, not to a specific word or basic sentence element.

    (1) The man, darkly handsome, took the package from his pocket, *a look of fear resting on his worried face.*
    (2) A small girl came into view slightly above them, walking quickly, *her knees bending abruptly.*

You will find more information on the function and possible uses of the absolute clause later in this appendix. At this point, don't worry very much about the specifics of sentence modifiers. Just familiarize yourself with the way the various kinds of sentence modifiers can be attached to the main elements of your sentences. Then, as you write and experiment, you'll have alternative ways of modifying in mind, and you will be able to choose from them to add variety, detail, and coordination to your sentences.

Here is a discussion and application of these modifying principles. Again, the sample sentence is the one that is based on Hopper's *Early Sunday Morning*.

> A row of red houses sets atop the stores and shops and peers across the city as the morning sun casts its golden rays upon the silent brick faces of the houses.

Basic Sentence Elements:

> S   V   V
> *row   sets* and *peers*

Sentence Modifiers: a prepositional phrase (across the city) linked to the basic sentence elements; an *adverbial clause* (as the morning sun cast its golden rays) with two supporting *prepositional phrases* (upon the silent brick faces of the houses).

This writer, let us suppose, wanted to have the reader experience the solitude he felt when he looked at the painting. He also wanted the reader to feel that he was receiving the details as he would if he had actually looked at the painting. As you look back over the painting, can you find details that would support a feeling of solitude? Consider this list of visual details.

> the dull red and green fronts of the houses
> the lonely images of the sidewalk—the hydrant and barber pole
> the still blue sky
> the fact that no human figure is in the painting
> the fact that nothing in the painting seems to be moving

We can pull these supporting details together in the following three sentences.

> We walked along the empty sidewalk and our eyes shifted up to the silent brick and glass front of the houses. They looked soberly out at

us, the windows partially shaded and curtained. The sky was a dull gray and formed a sharp contrast to the red brick.

These sentences include most of the details in the above list and several others. But, more importantly, they connect these details in sentences that are clearly ordered and carefully modified. Do you feel the solitude the writer tries to show as you read? Can you visualize the scene clearly? Locate the sentence modifiers, identify them, and try to see clearly how they are connected grammatically to the basic sentence elements.

As you read, your mind's eye moves easily from the house and store fronts to the windows and their shades and curtains and finally out to the sky beyond. You feel the solitude without being told to do so because the writer *shows* you solitude—the sober houses and storefronts, the still windows, the blue sky, the *empty* sidewalk. And he puts those details together in sentence modifiers that are always clearly related to basic sentence elements. Here is the paragraph reproduced with sentence modifiers in italics and arrows showing their clear relation to basic elements.

We walked *along the empty sidewalk* and our eyes shifted up *to the silent brick and glass fronts of the houses.* (This compound sentence has three prepositional phrases directly connected to the subject and predicate of both independent clauses.) They looked *soberly* out *at us,* the windows *partially* shaded and curtained. (This sentence includes two adverbs clearly connected to antecedent verbs and an absolute phrase that focuses the reader on a single detail—the windows of the houses.) The sky *beyond the flat roofs* was a *dull* gray and formed a *sharp* contrast *to the red brick.* (This compound sentence has two prepositional phrases and two single-word modifiers, both adjectives.)

The graphing of this paragraph shows why we find it easy to read. First, it *does* include details that *show;* the writer doesn't have to *tell* us that he feels solitude when he looks at the painting. Second, the showing details are included in sentence modifiers that the reader has no trouble connecting to the main objects of the painting, which are all included in basic sentence elements (subjects, verbs, and objects or complements). Third, the writer *varies* his sentence modifiers, using prepositional phrases, adjectives, adverbs, and an absolute phrase. Each is used to fit the detail that he is describing. Keep these hints in mind.

1. Find and use detail.
2. Relate the details to larger objects.

3. Vary the modifiers you use to include your detail. *Don't overuse adjectives; they often tell more than they show.*

Chapter 5, Reference 2: The cumulative sentence[1]

Many professional writers use the cumulative sentence to get moving action into their sentences. If you are looking for examples of good narrative sentences with some explanation of how they work, this section will provide some of these. Remember, the cumulative sentence is especially useful in getting action and detail into your writing. But it must be combined with information and summary sentences in most effective writing.

We began our analyses of sentences by separating base clauses from sentence modifiers. In the following example sentences, the base clauses are underlined and marked by a 1. Every sentence modifier that modifies a noun or verb in the base clause is marked with a 2, because that modifier is only one step removed from the main part of the sentence. Every modifier that modifies a word in level two is marked by a 3, since that modifier is two steps away from the base clause. Many sentences may contain many levels of sentence modifiers, as many as five or six levels removed from the base clause. But in such sentences, the writer must be sure that the reader can follow the way each level is related to the previous. And, finally, he must be sure that his readers can see that every level, even the last, relates back to the base clause. Otherwise his sentences lack unity, and the reader can't follow the action being described through all its details. Study the modifiers in these examples.

Example sentences

Single-level sentence modifier

1. *The jockeys sat bowed and relaxed,* 2 moving a little at the waist with the movement of their horses.

—Katherine Anne Porter

---

[1]Some of the principles and example sentences in this section are taken from Francis Christensen's explanation of the cumulative sentence in *Notes Toward A New Rhetoric* (New York, 1967).

Two sentences with two levels of modification

1. *Six boys came over the hill half an hour early that afternoon,*
    2. running hard,
    2. their heads down,
    2. their forearms working,
    2. their breath whistling.

—John Steinbeck

1. He could sail for hours.
    2. searching the blanched grases below him with his telescopic eyes
    2. gaining height against the wind
    2. descending in mile-long, gently declining swoops when he curved and rode back,
    2. never beating a wing.

—Walter van Tilburg Clark

Each second-level modifier in these sentences modifies the subject of the base structures.

Sentence with second- and third-level sentence modifiers

1. They regarded me silently,
    2. Brother Jack with a smile that went no deeper than his lips,
        3. his head cocked to one side,
        3. studying me with his penetrating eyes,
    2. the other blank-faced,
        looking out of eyes that were meant to reveal nothing and to stir profound uncertainty.

The second-level modifiers modify the subject of the base structure *they;* the third-level modifiers modify the nouns *Brother Jack* and *other* in the second-level modifiers.

Sentence with multilevel sentence modifiers

1. The group of men peered over the side of the bridge,
    2. their eyes furtive and quick,
        3. every glance like a sharp knife,
            4. diving to the black water below,
                5. which glistened in the night.

Every sentence modifier in this specific series adds detail to the general base clause of the sentence. But more importantly, the modifiers add detail in ways that naturally involve the reader in the action or scene described. In order to make the reader feel a part of the action being described, the writers use different kinds of sentence modifiers; they are careful to control the relationships among the modifiers and the base structure of the sentence.

The Katherine Anne Porter sentence develops in a way that encourages the reader to become the jockey. The added modifier is a verbal cluster—a present participial phrase that describes the jockeys as if they were immediately before the reader ("The jockeys sat bowed and relaxed, *moving a little at the waist with the movement of their horses.*") Verbal sentence modifiers usually help to add *action* to the sentence. Present participial phrases (you can find them by looking for -ing words followed by a series of words forming a phrase) make the action seem more immediate. Past participial phrases (-ed words) put the action in the past; the reader becomes more of an observer than a participator in the action.

The absolute phrase is one of the most effective means of adding detail to the base structure of a cumulative sentence. An absolute phrase has a dependent function in the sentence; but unlike most dependent phrases or clauses, the absolute does not modify a word in another structure. Rather, the absolute always refers to a preceding idea. Absolutes are useful when you want to focus attention on additional parts of a subject that you have already introduced in the base structure or in a lower level sentence modifier. Take the example sentence with several second-level modifiers: "Six boys came over the hill half an hour early that afternoon, *running hard, their heads down, their forearms working, their breath whistling.*" The first modifier is a present participial phrase; it tells us what the boys were doing as they came over the hill. It puts the boys into a specific physical action. Each successive sentence modifier is an absolute phrase that adds some specific physical detail to the subject of the base structure—*six boys.* Imagine how these added details would read if they were put in separate sentences.

> Six boys came over the hill half an hour early that afternoon. They were running hard. Their heads were down. Their forearms were working. Their breath was whistling.

When divided into separate sentences, the original action seems less intense, less dramatic to the reader. The decrease in dramatic intensity occurs because the action and description is artificially separated by the stops after each sentence; in the cumulative sentence, the absolutes impress themselves on the consciousness of the reader rapidly just as the sight of six running boys would impress itself simultaneously on the eyes of an observer. The absolute has five basic forms, all including a noun and one of the following forms. Learn to recognize and use them.

1. noun + participle or participial phrase	example: *their forearms working*
2. noun + verb	example: *their heads down*
2. noun + prepositional phrase	example: *every glance like a sharp knife*
4. noun + appositive (a phrase or word that functions as a contrast to a preceding word or phrase, usually in a way that gives us more detail about the preceding words)	example: *his body a twisted mess*
5. noun + adjective or adjectival phrase	example: *their eyes furtive and quick*

Of course, you need not memorize these forms. Practice using absolutes to add detail to your base structures and try, at least occasionally, to vary the forms of your absolute phrases.

The adjective phrase is another common type of large constituent sentence modifier. Like the absolute, the adjective phrase adds detail to the subject or nouns in the base structure or preceding modifiers in a cumulative sentence. Here is an example.

> Before today, Jody had been a boy dressed in overalls and a blue shirt, *quieter than most,* even suspected of being a little cowardly.
>
> —John Steinbeck

The italicized adjective phrase adds to what the reader knows about Jody, the subject of the base clause. The information comes to the reader, without the benefit of a verbal form (an action word such as a participle). If Steinbeck were to use *all* adjective phrase sentence modifiers, his sentences would be informative without conveying a sense of dramatic action. But Steinbeck is careful to vary the kinds of sentence modifiers he uses. In the above sentence, we find two past participial sentence modifiers combined with the adjective phrase modifier. As a result, the sentence combines specific physical detail with a sense of action and relationship. The verbal and adjective modifiers help bring together very specific physical details and a sense of action; Jody's conventional dress merges nicely with the way the observer describes his personality.

We've analyzed three different sentence modifiers—participial and absolute phrases and the adjective phrase. These are useful ways to show your reader in detail what you have introduced in the main parts of your sentence. Try these sentence exercises.

Activity Exercise

1. Add sentence modifiers to the following base clauses. Use at least two of the three modifiers we have just discussed. You may use as many levels of modification as you wish, but remember: *the reader must be able to follow the action you describe.* The modifiers have to be clearly related and unified. Think out what you want to have the subject of each sentence do *before* you write. Then find the right modifiers.

The young boy walked along . . .
He ate the peach rapidly . . .
After flying low over the plains, the pilot brought the plane up . . .

Now, look around you—out a nearby window, at your wife, roommate, or mother as he or she washes dishes, lifts a box, or runs the vacuum cleaner—and find an action you can describe very specifically in one or two sentences. Limit your subject and decide what you want to say first. Then try your hand at several cumulative sentences.

2. Rewrite the following short paragraphs into single cumulative sentences. Change every sentence after the first into a sentence modifier and change the first sentence into a base clause.

The sun was coming over the ridge. It was glaring on the whitewash of the houses and barns. It made the wet grass blaze softly. (Rewritten from John Steinbeck's *The Red Pony.*)

He approached the wall and then leaped. As he leaped, his feet flew out in front of him. His eyes were bulging. He looked like he was running through the air.

Journal Exercise

1. Find a comfortable place to observe people *in action.* Take notes, not only of physical characteristics, but of how actions and gestures are carried out. Then compose cumulative sentences which successfully

convey a sense of detail *and* action. Describe a person *as* he walks down a street or someone engaged in conversation.

2. Write a description of an activity—say, eating a meal by candle-light, riding on a train, walking through a garden—and try to appeal to at least two senses simultaneously. Describe, for example, how the garden smells as well as how it looks, or how a train ride feels as well as how the car you are riding in smells.

3. Rethink a recent experience, preferably one in which you were personally involved. Compose a narrative description that will make the reader feel as if the experience were actually happening as he reads. You'll probably need to use direct sensory appeal, cumulative sentences, and sentence modifiers that read rapidly and smoothly, without interrupt-ing the flow of the sentence.

A summary of principles on writing narrative sentences

1. Remember that *length* is not the measure of a successful sentence. Don't add modifiers merely to pad; add only when you feel that the reader can use the additional information, without confusion.

2. Don't place participial and adjective phrases too far from the words they modify. Absolute phrases usually include direct reference to the subject of the base structure; as a result, they can be safely placed away from the words or ideas they modify.

Example:

The cart moved across the field, its wheels bumping and turning roughly, its driver bouncing along, spewing out dust behind it.

Rewritten example:

The cart moved across the field, *spewing out dust behind it,* its wheels bumping and turning roughly, its driver bouncing along.

By moving the present participial phrase closer to the word it modifies—*cart*—the sentence is made clearer. The reader can easily relate each sentence modifier back to the subject of the base structure. The absolute phrases mention parts of the cart specifically—its wheels, its driver; the reader, as a result, has no trouble relating the absolutes to their antecedents.

3. Sometimes a periodic sentence better conveys the sequence of action that is desired than the cumulative sentence. A periodic sentence usually has the sentence modifiers arranged so that they build up to the main idea, which is expressed in a base structure at the end of the sentence.

Periodic example:

Filling his gullet for the third time, lowering the jug one instant ahead of the bright intact repetition, panting, indrawing the cool of air until he could breathe, he drank.

Such sentences arrange modifiers so that separate details lead up to a final action. Then, the final action—*he drank*—is emphasized while the other actions—the filling of the gullet, the indrawing of air, and so on —reproduce experience more naturally. That is probably why William Faulkner put the above sentence in a periodic structure.

Cumulative example:

He drank, filling his gullet for the third time and lowered the jug one instant ahead of the bright intact repetition, panting, indrawing the cool of air until he could breathe.

In this sentence, the writer presents the action much as a reader would perceive it in real life, the whole action received generally with the eye catching further detail *as* the action continues. There are occasions, however, when you will want to emphasize certain aspects of experience. Then, the periodic sentence should help you, because it will allow you to begin with subordinate details and build toward a main idea near the close of the sentence.

Chapter 7:
Specific transitional expressions

There are numerous specific transitional expressions. Some are single words, others are complete phrases or clauses. But, whatever the specific expression, transitional devices usually indicate one of the following three relationships between ideas.

First, they indicate that two ideas are *equal.* Such transitions *coordinate* or make clear the equality or simultaneity of two parts of a sentence or paragraph. Semicolons and *ands* are the most obvious coordinators.

A writer's style depends on the choices he makes; certain charac-teristic choices tell us what kind of person is writing and speaking. (The semi-colon here sets off two different and equal ways of saying the same thing)

He turned the corner sharply and riveted his attention on the side of the road. (Here *and* connects two actions, equal in importance, which occur simultaneously)

Second, transitions often indicate the degree of *similarity* and *difference* between two ideas.

As a symbol, the tiger has a ferocious attractiveness. The owl and the bat, *however,* because of their physical unattractiveness, usually signify the evil, stupid or ugly.

These sentences compare two classes of animals used as symbols. The *however* indicates that the idea in the second sentence is different from the idea in the first. The writer describes a contrast in the second sentence to the assertion he has made in the first sentence. Notice, however, how this transitional phrase expresses the similarity between two ideas.

Somebody who does something well enough to make what is difficult seem easy and natural usually has our admiration. The athlete, *in like manner,* displays real talent when he succeeds naturally, without obvious effort.

Finally, transitions often indicate *why* something happened (a causal relationship). The words *because* and *therefore* often function this way.

Because the trees were slightly green mixed with brown, we assumed the season was either fall or spring.

Such causal transitions should be used only when the cause or effect is complex enough to require elaboration or precise explanation. Don't insult your reader's intelligence by pointing out obvious causes in needless detail. Yet don't lose your reader by not clarifying through transitions the less obvious connections between your ideas.

Transitional expressions have another important, though separate, function. They often indicate to a reader that the writer is shifting from a universal to a particular, from a general statement to a specific example. Or they may indicate a shift from particular example to a general interpretation or influence. Probably most common are sentences that prepare the reader to share an example which is specifically related to a previous generalization.

Sometimes, as the old adage goes, three is a crowd. The other day, *for example,* I was able to corner someone I've wanted to talk to privately for the first time and another friend of mine immediately interrupted.

But often we work in the opposite direction, from example to generality.

And whenever I returned to that spot the horse was there waiting. *In sum,* I came to believe that he had trained himself to show up at that particular time, in that particular spot, everyday.

Here is a summary list of specific transitional devices along with their grammatical function. This list is by no means exhaustive. But it should help you understand the most common transitional words and their usual functions.

1. *Coordinate Conjunctions* (and, but, or, nor and for) usually point out similarity, difference or equality between two sentences or clauses. Often they connect independent clauses that might stand alone as sentences. When such clauses are connected rather than left in separate sentences, the result is a closer combination of the concepts and a more specific recognition of the relationship between the concepts that are represented in each clause.

2. *Conjunctive Adverbs* (likewise, however) usually relate the concept in one sentence to the concept in the previous sentence. They most often appear at the beginning or after the subject of a sentence; they clarify the sentence's relationship with the previous sentence. Conjunctive adverbs always point out similarity or difference.

3. *Transitional Phrases* (on the other hand, in contrast to, in the same manner) usually appear at the beginning of a sentence and they clarify the similarity or difference between two sentences. They tell the reader that an opposition or friction is being set up.

4. *Subordinating Conjunctions* (just, so, as, because) serve a more complex function. They allow the reader to clarify the relationships between clauses within a sentence. They, for example, tell the reader that something happened because of something else, or that one action was occurring simultaneously with another action. Subordinating conjunctions are especially important when you are arguing logically, when you wish to convince your reader that it is more likely that one sequence of events led to a situation than another.

5. *The Semicolon* usually connects two balanced clauses and enables the writer to rephrase in order to clarify. The semicolon usually sets off ideas that are of equal importance.

Remember that too many obvious transitional devices and expressions can clutter your writing with words that don't really *add* to your meaning. Don't resort to a *however, because* or to an *on the other hand* every time you want to connect ideas. Depend as well on more natural ways of connecting the parts of your writing—repetition of key terms and ideas, pronouns, and parallel structure.

Appendix II

The everyday eye:
On keeping a journal

These directions on how to keep a journal along with *The Writing Eye* are not to be taken as rules. Be flexible, discuss your journal entries and the entire process of keeping a journal often with your teacher. In fact, your teacher will probably read this appendix carefully since he may also be new to the idea of using and reading journals. How does your journal relate to the rest of what you do in this course?

Above all, a journal should help you write more. It should get you into the *habit* of writing. Then sitting down with your pen in hand and staring at a blank page won't seem as terrifying as it probably does now.

Also, your journal should encourage you to *experiment*. Imagine yourself in another person's skin once in awhile. Go out and take notes on what you see, carefully recording your sensory impressions. Try to find really specific words and modifiers just as a painter tries to find the right shades and tones of color as he sketches *before* actually painting on canvas. Experiment with different voices and styles. If, for example, you've just read a particularly hard-hitting editorial, try to find a controversial issue that interests you and apply a similar style to that issue in your journal. Experiment with very brief, perhaps one-sentence, entries as well as longer entries.

Your journal should also help you to *observe* and *perceive* more sensitively. Find a journal that you feel comfortable carrying almost anywhere. Be ready to analyze anything at anytime. Get use to paying close attention to how and why you see and feel the way you do. What are your prejudices and how do they influence what you are saying? Plan to observe some campus scene or object. Record what you *think* you'll find.

417

Then compare that with what you *do* find. Your journal should also help you to select and arrange concrete experience.

For example, go to a local street corner and observe carefully. Then write a general paragraph that you think captures the impression the scene left with you. Then go back over your original journal notes and observations and find and arrange concrete evidence in support of that impression. Such exercises should help you build whole compositions out of what at first seemed random and chaotic observations.

Finally, a journal should help you *integrate*. It should help you put things together in writing. Your specific observations from one day will, as you read and re-read and add new entries, begin to come together and form a design. You'll see more and you'll be able to connect more of what you see. Early in this course, you should be able to capture particular perceptions in sentences and notes. Hopefully, by the end of the course, you'll have experienced at least some success in composing, organizing and arranging those particulars into composite pictures.

A journal is *not* a diary. People record their feelings and ideas in very *personal* language in a diary. In fact, sometimes no one but the writer himself can get much out of a diary: "Today I went to Upshaw's. Big was there. We talked and then I left and went home and read." A reader has very little to go on here. It's like reading a secret code. Not only the experience is private, even the language is private.

A journal, however records personal observations, thoughts and experience in a language that can be read by others. Certainly your journal is *yours*. It captures your very personal experience in concrete, telling terms. But it should also make sense to others, although your journal entries will not need to follow the conventions of more formal writing situations. This is a good journal entry. It captures the writer's personality, gives you a peek into *his* mind and feelings and an idea of how he talks and acts in everyday life. It *communicates*.

> I met Professor Jones today. He's a tall Abe Lincolnish character with a gaunt eye and haggard brow. The lines on his face are deep. My roommate's description was pretty accurate but I had to see for myself. As I talked to Jones, I found my voice rising in excitement; his ideas were like tinder on the fire of my mind.

We know both Mr. Jones and the student-writer better after reading this entry. The writing is straight to the point; it sounds like talk without sacrificing precision. The eye for detail is sensitive and accurate and we are shown only what we need to build our impressions, not everything.

Here is a list to suggest entries for your journal. Use the list to generate ideas for other kinds of entries that appeal to you.

1. Put your ongoing responses to course readings in your journal. Begin by recording your immediate reactions. Every once in awhile go back and write a few paragraphs that pull together the immediate reactions and form more unified, overall impressions.

2. Be sure to try at least a few observation exercises. You are a professional writer on the lookout for material. Just take notes on what you see, be concrete and try to observe from several different perspectives.

3. Include some *personal feeling* entries. Describe how an experience makes you feel *inside*. Try to find words and a style that you think accurately convey feelings to your readers. Don't just say that something made you feel gloomy. Actually *show* in words how it feels inside to be gloomy.

4. Rewrite your descriptions of objects and people every once in awhile. For example, if you've observed and objectively described some person, try rewriting that description in more subjective language. Feel free to tell what you think of this person along with the objective detail. Imagine yourself a vase or a glass of milk. How do you feel?

5. Try writing a longer journal entry in the style of your favorite sports columnist, editorialist or political columnist. Better yet, write a series of fictional "Dear Abby" columns into your journal, letters and all.

6. Record your passing observations of current events—elections, local issues, general public events. Try to include entries from different perspectives, in varying styles.

7. Record little language tidbits that you find interesting or instructive. A particularly apt advertising slogan, a clever piece of irony you overheard at a party or in the student union, a short, descriptive poem or an excerpt from a popular song. Occasionally you might attach an explanation to what you record telling just why you like the selection.

8. Write some letters that you'll never send in your journal. A note introducing yourself to a classy girl you saw only briefly. An ironic note to a store clerk or college official that you feel treated you rudely. A "beef" letter to a public official or a teacher about some bothersome rule, convention or official policy.

9. You may discover as you begin your journal that one theme keeps recurring as you write. Maybe you are constantly referring to particular kinds of people. Perhaps you enjoy sketching in busy department stores more than anything else. Maybe you are interested in students rights, in how you are treated as a second-class citizen because you are a student. Then force yourself to make at least one entry, no matter how small, on that subject everyday. You might want to boil down all your entires into a single expository essay as the class comes to an end.

10. Every six or seven days you should go back over what you have written and write approximately a one-page entry that integrates or pulls together your individual entries. These longer entries should help you

unify your experience and give you some idea of what to look for and what to emphasise.

You are your first teacher. Your classroom teacher is your second teacher. Your journal is your third teacher. It gives you time to practice and experiment, to take risky chances in your writing, to make and correct mistakes, to use language in ways you might not use it in formal, academic situations. A journal makes writing an everyday, fun thing. Note what two experts on journal-writing say about the subject.

> The man who dreams of becoming a writer spends his time dreaming of becoming a writer. The man who intends to become a writer keeps a journal and works the mine. (1970)
>
> —Ken Macrorie

> Of all strange and unaccountable things this journalizing is the strangest. It will allow nothing to be predicted of it; its good is not good, nor its bad bad. If I make a huge effort to expose my innermost and richest wares to light, my counter seems cluttered with the meanest homemade stuffs; but after months or years I may discover the wealth of India . . . in that confused heap . . . (1841)
>
> —Henry David Thoreau

Rhetorical Index

421